MIGRATION AND DISRUPTIONS

UNIVERSITY PRESS OF FLORIDA

Florida A&M University, Tallahassee
Florida Atlantic University, Boca Raton
Florida Gulf Coast University, Ft. Myers
Florida International University, Miami
Florida State University, Tallahassee
New College of Florida, Sarasota
University of Central Florida, Orlando
University of Florida, Gainesville
University of North Florida, Jacksonville
University of South Florida, Tampa
University of West Florida, Pensacola

MIGRATION AND DISRUPTIONS

Toward a Unifying Theory of Ancient and Contemporary Migrations

EDITED BY

BRENDA J. BAKER AND TAKEYUKI TSUDA

University Press of Florida

Gainesville · Tallahassee · Tampa · Boca Raton

Pensacola · Orlando · Miami · Jacksonville · Ft. Myers · Sarasota

This book may be available in an electronic edition.

First cloth printing, 2015
First paperback printing, 2018

23 22 21 20 19 18   6 5 4 3 2 1

Library of Congress Cataloging-in-Publication Data
Migration and disruptions : toward a unifying theory of ancient and contemporary
migrations / edited by Brenda J. Baker and Takeyuki Tsuda.
pages cm
Includes index.
ISBN 978-0-8130-6080-4 (cloth)
ISBN 978-0-8130-6473-4 (pbk.)
1. Human beings—Migrations. 2. Social sciences—Emigration and immigration.
3. Emigration and immigration. I. Baker, Brenda J., editor. II. Tsuda, Takeyuki, editor.
GN370.M52 2015
304.8—dc23
2015004616

The University Press of Florida is the scholarly publishing agency for the State University
System of Florida, comprising Florida A&M University, Florida Atlantic University,
Florida Gulf Coast University, Florida International University, Florida State University,
New College of Florida, University of Central Florida, University of Florida, University of
North Florida, University of South Florida, and University of West Florida.

University Press of Florida
15 Northwest 15th Street
Gainesville, FL 32611-2079
http://upress.ufl.edu

Contents

Figures

Tables

Foreword

Migration has again become an immediate social concern, although it is a pattern as old as humanity itself. Studies of migration have become more numerous in recent years, no doubt in response to public interest in the issue. Fortunately the growing quantity of studies has also brought an improvement in the quality of academic studies—if not always in the quality of public discourse. At least as interesting is that the closer study of migration today is bringing greater understanding of migration in the past.

Migration itself fluctuates from year to year and from generation to generation. So also does the debate over migration. Given the present era of globalization, the analysis of migration is far more cosmopolitan than before. The multivalent amplification of communication, culture, and economics has made it easier to locate and analyze the complexities of migration and, indeed, other social phenomena. We are fortunate to experience an increased sophistication in social science analysis at several levels—within each discipline, in linking disciplines to each other, and across time and space.

The group that has assembled this volume, led by Brenda Baker and Takeyuki Tsuda, has taken an important step forward. That is, they link migration studies through the disciplines of archaeology and sociocultural anthropology, and through comparison of present-day migration with earlier migrations. This cross-disciplinary, cross-temporal research design yields new insights by helping to distinguish what is common to all migrations from what depends on specific situations. The collaboration of sociocultural anthropologists and archaeologists brings together two distinctive disciplines that, although they are often located administratively within the same academic department, do not always combine their insights on social problems. It is always good to see efforts in cross-disciplinary study and good to see detailed comparisons across time—so it is better yet to see the combination of the two types of collaboration at once.

Recent research has led logically to the advances of this book. One previous step was a survey of migration throughout human history, which led to the recognition that humans have relied since their beginnings on a common pattern of migration. Thus, young adults especially, in voluntary or involuntary migration, had to learn languages, customs, and perhaps other new ideas. Another advance in research was that specialists in several disciplines showed the distinctive contributions of each discipline to migration studies in general.

The further advance in this volume is the actual collaboration among disciplines. The studies in this volume focus tightly on observations in archaeology and sociocultural anthropology, and help specify the continuities and changes in migration over recent millennia. Among the overall results of this collaborative process is the recognition that social disruption—of various sorts—has launched waves of migration. The contributions of the book thus provide new knowledge on processes of migration, but they also provide a valuable example of expanding the scope of research through cross-disciplinary study.

Patrick Manning
University of Pittsburgh

Acknowledgments

The collaborative project that culminated in this volume was funded by the Late Lessons from Early History (LLEH) initiative in the School of Human Evolution and Social Change (SHESC) at Arizona State University and the Wenner-Gren Anthropological Research Foundation (Gr. CONF-573). We thank Sander Van der Leeuw, founding director of SHESC, for his support of the LLEH initiative and the incorporation of our project. The editors benefited immensely from the many discussions with core team members at ASU—George Cowgill, James Eder, Kelly Knudson, Jonathan Maupin, Lisa Meierotto, and Rachel Scott—and occasional participants such as Jane Buikstra. Graduate research assistants Charisse Carver, Kent Johnson, Claire Smith, and Skaidra Smith-Heisters were instrumental in creating an annotated bibliography of ancient and modern migration studies that was shared with all project members and workshop participants. The staff of Saguaro Lake Ranch facilitated our workshop in a comfortable setting that promoted group discussion. The workshop attendees included all contributors to the volume and T. Douglas Price. Our discussion of questions posed in advance of the workshop and the ensuing debates on key concepts in our intellectual framework helped guide the development of chapters in this book. The dedication of the contributors in revising their chapters based on the workshop and in response to our subsequent comments is greatly appreciated.

I

A CONCEPTUAL FRAMEWORK

Introduction

Bridging the Past and Present in Assessing Migration

BRENDA J. BAKER AND TAKEYUKI TSUDA

Migration has been integral to the development of human societies since the emergence of our species and has continually reshaped the economic, ethnic, and political dynamics of various societies over time. Despite the importance of migration throughout human history, little dialogue has occurred between scholars examining contemporary and past migrations. This temporal division has led to seemingly disparate views of migration, creating a conceptual gulf between those who focus on modern migration and those who study it in the past. Modern migration scholars have only studied recent population movements and have shown no interest in ancient migrations. They have been interested mainly in the socioeconomic and political causes of migration, migrant labor markets, gender relationships and migrant families, transnationalism and diasporas, and attitudes toward migrants in receiving societies (Tsuda 2011:315). In contrast, scholars investigating migration in the past have focused on documenting migratory flows to explain changes in material culture or settlement and subsistence patterns, the origins and composition of specific peoples and their biological relationships, as well as the development and collapse of states (see critiques of this focus by Adams et al. 1978; Anthony 1990; Burmeister 2000; Cabana 2011; and Cabana and Clark 2011a:3–4, among others). Such studies usually emphasize natural or social disruptions (e.g., climate change, conquest, socioeconomic collapse) as a primary cause of migration.

The tacit assumption is that current migratory patterns differ radically from those in the distant past and, therefore, are not comparable. Some archaeologists, in fact, have previously questioned or even rejected the relevance of modern migration to ancient migration (e.g., Clark 1994; Rouse 1986:161–163). Because people have always migrated, however, there is no distinct temporal or conceptual break between the past and present. Although "migration after the Industrial Revolution has been structured by capitalist wage-labor systems, modern nation-states and their immigration policies, as well as advanced transportation and communications technologies, none of which existed in antiquity" (Tsuda 2011:313; see also Anthony 1990:898; Beekman and Christensen 2003:115; Duff 1998:32; Rouse 1986:162), sufficient similarities and continuities exist to identify common patterns and dynamics involved in both past and present migration (O'Rourke 2012; Tsuda 2011).

According to world historian Patrick Manning (2006:48), contemporary migration is an acceleration of ancient processes rather than the development of entirely new ones. Similarly, two biological anthropologists, Ben Campbell and Michael Crawford (2012:2), state that, "while the scale and scope of migration has changed over time, its fundamental causes have not." In fact, an increasing number of archaeologists, bioarchaeologists, and biological anthropologists now argue that certain aspects of current population movements resemble those from the distant past and that studies of modern migration can be used to provide a better understanding of ancient migrations (Anthony 1990:898, 1997; Burmeister 2000:543; Cabana and Clark 2011a:4; Cameron 1995; Chapman 1997; Duff 1998:32; O'Rourke 2012).

The central conviction of this book is that scholars of recent and ancient migrations can benefit considerably by sharing their knowledge and learning from each other. Such dialogue is especially important because archaeologists and biological anthropologists are increasingly interested in investigating *why* people migrate and understanding migration as a dynamic *process* (e.g., Anthony 1990:895–896; Beekman and Christensen 2003:113–114; Clark 2011; Duff 1998; O'Rourke 2012) rather than a simple *explanation* for change or discontinuities found in the material record or the biological composition of past peoples. As Tsuda (2011:315) has noted, some archaeologists have, therefore, used modern migration theories (e.g., Anthony 1990, 1997; Burmeister 2000; Duff 1998). In fact, migration research has experienced a recent resurgence among archaeologists, bioarchaeologists, and biological anthropologists, an interest that never waned among scholars of contemporary migration. Additionally, as noted by O'Rourke (2012:528), "the ecological forces that motivate human migration also affect the genetic structure of human populations," so that "migration as a process links the natural and social sciences." The evolutionary perspective in biological anthropology provides a window into assessing how gene flow associated with migration affects skeletal morphology and the genetic composition of populations (see Bolnick 2011 for a recent overview). Although better methods are being used to detect and track past migration, including sourcing of raw materials, biogeochemical analyses of human bones and teeth, and ancient DNA analysis, it is still difficult to study the actual migratory process using the fragmentary material and skeletal record.

Unlike investigators of ancient migrations, modern migration scholars can observe migration directly as it occurs and can rely on a wealth of informant accounts, written documents, statistics, and mass media sources to analyze its complex social dynamics. However, they can also benefit from an intellectual collaboration with scholars studying migration in the past because their research covers a very limited time period (usually one or two years, in the case of ethnographic fieldwork). They cannot trace long-term changes in migratory patterns or their consequences, as archaeologists, bioarchaeologists, or many biological anthropologists do. Given the intensive and detailed ethnographic method that sociocultural anthropologists use, they must focus on community-level migrations, which makes it difficult to understand the broader structural impact of large migratory flows. The greater time depth and broader scope provided by studies of past migration can help modern migration specialists understand the common processes that operate in both the past and present and help project patterns of migration into the future.

This volume complements recent anthropological collections on migration (e.g., Cabana and Clark 2011b; Crawford and Campbell 2012). Although archaeologists and historians have commonly related migration to natural and social disruptions, those studying contemporary migration have not focused on disruption as a possible cause or consequence of migration. As a result, we decided to examine the role of disruption in migration. Contributors were asked to focus on this specific, but frequently invoked, aspect of migration and to consider two substantive questions in their own research areas:

1. To what extent have environmental and social disruptions been a cause of migration over time?
2. Did migratory flows lead to disruptive consequences for the societies that received them?

Each chapter articulates with a common, comprehensive framework developed by a working group of bioarchaeologists, archaeologists, and sociocultural anthropologists, which is delineated in chapter 1. Chapter authors, thus, aim to develop our understanding of the relationship between disruptions and population displacements to form a cohesive volume that bridges past and present.

Late Lessons from Early History

This book is the culmination of a project led by the editors that was part of a School of Human Evolution and Social Change (SHESC) initiative, Late Lessons from Early History (LLEH), at Arizona State University (ASU). The goal of the LLEH initiative, as promulgated by SHESC's then director, Sander Van der Leeuw, was to develop research projects to explore the past, present, and future by crosscutting traditional academic boundaries and promote intellectual fusion within the nascent school and beyond it. A group of bioarchaeologists, archaeologists, and sociocultural anthropologists coalesced through a series of meetings organized around the central concept of disruptions and their relationship to population movements throughout human history. The main goals initially were to investigate how environmental and social disruptions may cause human migration over time and the ways in which migrants themselves may produce environmental or social disruptions in various host societies. As our thinking progressed, these goals were refined to address the extent to which disruptions relate to migration, recognizing that not all disruptions may produce migration since local populations can choose to stay rather than leave despite an interruption of their normal lifeways. To develop a common approach to this issue, we held meetings to discuss relevant readings on migration and present our ongoing research related to the project. Faculty from other disciplines at ASU (e.g., historian Dirk Hoerder) and scholars from other universities (David Anthony, Patrick Manning, and Bartholomew Dean) also visited to present their research and discuss our project. We also employed graduate research assistants Charisse Carver, Kent Johnson, Claire Smith, and Skaidra Smith-Heisters to produce an annotated bibliography of both past and present migration literature.

During the 2010–2011 academic year, the ASU group drafted an integrative intellectual framework that could be used to analyze migration from prehistory to the present. This conceptual and analytical framework was also used to generate interest among international scholars who wished to develop the premises in collaboration with the ASU group. With funding from the Wenner-Gren Anthropological Research Foundation (Gr. CONF-573) and the ASU Late Lessons from Early History initiative, an international workshop, "Disruptions as a Cause and Consequence of Migrations in Human History," was held May 3–5, 2012, at a rustic lodge on Saguaro Lake, on the outskirts of Mesa, Arizona. An effort was made to recruit scholars from many disciplines whose research spanned prehistoric to modern periods. Although historians were invited, none of them was able to attend the workshop. Participants ultimately included the ASU faculty group and seven non-ASU scholars (three archaeologists, a bioarchaeologist, two sociocultural anthropologists, and one international development scholar who conducts ethnographic fieldwork). The composition of the group left an unintended gap of about 600 years in our coverage of ancient and modern migrations. The workshop consisted of general sessions, which were devoted to discussion of relevant themes and the project's intellectual framework, and more specific sessions for the discussion of case-study papers submitted in advance by workshop participants. Our many lively discussions were highly successful and were very helpful in revising our project framework. After the workshop, the editors provided extensive comments to participants to help guide revisions of papers and promote articulation with the project's intellectual framework. These papers, using different and sometimes multiple lines of evidence to address disruptive aspects of migration, are collected in this volume.

Organization of the Volume

The volume is divided into three parts. The first part provides the intellectual foundation on which the volume rests. The conceptual framework developed by the ASU group is presented in chapter 1. This chapter lays out the unifying themes and analytical framework discussed and developed over the course of this project to guide the contributors. Articulation with this conceptual framework was a key component of the May 2012 workshop presentations and subsequent discussion and revision of the chapters presented in this volume. The rest of the book is divided into two relatively equal parts consisting of chapters that investigate migration in past societies and those that examine contemporary population movements. Chapter authors were asked to stress connections between their work and those of others in both past and present settings.

Part II includes five chapters on migration and its relation to disruptions in sending or receiving societies in the past. Chapter 2, by Catherine Hills, addresses changing views of the magnitude of Anglo-Saxon migration to Britain in the fifth century. This chapter has several parallels with Sonia Zakrzewski's examination of the Islamic conquest of Spain (chapter 3). Both authors attempt to assess the magnitude of the disruptive migration accompanying a conquest, though they use different types of evidence. While Hills focuses largely on material culture in the archaeological record to evaluate the extent of change, Zakrzewski uses mortuary and skeletal data. Both Hills and Zakrzewski present two different models concerning the scale and impact of a conquest. In chapter 2, Hills confronts the debate concerning the number of immigrants. Did only a small number of elite Germanic immigrants impose their culture in certain areas they overtook without replacing the indigenous population, or did massive numbers of Anglo-Saxons arrive and replace the main population? Hills discusses changing interpretations of material culture as archaeology developed from a culture-historical to a theoretically informed discipline and evaluates cremation burials and grave goods, placing the large fifth-century cemetery at Spong Hill in this light. Her study shows the complexities of the Anglo-Saxon migration and its varied effects in different regions of Britain.

In Spain, as in Britain, the Islamic conquest has been viewed differently over time and used to justify politics and nationalism, as Sonia Zakrzewski discusses in chapter 3. Changes in mortuary practices, such as grave style, orientation, body position, skeletal evidence of repetitive activities associated with religious practices, and skeletal and isotopic indicators of population relationships are assessed in a large cemetery sample from Écija, near Seville, Spain, to address the scale of immigration and potential religious disruption associated with the Islamic conquest in the early eighth century. The diverse burial styles suggest a short period of social disruption, with skeletal nonmetric and craniometric analyses indicating biological diversity of those interred in the cemetery. Supplementary evidence derived from skeletal activity markers and isotopic analyses provides a multifaceted exploration of population and religious change in this area that Zakrzewski concludes was initially disruptive but subsequently led to a transformation of identity in this region.

In chapter 4, Christopher Beekman uses multiple lines of evidence to detect migration, and potential disruptive causes and consequences associated with it, in Epiclassic to Early Postclassic northwestern and central Mexico. Environmental reconstruction shows a long period of gradual drying in the Bajío region of Guanajuato, north of the Basin of Mexico. Beekman discusses initial attempts to mitigate its consequences, leading eventually to decisions concerning whether to stay and shift subsistence practices from agriculture to hunting and gathering or migrate out of the area. With the collapse of major centers like Teotihuacan, discussed in detail by George Cowgill in chapter 5, Beekman shows how elites in newly established centers used what he construes as "mass media" to distinguish their polity and attract new residents from surrounding areas. The complexities surrounding choices to stay or leave this area in Epiclassic Mexico have parallels to the situation discussed by James Morrissey (chapter 9) in highland Ethiopia today.

George Cowgill places the fall of Teotihuacan within a framework he lays out in chapter 5 for detecting and dating a migration, identifying disruptions and other motives for leaving a sending area, and for discerning disruptive and other types of impacts on a receiving society or region. Archaeological studies of material culture often overlook the importance of distinguishing imported items that are the product of "inheritance," in which a novice learns how to make the items from experienced individuals, and "emulation," in which copies are produced using local technology. Cowgill notes that differences in technological attributes are suggestive of migrants, while objects with a similar outward appearance produced with local technology show copying of external forms or styles without migration necessarily being involved. His critical evaluation of the evidence surrounding the fall of Teotihuacan provides a significant case study in detecting the disruptive causes and consequences of migration.

The last chapter on past migrations by Kelly Knudson and Christina Torres-Rouff shows the utility of combining biogeochemical analyses of bones and tooth enamel and biodistance studies of skeletal variations (nonmetric traits) to investigate residential mobility in the south-central Andes during a period of political and environmental change between AD 500 and 1400. Knudson and Torres-Rouff examine the disintegration of the Tiwanaku polity in the Lake Titicaca Basin in modern Bolivia and its impact on the inhabitants of the San Pedro de Atacama oases in northern Chile. Contrary to the expectation that collapse of Tiwanaku would increase out-migration from the core area, they find that migration actually decreased during the Late Intermediate period. They conclude that the disruption of social and economic networks that promoted migration during the preceding Middle Horizon impeded population mobility, despite political and ecological disruption.

Together, the chapters considering past migration exemplify the need to contextualize the archaeological record and use multiple approaches to unravel the complexities of group interactions and movements. The issues identified often relate to those discussed by authors of the subsequent six chapters, which investigate modern migration and its possible relationship to disruptions in sending or receiving groups.

Part III begins with a significant study of illegal immigration on the Arizona-Mexico border that combines archaeological and ethnographic methods to evaluate the disruption inherent in the migratory process and the toll it takes on the migrants themselves. In chapter 7, Jason De León, Cameron Gokee, and Anna Forringer-Beal bridge the gap between contemporary and past approaches by assessing the "use wear" and repurposing evident among items that migrants have left behind at way stations in the desert. Their evaluation of these sites and the artifacts within them is informed by ethnography. This chapter, therefore, is a powerful demonstration of how archaeological methods and approaches are relevant to current social processes and can shed light on issues that are not part of public or scholarly awareness. Beyond insights that archaeological investigations may reveal to those working on contemporary migration, chapter 7 suggests information that archaeologists may glean from this "material approach." The research presented by De León and coworkers also has close ties to other chapters in this section, especially Lisa Meierotto's (chapter 8) study of environmental impact associated with migration along the Arizona-Mexico border. The routinized, corporeal suffering of the migrants highlighted by De León, Gokee, and Forringer-Beal also relates to perceptions of sickness and health among undocumented migrants and their actual impact on the healthcare system, discussed by Jonathan Maupin in chapter 12.

Lisa Meierotto's (chapter 8) investigation of environmental disruption caused by illegal migration reinforces many of the findings presented in chapter 7. In her study of the Cabeza Prieta National Wildlife Refuge in southern Arizona, Meierotto shows how public perceptions about the migrants shape views of the environmental damage they cause to the receiving society, particularly concerning the "trash" left in the desert. Her historical overview of land use in this area is critical to evaluating contemporary environmental impacts. She then explains how, contrary to prevailing perceptions, the environmental degradation due to border crossers in this large wilderness area pales in comparison to that caused by the U.S. Border Patrol and adjacent U.S. Air Force base exercises.

Environmental degradation is also discussed in chapter 9 by James Morrissey, who challenges the notions of the "environmental refugee" and "disruptions," particularly in portrayals of environmental stress as a cause of migration. Morrissey emphasizes that the relationship between environmental stress and mobility is heavily influenced by many non-environmental variables, illustrating how these contextual factors shape mobility decisions in the highlands of northeastern Ethiopia. He suggests that we should not focus on whether environmental changes cause migration; instead, we should investigate the role played by environmental stress in mobility decisions to illuminate the interaction of environmental and non-environmental factors to achieve an understanding of the multiple causes of mobility. In this regard, Morrisey's chapter provides ethnographic examples that present a framework for evaluating the variety of push-and-pull factors involved in mobility decisions, as well as factors that may counteract them.

In chapter 10, James Eder compares two groups of migrants to Palawan Island in the southern Philippines. He examines the similarities and differences between these migrant streams and the disruptive impacts they have had on the receiving side. While objective measures show that agricultural migrants have been more numerous, caused more damage to the environment and livelihoods of indigenous peoples, and presented greater challenges to state control, the Muslim migrants are deemed a greater threat to the local populace. Eder demonstrates how ethnic, religious, and political differences between the two migrant groups and the receiving society dramatically influence how disruptive the newcomers are perceived to be by the local populace. His chapter, thus, has parallels to studies in this volume concerning the measurable, versus perceived, impact of illegal immigrants crossing the U.S.-Mexico border.

The issue of perceptions about the disruption caused by different groups of migrants in the United States is confronted directly by Takeyuki Tsuda in chapter 11. Comparison of the size, socioeconomic status, and education of immigrants from Mexico and Asia places public perceptions into perspective, particularly in relation to streams of illegal immigrants. Tsuda, like Eder in the preceding chapter, finds that perceived differences between migrants and the host population influence the perception of their disruptive impact. Despite their similar numbers, Mexican immigrants are viewed to be much more disruptive in the United States than their Asian counterparts. Tsuda presents the reasons for this disparity in public opinion through his examination of opinion polls, anti-immigrant publications and websites, and portrayals of immigrants in the media. In chapter 12, Jonathan Maupin focuses specifically on recent immigration legislation in Arizona and the perceived impact of undocumented migrants on the healthcare system. His survey of registered nurses (RNs) is compared to data from public opinion polls. Despite evidence that only a small portion of uncompensated healthcare costs result from undocumented immigrants, Maupin's study shows that RNs are overwhelmingly influenced by public perceptions that such immigrants are a burden to the healthcare system. As a result, they support hospital verification of citizenship or legal immigration status to receive federal or state aid, including coverage of healthcare costs. From these studies, it is clear that social perceptions in receiving societies are instrumental in determining whether migrants are deemed disruptive. As demonstrated by some papers in the section on past migrations, however, views of migrant groups may change over time to advance political agendas.

A concluding chapter by the editors highlights major themes that connect the studies in this volume. It elaborates upon the unifying conceptual and analytical framework presented in chapter 1 and identifies problems to be addressed by future research and collaborations. Because of the considerable amount of intellectual discussion and exchange involved in this project, our volume has conceptual unity and coherence. While focusing more narrowly on the relative contribution of disruptions to population movements, it builds upon other volumes that have begun to connect past and present perspectives concerning human migration (e.g., Cabana and Clark 2011b; Crawford and Campbell 2012; Lucassen et al 2010; Manning 2012).

References Cited

Adams, William Y., Dennis P. Van Gerven, and Richard S. Levy
1978   The Retreat from Migrationism. Annual Review of Anthropology 7:483–532.
Anthony, David W.
1990   Migration in Archeology: The Baby and the Bathwater. American Anthropologist 92(4):895–914.
Anthony, David
1997   Prehistoric Migration as Social Process. *In* Migrations and Invasions in Archaeological Explanation. John Chapman and Helena Hamerow, eds. Pp. 21–32. British Archaeological Reports International Series, 664. Oxford: Archaeopress.

Beekman, Christopher S., and Alexander F. Christensen

2003   Controlling for Doubt and Uncertainty Through Multiple Lines of Evidence: A New Look at the Mesoamerican Nahua Migrations. Journal of Archaeological Method and Theory 10(2):111–164.

Bolnick, Deborah A.

2011   Continuity and Change in Anthropological Perspectives on Migration: Insights from Molecular Anthropology. *In* Rethinking Anthropological Perspectives on Migration. Graciela S. Cabana and Jeffery J. Clark, eds. Pp. 263–277. Gainesville: University Press of Florida.

Burmeister, Stefan

2000   Archaeology and Migration: Approaches to an Archaeological Proof of Migration. Current Anthropology 41(4):539–567.

Cabana, Graciela S.

2011   The Problematic Relationship between Migration and Culture Change. *In* Rethinking Anthropological Perspectives on Migration, Graciela S. Cabana and Jeffery J. Clark, eds. Pp. 16–28. Gainesville: University Press of Florida.

Cabana, Graciela S., and Jeffery J. Clark

2011a   Introduction. Migration in Anthropology: Where We Stand. *In* Rethinking Anthropological Perspectives on Migration, Graciela S. Cabana and Jeffery J. Clark, eds. Pp. 1–15. Gainesville: University Press of Florida.

Cabana, Graciela S. and Jeffery J. Clark, eds.

2011b   Rethinking Anthropological Perspectives on Migration. Gainesville: University Press of Florida.

Cameron, Catherine M.

1995   Migration and the Movement of Southwestern Peoples. Journal of Anthropological Archaeology 14(2):104–124.

Campbell, Benjamin C., and Michael H. Crawford

2012   Perspectives on Human Migration: Introduction. *In* Causes and Consequences of Human Migration: An Evolutionary Perspective. Michael H. Crawford and Benjamin C. Campbell, eds. Pp. 1–8. New York: Cambridge University Press.

Chapman, John

1997   The Impact of Modern Invasions and Migrations on Archaeological Explanation. *In* Migrations and Invasions in Archaeological Explanation. John Chapman and Helena Hamerow, eds. Pp. 11–20. British Archaeological Reports International Series, 664. Oxford: Archaeopress.

Clark, Geoffrey A.

1994   Migration as an Explanatory Concept in Paleolithic Archaeology. Journal of Archaeological Method and Theory 1(4):305–343.

Clark, Jeffery J.

2011   Disappearance and Diaspora: Contrasting Two Migrations in the Southern U.S. Southwest. *In* Rethinking Anthropological Perspectives on Migration. Graciela S. Cabana and Jeffery J. Clark, eds. Pp. 84–107. Gainesville: University Press of Florida.

Crawford, Michael H., and Benjamin C. Campbell, eds.

2012   Causes and Consequences of Human Migration: An Evolutionary Perspective. New York: Cambridge University Press.

Duff, Andrew

1998   The Process of Migration in the Late Prehistoric Southwest. *In* Migration and Reorganization: The Pueblo IV Period in the American Southwest. Katherine A. Spielmann, ed. Pp. 31–52. Arizona State University Anthropological Research Papers, 51. Tempe: Department of Anthropology, Arizona State University.

Lucassen, Jan, Leo Lucassen, and Patrick Manning, eds.

2010   Migration History in World History: Multidisciplinary Approaches. Leiden and Boston: Brill.

Manning, Patrick

2006   Cross-Community Migration: A Distinctive Human Pattern. Social Evolution & History 5(2):24–54.

2012   Migration in World History. 2nd edition. London: Routledge.

O'Rourke, Dennis H.

2012   Why Do We Migrate? A Retrospective. *In* Causes and Consequences of Human Migration: An Evolutionary Perspective. Michael H. Crawford and Benjamin C. Campbell, eds. Pp. 527–536. New York: Cambridge University Press.

Rouse, Irving

1986   Migrations in Prehistory: Inferring Population Movement from Cultural Remains. New Haven: Yale University Press.

Tsuda, Takeyuki

2011   Modern Perspectives on Ancient Migrations. *In* Rethinking Anthropological Perspectives on Migration. Graciela S. Cabana and Jeffery J. Clark, eds. Pp. 313–338. Gainesville: University Press of Florida.

1

Unifying Themes in Studies of Ancient and Contemporary Migrations

TAKEYUKI TSUDA, BRENDA J. BAKER, JAMES F. EDER, KELLY J. KNUDSON,
JONATHAN MAUPIN, LISA MEIEROTTO, AND RACHEL E. SCOTT

In order to address the temporal and conceptual dichotomy in migration studies discussed in the introduction, the authors of this chapter (sociocultural anthropologists and archaeologists/bioarchaeologists) engaged in direct dialogue to develop a shared set of definitions and concepts. Our goal was to develop a comprehensive intellectual framework for investigating both the causes and consequences of migration throughout human history.

Unifying Concepts: Disruptions and Migration

Admittedly, many of the primary issues that interest modern migration specialists may not have existed in antiquity or often cannot be studied using the fragmentary material and skeletal record (such as immigration policies and politics and public and media reactions toward immigrants, transnational migrant communities, and immigrant citizenship). Nonetheless, because scholars interested in past migration are moving beyond the basic objective of detecting its occurrence to developing an understanding of the actual social dynamics of migration, there are now areas of considerable topical overlap with specialists in contemporary migration. According to Clark (2011:86), archaeologists are interested not only in identifying the occurrence of migration, but also in its *causes* ("motivation"), the *process* of migratory movement ("logistics/organization during movement)," which he notes are difficult to study archaeologically due to the "ephemeral character of emigrant settlements on the move," and its impact or *consequences* (usually in the destination area). As Tsuda (2011:315) notes, contemporary migration scholars have studied these issues extensively. Archaeologists have, therefore, drawn on the substantial modern migration literature to elucidate the motivations for and impacts of past migrations (Anthony 1990:898, 899–901; Burmeister 2000:543–547; Duff 1998:32–33).

Our project and the chapters in this volume examine the causes and consequences of migration by employing the unifying concept of disruptions (we do not focus much on the process of migratory movement).[1] As outlined by Baker and Tsuda in the introduction, migration of past populations is often attributed to upheavals resulting from natural perturbations or political, economic, or religious change. Such disruptions have drawn little attention from modern migration specialists. Migration is, in fact, increasingly recognized as a fundamental attribute of humankind (e.g., Cabana and Clark 2011b; Crawford and Campbell 2012; Lucassen et al. 2010; Manning 2012). We, therefore, wish to analyze the extent to which environmental and social disruptions have been a cause of migration over time and whether these migratory flows have in turn led to disruptive consequences for the societies that receive them. We do not automatically equate migration with disruptions or assume that migration is primarily caused by disruptions. Nor do we expect that most of the consequences of migration for host societies are disruptive. Instead, we wish to examine the *relative importance* of disruptions in human migration by asking why certain migrations are associated with disruptions to some degree while others are not.

Chapter 7, by De León et al., is the only one in our book that considers the potentially disruptive impact of migration on the migrants themselves. Although research on contemporary migrants has examined the disruptive effects of migration on their mental health, families, occupations, and identities (e.g., Clark et al. 2009; Landale and Ogena 1995; Lin 1986; McAllister 1995; Mirsky et al. 2007; Tsuda 2003), such micro-level disruptions are harder to study and document for ancient migrations. We are also less interested in comparing migrations in the past and present in order to determine how contemporary migrations differ from or are similar to those in the past (e.g., whether disruptions were a greater cause and/or consequence of migration than they are now). Such vast generalizations encompassing huge time periods of human history and all societies across the globe are always suspect. Instead, we have developed a common framework of analysis that can be used for case studies of migratory disruption in specific societies during certain time periods. With this general objective in mind, we agreed upon a set of unifying concepts and definitions that can be applied broadly to studies of both modern and ancient migration.

Disruptions

We define *disruptions* as substantial interruptions that disturb the accustomed activities of a society and have a significant structural impact from the macro level of civilizations, nations, and cities to the meso level of ethnic groups/tribes, institutions, and families.[2] They may be abrupt or more gradual and long-term changes (although abrupt changes generally tend to be more disruptive). Disruptions are relevant to both the migrant-sending and -receiving societies, since various environmental or social disruptions can cause migrants to out-migrate from a certain area and in-migrations can also be socially or environmentally disruptive to host societies. Because disruptions have been connected with population movements throughout human history, this concept is an appropriate way to bring researchers studying modern and ancient migrations together.

The concept of disruptions is equivalent to what is called "disturbances" in the complex socioecological systems literature (Carpenter et al. 2001; Gunderson et al. 2006; Holling 1973; Walker et al. 2004). Although usually understood to be external shocks to the system (Burt 2007:737; Walker et al. 2004), such disturbances can be generated internally as well. Although disruptions have been defined by certain researchers as events that have negative and adverse consequences, such as social disorder, conflict, and disintegration (Burt 2007:732; Park and Stokowski 2009:905–907), we have chosen not to conceive of disruptions in a purely negative manner, for two reasons. First, such definitions are ultimately susceptible to normative value judgments. In the case of migration, for example, who decides whether an immigrant flow has a negative (versus a neutral or positive) impact: the host society, the immigrants, or the researcher? Second, although it is undeniable that certain disruptive events can indeed have some quite negative consequences, they do not always lead to such adverse outcomes.

Disruptions, therefore, must be distinguished from disasters, which are extreme and severe events, as opposed to more chronic and everyday risks (Hewitt 1997:5–8). In addition, the literature on disasters is usually limited to natural catastrophes, such as earthquakes, hurricanes, and floods, or technological calamities, including toxic, chemical, or nuclear hazards (Bolin 1998; Kreps 1984; Oliver-Smith 1996). Although disruptions can certainly include disasters, "disruptions" is a much broader concept. In addition, disaster research does not seriously examine out-migration as one of the major ways in which vulnerable populations respond and adapt to disasters (Hewitt 1997, Kreps 1984, Oliver-Smith 1996, Wisner et al. 2004), though some literature examines the connection between hazards and migration (e.g., Hunter 2005).

We generally distinguish between two general types of disruptions. The first are environmental, affecting the habitat and availability of natural resources for human societies. These disruptions can be the result of natural processes, such as droughts, floods, hurricanes, earthquakes, tornados, tsunamis, etc., or pathogens and pests that endanger livestock, crops, and other food sources. Environmental disruptions are also often the product of human activities that lead to environmental degradation, resource over-exploitation, and (in today's world), technological hazards and pollution. The second type can be broadly called social disruptions. These include disruptions of economic systems and subsistence patterns, political systems (governance and state systems through conflict, warfare, and invasions/conquests), social structures (kinship, ethnic, class, or gender systems), and cultural systems (ideologies, belief/symbolic systems, religions, languages, identities). Of course, environmental and social disruptions are often intertwined since sociopolitical conflict and warfare can often have detrimental impacts on the environment, and environmental disruptions can threaten economic livelihoods and subsistence as well as lead to sociopolitical conflicts over limited resources. Disruptions that cause a dramatic change in population size or structure, such as epidemics or illnesses that threaten human health and populations, and psychological disruptions that affect mental health, may be related to both environmental and sociocultural circumstances.

Finally, we stress the socially relative nature of disruptions, since the disruptions that are the causes and consequences of migration are experienced differently by different social groups. An environmental or social disruption may be very disruptive to certain vulnerable groups and cause them to migrate, whereas more resilient groups are not as affected and do not migrate. Likewise, a migratory inflow may be experienced and perceived as disruptive by certain segments of a host society but not by others. Nonetheless, despite the socially relative nature of disruptions, certain changes can be characterized clearly and objectively as disruptive (for example, when the causes or consequences of migration are warfare, violence, social/ethnic conflict, political collapse, disease, death, population loss, environmental degradation/resource depletion, economic decline, increase in poverty or economic costs, etc.).

Migration

We define migration as the movement of people across significant *socio-cultural, political, or environmental boundaries* that involves uprooting and *long-term relocation*.[3] Our definition of migration does *not* include two types of population movements: 1) internal, localized movements within a cultural/political/environmental boundary or area; and 2) circular, temporary, seasonal movements ("seasonal rounds") in which migrants return home after a short period, even if they cross significant boundaries. Our definition of migration is similar to those adopted by other archaeologists (for example, see Adams et al. 1978:486; Cabana and Clark 2011a:5; Cameron 1995; Duff 1998:32; Rouse 1986:9, 176), who emphasize its large-scale, long-distance, and long-term nature. In contrast, seasonal or circular, short-term movements within localized areas by small groups or individuals are often excluded by these scholars as "not migration" or "background noise" and, therefore, not a subject of study (Cabana and Clark 2011a:5; Cameron 1995; Clark 2011:85; Duff 1998:32; Rouse 1986).

For modern migration specialists, it may seem rather strange that we are adopting such a restrictive definition of migration, since they often consider internal, circular movement of peoples to be migration as well. Although a number of archaeologists differentiate large-scale migrations from smaller-scale, localized migrations (e.g., Chapman and Hamerow 1997:1; Cabana and Clark 2011a; Duff 1998:32; Rouse 1986:9, 176), they tend not to focus on the latter for methodological reasons. Archaeologists relying on the material and skeletal record from the distant past can generally only detect major, long-term population movements over significant boundaries that create significant change in a region's material culture or settlement patterns (Clark 2001:6) or affect a population's skeletal morphology or genetic composition (Bolnick 2011). In contrast, short-term and localized migrations below the community level are hard, if not impossible, to track (Adams et al. 1978:488–489; Anthony 1990:901–902; Burmeister 2000:547; cf. Beekman and Christensen 2003:154–155; Clark 2001:6, 2011:86) and only the aggregate, macro-level effects of such individual migratory actions can be documented through the archaeological record (Burmeister 2000:547; cf. De León et al., chapter 7). Bioarchaeologists who use biogeochemical signatures of human bone and tooth enamel to study ancient (even small-scale) migrations can now detect immigrants at the level of the individual, but such analyses generally involve relatively long-distance movements from distinct geological regions that differ in strontium or oxygen isotope signatures (for example, see Bentley 2006; Buzon and Bowen 2010; Buzon and Simonetti 2013; Dupras and Schwarcz 2001; Knudson and Price 2007; Knudson and Torres-Rouff, chapter 6).

Although modern migration specialists can certainly observe and study localized, short-term population movements, most of the migrations they study do cross significant boundaries. Despite the fact that the total volume of internal migration is much greater than international migration, most research is about international migration across national borders. In addition, a majority of the world's internal migration consists of rural to urban population movements (International Organization for Migration 2008:173–183), on which most research has focused (e.g., Afsar 2000; Cole and Sanders 1985; Davin 1999). In contrast, internal movement within the same geographical area that does not cross significant cultural, economic, or ecological zones is often not considered to be migration (for instance, urban to urban migration within one province or state). Therefore, the only major difference between archaeological and contemporary understandings of migrations is that the latter includes circular, temporary population movements, such as seasonal rural to urban migrants, international sojourners/target earners who migrate abroad for only a few years, and even commuter migrants who cross international borders on a daily basis for work.

Boundaries and Borders

We also find it useful to distinguish between boundaries and borders, which are often used interchangeably in the literature (e.g., Kearney 1991; Newman 2001). Boundaries separate different environmental, cultural, linguistic, economic, or political areas or zones and generally permit more flexible movement across them. A border is a specific type of boundary that delineates political territories, such as those found between nation-states, polities, and empires (see also Nevins 2002:8–9). Political borders often correspond with linguistic and cultural boundaries, but they less frequently correspond with ecological, geographical, or economic boundaries. As noted previously, population movements that occur within territorial borders (contemporary internal migration within one nation-state, for example) can still be migration if they cross significant ecological, economic, or social boundaries (such as rural to urban migration).[4]

Although political borders are not simply the product of modernity, they have become more prominent with the rise of nation-states. Not only are they more clearly delineated in modern times, but migratory movement across them is restricted to a certain extent, especially by rich, developed countries that wish to deter immigration from poorer ones.[5] Even in ancient times, however, empires and states sometimes tried to prevent others from crossing their territorial borders. When such borders do not correspond with geographical barriers (mountains, oceans, etc.), various polities have constructed vast walls and fences to keep out undesired immigrants, which have often had limited effect and mainly served as symbolic territorial markers.[6]

Types of Migrants

Although the modern immigration studies literature is replete with various typologies of the different kinds of contemporary migrants, we propose the following typology that applies to both the present and the past and note that the impact on the sending and receiving societies may depend on the type of migrant involved.

Conquerors—migrants who intend to seize power politically/culturally/socially and dominate the host society.

Colonizers/settlers—migrants who remain for the long term, if not permanently, but do not intend to seize power.

Elite migrants—those who are from the political ruling class and/or are economically well-off (including those called high-skilled/professional migrants in the modern migration literature).

Commoner migrants—those who seek better economic opportunities and livelihoods elsewhere (currently called unskilled migrants or economic labor migrants).

Refugee migrants—those who, under duress, flee ethnopolitical conflict or persecution or environmental disaster.

Disruptions and the Causes of Migration

Although not all migrations are caused by a specific type of disruption, it is clear that one way in which human populations have always responded to environmental and social disruptions is by moving out of the affected area. From the perspective of the migrant-sending society, the main questions we wish to ask are: Why do disruptions cause some populations to out-migrate while others do not? What is the threshold at which a disruption becomes serious enough to push people out of a sending society? We suggest that whether or not disruptions actually result in out-migration depends on both their severity and the resilience of societies to withstand them. In addition, the relative importance of disruptions in causing out-migration must be considered alongside other forces that influence migratory patterns, including pull factors that draw and attract migrants to a receiving society.

At the most basic level, it could be argued that the more severe an environmental or social disruption, the more likely it is to instigate out-migration. Among the variables that determine the magnitude or severity of a disruption are its *size and scale* (the number of people affected and the extent of the damage), its *duration* (how long a disruption lasts), and its *frequency* (how often a disruption occurs). Ultimately, the severity of a disruption depends on the interrelationship among these three variables. Even if a disruption occurs more frequently and has a longer duration, it may be less severe if it is small-scale and low-intensity, or is potentially reversible, thereby enabling societies to absorb its impact without resorting to out-migration. On the other hand, a disruption that occurs only once (low on frequency) and is brief (low on duration) but is large in scale may be severe enough to cause out-migration.

Whether an environmentally or socially disruptive event causes out-migration is not simply a mechanical reflection of its disruptive severity but also depends on various contextual social factors that influence a specific population's resilience or vulnerability to disruptions (see Morrissey, chapter 9). The socioeconomic, political, and cultural resources of specific social groups and communities can increase their resilience to withstand even severe disruptions without the need to migrate. Those who lack such resources may be especially vulnerable and may leave their homes even in response to less severe disruptions.

In addition, there are other factors that may encourage or discourage people to migrate when faced with disruptions. Certain groups may face social barriers that prevent them from migrating (or render them relatively immobile) even if they are confronted by significant disruptions. In most cases, there are significant pull factors that attract migrants to a specific receiving society, which may encourage people to move even if the disruptive push factors are moderate. Therefore, the relationship between disruptions and migration is not simply the product of simple causal dynamics but is usually more complex since the impact of disruptions is mediated by contextual social factors that determine a community's resilience and is also influenced by pull forces unrelated to disruptions. These issues will be discussed more extensively in the concluding chapter.

Disruptions as a Possible Consequence of Migration

Not only have humans responded to disruptions throughout history by out-migrating, these population movements themselves have become potential sources of both environmental and social disruption as migrant-receiving societies experience the sudden influx of alien populations that may overburden limited economic and environmental resources and cause sociopolitical and ethnic conflict and instability. In other cases, however, receiving societies have been able to absorb and adapt to population influxes without significant or long-term disruptive consequences. From the standpoint of the receiving society, the central question we wish to ask is: What factors determine whether certain migrations are more disruptive to the receiving society than others, and why are certain migratory groups not disruptive? This question can be illustrated effectively by comparing different immigrant groups (either within one society and country or the same migrant ethnic group in different societies and countries) to see why certain groups are more disruptive than others (see, for example, Eder, chapter 10; Tsuda, chapter 11).

Again, we hypothesize that the relative impact of a migratory disruption depends on its severity and the resilience of the host society. The severity of migratory disruptions depends on their size and scale, duration, frequency, and the type of migrant involved. Apparently, population inflows will be more disruptive for receiving societies if they are larger, last longer, and occur more often. In addition, migrants are more likely to be disruptive when the actual or perceived *differences* between them and the receiving population are greater (in terms of language, culture and ethnicity, socioeconomic status, subsistence patterns, etc.), which makes their smooth (nondisruptive) social integration into the host society difficult. Immigrants who are unwilling or unable to assimilate culturally and socially (and thus retain their differences) generally tend to be more disruptive than those who assimilate. The actual disruptive severity of migrations for the host society is again influenced by the interrelationship among these variables. Even if migratory inflows occur often and over extended periods of time (high frequency and long duration), they are not likely to be disruptive if they are small trickles of similar peoples. On the other hand, a migration that occurs only once over a short period but is large and consists of very different people will likely have more disruptive consequences. In addition, certain types of migrants (such as conquerors, refugees, illegal immigrants) may be inherently more disruptive than others.

In addition to the characteristics of the migrants themselves, the nature of the receiving society has a significant influence on the amount of disruption caused by immigration. The most important is its resilience, which is defined as the ability to withstand disruption without fundamental structural change (Carpenter et al. 2001:765; Gunderson et al. 2006; Holling 1973:17; Walker et al. 2004). Instead of defining resilience as simply the ability of a system to persist without fundamental change, however, we prefer to view it as the ability to withstand and recover from a disruption by returning to a state of stable equilibrium (see also Carpenter et al. 2001:766; Walker et al. 2006).[7] Even if migration temporarily disturbs social equilibrium, its long-term outcomes are not necessarily disruptive if the host society is resilient. First, its effects may be reversible and the status quo restored (for example, if migrant newcomers assimilate rapidly). Therefore, a dramatic change caused by migration that initially appears to be disruptive to the host society may not be as disruptive in the long term, because it does not lead to significant structural changes. Such social reproduction (maintenance of the status quo) does not imply a complete lack of change but can involve surface changes in a stable system that do not affect underlying structures. The second possibility is that the initially disruptive changes introduced by migration eventually may become incorporated into the accustomed activities of the host society, so that a new, stable status quo and equilibrium is established. In other words, a short-term disruption may lead to a nondisruptive, *transformative* structural change over time. Although transformation is a fundamental structural change (Walker et al. 2004), some underlying stability must be maintained through the establishment of a new status quo and equilibrium, since too much repeated upheaval of foundational structures can lead to disorder and collapse (for example, see Sahlins 1981:43–64). Consequently, resilience should not be seen as opposed to transformative change, as some scholars suggest (see Prosperi and Morgado 2011:819). It is only when equilibrium and stability cannot be reestablished after a disruption (i.e., the society cannot return to the status quo or transform to a new stable state) that it can then be threatened with long-term disorder, decline, and even possible collapse.

Although there are many factors that determine the resilience of a society to migratory disruptions, those that we highlight are its access to resources and wealth and sociocultural diversity. We also wish to emphasize the importance of host-society perceptions when it comes to the potentially disruptive consequences of immigration. Even if immigration is not disruptive according to the measures we have outlined, it may become disruptive and lead to social conflicts if the host populace *perceives* it to be disruptive (see examples in Meierotto, chapter 8; Eder, chapter 10; Tsuda, chapter 11; Maupin, chapter 12). On the other hand, even if immigration is disruptive based on objective measures, its effects may be mitigated if the host populace does not perceive it as disruptive (see Eder, chapter 10; Tsuda, chapter 11). Deciphering such perceptions in the past, however, is a challenge given the reinterpretations that may ensue decades and centuries later (see Hills, chapter 2; Zakrzewski, chapter 3).

The contributors to this volume address various aspects of this intellectual framework, providing illustrations of these definitions and concepts in their case studies. This conceptual and analytical framework will, therefore, be revisited in the concluding chapter of the volume, in which common themes and problems identified in the chapters of this book are addressed further.

Acknowledgments

This chapter stems from discussions among a working group of faculty supported by the Late Lessons from Early History (LLEH) initiative in the School of Human Evolution & Social Change at Arizona State University. We thank George Cowgill for his participation and insightful comments in these discussions. Participants in the May 2012 workshop, "Disruptions as a Cause and Consequence of Migrations in Human History," supported by LLEH and the Wenner-Gren Anthropological Research Foundation (Gr. CONF-573), also provided invaluable feedback on this conceptual framework.

Notes

1. In fact, even in the modern migration literature, there are few studies of the actual process of migratory movement and relocation. Virtually all research focuses on either immigrants in the receiving society or (much less often) migrant-sending societies.

2. We generally do not consider micro-level individual or psychological disruptions in this book.

3. Our definition of migration is therefore similar to what Patrick Manning (2006; 2012:ch. 1) calls "cross-community migration," which is the type of population movement that is most important for his historical analysis.

4. For political territories that are divided into semiautonomous cultural or ethnic regions (for example, the United Kingdom, Spain, China, etc.), internal migration can traverse cultural boundaries as well.

5. Our definition of these two concepts is almost the opposite of David Anthony's (2010:102), for whom borders have a more general and neutral connotation and boundaries are sharply defined borders that limit movement in some way.

6. The Great Wall of China never kept out the barbarians and neither did the various walls built by the ancient Roman Empire, such as Hadrian's Wall—they were more notable as ways to delineate the empire's political borders. The extensive fences, walls, and fortifications that the United States has built on its southern Mexican border has not kept out illegal immigrants and has been more effective as a political symbol of the government's efforts to defend the country's sovereignty (Andreas 2000; Cornelius and Tsuda 2004).

7. This definition of resilience is similar to C. S. Holling's (1973:17) concept of stability.

References Cited

Adams, William Y., Dennis P. Van Gerven, and Richard S. Levy
1978   The Retreat from Migrationism. Annual Review of Anthropology 7:483–532.
Afsar, Rita
2000   Rural-Urban Migration in Bangladesh: Causes, Consequences, and Challenges. Dhaka, Bangladesh: University Press Limited.
Andreas, Peter
2000   Border Games: Policing the U.S.-Mexico Divide. Ithaca: Cornell University Press.
Anthony, David W.
1990   Migration in Archeology: The Baby and the Bathwater. American Anthropologist 92(4):895–914.
2010   The Horse, the Wheel, and Language: How Bronze-Age Riders from the Eurasian Steppes Shaped the Modern World. Princeton: Princeton University Press.
Beekman, Christopher S., and Alexander F. Christensen
2003   Controlling for Doubt and Uncertainty Through Multiple Lines of Evidence: A New Look at the Mesoamerican Nahua Migrations. Journal of Archaeological Method and Theory 10(2):111–164.
Bentley, R. Alexander
2006   Strontium Isotopes from the Earth to the Archaeological Skeleton: A Review. Journal of Archaeological Method and Theory 13(3):135–187.
Bolin, Robert, with Lois Stanford
1998   The Northridge Earthquake: Vulnerability and Disaster. London: Routledge.
Bolnick, Deborah A.
2011   Continuity and Change in Anthropological Perspectives on Migration: Insights from Molecular Anthropology. In Rethinking Anthropological Perspectives on Migration. Graciela S. Cabana and Jeffery J. Clark, eds. Pp. 263–77. Gainesville: University Press of Florida.
Burmeister, Stefan
2000   Archaeology and Migration: Approaches to an Archaeological Proof of Migration. Current Anthropology 41(4):539–567.

Burt, George
2007   Why Are We Surprised at Surprises? Integrating Disruption Theory and System Analysis with the Scenario Methodology to Help Identify Disruptions and Discontinuities. Technological Forecasting and Social Change 74(6):731–749.

Buzon, Michele R., and G. J. Bowen
2010   Oxygen and Carbon Isotope Analysis of Human Tooth Enamel from the New Kingdom Site of Tombos in Nubia. Archaeometry 52(5):855–868.

Buzon, Michele R., and Antonio Simonetti
2013   Strontium Isotope ($^{87}Sr/^{86}Sr$) Variability in the Nile Valley: Identifying Residential Mobility During Ancient Egyptian and Nubian Sociopolitical Changes in the New Kingdom and Napatan Periods. American Journal of Physical Anthropology 151(1):1–9.

Cabana, Graciela S., and Jeffery J. Clark
2011a Introduction. Migration in Anthropology: Where We Stand. In Rethinking Anthropological Perspectives on Migration, Graciela S. Cabana and Jeffery J. Clark, eds. Pp. 1–15. Gainesville: University Press of Florida.

Cabana, Graciela S. and Jeffery J. Clark, eds.
2011b Rethinking Anthropological Perspectives on Migration. Gainesville: University Press of Florida.

Cameron, Catherine M.
1995   Migration and the Movement of Southwestern Peoples. Journal of Anthropological Archaeology 14(2):104–124.

Carpenter, Steve, Brian Walker, J. Marty Anderies, and Nick Abel
2001   From Metaphor to Measurement: Resilience of What to What? Ecosystems 4(8):765–781.

Chapman, John, and Helena Hamerow
1997   On the Move Again: Migrations and Invasions in Archaeological Explanation. In Migrations and Invasions in Archaeological Explanation. John Chapman and Helena Hamerow, eds. Pp. 1–10. British Archaeological Reports International Series, 664. Oxford: Archaeopress.

Clark, Jeffery J.
2001   Tracking Prehistoric Migrations: Pueblo Settlers Among the Tonto Basin Hohokam. Anthropological Papers of the University of Arizona, 65. Tucson: University of Arizona Press.

2011   Disappearance and Diaspora: Contrasting Two Migrations in the Southern U.S. Southwest. In Rethinking Anthropological Perspectives on Migration. Graciela S. Cabana and Jeffery J. Clark, eds. Pp. 84–107. Gainesville: University Press of Florida.

Clark, Rebecca L., Jennifer E. Glick, and Regina M. Bures
2009   Immigrant Families Over the Life Course: Research Directions and Needs. Journal of Family Issues 30(6):852–872.

Cole, William, and Richard Sanders
1985   Internal Migration and Urban Employment in the Third World. American Economic Review 75(3):481–494.

Cornelius, Wayne A., and Takeyuki Tsuda
2004   Controlling Immigration: The Limits of Government Intervention. *In* Controlling Immigration: A Global Perspective. 2nd edition. Wayne A. Cornelius, Takeyuki Tsuda, Philip L. Martin, and James F. Hollifield, eds. Pp. 3–48. Stanford, California: Stanford University Press.

Crawford, Michael H., and Benjamin C. Campbell, eds.
2012   Causes and Consequences of Human Migration: An Evolutionary Perspective. New York: Cambridge University Press.

Davin, Delia
1999   Internal Migration in Contemporary China. New York: St. Martin's Press.

Duff, Andrew
1998   The Process of Migration in the Late Prehistoric Southwest. *In* Migration and Reorganization: The Pueblo IV Period in the American Southwest. Katherine A. Spielmann, ed. Pp. 31–52. Arizona State University Anthropological Research Papers, 51. Tempe: Department of Anthropology, Arizona State University.

Dupras, Tosha L., and Henry P. Schwarcz
2001   Strangers in a Strange Land: Stable Isotope Evidence for Human Migration in the Dakhleh Oasis, Egypt. Journal of Archaeological Science 28(11):1199–1208.

Gunderson, Lance H., Steve R. Carpenter, Carl Folke, Per Olsson, and Garry Peterson
2006   Water RATs (Resilience, Adaptability, and Transformability) in Lake and Wetland Social-Ecological Systems. Ecology and Society 11(1):Art. 16.

Hewitt, Kenneth
1997   Regions at Risk: A Geographical Introduction to Disaster. London: Longman.

Holling, C. S.
1973   Resilience and Stability of Ecological Systems. Annual Review of Ecology and Systematics 4:1–23.

Hunter, Lori M.
2005   Migration and Environmental Hazards. Population and Environment 26(4):273–302.

International Organization for Migration
2008   World Migration Report 2008: Managing Labour Mobility in the Evolving Global Economy. IOM World Migration Report Series, vol. 4. Geneva: International Organization for Migration.

Kearney, Michael
1991   Borders and Boundaries of State and Self at the End of Empire. Journal of Historical Sociology 4(1):52–74.

Knudson, Kelly J., and T. Douglas Price
2007   Utility of Multiple Chemical Techniques in Archaeological Residential Mobility Studies: Case Studies from Tiwanaku- and Chiribaya-Affiliated Sites in the Andes. American Journal of Physical Anthropology 132(1):25–39.

Kreps, G. A.
1984   Sociological Inquiry and Disaster Research. Annual Review of Sociology 10:309–330.

Landale, Nancy S., and Nimfa B. Ogena
1995   Migration and Union Dissolution among Puerto Rican Women. International Migration Review 29(3):671–692.

Lin, Keh-Ming
1986   Psychopathology and Social Disruption in Refugees. *In* Refugee Mental Health in Resettlement Countries. Carolyn L. Williams and Joseph Westermeyer, eds. Pp. 61–73. Washington, DC: Hemisphere Publishing Corporation.

Lucassen, Jan, Leo Lucassen, and Patrick Manning, eds.
2010   Migration History in World History: Multidisciplinary Approaches. Leiden and Boston: Brill.

Manning, Patrick
2006   Cross-Community Migration: A Distinctive Human Pattern. Social Evolution & History 5(2):24–54.
2012   Migration in World History. 2nd edition. London: Routledge.

McAllister, Ian
1995   Occupational Mobility among Immigrants: The Impact of Migration on Economic Success in Australia. International Migration Review 29(2):441–468.

Mirsky, Julia, V. Slonim-Nevo, and L. Rubinstein
2007   Psychological Wellness and Distress among Recent Immigrants: A Four-year Longitudinal Study in Israel and Germany. International Migration 45(1):151–175.

Nevins, Joseph
2002   Operation Gatekeeper: The Rise of the "Illegal Alien" and the Making of the U.S.-Mexico Boundary. New York: Routledge.

Newman, David
2001   Boundaries, Borders, and Barriers: Changing Geographic Perspectives on Territorial Lines. *In* Identities, Borders, Orders: Rethinking International Relations Theory. Mathias Albert, David Jacobson, and Yosef Lapid, eds. Pp.137–152. Minneapolis: University of Minnesota Press.

Oliver-Smith, Anthony
1996   Anthropological Research on Hazards and Disasters. Annual Review of Anthropology 25:303–328.

Park, Minkyung, and Patricia A. Stokowski
2009   Social Disruption Theory and Crime in Rural Communities: Comparisons Across Three Levels of Tourism Growth. Tourism Management 30(6):905–915.

Prosperi, David C., and Sofia Morgado
2011   Resilience and Transformation: Can We Have Both? *In* Change for Stability: Lifecycles of Cities and Regions. Manfred Schrenk, Vasily V. Popovich, and Peter Zeile, eds. Pp. 819–829. Proceedings, 16th International Conference on Urban Planning, Regional Development and Information Society, Real Corp 2011. http://programm.corp.at/cdrom2011/papers2011/CORP2011_92.pdf, accessed June 17, 2014.

Rouse, Irving
1986   Migrations in Prehistory: Inferring Population Movement from Cultural Remains. New Haven: Yale University Press.

Sahlins, Marshall
1981   Historical Metaphors and Mythical Realities. Ann Arbor: University of Michigan Press.

Tsuda, Takeyuki
2003   Strangers in the Ethnic Homeland: Japanese Brazilian Return Migration in Transnational Perspective. New York: Columbia University Press.
2011   Modern Perspectives on Ancient Migrations. *In* Rethinking Anthropological Perspectives on Migration. Graciela S. Cabana and Jeffery J. Clark, eds. Pp. 313–338. Gainesville: University Press of Florida.

Walker, Brian, C. S. Holling, Stephen R. Carpenter, and Ann Kinzig
2004   Resilience, Adaptability and Transformability in Social-Ecological Systems. Ecology and Society 9(2):5.

Walker, Brian H., John M. Anderies, Ann P. Kinzig, and Paul Ryan
2006   Exploring Resilience in Social-Ecological Systems Through Comparative Studies and Theory Development: Introduction to the Special Issue. Ecology and Society 11(1): Art. 12.

Wisner, Ben, Piers Blaikie, Terry Cannon, and Ian Davis
2004   At Risk: Natural Hazards, People's Vulnerability and Disasters. 2nd edition. London: Routledge.

II

PAST PERSPECTIVES

2

The Anglo-Saxon Migration

An Archaeological Case Study of Disruption

CATHERINE HILLS

"The Migration Period" is one of the names given to the period of European history that saw the collapse of the western Roman Empire, mainly during the fifth century AD. This collapse has always been viewed as one of the most dramatic disruptions in European history, associated with the invasion and migration of barbarians into the disintegrating empire. It is therefore appropriate that a case study from this period be included in this work.

The causes, character, and consequences of the fall of Rome were complex, and are still much debated (Halsall 2007; Ward-Perkins 2005). Accounts of this period continue to have political resonance, because they are the starting point for discussion of the identities, now and in the past, of the peoples who inhabit Europe today. Here, one specific migration, by the Anglo-Saxons, is chosen for detailed analysis, mainly from an archaeological perspective. This chapter addresses some of the same issues as those discussed by Zakrzewski (chapter 3), and identifies some of the same problems in assessing the scale and impact of past migration/invasion.

The Anglo-Saxon migration during the fifth century AD from north Germany and southern Scandinavia to Britain seems at first like a straightforward example of a historical migration that can usefully contribute to wider discussion of the phenomenon of migration. "Disruption" is not a term often used in discussion of this process, because it is taken for granted that there was considerable disruption, involving change in all aspects of society, during the transition from Roman Britain to Anglo-Saxon England. However, the character, scale, and impact of the changes that took place, and their causes, have been, and continue to be, the subject of much debate.

The key question is the extent to which there was migration by Germanic people from northern Europe to Britain, and whether that took place on such a scale that the migrants replaced the native British population in what became England. This question has political resonance to this day because it underlies perceptions of the relationships between the existing peoples of the British Isles. When the English are seen as different and separate from the other peoples of Britain—the Scots, Welsh, and Irish, that is, the "Celtic" peoples—an explanation can be sought in differing origins. The British, in this version, are ancestral to the other peoples, but not to the English, who were once immigrant Anglo-Saxons. The alternative scenario is that a small number of incomers took over at an elite level, imposing their material culture and language on the indigenous population. In this version, the peoples of Britain share the same ancestry.

It is clear from historical and archaeological evidence that at an elite level there was political, institutional, social, and economic disruption. What were provinces within a centrally administered empire in the fourth century had, by the end of the sixth century, become a series of small kingdoms, with rulers of various ancestries. However, it is less clear how extensively the population and its basic subsistence strategies were disrupted. Differing views are supported by different interpretations of the same historical, linguistic, archaeological, and bioarchaeological evidence (see Hills 2003 and Härke 2011 for reviews from different perspectives and detailed bibliographies). The arguments have been both about the scale of change reflected in different kinds of evidence and the degree to which those changes can be explained as the results of large-scale migration of new people or, alternatively, as indigenous response to new ideas transmitted by small numbers of immigrants. The purpose of this chapter is to explain this situation and to offer some cautious conclusions based mainly on recent archaeological research. It is also to show that this migration is not an unproblematic historical event but a complex and not fully understood process, which varied considerably in its impact both regionally and chronologically. It cannot be treated as one single process that can be explained by the application of any one explanatory model, nor can it be used without due caution in the construction of historical models of migration—although such models may bring valuable clarity to the debate.

Perspectives on the Debate

The starting point for this debate has always been the well-known account of the arrival and origins of the Anglo-Saxons given by Bede, writing at Jarrow in the early eighth century AD. According to Bede they were invited as military allies by the British leader Vortigern around AD 449, arriving at first in three ships and then joined by a larger fleet. "They came from three very powerful Germanic tribes, the Saxons, Angles and Jutes" (Bede, HE 1.15). This narrative is usually coupled to the account by the earlier writer Gildas—quoted by Bede—of the violent incursion of barbarians who laid waste to town and country from sea to sea. The linguistic and archaeological evidence appear to support this story of violent incursions and settlement of new people: English replaced Celtic and Latin, the Roman cities were abandoned, and the burials, pots, and houses datable to the fifth and sixth centuries AD do look like those found in northern Germany rather than in late Roman Britain. So why has this nice, clear picture been questioned?

The answer lies partly in the changing political perspectives of historians and others from the days of Gildas to the present, partly in the source-critical and theoretical approach that dominated all fields of humanities scholarship, including archaeology, in the second half of the twentieth century, and partly in the reality that things were indeed not so simple in the fifth century AD. Here, I look at the historical sources and their changing interpretation, more recent scientific approaches, and, finally, archaeological evidence and its interpretation. I will not focus on the linguistic evidence, as it is outside my own expertise, but simply note that the rate at which English replaced Latin and Celtic as the language of the majority of the population of what became England is difficult to assess, and that language change is driven by social, political, and economic factors, as well as by the number of speakers of a specific language. The spread of English around the world in recent centuries has happened in various ways, with and without population replacement.

Historical Sources

The key historical sources are the two referenced previously, Bede and Gildas (Colgrave and Mynors 1969; Winterbottom 1978). There are other brief sources, but these two have dominated discussion because they are substantial narrative accounts. Neither of these authors set out to provide answers to the questions asked by modern scholars. Gildas is a near contemporary of the events he described, but he is writing as a prophet of doom, calling to account the British rulers of his own day, whose wickedness, he predicted, would bring down on their heads the wrath of God, who would punish them as a generation before their ancestors had been punished by barbarian invaders. The gist of the story must be true, because Gildas could not have used it if it was not based in reality: violent invasions caused great destruction in Britain after it ceased to be part of the Roman Empire. Exactly when this invasion happened, or when and where Gildas was writing, is not clear, despite generations of scholarly argument devoted to the subject. The chronology Gildas gives in his work is not externally fixed, though the decades on either side of AD 500 are generally accepted as the time he was writing. We are left unclear on how much of Britain had fallen under foreign control by Gildas's day.

Bede, writing three centuries later than the events he describes, draws heavily on Gildas. Bede takes the story of violent barbarian invasions from Gildas and adds tribal origins from another (unknown) source. Most of his work is then concerned with showing how Christianity came to the "gens Anglorum," to which he belonged himself. From Bede we learn much about the history of sixth- to early eighth-century England, a period for which he had direct and indirect witness accounts. The Angles, Saxons, and Jutes were settled in the southern and eastern parts of Britain, occupying small territories that were becoming consolidated into larger kingdoms. His account focuses on royalty and holy men and women, rather than the population at large. Bede says that five languages were spoken on the island, English, British, Irish, Pictish, as well as Latin, which was in use among everyone because of the Scriptures. However, he does not explain whether, for example, everyone in Northumbria in his lifetime spoke English or if only the elite did.

Bede and Gildas provide clear evidence for violent incursions into Britain at some time after the beginning of the fifth century AD. From Bede it is clear that by the eighth century those in the dominant stratum of the population in what had been south and east Britain identified themselves as of Germanic ancestry, differentiated from the British populations of the west and north. Royal genealogies preserved in later compilations confirm this self-perception. An origin in north Germany was also recognized and was the reason for the interest of the English Saxons in the conversion of the continental German Saxons, a process to which many English missionaries contributed. Neither of these authors was primarily interested in the ancestry of the population at large.

Over subsequent centuries, interpretation changed according to contemporary politics, remaining top-down, concerned mainly with the deeds and ancestry of rulers, not their people. Following the Norman conquest of 1066 there was little incentive for the Norman elite to emphasize descent from Anglo-Saxon invaders, and the popular version of British history throughout much of the Middle Ages was that of Geoffrey of Monmouth, who focused instead on the British king Arthur, putative heroic defender of Britain against Anglo-Saxon invaders. In later centuries, however, the Anglo-Saxons were again seen as having played a significant role in the history of England. The Reformation in the sixteenth century led to the rediscovery of the Anglo-Saxon language, literature, and theology, seen as the origin of the true English church before corruption by later medieval Catholicism. The Parliamentarians of the seventeenth century found support for their cause in Anglo-Saxon law, while philologists demonstrated the links between the German and English languages. In the nineteenth century some historians suggested that the English were a superior race, peculiarly fitted to rule an empire, including controlling the Celtic peoples of Britain.

Alternatively, more recently, the dissolution of the United Kingdom and the separation of Scotland, Wales, and England can be justified in terms of the differences among those nations. Both arguments start from a maximalist version of the Anglo-Saxon migration: there was substantial population change that made the English different. From the 1960s to the 1980s, another view prevailed. We were all British, all one people, and since we had not been invaded by Germany in the 1940s, maybe that had not happened in the 440s either. Invading war bands, of varied ancestry, may have taken over some territories, imposing their culture but not replacing the main population. In this version, English, Scots, and Welsh were differentiated by later history and politics, not by ancestry. Now the pendulum has swung back to argue for more migrants in the past, maybe because we see so many migrants today. It is important to take into account the context of the debate along with the substance of it. I am more willing to see more immigrants now than I was 30 years ago partly because I cannot escape from current trends of thought, although I would like to think that it is because the weight of new evidence is moving in that direction and forcing me to modify my views.

Archaeological Theory

Archaeology began to contribute to this debate in the nineteenth century, and for a long time it seemed to provide clear confirmation of Bede's account, because there is visible change in many aspects of material culture from fourth-century Romano-British to sixth-century Anglo-Saxon and British. We do not see large numbers of slaughtered Britons, or even many skeletons with signs of battle injuries, but Roman cities and houses decayed and were either abandoned or built over, stone and tile gave way to timber and thatch as the main building materials, and wheel-thrown pottery and coinage disappeared. Burials changed from inhumation with very few grave goods to a mix of cremation and inhumation, both often associated with new kinds of jewelry, pots, and weapons. Within a culture-historical framework of interpretation of archaeological evidence, this change seemed clear evidence of the appearance of new people. This is based on the idea that individual peoples in the past were defined by specific types of houses, pots, or metalwork and that they are therefore recognizable in the archaeological record. Plotting the geographical and chronological distributions of different artifact types would show where separate peoples had existed in time and space. Thus "prehistory" could be written very much like traditional history—only with beaker folk and battle-ax people instead of Romans and Normans. This interpretative framework was discredited in European scholarship by the misuse made of it by Nazism, but the underlying idea is still present in archaeological interpretation across much of the world—and as a popular "common sense" explanation in the United Kingdom outside university archaeology departments. In relation to early Anglo-Saxon England, or the European Migration Period more widely, it has seemed to make very good sense. We have written accounts of movements of Anglo-Saxons, Goths, Franks, Huns, Lombards, etc., and we can see artifacts, mostly brooches, of different shapes, with regional and chronological variation that can be linked plausibly to those recorded movements. Thus, a brief historical mention of people moving into a territory could be expanded by plotting all the brooches of each type to argue that their presence either confirmed the historical account or meant that the relevant people were there earlier or sooner and in greater or lesser force than the written source suggested. A large and complex body of literature has developed on this basis. In England it is even possible to see Bede's Angles, Saxons, and Jutes. The material culture of the regions distinguished by Bede does differ broadly in line with his account: East Anglia,

Lincolnshire, and Yorkshire can be distinguished from the regions south of the Thames as respectively "Anglian" and "Saxon," while Kent and the Isle of Wight, the "Jutish" areas, are different again and similar to each other. The archaeological material from both sides of the North Sea during the fifth and sixth centuries, including brooches, weapons, pots, and types of houses, shows many detailed similarities, which might be explained as having been brought en masse from north Germany to eastern England by Anglo-Saxon immigrants.

Developments in theoretical archaeology, however, have cast doubt on this whole edifice of scholarship. In the 1960s and 1970s "New" archaeology (which became "processual" once it was no longer new) took a radical ax to the culture-historical tree. Understanding cultural systems, their evolution, and their interaction with the environment, replaced description and chronology, and anthropology replaced history as the preferred ally. It was emphasized that material culture patterning is caused by many factors—economic, social, technological, and ideological—and not primarily driven by membership of an ethnic or national group. Migration as an explanation for change in the past was downplayed, and in England this coincided with the prevalence of the idea that the inhabitants of modern Britain had much common ancestry, and that there had not been large-scale population change in the fifth century. This has caused rethinking of the Migration Period as a whole (Halsall 2007; Hakenbeck 2007).

Change in material culture clearly is not driven solely by migration: an example described by Härke is the westernization of Russia after 1989 (Härke 2007). In Britain during the first millennium AD, both the Roman military conquest and the conversion of the Anglo-Saxons to Christianity caused significant change in material culture, disrupting to some extent previous political, economic, and religious structures. Neither of these processes involved mass migration, although key external personnel did arrive: soldiers, tax collectors, slaves, and traders in Roman Britain, which recent isotopic analysis shows to have had an urban population with diverse origins (Chenery et al. 2011), or the monks, stonemasons, and glaziers in Anglo-Saxon Northumbria recorded by Bede. On the other hand, change and regional variation in material culture are not always externally driven. The "Anglian," "Saxon," and "Jutish" regional distinctions visible in sixth-century burials do not in fact represent transfers of material culture packages from the relevant homelands, but were created within Britain, drawing on a mixture of local indigenous traditions and new ideas from many different parts of the continent. "Jutish" Kent has most similarity to what is now northern France, caused by close political and economic links across the English Channel; "Anglian" dress fasteners develop from earlier artifacts found in different regions around the North Sea, combined to create a new English dress code; "Saxons" favored round brooches whose antecedents occurred within and outside the Roman empire. The identities visible in the sixth-century burials probably were related to the tribal divisions recorded by Bede in the eighth century, but they do not have a simple explanation in the specific origins of immigrants.

Since the 1970s it has also been apparent that the population of Roman Britain was too substantial to have vanished overnight. Ancient demography is a very imprecise subject, but settlement patterns give a relative scale. Aerial photography and field surveys showed that the late prehistoric and Roman rural settlement pattern was comparable to the medieval one, reflecting population sizes of a comparable magnitude. More recent research using metal-detected finds and geophysical surveys has strengthened this picture. This densely settled agricultural landscape was very different from the deserted woodland waiting to be cleared by pioneering Saxons envisaged by traditional historical accounts. The same evidence has been used to map early Anglo-Saxon settlement patterns, showing regional variation, with some areas having comparable density and distribution of settlement in Roman and Anglo-Saxon periods and others having a decline in intensity of settlement with a shift from arable to pastoral farming, which probably does reflect population decline in some regions, but not universally (Chester-Kadwell 2009).

A critique of processual archaeology suggested that it did not pay enough attention to change, to nonfunctional causation, or to the individual. There was a tendency to study societies as a set of interlocking systems, with change, if it happened at all, caused by imbalance in the relationship between those systems rather than by an external force such as migration. Post-processual archaeology has not adopted a monolithic theoretical paradigm, which is why it is still defined by that name. Many different ways of understanding and interpreting the material record exist, but there is a focus on identity—gender, age, ethnicity, social hierarchy, religious affiliation, or ideology. This emphasis has been very influential in early Anglo-Saxon archaeology because much of the evidence for this period comes from graves, which are well suited to explorations of the kinds of identity listed previously (see papers in Semple and Williams 2007; Lucy 2002).

The overall impact of developments in theoretical archaeology on the study of migration in the past has been to make the evidence seem more

difficult and complex. If an "Anglo-Saxon" brooch does not necessarily sig-
nify that the person who wore and was buried with it was of Anglo-Saxon
descent, what can we say about it and what use is archaeological evidence in
interpretation of the historical sources? Frustration with the uncertainties
of current archaeological interpretation has led to attempts to get answers
from science.

Osteology and Molecular Biology

Various methods are now being applied to skeletal material to identify local
or nonlocal populations and other information, such as family groupings.
Osteology, long used to study age and sex structure, and health within populations, has also been applied to the question of population change, using
patterns of metric and nonmetric traits. Heinrich Härke (1992) argued that
it is possible to identify taller weapon-bearing men and shorter men without weapons as of Germanic and British origin, respectively, although they
are buried in the same "Anglo-Saxon" cemeteries. However, the equivalent
women did not show a similar pattern. If tall incoming Germanic warriors
did not have similarly tall wives, their sons should not have maintained the
height differential into the next generation unless some other factor were
at play, such as diet or selection of tall men of any ancestry as warriors. A
height differential between Romano-British and Anglo-Saxon populations
has been detected by other researchers, but not conclusively explained. In
her study of burials from the Upper Thames region, Becky Gowland (2007)
suggested that variation was related more to age, gender, and local practice
than to ethnicity. In the fifth century in eastern England, cremation was
the dominant burial practice, and cremated bone is more limited in the
information it can provide, but some demographic information about life
expectancy can be recovered (McKinley 1994).

Molecular biology recently has been seen as a way of circumventing the
complexities of historical and archaeological evidence (Hedges 2011). This
is very attractive: information extracted from ancient skeletons should give
direct insights into ancient peoples and provide the basis for real historical
demography. However, media reports have exaggerated the success of these
techniques so far. Ancient DNA (aDNA) has been extracted from animal
and human skeletons, but initial research was compromised by the contamination of aDNA by the modern DNA of the researchers. New techniques
now offer much better hope of avoiding contamination and achieving success, but it will be a slow and expensive process to amass a database large

enough for demographic patterns to become evident. Another approach is the analysis of isotopes preserved in teeth. These can indicate diet and also show whether an individual had spent their childhood near where they were buried. However, although it is possible to identify individuals who were not born in the same place that they were buried, it is much more difficult to pinpoint the origin of nonlocal individuals, because there is usually a wide geographical area that would provide comparable isotopic evidence. For example, the isotopic signature of burials originating on either side of the North Sea might not be very different (Brettell et al. 2012). These approaches are a work in progress, in need of further critical methodological research, and then, hopefully, assembly of data that will yield real answers.

Most current and recent research on ancient population genetics actually depends on analysis of modern DNA. Large databases of modern samples now exist, which show patterns of genetic variation around the world. Back-projecting these patterns is the tool used to study past population movement, but the premises on which the conclusions are based sometimes fail to take key historical issues into account. This problem is apparent in a study claiming to show that a significant number of Frisian men invaded England during the fifth century, exaggerated by the media as genocide of Britons by Frisians. In follow-up papers it was argued that the dominance of the invaders had been secured by an apartheid-style policy of segregated marriage so that the invaders had more sons and grandsons than the indigenous men, allowing an initially relatively small number of immigrants to become genetically dominant in the eventual population (Thomas et al. 2006; Weale et al. 2002) This research at first appears well-founded, and it has been reported widely in recent literature, but if examined more closely, the conclusions are problematic (Hills 2009). The samples were taken from an east-west transect across England into Wales, from men whose grandfathers had been born locally (in order to avoid recent immigrants). Small towns were chosen, again to avoid the population dislocation caused by the Industrial Revolution. The English samples proved to differ from the Welsh and to be closer to Frisian samples. So far so good, but several problems emerged. First, the size of the samples was not very large: rerunning with more data might answer this criticism. Second, if the pattern is real, there are contexts other than the fifth century that might explain it. The Danish Viking settlement of the tenth century is the most obvious: all of the English samples came from within the Danelaw, and the continental homelands of Frisians, Anglo-Saxons, and Danes lie close to each other around the eastern North Sea coast. The researchers later conceded that they could not distinguish between Danish and Anglo-Saxon invaders. There are also other times when significant movement across the North Sea took place—for example, Flemish weavers moving to East Anglia in the sixteenth century. The specifically "Frisian" origin is also problematic, since in the fourth century the coastal regions of what is now the northern Netherlands seem to have been very thinly populated, and were partly resettled by the same Anglo-Saxons who were also arriving in England, which might explain any similarity. Even the difference between Welsh and English might be explicable in terms of later centuries of separate political and economic development—or the precise character of the samples chosen. Even small towns were subject to substantial immigration during the nineteenth and twentieth centuries, if not before, so even the local grandfather was not an infallible selection criterion. This research has not provided secure conclusions about the Anglo-Saxon impact on Britain, but similar future reframed research projects may do so. The conclusion to be drawn is that there are new scientific tools that will, when thoroughly tested and critically deployed, provide new information, but it is unlikely to come in the form of simple answers.

Recent Archaeological Research

Anglo-Saxon archaeological research in recent decades has tended to downplay migration, whatever theoretical slant is taken. Social structure and identity have been the frameworks for interpretation, with sudden catastrophic change, including migration/invasion, consigned to the culture-historical scrap heap. However, this is less true of German scholarship, which has a strong influence on English scholarship of this period. Awareness of parallels between English and German artifacts goes back to the nineteenth century, when J. M. Kemble excavated burial urns in Germany that he rightly pointed out were very like those found in England. Between the 1930s and 1980s these parallels were pursued by J. N. L. Myres, who found many very similar cremation urns in eastern England and north Germany, interpreting them in terms of invasion and settlement (Myres 1969). There is mobility of ideas and people across the North Sea in this research field today, whatever the situation in the past. Some scholars have applied modern migration theory to the problem, which helps in clarifying issues and thinking about the scale and duration of population movement (Burmeister 2000; Hamerow 1997). The analytical framework applied by Burmeister is interesting, but some of the specifics of the data he used can be queried. A key issue is establishing a chronology for the fifth century. There is a hiatus of up to a century between clearly definable and dateable late fourth-century Roman material culture and equally clearly definable furnished Anglo-Saxon inhumation burials attributable mostly to the sixth century. How to fill the gap? Different specialists, classicists, and medievalists study each end of this gap with different agendas and perceptions. Until recently, the mid–fifth century date given by Bede for the arrival of the Anglo-Saxons was taken as a fixed point in archaeological chronologies, the changeover point for Romanists and Anglo-Saxonists, which therefore necessarily confirmed it as a significant dividing point.

One way forward might be to extend the Roman period. The buildings, pottery, coins, and infrastructure of fourth-century Roman Britain fall into disuse and disappear, but when? Different types of evidence allow different conclusions. Coinage ceases to arrive as pay for soldiers, and does not remain in circulation, although there are fifth-century coins in Britain, most notably the Patching hoard, with coins dating up to 470 (White et al. 1999). The market economy collapses, so the potters cease to operate, as do many other craftspeople and tradespeople. On the other hand, some buildings show signs of rebuilding and use long after an initial late fourth-century construction. Also, a finer chronology for late Roman artifacts shows change in fashion in pottery and jewelry within the fourth century, with indications of the kind of material that might have continued to be used into the fifth century (Cool 2000).

The history of land use can be reconstructed to some extent from dated pollen cores, which give an indication of the fluctuations in forest, arable land, and pasture. The picture here is complicated by variable preservation of suitable samples whose interpretation is also not always straightforward. Around Hadrian's Wall some regeneration of woodland in the early fifth century has been attributed to the departure of the army making less demand on local food resources, while in the southwest it seems that dramatic change in land use may not have taken place until much later, perhaps not until the eighth to tenth centuries (Fyfe and Rippon 2004). In East Anglia we lack good dated cores partly because the dry sandy soils are not conducive to good preservation. Clearly there was regional variation, and at least we can no longer suggest abandonment of most arable land in lowland England, although some may have been converted to pasture. Maps of pre-twentieth-century field systems give some support for the argument that later prehistoric boundaries continued to be in use during Roman, Anglo-Saxon, medieval, and early modern periods, indicating some degree of continuity of use. New arrivals came into a settled farmed landscape full of field boundaries, settlements, and at least some of their inhabitants.

Yet there is surprisingly little direct evidence of interaction. The best example so far is found in the West Midlands, at Wasperton, in Warwickshire, where a late Roman cemetery continued to be used into the Anglo-Saxon period (Carver et al. 2009). Typical late Roman burials, largely unfurnished except for hobnailed boots, some in coffins, were succeeded by typical "Anglo-Saxon" furnished inhumations, with jewelry and weapons of the same types as those found farther east. Analysis of the chronology and the material culture of these burials shows that the cemetery was in use from the fourth to the seventh centuries, with change driven by social and religious factors as much, or more than, population change. Some Germanic people must have arrived, together with their ideas about burial, dress, and weaponry, but it does not seem that they completely displaced and replaced the local people.

Unfortunately this situation has not been observed elsewhere, and in south and eastern Britain it is difficult to identify anyone who is not using Anglo-Saxon material culture from the later fifth century onward. This has often been interpreted as meaning Britons were indeed overwhelmed and largely replaced by Germanic invaders. But since it is no longer believed that ethnicity can be clearly read from material culture, an alternative hypothesis is that elite Britons took on Germanic material culture, just as in previous centuries they had taken on Roman styles of clothing and houses. This would explain the British names in the genealogies of West Saxon kings, such as Cerdic or Caedwalla. The peasantry might be barely visible anywhere because of the poverty of their material possessions. It is important to remember that the archaeological record for this period is biased toward burial, which is not a simple reflection of the living society that created it. Unfurnished inhumation is a burial rite prevalent in the fourth century throughout the Roman Empire, identifiable on the continent well into the fifth century. Furnished burial might be seen as an aberrant practice of the sixth and seventh centuries, after which grave goods disappeared again. The lack of dateable material culture is not only a feature of the parts of Britain that became Anglo-Saxon. In the west it is also difficult to find fifth- to sixth-century material culture, apart from pottery imported from the Mediterranean, so there is little specifically "British" material culture in the west, where it must have existed, that is not obscured by Anglo-Saxon material culture, as it is in the east—if it existed. Lack of obviously durable material culture does not necessarily mean an impossibly low living standard. Many of the categories of material on which archaeologists seem to depend are not in fact essential for existence. Pottery, for example, if poorly made and fired, is not functional for many purposes, and burials need not be equipped with durable equipment. Unfurnished burials, timber buildings, textiles, and wood or leather containers all leave little trace, and metal can be recycled and eventually rust away—only an elite still able to acquire imported tableware and glass vessels and make the occasional stone monument can be seen in the record in the west of Britain, while their equivalents, of whatever ancestry, in the east, together with a good proportion of the rest of the population, were dressed and buried with brooches, pots, and weapons of types usually identified as Anglo-Saxon. Absence of evidence is not conclusive evidence of absence (or presence) of British inhabitants of south and eastern England during the fifth century or later.

Another approach is to push back the arrival of the Anglo-Saxons, or at least the appearance of Anglo-Saxon material culture, before the traditional mid–fifth century Adventus Saxonum. This has now been demonstrated for East Anglia, through the analysis of the large cremation cemetery of Spong Hill, in central Norfolk. This site was completely excavated in the 1970s, published between 1976 and 1994, by a team led from 1975 by the author of this chapter. It produced 2,500 cremations and 57 inhumations. Renewed research in recent years by this author, Dr. Sam Lucy, and others has produced a relative chronology for the site showing that its latest phase includes inhumation burials that can be dated by reference to recent chronologies for East Anglia to the later fifth and early sixth centuries AD (Hills and Lucy 2013). The majority of the cremation burials belong to earlier phases, dating therefore before the end of the fifth century. The Spong Hill cremations have many direct parallels with cemeteries in north Germany, which come into use during the later fourth century and continue through much of the fifth century. Pottery and grave goods all show close similarities, indicating ongoing contact for several generations. We conclude that the Spong Hill cemetery came into use in the first half of the fifth century and maintained contact with the continent while developing locally specific styles of pottery and burial practices, and went out of use during the first half of the sixth century. The Spong Hill evidence is supported by the wealth of material of this period found in recent decades by metal detectorists (Worrell et al. 2010). In Norfolk and Lincolnshire, and neighboring areas, the density of early Anglo-Saxon metalwork is far higher than elsewhere. More than a thousand cruciform brooch fragments have been recorded for Norfolk, the majority probably from disturbed burials. Other parts of England produce few fifth-century finds, apart from small concentrations in the Upper Thames and east Kent (McLean and Richardson 2010). Analysis of the distribution of cremation burials shows that there is a strong concentration in the region outlined previously, Norfolk, Lincolnshire, and immediately adjacent areas. Here there were cremation burials like those from Spong Hill, with elaborately decorated pots, cruciform brooches, antler combs and playing pieces, and sets of miniature toilet items, all closely paralleled in north Germany. A small number of similar cremations are scattered across southern England, for example at Abingdon in the Upper Thames. But most cremations found elsewhere are in undecorated pots, with few grave goods, and range in date from the late fifth to early eighth century. They may derive partly from local native tradition as well as from Anglo-Saxon influence, and suggest a much later and less numerous immigration.

What does this mean for interpretation of the Anglo-Saxon migration? In part it supports the traditional account of migration from north Germany. The detailed similarities between Spong Hill and north German cemeteries such as Issendorf, and the scale of fifth-century material found in East Anglia, suggest the transfer of ideas about burial and pottery and metalwork technology and styles on a scale that must have involved the movement of people, as does the use of the distinctive type of house, the "grubenhaus." This was not a one-off journey across the North Sea—an unlikely proposition in any case, for a sea that in other periods has rightly been seen as a route for communication and commerce rather than a barrier. Long-term reinforcement of ideas fits some models for migration, initial pioneers being followed by others, with two-way traffic between homeland and new settlements.

What is clear is that there was a strong regional character to what happened. One explanation does not fit all of England. This has always been broadly recognized, in that Wales never became Anglo-Saxon and the southwest did so only after centuries of expansion by the West Saxons. The new evidence suggests that there were a range of different regional histories between the extremes of west and east, and that that events in Norfolk, for example, followed a different course from the midlands or south of the Thames.

In a fairly precisely defined region in eastern England, centered on Norfolk and Lincolnshire, a significant number of people from the other side of the North Sea do seem to have arrived early in the fifth century and established territories where Germanic material culture and, especially, burial practice were dominant. This area formed the basis for the "Anglian" zone of later Anglo-Saxon England. The population may indeed have included a substantial number of people with Germanic ancestry as well as an as yet unspecifiable proportion of the native British population. However, elsewhere in England, the local population seems to have survived more substantially, Anglo-Saxon material culture arrived later, and there is a stronger case for interpreting the transition as one of takeover rather than population replacement. There was not one "Anglo-Saxon migration" that had the same impact in all of England; therefore, any use of the "Adventus Saxonum" in a summary discussion of migration must take account of this and define precisely the sources and character of the evidence used. There is not one story of early English ancestry but many different regional trajectories.

References Cited

Brettell, Rhea, Jane Evans, Sonja Marzinzik, Angela Lamb, and Janet Montgomery
2012   'Impious Easterners': Can Oxygen and Strontium Isotopes Serve as Indicators of Provenance in Early Medieval European Cemetery Populations? European Journal of Archaeology 15(1):117–145.
Burmeister, Stefan
2000   Archaeology and Migration: Approaches to an Archaeological Proof of Migration. Current Anthropology 41(4):539–567.
Carver, Martin, Catherine Hills, and Jonathan Scheschkewitz
2009   Wasperton: A Roman, British and Anglo-Saxon Community in Central England. Woodbridge: Boydell.
Chapman, John, and Helena Hamerow, eds.
1997   Migrations and Invasions in Archaeological Explanation. British Archaeological Reports International Series, 664. Oxford: Archaeopress.
Chenery, Carolyn, Hella Eckardt, and Gundula Müldner
2011   Cosmopolitan Catterick? Isotopic Evidence for Population Mobility on Rome's Northern Frontier. Journal of Archaeological Science 38:1525–1536.
Chester-Kadwell, Mary
2009   Early Anglo-Saxon Communities in the Landscape of Norfolk. British Archaeological Reports British Series, 481. Oxford: Archaeopress.
Colgrave, Bertram, and R. A. B. Mynors, eds. and trans.
1969   Bede's Ecclesiastical History of the English People. Oxford: Clarendon.
Collins, Rob, and James Gerrard, eds.
2004   Debating Late Antiquity in Britain AD 300–700. British Archaeological Reports British Series, 365. Oxford: Archaeopress.

Cool, H. E. M.

2000   The Parts Left Over: Material Culture into the Fifth Century. *In* The Late Roman Transition in the North. Tony Wilmott and Pete Wilson, eds. Pp. 47–65. British Archaeological Reports British Series, 299. Oxford: Archaeopress.

Fyfe, Ralph, and Stephen Rippon

2004   A Landscape in Transition? Palaeoenvironmental Evidence for the End of the 'Romano-British' Period in Southwest England. *In* Debating Late Antiquity in Britain AD 300–700. Rob Collins and James Gerrard, eds. Pp. 33–42. British Archaeological Reports British Series, 365. Oxford: Archaeopress.

Gowland, Rebecca

2007   Beyond Ethnicity: Symbols of Social Identity from the Fourth to Sixth Centuries in England. *In* Early Medieval Mortuary Practices. Sarah Semple and Howard M. R. Williams, eds. Pp. 56–65. Anglo-Saxon Studies in Archaeology and History, 14. Oxford: Oxford University School of Archaeology.

Hakenbeck, Susanne

2007   Situational Ethnicity and Nested Identities: New Approaches to an Old Problem. *In* Early Medieval Mortuary Practices. Sarah Semple and Howard M. R. Williams, eds. Pp. 19–27. Anglo-Saxon Studies in Archaeology and History, 14. Oxford: Oxford University School of Archaeology.

Halsall, Guy

2007   Barbarian Migrations and the Roman West, 376–568. Cambridge: Cambridge University Press.

Hamerow, Helena

1997   Migration Theory and the Anglo-Saxon 'Identity Crisis.' *In* Migrations and Invasions in Archaeological Explanation. John Chapman and Helena Hamerow, eds. Pp. 33–44. British Archaeological Reports International Series, 664. Oxford: Archaeopress.

Hamerow, Helena, David A. Hinton, and Sally Crawford, eds.

2011   The Oxford Handbook of Anglo-Saxon Archaeology. Oxford: Oxford University Press.

Härke, Heinrich

1992   Changing Symbols in a Changing Society: The Anglo-Saxon Weapon Burial Rite in the Seventh Century. *In* The Age of Sutton Hoo. Pp. 149–165. Martin Carver, ed. Woodbridge: Boydell.

2007   Invisible Britons, Gallo-Romans and Russians: Perspectives on Culture Change. *In* Britons in Anglo-Saxon England. N. J. Higham, ed. Pp. 57–67. Woodbridge: Boydell.

2011   Anglo-Saxon Immigration and Ethnogenesis. Medieval Archaeology 55:1–28.

Hedges, Robert E. M.

2011   Anglo-Saxon Migration and the Molecular Evidence. *In* The Oxford Handbook of Anglo-Saxon Archaeology. Helena Hamerow, David A. Hinton, and Sally Crawford, eds. Pp. 79–90. Oxford: Oxford University Press.

Higham, N. J., ed.

2007   Britons in Anglo-Saxon England. Woodbridge: Boydell.

Hills, Catherine M.
2003   Origins of the English. London: Duckworth.
2009   Anglo-Saxon DNA? *In* Mortuary Practices and Social Identities in the Middle Ages. Duncan Sayer, and Howard Williams, eds. Pp. 123–140. Exeter: University of Liverpool Press.

Hills, Catherine M., and Sam Lucy
2013   Spong Hill Part IX. Synthesis and Chronology. Cambridge: McDonald Monograph Series.

Hills, Catherine M., and O'Connell, T. C.
2009   New Light on the Anglo-Saxon Succession: Two Cemeteries and their Dates. Antiquity 83:1096–1108.

Lucy, Sam
2002   Burial Practice in Early Medieval Eastern England: Constructing Local Identities, Deconstructing Ethnicity. *In* Burial in Early Medieval England and Wales. Sam Lucy and A. J. Reynolds, eds. Pp. 72–87. London: Society for Medieval Archaeology, monograph 17.

Lucy, Sam, and A. J. Reynolds, eds.
2002   Burial in Early Medieval England and Wales. London: Society for Medieval Archaeology, monograph 17.

McKinley, J.
1994   The Anglo-Saxon Cemetery at Spong Hill, North Elmham, Part VIII: The Cremations. East Anglian Archaeology Report, 69. Gressenhall: Norfolk Museums Service.

McLean, Laura, and A. Richardson.
2010   Early Anglo-Saxon Brooches in Southern England: The Contribution of the Portable Antiquities Scheme. *In* A Decade of Discovery. Proceedings of the Portable Antiquities Scheme Conference 2007. Sally Worrell, Geoff Egan, John Naylor, Kevin Leahy, and Michael Lewis, eds. Pp. 156–171. British Archaeological Reports British Series 520. Oxford: Archaeopress.

Myres, J. N. L.
1969   Anglo-Saxon Pottery and the Settlement of England. Oxford: Oxford University Press.

Sayer, Duncan, and Howard Williams, eds.
2009   Mortuary Practices and Social Identities in the Middle Ages. Exeter: University of Liverpool Press.

Semple, Sarah, and Howard M. R. Williams, eds.
2007   Early Medieval Mortuary Practices. Anglo-Saxon Studies in Archaeology and History, 14. Oxford: Oxford University School of Archaeology.

Thomas, Mark G., Michael P. H. Stumpf, and Heinrich Härke
2006   Evidence for Apartheid-like Social Structure in Early Anglo-Saxon England. Proceedings of the Royal Society B 273(1601):2651–2657.

Ward-Perkins, Bryan
2005   The Fall of Rome: And the End of Civilization. Oxford: Oxford University Press.

Weale, Michael E., Deborah A. Weiss, Rolf F. Jager, Neil Bradman, and Mark G. Thomas
2002   Y Chromosome Evidence for Anglo-Saxon Mass Migration. Molecular Biology and Evolution 19:1008–1021.

White, Sally, John Manley, Richard Jones, John Orna-Ornstein, Catherine Johns, and Leslie Webster.
1999   A Mid Fifth-century Hoard of Roman and Pseudo-Roman Material from Patching, West Sussex. Britannia 30:301–315.

Wilmott, Tony, and Pete Wilson, eds.
2000   The Late Roman Transition in the North. British Archaeological Reports British Series 299. Oxford: Archaeopress.

Winterbottom, Michael, ed. and trans.
1978   Gildas, The Ruin of Britain and Other Works. Chichester: Phillimore.

Worrell, Sally, Geoff Egan, John Naylor, Kevin Leahy, and Michael Lewis, eds.
2010   A Decade of Discovery. Proceedings of the Portable Antiquities Scheme Conference 2007. British Archaeological Reports British Series, 520. Oxford: Archaeopress.

3

Religious Disruption and the Islamic Conquest of Andalucía

SONIA ZAKRZEWSKI

Moorish Iberia has been described as a "lost civilization" (Boone 2009:title). The start of the medieval Islamic period is marked by a known migration, but its impact and magnitude are much debated by both historians and archaeologists. The extent of the associated disruption, in social and religious terms, is evaluated using bioarchaeological methods. As such, this chapter develops a framework for the use of bioarchaeology in developing historiography and the recognition of historical disruption from religious change.

Medieval Spain was a religious melting pot existing in a "dynamic tension" (Boone 2009). It was a veritable multicultural society, with peoples of different faiths, ethnicities, languages, and customs (Fletcher 1992). These different groups coexisted and interacted with one another, albeit with differing relations and power structures between them. Iberia was one of the richest areas of the Western Roman Empire, but, following that period, for the three centuries preceding the Islamic conquest, it had been ruled by warrior groups such as the Visigoths (Kennedy 1996). The Visigothic kingdom in Spain was highly Romanized (Fletcher 1992) and, as such, maintained aspects of Roman administrative practices and order, including Arian Christianity. However, the functioning of these Romanized practices depended on active administration by local elites, and hence the Visigothic rulers of Spain had relatively limited actual control over their subjects. The Visigoths themselves were immigrants to Spain, having migrated there in the fourth and fifth centuries (Jotischky and Hull 2005). Preceding the Islamic conquest of Spain, the Iberian population comprised groups derived from North Africans, Northern European "Celts," Jews originating from the Near East, people from the Roman Empire, and barbarian tribes, including Vandals from the Baltic, Alans from the Russian steppe, Germanic Sueves, and the Visigoths deriving originally from the (modern) Greek/Turkish border area near the Black Sea (Lowney 2005). In addition to these groups, preexisting semi-independent peoples continued to exist on the Iberian periphery, such as Basques and Galicians, maintaining their own languages and traditions.

In April of AD 711, the governor of Arab-held North Africa, Musa ibn Nusayr, sent an army under the command of Tariq to invade Spain, which was followed the next year by an army led by the governor himself (Boone 2009; Fletcher 1992; Glick 1979, 1995; Jotischky and Hull 2005; Kennedy 1996). The initial invasion by Tariq followed a series of previous raids and incursions. These armies fought against King Roderick's Visigothic armies, although it is thought that most of the Visigothic armies had been in northern Spain, and so were unable to counter the initial invasion until the summer (Kennedy 1996). A battle was fought in Écija (fig. 3.1) in 711 (Jotischky and Hull 2005), followed by what were apparently decisive battles the following year (Fletcher 1992). By 714, most of the Iberian peninsula had come under Muslim control, although conquest was not complete (Kennedy 1996). The composition of Tariq and Musa's armies is uncertain, but it is likely that they comprised some Arabs, but primarily Berbers. The Berbers were the indigenous inhabitants of North Africa, with an apparently tribal and kin-organized social structure. The Berbers converted to Islam from paganism, and appear to have received a share of all booties from the Islamic conquest of both Spain and the rest of North Africa (Kennedy 1996).

The reason for the rapid success of the Muslim conquest has been much debated, with its organization and the Visigothic kingdom's lack thereof frequently being blamed (Fletcher 1992; Kennedy 1996). The impacts and interactions of differing religions must be considered. The Visigoths were anti-Semitic, and ultimately offered the Jews of Spain a choice among conversion to Christianity, exile, or slavery (Lowney 2005). In addition, the Visigoths did not have a well-equipped standing army, relying instead on poorly trained and equipped men called up by summons from their regional chieftain.

Historiography of Islamic Spain

Like all other "histories" (McPherson 2003), the historical view of the Islamic period is affected by the prevailing political norms and beliefs (Boone

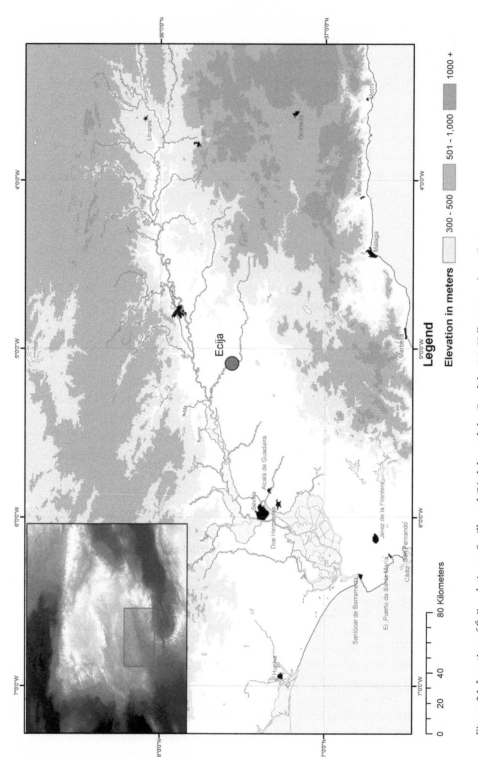

Figure 3.1. Location of Écija relative to Sevilla and Córdoba and the Guadalquivir Valley in southern Iberia.

2009). The period was almost ignored and treated as a "lost civilization" (Boone 2009), considered potentially "lost in our own historiography" (Barceló, paraphrased in Boone 2009:10). For much of the early modern period, the Islamic period was almost considered an aberration in the historiography of Iberia, rather than a period of tremendous scientific development. This idea culminated in the view that the Visigoths formed part of a direct line between the Romans and the Hapsburg monarchs. Some aspects of this view of history developed as a result of the rereading of works by early Spanish historians predating the Islamic period, such as San Isidro de Sevilla (AD 560–636), and the interaction with the political ascendancy of Castile and León during the reign of Fernando and Isabella (AD 1479–1504) and Carlos I [V] (Boone 2009). By the twentieth century, Spanish history was viewed in more nuanced terms but was primarily conceived of in two opposing ways. The first was essentially nationalist and continued the preceding model of history, with the Spanish identity viewed as having been threatened by immigrants, including both Jews and Muslims. Unsurprisingly, this view dominated during the late nineteenth century and during the period of the Franco regime. The second model views the Islamic period as one of religious harmony and prosperity, and sees the period of *convivencia* as a potential model for religious coexistence in modern Europe (Boone 2009).

Similarly to views of the Anglo-Saxon migration (see Hills 2009, chapter 2), these two differing historical models affect ideas as to the composition of the modern Spanish population. The former model posits the view that the vast majority of the population during the Islamic period was of indigenous descent, with only small numbers of Arab and Berber immigrants arriving and being rapidly assimilated into the Spanish population. Following this model, the Spanish population has its origins in the pre-Roman period, but with small-scale interactions resulting from the Roman, Visigothic, and Muslim periods. This first approach was even developed by the philologist Ramón Menéndez Pidal to argue that Spain Hispanicized Islam (Kamen 2007), and historian Ignacio Olagüe (1969, 1974) went so far as to argue that Arabs never actually invaded Spain, but rather that the Spanish peoples adopted Islam independently to form a distinctive indigenous Andalucían culture (Boone 2009). The second model, most strongly argued by Guichard (1976), posits that the number of immigrating Arabs and Berbers was large. This model argues that, given the differing marriage patterns of the preceding Christians and the invading Muslims,[1] there was little acculturation, with the Muslim groups eventually becoming the majority population in Iberia. The development of this model coincided with the end of the Franco regime and led to the rewriting of Spain's national history (Boone 2009; Glick 1995). Guichard and Cuvilier (1996:338) go so far as to argue that "the practices of exogamy and homogamy were essential to [a group's] . . . social cohesion." Guichard's model, as it was based on differences in structural social organization (at the family and household level), enabled the development of Iberian Islamic archaeology, with specific focus being placed on family organization and village and rural settlement patterns (Boone 2009). As a result, the model argues for relationships with the local landscape, and develops a positive and potentially idealized view of religious coexistence.

Who were the initial conquerors and where did they come from? It is most likely that the greatest number of immigrants to Iberia post-711 were Berber, including people deriving from groups newly converted to Islam and located in Morocco, Algeria, and Tunisia (Glick 1979, 1995; Fletcher 1992; Reilly 1993). Furthermore, one would expect that after the initial invasions, many more Berber settlers would have crossed from North Africa to join others from their clans or tribes (Boone 2009). There is much debate as to the extent to which both the Berbers and the Arab warriors brought their families and slaves with them, but it is thought that the initial conquest by Berbers probably involved only small numbers of men, along with their families and slaves (Brett and Forman 1980; Fletcher 1992; Glick 1995; Reilly 1993).

Population and Religious Boundaries in Early Medieval Spain

In medieval Iberia, religion operated within a framework that separates and distinguishes between individuals and groups. But religion may comprise perceived ethnic or other "typological" grouping or aspects of actively practiced and ritually performed activity (Insoll 2004). How might these separations be distinguished and identified? In the culture-historical approach to archaeology, discrete, bounded, and apparently homogeneous "material culture" units were assumed to correlate directly with specific ethnic groups, races, and/or tribes (Jones 1997). Transmission of specific cultural traits or forms was thus assumed to be a function of the interaction between these differing groups. More recently, post-processual archaeological thought has suggested that these material culture typologies do not map directly on to specific population or other groupings, so that material culture cannot be used as a direct normative marker of past population or other boundaries (for more detail, see Beck 1995; Jones 1997; Zakrzewski 2011).

Given that religious entities are socially constructed through repeated practice and tradition (Edwards 2005; Insoll 2004), religion forms one of the boundaries between differing social and cultural groups. Religious practice might transmit boundary information in the form of archaeo-logically recognizable signatures, such as within material culture or bio-archaeological patterning. In this sense, the group or religious boundary is recognized through different patterns rather than absolute typologies or traits.

Certain aspects of material culture can act as distinct flags. Bilingual gold dinar coins appear to have been struck within a year of the conquest (Boone 2009). These may act as potential typological markers of coloniza-tion and conquest, but not of religious or social grouping. Early forms of the coins bear only Latin text, but later ones were marked *solidus* in Latin on one side and *dinar* in Arabic on the other. These coins also stylistically resemble those minted in North Africa under Musa's governorship (Boone 2009) and therefore signal the intentional nature of the conquest and gov-ernment resulting from the migration into Iberia, but do not indicate reli-gious control.

Other aspects of archaeological evidence may enable the demarcation of other potential boundaries and disruptions. It has traditionally been thought that the Arab and Berber conquerors and settlers took possession of different areas of land, with the Arabs taking the more valuable irri-gable lands, such as the Guadalquivir Valley, with the Berbers settling and farming in the more arid areas (Boone 2009). Associated with this was a change in the structure of the city, including public architecture and cem-etery location. In addition, Islamization also operated at a household level, and archaeologically was reflected in the spatial organization and ceramic assemblages. Tax revenue figures indicate that between the middle of the eighth century and the middle of the tenth century, the population of al-Andalus underwent a dramatic increase, rising from 5–7 million to over 10 million (Chalmeta 1994). This is mirrored by an increase in settlement den-sity, but no corresponding change in rural material culture is recognized archaeologically (Boone and Worman 2007).

Bioarchaeology and Religion

Religion forms an aspect of identity within the individual social persona (Beck 1995), but religions vary in their expression and in the activeness of their membership, and hence in the plasticity and malleability of religious group membership. Aspects of behavior that are ritually performed may identify such religious group membership (Insoll 2004) and, hence, may imprint upon the biological body in some manner. "Within many Muslim societies distinctions can be made between practices and beliefs that may be classified as religion . . . and customary practices" (Edwards 2005:123), but, within Islam, it is active practice that identifies membership of the *Ummah* (the "Community of the Believers" [Insoll 1999]).

Through the use of both the body and its funerary treatment, bioarchaeology has the potential to identify disruptions within and between religious groupings (for further discussion regarding religion and ethnicity, see Zakrzewski 2011). Funerary archaeology may identify grave goods, such as jewelry or ceramics, or, using an *anthropologie de terrain* or *archaeothanatological* approach (Duday 2009; Nilsson Stutz 2006), may enable mortuary treatment to be identified, such as excarnation or deliberate bodily wrapping. These methods stress the integration of the social and biological components of death. This approach permits bioarchaeologists to identify and separate the natural effects of decomposition and putrefaction from the signals of funerary practices, such as the preparatory treatments of the body and positioning of the corpse, in the space in which the body decomposed. But humans are not necessarily buried with material culture that demarcates ethnic or religious grouping.

Beyond the burial context itself, humans are also able to manipulate or modify their bodies to display upon themselves (or their offspring) a marker of their religious or other group membership. Most simply, this marking occurs at a superficial level through clothing or hairstyles, such as the skullcap (called a yarmulke or *kippah*) and long sideburns (*payot*) for males in Judaism or the covering of the hair (hijab) or face (niqab) for females in Islam. These rarely leave archaeological traces, but tattooing (forbidden in both Judaism and Sunni Islam), body piercing (such as of the nose for Hindu women) or the binding or modification of the head may also signal religious group affiliation. These are intentional artificial (and much more permanent) changes made to the body that enable religious group membership to be identified by those who are able to "read" the signs.

There are, however, other bodily traits (including skeletal and dental traits) that also provide an indication of group membership and hence link to biological affinity and through this to religious affiliation. These latter traits, such as measurements of specific portions of the body or the presence (or absence) of specific minor skeletal or dental anomalies, cannot (generally) be manipulated by the individual or by their parent through bodily or cultural modification. The traits usually have both genetic and environmental components (for detailed discussion, see Larsen 1997) and so cannot provide a definitive answer as to religious or population grouping, but rather provide a guide to biological affinity (see also Knudson and Torres-Rouff, chapter 6, for discussion of nonmetric traits as markers of biodistance). The body is plastic, and such traits are not fixed. Aspects of biological and religious affinity might be viewed similarly to discussions of race. Although race is considered a socially constructed phenomenon, biological affinity, to which it is commonly uncritically linked, acknowledges the plasticity of human morphology and comprises the embodiment of ancestry. In this sense, the body provides indicators of population grouping. These groupings can themselves be linked, albeit not on a direct correspondence basis, with religious groupings.

As noted earlier, religious group membership[2] is actively performed. The "Pillars of Islam" are five basic acts considered obligatory for all Muslims, so their active performance enables reidentification and reconstruction of Islamic identify. These activities include the ritual prayers, called Ṣalāh or Ṣalāt, which must be performed five times daily. Given the plastic nature of the body, and especially of bone, prolonged repetition of specific activities may leave an imprint upon the body. In some modern Muslim groups, the presence of a prayer "bump" or scar on the forehead (zebibah), resulting apparently from repeated friction between the forehead and the prayer mat during the Ṣalāh, is considered to be a sign of piety and devotion (Slackman 2007). Again, this feature is unlikely to leave an archaeologically recognizable signature unless the frontal bone was affected. Within bioarchaeology, the effects of repetitive activity on the bone usually have been considered in terms of musculoskeletal stress markers or markers of occupational stress (for discussion, see Kennedy 1998; Larsen 1997). Musculoskeletal stress markers (MSM) can provide insight into the ways in which a muscle or group(s) of muscles were used during life and, therefore, can hint at the types of movements in which the individual engaged when alive. Repeated and strenuous activity of muscles leads to bone remodeling at sites of tendon-to-bone and muscle-to-bone attachments. Pathology from kneeling, such as arthritic changes at the knee and ankle, have been noted in a Byzantine monastic community (Sheridan 1997). During prayer, a Muslim will hyperflex the knee and hyperdorsiflex the metatarsophalangeal joints (extreme backward bending of the joints between the ball of the foot and the toes). Given that the Ṣalāh are performed five times daily, a Muslim person will undertake these movements more than thirty times each day, so a skeletal reaction might be expected at the joints involved. This reaction would be religious activity–related skeletal change.

Case Study: The *Maqbara* at Écija

The rest of this chapter explores the use of bioarchaeology to identify migration and/or disruption patterning in Andalucía, employing the population from a *maqbara* (cemetery) at Écija as a case study. The modern town of Écija is located 80 kilometers east of Sevilla. Excavations in the Plaza de España between 1997 and 2002 uncovered the medieval Muslim *maqbara*, which yielded in excess of 4,500 inhumed individuals (Jiménez, n.d.; Ortega, n.d.; Román, n.d.). As noted earlier, the medieval walled town of Écija was important not only as the site of a major battle in AD 711 but also because of its location in the Guadalquivir Valley, between Sevilla and Córdoba, with some control over the olive oil trade. The *maqbara* was an exclusively Islamic cemetery, with use starting immediately post-conquest and lasting until the eleventh century (Jiménez, n.d.; Ortega, n.d.; Román, n.d.).

Funerary Archaeology and Bioarchaeology at Écija

During the Visigothic period preceding the Islamic conquest, burials in Iberia were primarily in row-grave cemeteries. The burials of men contained few grave goods, although women were sometimes accompanied by specific brooches or buckles. As graves are not intercut, surface grave markers are hypothesized to have been present (Boone 2009).

Similarly, Islamic burials are characterized by their simplicity (Insoll 1999) in cemeteries designated for Muslim use only (Al-Kaysı 1999). Graves may be marked, albeit without ornamentation (Leisten 1990), but the key mortuary feature is that the body is placed into the grave so that it lies on its right side, with the head facing toward Mecca. Furthermore, graves tend to be shallowly dug to ensure that the deceased is still able to hear the calls to prayer from the *muezzin* (Insoll 1999).

Although Écija does not have a preceding row-grave cemetery, most of the Islamic burials in the *maqbara* followed the prescribed norm. There are, however, some exceptions to the Muslim burial tradition, as some individuals were buried in coffins, and a few multiple burials and ossuaries were recovered. Bodies were found lying on their right sides, leading to bilateral patterning in the degree of skeletal preservation (Inskip et al., in press). This basic funerary analysis indicates that the burials within the *maqbara* do indeed follow the established Islamic norms, and are distinct and clearly archaeologically recognizable.

The bodies themselves also indicated aspects of religious identity. During prayer, the knees are hyperflexed and the metatarsophalangeal joints are hyperdorsiflexed. Osteochondritic imprints (Capasso et al. 1999) were found on the posterior of the femoral condyles (Inskip 2009), which likely developed as a result of pressure from the proximal portion of the tibia upon the posterior of the femora during the knee hyperflexion period of kneeling. Furthermore, during kneeling, the vastus lateralis tendon (part of the quadriceps femoris muscle group) may undergo stress and lead to the formation of a patellar vastus notch (Finnegan 1978). Given severe stress, it is possible that a portion of the superior portion of the patella may be pulled away (and be resorbed by the body). In addition, a secondary ossification center should also develop in this location (Anderson 2002). Should this part not fuse to the rest of the patella because of stress acting upon it in childhood, for example, an emarginate patella forms (Finnegan 1978). Of a sample of 129 individuals from the *maqbara*, 19 left vastus notches (of 62 scorable patellae) and 20 right ones (65 patellae) were recorded. In addition, two left and three right emarginate patellae were recorded (fig. 3.2) and 30–35 percent of patellae exhibited morphological variation that might be linked with knee hyperflexion.[3] Variation is noted in the directions of the muscle fibers within the vastus lateralis muscle (Reider et al. 1981), which has been suggested to be gender-driven (Sakai et al. 1996). The movements of the knee joint are complex and much discussed (e.g., Garth 2001; Mesfar and Shirazi-Adl 2005; Sakai et al. 1996) so, although we cannot be certain that the repeated movements associated with praying led to the high prevalence of emarginated patellae and vastus notches within the Écija *maqbara*, it is likely. In addition, both tibial and talar squatting facets (Boule 2001) and metatarsal facet extensions (Molleson 1989; Ubelaker 1979) were noted (Inskip 2009), and are likely the result of the metatarsophalangeal hyperdorsiflexion occurring during prayer.

Recent bioarchaeological studies of migration and mobility have focused on analyses of radiogenic isotopes of archaeological tooth enamel

Figure 3.2. Example of an emarginate patella.

and bone, most commonly strontium (Bentley 2006; Knudson and Torres-Rouff, chapter 6; Price et al. 2001). These studies operate on the principle that if "local" strontium is incorporated into the body (through consumption in the diet or from drinking water), the $^{87}Sr/^{86}Sr$ values in the body will reflect this local geology. Isotopic studies of a small sample of individuals from the *maqbara* have been previously reported and indicated a relative homogeneity in strontium signal (Zakrzewski 2011), implying that the individuals studied likely grew up in similar geological locales. The strontium signals for humans differed from some of the contemporary comparative faunal samples, suggesting that the humans and animals grew up in differing locations. It is therefore most likely that the individuals studied did not spend their childhood in the local area and were instead immigrants to Écija. More recent studies have found that one young female has a very clear and distinct $^{87}Sr/^{86}Sr$ signature[4] and very definitely spent her childhood in an area with a very different geological baseline.

Analysis of craniofacial form can provide a guide to the population history and affinities of the skeletal sample (e.g., Howells 1973, 1989). Preliminary analyses of 122 crania (comprising 73 males, 48 females, and one individual of unknown sex) have been previously reported (Zakrzewski 2011) and have shown the Écija *maqbara* population to be morphologically heterogeneous. This finding implies that the Écija sample includes people deriving from a variety of craniomorphological patterns, and hence is biologically and genetically heterogeneous. This morphological and hence biological heterogeneity has also been noted in later medieval Spanish skulls (Ubelaker et al. 2002) and a cadaveric Spanish sample (Ross et al. 2011). Comparison of cranial measurements with sample means is possible using data published by Lalueza Fox et al. (1996), and indicates the morphological diversity of the Écija *maqbara* (fig. 3.3). Comparative sample means for medieval Islamic males and females are marked with open diamonds, medieval Christians in squares of shades of gray, and medieval Jews in gray circles. Although the Écija sample is morphologically diverse, the sample means by sex (open circles) for the *maqbara* are clustered within the other sample means, but surprisingly do not cluster particularly close to the contemporaneous Islamic sample from Granada. They do, however, demonstrate some similarity with the preceding Visigothic samples, suggesting at least some degree of population continuity rather than abrupt population disruption associated with the Islamic conquest. This analysis should only be considered as a simple outline evaluation due to the varying nature of the data (individuals relative to sample means with greatly varying sample sizes), but it does demonstrate the method's potential.

As mentioned earlier, nonmetric traits are thought to be inherited in a primarily genetic manner, such as retention of the metopic suture or bridging of the mylohyoid canal. Previous studies within the Écija *maqbara*, such as noting the high frequency of septal apertures, have demonstrated similarities between the individuals buried and certain North and West African groups, thereby suggesting extra-European components within the assemblage (Zakrzewski 2011).

Although genetic studies of modern living people may enable biological groupings, such as DNA haplogroups, to be recognized, these can rarely be matched with religious affiliation. An exception exists, however, within Jewish groups, such as the Cohanim (Thomas et al. 1998) and the Lemba (Thomas et al. 2000). No such clear patterning has been described for Muslim subgroups. It has been estimated that ten percent of the mtDNA haplotypes and Y chromosome forms currently found in Iberia are of African origin (Bosch et al. 2001; Côrte-Real et al. 1996). This pattern has been attributed both to the Islamic conquest (Bosch et al. 2001) and to earlier migrations from northwest Africa (Alzualde et al. 2006; Brion et al. 2003; Flores et al. 2004). Given the high temperatures in Andalucía, ancient DNA is rarely preserved; hence, genetic comparison between modern and past populations is difficult. Ancient DNA has been extracted successfully from archaeological samples farther north in Iberia (e.g., Aldaieta in Basque Country (Alzualde et al. 2006) and Segovia (Gamba et al. 2011)). There has been one successful attempt at recovery of ancient DNA from medieval Islamic material in Spain, from neighboring Córdoba, which indicated that

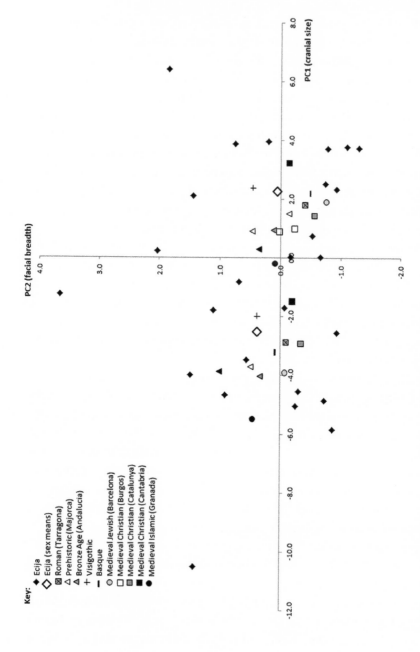

Figure 3.3. Plot of principal components analyses of Écija crania relative to comparative sample means.

the medieval Islamic sample studied demonstrated greater genetic affinities to modern North African than to modern Iberian samples (Casas et al. 2006).

Bioarchaeology and Disruption at Écija

Recognizing and identifying religious disruption is not simple. In the case of medieval Andalucía, either individuals migrate with Islam or indigenes convert to Islam. Bioarchaeological studies have permitted a more nuanced view of the Islamic conquest to be developed. Bioarchaeology enables human variability and diversity to be detected. The funerary archaeology notes the diversity of burials, with most following the prescribed Islamic burial pattern, but some individuals are buried in coffins, multiple inhumations, or ossuaries. Deviations from the prescribed burial norm are most likely to occur during short-term periods of social disruption, followed by returns to the norm after periods of transformation, and greater temporal resolution may enable this process to be assessed.

The craniometric and nonmetric traits studies, acting as proxies for genetic studies, indicate the genetic diversity of the *maqbara* population, and some associated extra-European component to it. They also, however, demonstrate some degree of population continuity from the preceding Visigothic period. These results are both contradictory and complementary. The nonmetric trait similarity to North African groupings and the comparable genetic results from medieval Córdoba (Casas et al. 2006) and modern Iberia (Adams et al. 2008) imply that the initial migratory disruption became a transformation, with the new migrants and religion incorporated into the Iberian population dynamic. Furthermore, the isotopic studies demonstrate that individuals migrated into the area, and that these people came primarily from one localized region. However, there were also some unusual individuals, and these (likely) more distant migrants may have had the potential to cause greater short-term (or even disproportionate) disruption of the social group. Only one such individual (a young female) has so far been identified, and so their impact on social cohesion within the local population is, as yet, unknown. This one female, however, may be indicative of a different (exogamous) marriage pattern relative to the rest of the Écija population, and suggests that Guichard's model of endogamy associated with *convivencia* might have been the norm.

Similarly to the Byzantine monastic sample from Judea mentioned earlier (Sheridan 1997), the *maqbara* assemblage demonstrates that religious practice, such as repeated ritualized prayer, has the potential to imprint group membership on the body. It is, however, unable to inform as to whether this demarcation of religious group membership led to social disruption within the autochthonous Andalucían population, but simply suggests the active performance of group delineation.

Disruption and the Historiography of Andalucía

As in Britain (Hills, chapter 2), the changing political perspectives of historians clearly affect the interpretation of population dynamics within Iberia. The proportion of immigrants in the Iberian population is debated, and the long-term structural impact is uncertain. A portion of this uncertainty results from historical amnesia, potentially heightened as a result of both the civil war and Franco periods, but more recently the Islamic period has been viewed as incorporated to form the new history of the Spanish state.

The bioarchaeology traces aspects of these different models of Iberian history. The very fact that religious practice imprints upon the body suggests the distinctiveness and separation of the Islamic peoples from the autochthonous individuals. It further suggests that religion might act as a disruptor to social cohesion. The genetic continuity seen in Écija, but associated with admixture and integration of North African individuals, suggests that the migration and colonization period was not as disruptive as presupposed, but rather that the initial disruption turned into Hispanic transformation, with Iberian identity coalescing with Islamic identities. Furthermore, the fact that individuals are seen to move to another locale en masse but with only one female migrating from a vastly different area supports Guichard's model of *convivencia*. This model suggests a large migration associated with an initial period of social, cultural, and religious disruption, followed by transformation, as both religion and the populations are incorporated to form the Andalucían history. Given greater time resolution within the *maqbara*, it might be possible to identify this period of initial disruption when burial practice changes toward the Islamic funerary norm, associated with greater numbers of anomalous (and potentially disruptive) burials. Following this approach, the Islamic conquest of Iberia should rather be viewed as a period of initially disruptive colonization or settlement, followed by some degree of social interaction that, over a prolonged temporal duration, led to *convivencia* and increasing social cohesion. The Islamic religious boundary in medieval Iberia is thus initially disruptive, but the effect of the migration is eventually transformative for Andalucía.

Acknowledgments

I would like to thank Antonio Fernández Ugalde, José-Manuel Rodriguez Hidalgo, Ana Romo, Sergio Garcia Dils, and the Museo Histórico Municipal de Écija for access to the skeletal material and for support during data collection at Écija. Skeletal data were collected by the author and Lisa Cashmore, Sarah Inskip, Emma Pomeroy, Jolene Twomey, and Jennifer Wainwright. Fraser Sturt is thanked for the production of the map and Sarah Inskip for photographing the patella. This work was partially funded by the British Academy (SG-42094). Finally, I would also like to thank the organizers and all the participants in the Disruptions as a Cause and Consequence of Migration in Human History Workshop, held May 4–5, 2012, for stimulating discussions and their helpful comments on this work.

Notes

1. Arab and Berber marriage patterns were based on endogamy and so discouraged marriage with the "indigenous" Christian population (Boone 2009). Guichard (1976) also argues that family structure and the lineage descent pattern also encouraged population growth.

2. From here onward, *religion* refers to religious belief rather than ethnicity (such as may be common within many western societies, e.g., North American Jews).

3. For comparison, vastus notches were recorded in five percent of patellae at Ban Chiang in Thailand (Pietrusewsky and Douglas 2002) and in six percent of patellae at medieval Canterbury, UK (Anderson 2002).

4. Her Sr ratio was 0.7166, with the normal Écija range being approximately 0.7080 to 0.7100, albeit with a few outliers.

References Cited

Adams, Susan M., Elena Bosch, Patricia L. Balaresque, Stéphane J. Ballereau, Andrew C. Lee, Eduardo Arroyo, Ana M. López-Parra, Mercedes Aler, Marina S. Gisbert Grifo, Maria Brion, Angel Carracedo, João Lavinha, Begoña Martínez-Jarreta, Lluis Quintana-Murci, Antònia Picornell, Misericordia Ramon, Karl Skorecki, Doron M. Behar, Francesc Calafell, and Mark A. Jobling
2008   The Genetic Legacy of Religious Diversity and Intolerance: Paternal Lineages of Christians, Jews, and Muslims in the Iberian Peninsula. American Journal of Human Genetics 83:725–736.

Al-Kaysı Marwān I.
1999   Morals and Manners in Islam. Leicester: The Islamic Foundation.
Alzualde, Ainhoa, Neskuts Izagirre, Santos Alonso, Antonio Alonso, Cristina Albarrán, Agustin Azkarate, and Concepción de la Ruá
2006   Insights into the "Isolation" of the Basques: mtDNA Lineages from the Historical Site of Aldaieta (6th–7th centuries AD). American Journal of Physical Anthropology 130:394–404.
Anderson, T.
2002   A Bipartite Patella in a Juvenile from a Medieval Context. International Journal of Osteoarchaeology 12:297–302.
Beck, Lane A.
1995   Regional Cults and Ethnic Boundaries in "Southern Hopewell." *In* Regional Approaches to Mortuary Analysis. Lane A. Beck, ed. Pp. 167–187. New York: Plenum Press.
Bentley, R. Alexander
2006   Strontium Isotopes from the Earth to the Archaeological Skeleton: A Review. Journal of Archaeological Method and Theory 13(3):135–187.
Boone, James L.
2009   Lost Civilization: The Contested Islamic Past in Spain and Portugal. London: Duckworth.
Boone, James L., and F. Scott Worman
2007   Rural Settlement and Soil Erosion from the Late Roman Period through the Medieval Islamic Period in the Lower Alentejo of Portugal. Journal of Field Archaeology 32:115–132.
Bosch, Elena, Francesc Calafell, David Comas, Peter J.Oefner, Peter A. Underhill, and Jaume Bertranpetit
2001   High-Resolution Analysis of Human Y-Chromosome Variation Shows a Sharp Discontinuity and Limited Gene Flow between Northwestern Africa and the Iberian Peninsula. American Journal of Human Genetics 68:1019–1029.
Boule, Eveline
2001   Osteological Features Associated with Ankle Hyperdorsiflexion. International Journal of Osteoarchaeology 11:345–349.
Brett, Michael, and Werner Forman
1980   The Moors: Islam in the West. London: Orbis.
Brion, M., A. Salas, A. González-Neira, M. V. Lareu, and A. Carracedo
2003   Insights into Iberian Population Origins through the Construction of Highly Informative Y-Chromosome Haplotypes Using Biallelic Markers, STRs, and the MSY1 Minisatellite. American Journal of Physical Anthropology 121:147–161.
Capasso, Luigi, Kenneth A. R. Kennedy, and Cynthia A. Wilczak
1999   Atlas of Occupational Markers on Human Remains. Teramo, Italy: Edigrafital.
Casas, María J., Erika Hagelberg, Rosa Fregel, José M. Larruga, and Ana M. González
2006   Human Mitochondrial DNA Diversity in an Archaeological site in *al-Andalus*: Genetic Impact of Migrations from North Africa in Medieval Spain. American Journal of Physical Anthropology 131:539–551.

Chalmeta, Pedro

1994   An Approximate Picture of the Economy of al-Andalus. *In* The Legacy of Muslim Spain. Salma Khadra Jayyusi, ed. Vol. 2, Pp. 741–758. Leiden: Brill.

Côrte-Real H.B.S. M., V. A. Macaulay, M. B. Richards, G. Hariti, M. S. Issad, A. Cambon-Thomsen, S. Papiha, J. Bertranpetit, and B. C. Sykes

1996   Genetic Diversity in the Iberian Peninsula Determined from Mitochondrial Sequence Analysis. Annals of Human Genetics 60:331–350.

Duday, Henri

2009   The Archaeology of the Dead: Lectures in Archaeothanatology. Anna Maria Cipriani and John Pearce, trans. Oxford: Oxbow.

Edwards, David N.

2005   The Archaeology of Religion. *In* The Archaeology of Identity. Margarita Díaz-Andreu, Sam Lucy, Staša Babić, and David N. Edwards, eds. Pp. 110–128. London: Routledge.

Finnegan, Michael

1978   Non-Metric Variation of the Infracranial Skeleton. Journal of Anatomy 125:23–37.

Fletcher, Richard

1992   Moorish Spain. Berkeley: University of California Press.

Flores, Carlos, Nicole Maca-Meyer, Ana M. González, Peter J. Oefner, Peidong Shen, Jose A. Pérez, Antonio Rojas, Jose M. Larruga, and Peter A. Underhill

2004   Reduced Genetic Structure of the Iberian Peninsula Revealed by Y-Chromosome Analysis: Implications for Population Demography. European Journal of Human Genetics 12:855–863.

Gamba, Christina, Eva Fernández, Mirian Tirado, Francisco Pastor, and Eduardo Arroyo-Pardo

2011   Brief Communication: Ancient Nuclear DNA and Kinship Analysis: The Case of a Medieval Burial in San Esteban Church in Cuellar (Segovia, Central Spain). American Journal of Physical Anthropology 144:485–491.

Garth, William P., Jr.

2001   Clinical Biomechanics of the Patellofemoral Joint. Operative Techniques in Sports Medicine 9:122–128.

Glick, Thomas F.

1979   Islamic and Christian Spain in the Early Middle Ages. Princeton: Princeton University Press.

1995   From Muslim Fortress to Christian Castle: Social and Cultural Change in Medieval Spain. Manchester: Manchester University Press.

Guichard, Pierre

1976   Al-Andalus: Estructura Antropológica de Una Sociedade Islámica en Occidente. Breve Biblioteca de Reforma, 16. Barcelona: Barral Editores.

Guichard, Pierre, and J. P. Cuvilier.

1996   Barbarian Europe. *In* A History of the Family. Andre Burguière, Christiane Klapisch-Zuber, Martine Segalen, and Francois Zonabend, eds. Pp. 318–378. Oxford: Polity Press.

Hills, Catherine M.

2009   Anglo-Saxon DNA? *In* Mortuary Practices and Social Identities in the Middle

Ages. Duncan Sayer and Howard Williams, eds. Pp. 123–140. Exeter: University of Liverpool Press.

Howells, W. W.

1973   Cranial Variation in Man: A Study by Multivariate Analysis of Patterns of Difference among Recent Human Populations. Cambridge: Papers of the Peabody Museum of Archaeology and Ethnology, Harvard University, 67.

1989   Skull Shapes and the Map: Craniometric Analyses in the Dispersion of Modern Homo. Cambridge: Papers of the Peabody Museum of Archaeology and Ethnology, Harvard University, 79.

Inskip, Sarah

2009   Changing Faiths, Changing Identities: The Use of Activity Related Skeletal Modifications as an Indicator of Religious Change. Poster presented at the annual meeting of the British Association for Biological Anthropology & Osteoarchaeology, Bradford.

Inskip, Sarah A., Sonia R. Zakrzewski, and A. S. Romo Salas

In press   Taphonomy of the Islamic Burials from Plaza de España. Astigi Vetus.

Insoll, Timothy

1999   The Archaeology of Islam. Oxford: Blackwell.

2004   Archaeology, Ritual, Religion. London: Routledge.

Jones, Siân

1997   The Archaeology of Ethnicity. London: Routledge.

Jiménez, A.

N.d.   El Sector Noroeste. Intervención Arqueológica en la Plaza de España, Écija. In Memoria Final. Volumen 1: Memoria 1. A. Romo, ed. Unpublished MS. pp. 183–193. Consejería de Educación, Cultura y Deporte, Junta de Andalucía.

Jotischky, Andrew, and Caroline Hull

2005   The Penguin Historical Atlas of the Medieval World. London: Penguin.

Kamen, Henry

2007   The Disinherited: Exile and the Making of Spanish Culture. New York: Harper Collins.

Kennedy, Hugh

1996   Muslim Spain and Portugal: A Political History of al-Andalus. London: Longman.

Kennedy, Kenneth A. R.

1998   Markers of Occupational Stress: Conspectus and Prognosis of Research. International Journal of Osteoarchaeology 8:305–310.

Lalueza Fox, C., A. González Martín, and S. Vives Civit

1996   Cranial Variation in the Iberian Peninsula and the Balearic Islands: Inferences about the History of the Population. American Journal of Physical Anthropology 99:413–426.

Larsen, Clark S.

1997   Bioarchaeology. Cambridge: Cambridge University Press.

Leisten, Thomas

1990   Between Orthodoxy and Exegesis: Some Aspects of Attitudes in the Shariʿa toward Funerary Architecture. Muqarnas 7:12–22.

Lowney, Chris
2005   A Vanished World: Muslims, Christians, and Jews in Medieval Spain. Oxford: Oxford University Press.

McPherson, James
2003   Revisionist Historians. Perspectives on History 41(6). http://www.historians.org/perspectives/issues/2003/0309/0309pre1.cfm, accessed May 26, 2014.

Mesfar, W., and A. Shirazi-Adl
2005   Biomechanics of the Knee Joint in Flexion under Various Quadriceps Forces. The Knee 12:424–434.

Molleson, Theya
1989   Seed Preparation in the Mesolithic: the Osteological Evidence. Antiquity 63:356–362.

Nilsson Stutz, Liv
2006   Unwrapping the Dead: Searching for Evidence of Wrappings in the Mortuary Practices at Zvejnieki. In Back to the Origin: New Research in the Mesolithic-Neolithic Zvejnieki Cemetery and Environment, Northern Latvia. Lars Larsson and Ilga Zagorska, eds. Pp. 217–233. Acta Archaeologica Lundensia Series, 52. Stockholm: Almqvist & Wiksell.

Olagüe, Ignacio
1969   Les Arabes n'ont Jamais Envahi l'Espagne. Paris: Flammarion.
1974   La Revolucíon Islámica en Occidente. Barcelona: Fundacíon Juan March.

Ortega M.
N.d.   El Sector Noreste. Intervención Arqueológica en la Plaza de España, Écija. In Memoria Final. Volumen 1: Memoria 1. A. Romo, ed. Pp. 117–182. Unpublished MS. Consejería de Educación, Cultura y Deporte, Junta de Andalucía.

Pietrusewsky, Michael, and Michele Toomay Douglas
2002   Ban Chiang: A Prehistoric Village Site in Northeast Thailand, vol. I: The Human Skeletal Remains. Philadelphia: University of Pennsylvania Museum of Archaeology & Anthropology.

Price, T. Douglas, R. Alexander Bentley, Jens Lüning, Detlef Gronenborn, and Joachim Wahl
2001   Prehistoric Human Migration in the Linearbandkeramik of Central Europe. Antiquity 75:593–603.

Reider, B., J. L. Marshall, B. Koslin, B. Ring, and F. G. Girgis
1981   The Anterior Aspect of the Knee Joint. Journal of Bone and Joint Surgery [American], 63-A:351–356.

Reilly, Bernard F.
1993   The Medieval Spains. Cambridge: Cambridge University Press.

Román, L.
N.d.   El Sector Suroestse. Intervención Arqueológica en la Plaza de España, Écija. In Memoria Final. Volumen 1: Memoria 1. A. Romo, ed. Pp. 195–233. Unpublished MS. Consejería de Educación, Cultura y Deporte, Junta de Andalucía.

Ross, A. H., D. H. Ubelaker, and E. H. Kimmerle
2011   Implications of Dimorphism, Population Variation, and Secular Change in Es-

timating Population Affinity in the Iberian Peninsula. Forensic Science International 206 (2011) 214.e1–214.e5.

Sakai, Naotaka, Zong-Ping Luo, James A. Rand, and Kai-Nan An

1996   Quadriceps Forces and Patellar Motion in the Anatomical Model of the Patello-femoral Joint. The Knee 3:1–7.

Sheridan, Susan G.

1997   Biocultural Reconstruction of Kneeling Pathology in a Byzantine Judean Monastery. American Journal of Physical Anthropology Supplement 24:209.

Slackman, Michael

2007   Memo from Egypt: Fashion and Faith Meet, on Foreheads of the Pious. New York Times, December 18. http://www.nytimes.com/2007/12/18/world/africa/18egypt.html?pagewanted=all&action=click&module=Search&region=searchResults&mabReward=relbias%3Ar&url=http%3A%2F%2Fquery.nytimes.com%2Fsearch%2Fsitesearch%2F%23%2FSlackman%252C%2BFashion%2Band%2BFaith%2F&_r=0, accessed May 26, 2014.

Thomas, Mark G., Tudor Parfitt, Deborah A. Weiss., Karl Skorecki, James F. Wilson, Magdel le Roux, Neil Bradman, and David B. Goldstein

2000   Y Chromosomes Traveling South: The Cohen Modal Haplotype and the Origins of the Lemba—the "Black Jews of Southern Africa." American Journal of Human Genetics 66:674–686.

Thomas, Mark G., Karl Skorecki, Haim Ben-Ami, Tudor Parfitt, Neil Bradman, and David B. Goldstein

1998   Origins of Old Testament Priests. Nature 394:138–140.

Ubelaker, Douglas H.

1979   Skeletal Evidence for Kneeling in Prehistoric Ecuador. American Journal of Physical Anthropology 61:679–686.

Ubelaker, Douglas H., Ann H. Ross, and Sally M. Graver

2002   Application of Forensic Discriminant Functions to a Spanish Cranial Sample. Forensic Science Communications 4(3). http://www.fbi.gov/about-us/lab/forensic-science-communications/fsc/july2002/ubelaker1.htm/, accessed May 26, 2014.

Zakrzewski, Sonia R.

2011   Population Migration, Variation and Identity: An Islamic Population in Iberia. In Social Bioarchaeology. Sabrina C. Agarwal and Bonnie A. Glencross, eds. Pp. 183–211. Chichester: Wiley-Blackwell.

4

Causes and Consequences of Migration in Epiclassic Northern Mesoamerica

CHRISTOPHER S. BEEKMAN

This chapter will use a Mesoamerican case study of migration to assess its association with disruptions at its origin and destination by making use of archaeological, biological, linguistic, iconographic, and historic data. Archaeology requires supporting evidence to isolate a migration, as it is widely recognized that biology, language, ethnicity, and material culture do not neatly coincide. Thus, instead of using migration as an explanation for an archaeological pattern, I see our task as studying the social context framed by other data sets to understand better how people chose to use material culture as they moved across cultural boundaries and interacted with other people. Therein lies the ability to study the interaction between migration and disruption. I first summarize my past research and then, in the second and third parts, discuss migration's relationship to disruption.

The case of migration that has attracted most of my attention is that associated with the Epiclassic period (AD 500–900), between the Mesoamerican Classic (AD 200–500) and Postclassic (AD 900–1550) periods.[1] I noted significant changes in public architecture, mortuary customs, and both ritual and quotidian ceramics at the onset of the Epiclassic period along the northern margins of Mesoamerica from western to central Mexico (Beekman 1996; fig. 4.1). Christensen (1997, 2001) was simultaneously examining available skeletal collections and published data for the same region, with the aim of evaluating population affinities using cranial nonmetric and anthropometric data. We saw the relevance of our findings for the widespread legends of ancient migrations recorded in the early years after the Spanish conquest. Our collaboration incorporated a review of the linguistic and ethnohistoric data (Beekman and Christensen 2003).

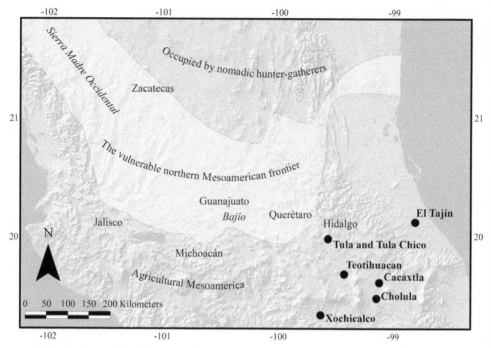

Figure 4.1. Map of northern Mesoamerica, showing states, sites, and regions mentioned in the text.

We concluded that sedentary farmers from the Bajío region of Guanajuato moved into neighboring areas of Mesoamerica at least partly in response to long-term drought (see a brief update in Beekman 2010). We have since pursued more detailed analyses of specific destinations of the migrants, concluding that the populations intruding into central Mexico were less organized family- or barrio-level groups (Beekman and Christensen 2011), while those intruding into central Jalisco showed considerably greater social and political cohesion and could be considered a military expansion (Beekman 2012). These analyses are in accordance with some prior proposals that migrations emanated from Zacatecas or Guanajuato during the Epiclassic period (Armillas 1969; Braniff 1972; Mastache and Cobean 1989; Hers 1989), but following a more explicitly theoretical perspective.

Our most basic methodological point is that each discipline that has contributed to our analyses has its own strengths and weaknesses, and that any single approach has only succeeded in narrowing down the range of interpretations. Used alone, even ironclad biological data will only explain a narrow aspect of migration and its potentially disruptive characteristics. The integration of data sets has resulted in conclusions that were rarely evident from any one of them, something equally evident in Hills' (chapter 2) and Zakrzewski's (chapter 3) studies. It is therefore worth summarizing the process of integrating these data.

The Case Study

Any discussion of migration in the last centuries of pre-Columbian Meso-american history begins with the ethnohistoric record. In pictorial and tex-tual documents dating to the decades immediately following the Spanish conquest, a frequent theme is the Postclassic migration of populations out of northern Mexico, or an earlier wave of migrations associated with the city of Tula, Hidalgo (Brotherston 1995). Tula was a multiethnic urban cen-ter, with Nahuatl being the dominant language from AD 900–1100, and mi-grations were associated with both its rise and its fall. Hence migrants took part in state-building, but Tula's political collapse also triggered further population dispersals to other centers. To take the documentary record at face value, we would have to conclude that populations moved frequently to avoid political persecution, to seek new protectors or new lands, or fol-lowing the proclamations of gods promising political greatness and a spe-cial place in history. Scholars have recognized that these tales were clearly interwoven with origin myths and formed the justification for Postclassic political charters, and it is these topics rather than the historicity of the tales that dominate current research. Moreover, ethnicity in the Postclassic period was complex (Berdan et al. 2008; Brumfiel 1994). Other social cat-egories, such as civilized (*Toltec*) versus non-civilized (*Chichimec*) crosscut language families along the northern edge of Mesoamerica (Viramontes 2000) and make it difficult to interpret the historical records too closely.

Viewed alongside linguistic data, however, these stories take on addi-tional significance. The Nahuatl language so closely associated with the dominant political centers of the Postclassic period is an offshoot from its nearest relatives far to the west. Nahuatl belongs to the southern Uto-Aztecan language group, which is predominantly located along the Sierra Madre Occidental of northwestern Mexico. The language of the Caxcanes of Jalisco in particular is considered very closely related to Nahuatl (Dávila Garibi 1940, 1950). Nahuatl spread further after its arrival as a prestige lan-guage used by successive empires, but beyond central Mexico only a string of isolated Nahuatl-speaking communities stretched southeastward to El Salvador and Nicaragua, where they recounted migration legends detail-ing their escape from central Mexican overlords (Fowler 1989). Although most considerations of the ethnohistoric migration legends focus on those pertaining to the founders of Late Postclassic polities, it is the earlier migrations, prior to the founding of Tula, that are more clearly associated with the separation of the Nahuatl language from its western cousins and its arrival in central Mexico.

Confirmation comes from epigraphic data. Rebus writing interpreted as using Nahuatl occurs at the new central Mexican Epiclassic centers of Cacaxtla and Xochicalco (Berlo 1989; Dakin and Wichmann 2000:68; Hirth 1989; Wichmann 1998:302). There are also proposed Nahuatl loanwords in a handful of inscriptions in the Maya cities of Guatemala and southeastern Mexico that more precisely situate contact with Nahuatl speakers by AD 650–750 (Macri 2005; Macri and Looper 2003). Earlier than this, the evidence becomes significantly more controversial (Dakin and Wichmann 2000; Kaufman and Justeson 2007), and Nahuatl's arrival in central Mexico, should not have occurred much before this date.

There are multiple means by which a language shift can occur. But available biological data point to the physical migration of people within this general time range. Nonmetric and anthropometric data document a significant population influx into central Mexico from northwestern Mexico sometime during the Classic to Early Postclassic period (AD 200–1200) (Beekman and Christensen 2003:127–133) or Epiclassic to Early Postclassic period (AD 500–1200) (González-José et al. 2006), depending on the analysis. Very limited DNA work at Tula has been used to support an Early Postclassic migration (Fournier and Vargas Sanders 2002), but there is no indication whether multiple origins for the population were considered and hence how samples might have been selected. The biological data, therefore, do not challenge the finding from the linguistic and historical record that a migration brought Nahuatl speakers (and probably others) into central Mexico by AD 650 and possibly earlier.

The limitations of each of these data sets are evident, and the integration of archaeological data can tell us about the social context in which the migration took place and the degree to which material culture was used to express ethnic identity during this period. My original study (Beekman 1996) identified related material culture in the form of public architecture, ceramics, and burial patterns that cut a swath along the northern perimeter of Mesoamerica from Zacatecas to Mexico State (an observation also made by Cowgill, chapter 5). Our joint analysis (Beekman and Christensen 2003) acknowledged that it was unlikely that the new material culture corresponded in a one-to-one manner with migrants, although it did appear to delineate quite well the zone in which migration and disruption took place. Our more specific analysis of the Tula area of Hidalgo exposed a complicated process (Beekman and Christensen 2011) in which the earliest migrants settled in the hills nearly a century prior to founding a city on the valley floor (agreeing with Mastache and Cobean 1989), at which point a single ceramic complex was in use by a multiethnic population. Ceramics thus became a social tool by which migrants and indigenous populations suppressed social differences to mitigate disruption in favor of an accommodation of some kind.

As we have pointed out (Beekman and Christensen 2011), the archaeological data do not in and of themselves prove that a migration occurred, producing a significant interpretive problem for the study of migration through archaeology alone. If we take seriously the critique within archaeology (Hodder 1977, 1979) that material culture can be selectively adopted or avoided by social actors, practically or discursively (the recognition of which took place in ethnography by at least Barth's time [1969]), then there is no simple definition for the presence or absence of migration.[2] Alternate explanations for the archaeological evidence discussed here may well be identified, but that does not automatically rule out a migration as part of the reconstruction. Let me clarify this issue, as it has been a sticking point with some skeptics. Virtually any alternate explanation we may propose (the spread of a new religion, the imposition of new customs by political authorities, the "interaction" or exchange among related polities) could occur with or without a demographic component. This issue is in fact what this project is about—to examine the relationship between migration and disruption—yet many archaeologists would prefer instead to use economic or political disruption as *an alternate explanation* to migration (e.g., Jiménez Betts 2006, 2007). Such a restrictive view of migration as a human strategy would relegate comparative research to only those examples in which the migration had no associated social, political, or economic impacts.

An alternate approach to analysis is to frame the period of migration using other data sets and then to analyze contextual details using the archaeological data. Material culture is not an independent variable that tells what people really did but a dependent variable that can be altered by human agency; the relationship between the migrants and the people they encounter at their destination will encourage (or discourage) them to emphasize their social identity through material culture. Building on the work of Stone (2003), we (Beekman and Christensen 2011) elaborated on variables that could be used to predict increased archaeological visibility of migrants: the size and social cohesion of the migrant group, difficulties of integration with local societies, more rigid social categories, and the lack of prior contact between migrants and locals. Other aspects are certainly involved, but these basic four clarify why some migrations will not be archaeologically visible. Small or socially incomplete groups are unlikely to maintain a visible social identity and are more likely to assimilate, though their presence may still be captured by biological, historical, or other data. It is quite possible, therefore, to have no material evidence of a migration, despite the existence of biological, linguistic, etc., evidence confirming that it took place, and that in itself tells us a great deal about the migrants.

These variables used to understand migration overlap with those associated with evaluating disruption. The overall statement by the Arizona State University working group (chapter 1) distinguishes between disruptions and transformations as potential consequences of migration. The scale of a migration, the vulnerability of a receiving population, and other elements used to evaluate the potential impact of migrants also play a role in defining the archaeological visibility of the migrants themselves. A full evaluation would require a much longer introduction, but there is reason to suggest that the most visible migrations are also the ones most likely to have disruptive consequences.

Disruption as a Trigger of Migration

The proposed source of the Epiclassic migration is the Bajío, a series of fertile valleys in the state of Guanajuato, and perhaps including the adjoining Los Altos area of Jalisco. During the Classic period, small polities began to centralize around distinctive public architecture based on enclosed patios, often with pyramids and rooms atop the encircling substructure (Cárdenas García 1999; Ramos de la Vega and Crespo 2005). Major centers have been excavated and dated in recent years (Castañeda López et al. 2007; Migeon and Pereira 2007), establishing their continuous presence over the course of the Classic period. The region experienced marked population growth in the Epiclassic period (Brambila Paz and Crespo 2005) even as its hallmark architecture and similar ceramics begin to be found in the adjoining regions. Yet this period of expansion and consolidation grinds to a halt after AD 700 or 900 (Filini and Cárdenas 2007), shifting to nearly complete abandonment or effective invisibility in the Early Postclassic (Castañeda López et al. 1988, 1989). Southern Querétaro was largely abandoned as well (Mejía 2005). The destinations of these migrants primarily appear to be to the west into central Jalisco, south into Michoacán, and east into Hidalgo, followed by Mexico State and beyond. As noted elsewhere (Beekman and Christensen 2003), these are areas with which the Bajío polities had ongoing interaction during the Classic period, so migrants followed well-worn paths to areas about which they had some prior information and where they perhaps had trade partners.

Substantial evidence exists for a major role in climate change in provoking these migrations, with the caveat that the social reactions were more complex than a simple "drought→migrate" model. Paleoclimatological researchers have gathered, over the past 20 years, a series of cores taken from the surviving lakes of the Mexican highlands, including the states of Nayarit, Jalisco, Guanajuato, Michoacán, and Mexico (most recently summarized in Metcalfe 2006; Metcalfe and Davies 2007; Metcalfe et al. 2007). The analysis of pollen and ostracods from these cores provides a combined record of climatic change and human impact across multiple basins. Variation is clearly apparent across the region at different points over time, but one period that shows consistent evidence of extreme aridity across the lake core record is AD 700–1200, in several cases following centuries of progressive drying. Metcalfe and Davies (2007:169) have characterized this span as "probably the driest of the Holocene," and it corresponds to a global period of aridity dated to AD 800–1000 (Mayewski et al. 2004). The pollen, ostracod, and other data correspond well to the better-known evidence for drought in the Yucatán peninsula (Escobar et al. 2010; Hodell et al. 2005), more recent high-resolution speleothem records from southern Mexico (Bernal et al. 2011; Lachniet et al. 2012), and a bald cypress dendrochronology from Querétaro (Stahle et al. 2011).[3] At least one of the speleothem records documents a long-term trend toward aridity that peaks at AD 770, a picture now supported by a recent geomorphological study in central Jalisco (Anderson et al. 2013).

This point is important. In our previous analysis (Beekman and Christensen 2003), our attention was drawn to the apparent contradiction between a period of aridity and intensified political activity among the Bajío polities. But reconstructions that see this period as the culmination of a centuries-long trend provide the basis for an alternative narrative, one that receives theoretical support from Morrissey's (chapter 9) discussion of the importance of perception and cultural definitions of a normal environment. As the long-term trend toward aridity progressed incrementally over the Classic period, initial reactions may have been to intensify cultural activities perceived as having a desirable effect on the weather. Farmers may have intensified public ritual, with the aim of influencing rainfall and agricultural harvests, while political elites may have encouraged this strategy for their own ends. Political elites could have exploited this activity in order to insert themselves into a mediating position between humans and the supernatural, adding to their prestige and authority. The initial stage of response to a gradual climatic downturn, therefore, actually may have contributed to intensified political activity and even the centralization of authority. I consider the central Jalisco case study to correspond to this first stage. The evidence for a migration from the Bajío began by AD 500 and appears to have been highly organized. Entire polities were quickly established in prime lands, demonstrating a high degree of organization and social cohesion. Despite evidence for prior contact between origin and destination, the rupture in material culture was nearly total, and a new material culture assemblage replaced its predecessor within a very short period of time (Beekman 2012). Local populations either abandoned their material culture entirely or disappeared. The introduction of new and specialized techniques for architecture and for pottery decoration implies that crafts specialists were part of this migration, intermingled with elites and farmers.

But political intensification would only work for so long if the trend toward aridity continued and the solutions sought had no real material impact. The northern margins of Mesoamerica corresponded to the limits of rainfall agriculture and its ability to support complex social and political formations, and if that vulnerable northern fringe were to suffer sustained drought, then these activities eventually became unsupportable as well. If farming continued to fail as drought intensified, then two options open to farmers included the abandonment of agriculture in favor of hunting-and-gathering adaptations, or migration toward better-watered areas. This second stage of response is evidenced in the Tula area (Beekman and Christensen 2011), where in-migration is dated to AD 550 (Mastache and Cobean 1989). New communities were established in marginal hilltop locations while the lowlands remained occupied, and they had multiple foci of public architecture serving heterogeneous social communities less organized than those in Jalisco. A century passed before some accommodation was reached between migrants and the indigenous population (thought to be partially instantiated in a new ceramic complex), allowing the new multiethnic center of Tula Chico to be founded in better farmland. New techniques associated with craft production do not appear to have been introduced, suggesting that a narrower range of social classes comprised these migrant groups.

Pedro Armillas (1969) was the first to suggest that climatic change led to the abandonment of the northern Mesoamerican frontier. He noted that even a relatively sparse population in the affected areas could result in the displacement of many tens of thousands of people overall. Even a low estimate of one person per square kilometer across the perhaps 70,000 square kilometers that were abandoned by the Early Postclassic period would create a profound demographic problem. This would be particularly the case if some of those individuals adopted a raiding strategy to take food stores from other farmers. There is limited evidence for populations that continued in situ. A greatly reduced population remained in some areas of Zacatecas (Jiménez Betts and Darling 2000; Kelley 1971), and two major centers remained for a time in the highland Sierra Gorda of northern Querétaro, evidently supported by a specialized mining economy (Mejía 2005). Those who chose to stay and adopt hunting and gathering are far less visible and less well studied. We can currently say little about those who may have chosen to remain as hunter-gatherers, but that is partly because these are questions that have not been addressed.

Disruption as a Consequence of Migration

Migrants are also associated with or blamed for disruption at their destination. Of the many areas impacted by the Epiclassic migrations, central Mexico presents the most data and the most opportunity for a consideration of the wider effects. This period is certainly one of political disruption, with the collapse of the urban center of Teotihuacan (see Cowgill, chapter 5) and the rise of its successors. While Cowgill considers the near simultaneous occurrence of migration and disruption, here I pursue the disruptive aftermath of migration a century or two later. I hope to narrow the gap between ancient and modern migration research by considering the possible rise in the social status of commoners and the resulting emergence of "migration policies" among the successor states of Teotihuacan in Epiclassic central Mexico. While these might be considered transformations rather than disruptions (see Tsuda et al., chapter 1), I will argue that the changes to commoners' perceptions of stability versus mobility were profound social disruptions.

The Epiclassic period in central Mexico begins in the sixth or seventh century AD, with the rapid decline of Teotihuacan as a populous urban center followed by the rejection of the distinctive style of material culture and artwork previously associated with the Teotihuacan state. The population of Teotihuacan, which Cowgill (chapter 5) estimates to have been in the neighborhood of 80,000–100,000 at the city's height in the Xolalpan phase (circa AD 350–550), plummeted to 35,000 by the Coyotlatelco phase (AD 650–850). Depending on whether Teotihuacan was totally abandoned and then reoccupied by other populations or whether the population simply rejected Teotihuacan-style material culture in favor of the newer Coyotlatelco ceramics, tens of thousands of people may have been displaced from the city alone, and that is without even considering the less-studied rural zones. Populations very much of the same order of magnitude as the initial movement out of the Bajío were now in search of new homes and lands within the general central Mexican region. As Cowgill notes, Teotihuacan's population decline could alternatively have resulted from changing demographic rates of births and deaths or even widespread massacres, but the Epiclassic emergence of multiple small successor states with substantial populations instead suggests that population was newly redistributed within central Mexico as a whole.

This point is critical, because Mesoamerican polities, like many polities elsewhere, would have derived their power and authority from the populations that they could draw into their orbit. Governments were dependent on people for foodstuffs, construction labor, soldiers, and the products of skilled labor, such as textiles or lapidary work. Although rarely singled out as something requiring theoretical explanation, the rise and fall of many Mesoamerican centers as far back as circa 1400 BC essentially involved the attraction and eventual loss of population. Mesoamerica's first experiment with centralized political authority at the Gulf Coast center of San Lorenzo attracted an estimated 10,000 people to the site proper and another 15,000 in its immediate sustaining area by its peak in the Early Formative period (Clark 2007:figure 2.12). Its collapse and near abandonment occurred a bare 200 years later, while a successor polity at nearby La Venta underwent a rapid rise most likely fed by San Lorenzo's misfortune. Arthur Joyce's research in Oaxaca (e.g., Joyce 2000) has been particularly evocative on this topic. He characterizes emerging elites at the major Formative period centers of San José Mogote and Monte Albán as deliberately drawing on and modifying prior efforts to develop an attractive religious and artistic program that would effectively present political ideology. A successful "media campaign" meant an increase in tributaries, a plentiful labor supply, and access to the works of skilled crafts specialists. Failure meant the defection of farmers to other centers, loss of resources, and political decline. The comparative demographic stability of the Late Formative–Classic period cities, such as Teotihuacan, that built upon these initial efforts at state-building suggests that people had become socially habituated to long-term settlement in a single location. As Morrissey (chapter 9) argues, sedentism is not a default adaptation, and migration is not solely a response to a disruption of "normal" conditions. Long-term sedentism is something that can be inculcated socially or politically, while even deeply ingrained tendencies may be broken by sufficiently disruptive events.

The Epiclassic period (re)introduced that prior demographic volatility, because elites were forced to start anew in establishing legitimate ideologies and because commoners were no longer tied to a particular location and polity. First, the elites of the successor states to Teotihuacan would have been more vulnerable and held fewer claims to legitimacy via deep and glorious genealogical ties to gods or past rulers. This situation is reflected in the vigorous trade in novel and exotic prestige goods at this time, as new elites scrambled to legitimize their status by obtaining powerful imported objects with innovative iconography as new symbols of authority (Beekman and Christensen 2003: 145–149; Pollard and Cahue 1999). New or increased exchange in turquoise, metalwork, and other exotics was widespread in the Epiclassic period (Holien 1977; Schiavitti 1996; Weigand 1982; Weigand and García de Weigand 2001). The increased trade in symbolic capital was not a sign of strong states obtaining luxury goods. Rather, the preoccupation with obtaining and displaying such items underlines the weakness and vulnerability of the new political elites, as prior ideologies associated with the Teotihuacan state were downplayed and new ones were sought.

A second difference was that commoners would have been the objects of competition among the new polities, such as Cacaxtla, Xochicalco, and Tula Chico. The displacement of people from the Bajío and of other populations from the Valley of Mexico would have undermined the secure demographic base of tribute-payers previously enjoyed by earlier and more stable polities like Teotihuacan. Farmers and others who had previously been socially habituated to assume stability over movement would have become newly aware of their social value and their capacity to vote with their feet. The multiethnic successor states of the Epiclassic all absorbed some combination of the displaced populations of Teotihuacan and the migrants from Guanajuato, providing a greater degree of choice for commoners than probably existed in the Classic period. But how would the new elites have enticed valuable tribute-paying farmers and crafts specialists to come to their center instead of going to others?

I suggest that the changed conditions of the Epiclassic period drove new elites to engage in a kind of migration policy, in which competing centers wooed newly mobile populations with novel interpretations of Mesoamerican ideology. There may have been economic incentives as well, and improving commoner standards of living may be evaluated by archaeologists in the future. But, in the absence of those data, what I wish to demonstrate here are the distinctive artistic styles instantiated in sculpture, architectural decoration, painted murals, and portable artifacts such as pottery that were the pre-Columbian equivalent of mass media. In the absence of twenty-first-century methods for disseminating messages or advertising, Epiclassic centers relied on public artwork utilizing an array of commonly understood symbols and explicit imagery to reach audiences who would have spoken a variety of languages. State-sponsored art programs are deliberate and selectively crafted choices about messages to present to the viewer and cannot be meaningfully analyzed as artifacts might, in terms of emulation versus inheritance (Nagao 1989). Rather, the content of Epiclassic artwork diverged from Classic Teotihuacan art because it was the result of parallel attempts by different centers to set their city apart from others by experimenting with reinterpretations of prior beliefs, much as modern secular cities attract citizens and businesses through beautification programs, organized sports, and economic incentives.[4] What follows is a very brief rundown of some of the distinctions to be found among four contemporary centers that emerged in the valleys surrounding the Basin of Mexico.

Tula Chico (AD 650–850) was a predecessor to Tula, Hidalgo, and lies northwest of Teotihuacan (Mastache and Cobean 1989). It was established within a century of the first migrants' arrival in the surrounding Mezquital Valley, and it became the major ceremonial center of the valley for the duration of the Epiclassic period. Based on our analysis of parallel data sets, we (Beekman and Christensen 2011) interpreted the site as having been occupied by Nahuatl and Otomi speakers during its occupation. Architecture at the site has seen limited excavation, but distinctive reclining figures on sculpted panels at both Tula Chico and Tula are interpreted as portraits of dead kings or warriors (Kristan-Graham 1999, 2011), suggesting an ancestral focus to the ideological narratives on display.

The center of Xochicalco is located in Morelos, south of Teotihuacan.

Beginning circa AD 650, the site grew extremely rapidly to reach a population of 10,000–15,000, only to collapse circa AD 900 (Hirth 2000). Architectural elements and sculptural style both indicate a mixture of strictly visual links (i.e., without meaning) to Oaxaca, Teotihuacan, and the Maya region far to the southeast, but without any directly derived examples (e.g., a pose depicted in sculpture is more akin to a pose found elsewhere on portable objects) (Nagao 1989). Rebus writing at the site probably indicates the presence of the Nahuatl language (Hirth 1989; Wichmann 1998:302) and may suggest that Nahuatl speakers held a dominant role here. The imagery depicts warriors and tribute payment by conquered communities (Hirth 1989), but there are numerous individuals without weaponry and possibly holding priestly equipment, particularly on the Pyramid of the Plumed Serpent. One sculpted panel, known as the Lápida Palacio, looks very much like a representation of a migration in one of the later Postclassic codices (Berlo 1989).

El Tajín was a major primate center on the northern Gulf Coast occupied primarily from AD 650–1000 by 15,000–30,000 people (Koontz 2009a). Koontz (2002, 2009a, 2009b) describes the artwork as a local evolution out of earlier visual styles. A unique interpretation of the common Mesoamerican architectural form of the pyramid showcases niches all over the exterior. Another common form of public architecture—the ball court—shows up at least 11 times within the bounds of the site, suggesting a uniquely central ideological role for the rubber ballgame. Associated decorated panels depict ballplayer sacrifice, political accession, and the creation of humans through self-sacrifice by gods. Comparisons have been made to contemporaneous scenes at sites like Chichén Itzá and Tula. Other themes in the artwork at the site include military banner raising, alliances among military figures, and references to the feathered serpent god depicted earlier at Teotihuacan and to stories of Coatepec, the "Snake Mountain."

Cacaxtla was a fortified hilltop center in central Mexican style found southeast of Teotihuacan in Tlaxcala and was probably the smallest of the centers described here. It also dates to AD 600–850. Although other artwork is present at the site, it is the spectacular painted murals that have received the most attention for their modes of representing the human figure, particularly the notable similarity to art from the southern Maya lowlands (Foncerrada de Molina 1993; McVicker 1985; Nagao 1989). The subject matter depicted includes a bloody battle scene, with symbols of rulership and sacrifice appearing in contexts that suggest some understanding of their meaning (Baird 1989). Whether the battle scene depicts a real event or not is less important than to note that battles (and Maya individuals) were a topic chosen by Cacaxtla elites for depiction in public buildings.

Epiclassic artwork has been described by some authors as eclectic yet also "international" (McVicker 1985; Robertson 1970), suggesting both local borrowing from disparate regions to produce new combinations and shared meanings across Mesoamerica. Viewed in terms of individual symbols or elements, the centers described previously do indeed share a common visual language (e.g., snakes as sky bands, crosses as references to Venus, etc.), though some would dispute even this (Meissner 2006). However, the style of imagery (e.g., roundedness or blockiness of figures, frontal versus side views, etc.) differs from center to center, and most importantly, the subject matter being depicted and the messages conveyed show significant differences. As opposed to Tula Chico elites' decision to emphasize ancestral ties, the emphasis on military dominance at Xochicalco, or El Tajín elites' preference for the symbolism and mythology of the ritual ballgame, those at Cacaxtla chose to depict their military figures in the act of conquest. These are quite different themes being chosen for emphasis, and none of them attempts to tie elites to agricultural success, as was common in the preceding Classic period (Beekman 2003a, 2003b, 2009; Fields 1989; Freidel and Schele 1988; Headrick 2002; Joyce 2000).

Each of these political centers developed a very distinct focus for its public artwork, which leaned toward different narratives, even if the actors (e.g., the Rain God) might be the same. Common topics relating to religion, sacrifice, warfare, etc., are depicted in the public art, but with slightly different "spins" or emphases at each center (e.g., ballgames versus military orders). Styles and subject matter have also been shown to have little to do with where the economic ties of any given center may lie (Nagao 1989); i.e., each center is being very deliberate and selective of the style and subject matter being used, and it is not based solely on the styles of their neighbors or interaction partners. The religious stories and doctrines being disseminated seem to have reshuffled older concepts into different combinations during what looks like a period of experimentation with public political messages, an argument that Joyce (2000) has made for Oaxaca in an early period when emerging elites were in a similar period of political instability and negotiation.

Some authors have recently argued that the Epiclassic in Mesoamerica was a period when a single religion became widespread (López Austin and López Luján 1999; Ringle et al. 1998), accounting for the "international style" mentioned previously. We might ask how Christianity would appear in the archaeological record from its origins to the present day. If we merely became fixated on common features in the imagery, such as a baby in a manger or a man bound to a cross, we would completely miss the profound disagreements and competition over followers to be found among Roman Catholicism, Orthodoxy, and the Protestant denominations. And this would not even touch upon the contrasting views of monotheism found among Judaism, Christianity, and Islam. So even if a single religion did spread throughout Epiclassic Mesoamerica, we need to acknowledge that the associated myths were being selected by political and religious elites to tell different stories. Why? To compete with other versions being told in order to draw in followers using the most aesthetic, most efficacious, or most compelling versions. This does not imply outright manipulation by cynical omnipotent elites but merely selectivity in the tales and lessons chosen based on local concerns.

This method of getting a message to large numbers of individuals was not sufficiently nuanced to allow pre-Columbian polities to select the kinds of migrants that they wanted to attract. In that sense, these efforts were rough, and they were more limited than those of later Italian city-states to attract weavers, artists, merchants, or other crafts specialists. On the other hand, this may be underestimating the perceived value of everyday farmers and their worth as food producers during a climatic downturn. Perhaps these individuals were the real targets of this early mass media, although there seems to be limited emphasis on agricultural success in the sculptural record. Competing claims to provide a secure environment seem to be more consistent themes across the different centers discussed.

With the end of the Epiclassic around AD 900 and the beginning of the Early Postclassic period, most of these centers declined into obscurity. Cholula emerged as a new pilgrimage center southeast of the Basin of Mexico. A new and important power arose at Tula and became the center of a populous state that would be successful for the next two hundred years. Tula's art style borrowed from its predecessors to present a narrowly focused visual narrative glorifying warriors, warrior societies, and human sacrifice (Mastache et al. 2009). This template would be developed in the later Aztec empire (Conrad and Demarest 1984), and was evidently a highly successful and motivating ideology that bore limited relationship to Classic period artwork stressing agricultural fertility. Perhaps the failure of political elites to deal effectively with climate change undermined the ideology that had justified their right to power.

Disruptions and Migration

The relationship between disruption and migration in the case described here is a classic dialectic, with disruption triggering migration and migration triggering disruptions of an altogether different kind. In the case of the source area in the Bajío, climatic factors well outside of the control of local populations presented a gradually worsening situation for rainfall agriculturalists. A sudden reversal from a wet to a dry period would likely have generated a very different response. But the gradual onset of drought over the Classic period was met first with attempts to ameliorate the problem through the only means available to farmers and political elites—expansion of ritual and of political powers, including perhaps the military conquest of better lands in western Mexico. Within another hundred years, more drastic responses were engaged, namely out-migration for some or a shift in subsistence practices toward hunting and gathering for those who stayed behind. By the Early Postclassic period, a vast territory crossing four Mexican states had been abandoned by sedentary populations.

The impact of migrants on their destinations was more complex and requires greater attention to the unfolding of disruption over an extended period. Disruptions in the short term were largely military and political in nature, with the collapse of some centers and the decline of others. Changes over the next century or two may be more subtle in appearance, as ideologies were delegitimized and the social habituation toward long-term sedentism was undermined. The social and political consequences of people made increasingly aware of their own mobility and capacity for choice were profound and disruptive. People became objects of value that had to be convinced to support one center or another, leading elites to employ a form of mass media to convey competitive religious ideologies and political charters. The Epiclassic period has long been recognized as a major watershed in Mesoamerican history, but the interwoven themes of migration and disruption are deeply entangled.

Notes

1. The Epiclassic has traditionally been considered the period between the fall of Teotihuacan in the Classic and the rise of the Tula polity in the Early Postclassic, and defined by the ceramics known as Coyotlatelco in the central Valley of Mexico. My dating tends to differ somewhat from others' for the Epiclassic, because I base my discussion in western Mexico, where these events begin earlier. I define the period by disruptive social and political events that begin circa AD 500 in western Mexico but are closely connected with

the Coyotlatelco complex in central Mexico. This definition has the effect of shortening the "Classic" period.

2. Cowgill's (chapter 5) derivation framework recognizes the same processes of human interaction with material culture, but the approach I pursue here is more closely tied to the theoretical assumptions and language of practice theory (Bourdieu 1990).

3. One multi-proxy study in Zacatecas (Elliott et al. 2010) interestingly reports no evidence of aridity during the period in question and suggests some local variation against the background of the regional and global data.

4. My university's efforts at "branding" are a good example of this argument. A new and consistent set of logos and photographic advertisements (visual symbols) are marshaled to present an image of the university that is meant to attract students. The visual aspects are at least as important as any written or verbal descriptions of the university, and the logos possess no actual *content*.

References Cited

Anderson, Kirk, Christopher S. Beekman, and Verenice Yunuen Heredia Espinoza
2013   The Ex-Laguna de Magdalena and pre-Columbian settlement in Jalisco, Mexico: The integration of archaeological and geomorphological datasets. Paper presented in the session "Human-environment interactions in the Neotropics: historical impact to current challenges," organized by Sarah Metcalfe, Elizabeth Rushton, and John Carson for the Royal Geographical Society (with the Institute of British Geographers), London, August 29.

Armillas, Pedro
1969   The Arid Frontier of Mexican Civilization. Transactions of the New York Academy of Sciences, Series 2, 31:697–704.

Baird, Ellen
1989   Stars and War at Cacaxtla. *In* Mesoamerica after the Decline of Teotihuacan, AD 700–900. Richard Diehl and Janet Berlo, eds. Pp. 105–122. Washington, D.C.: Dumbarton Oaks.

Barth, Frederik
1969   Ethnic Groups and Boundaries. Oslo: Universitetforlaget.

Beekman, Christopher S.
1996   El Complejo El Grillo del Centro de Jalisco: Una Revisión de su Cronología y Significado. *In* Las Cuencas del Occidente de México: Época Prehispánica, Eduardo Williams and Phil C. Weigand, coordinadoras. Pp. 247–291. Zamora, México: Colegio de Michoacán.
2003a   Agricultural Pole Rituals and Rulership in Late Formative Central Jalisco. Ancient Mesoamerica 14(2):299–318.
2003b   Fruitful Symmetry: Corn and Cosmology in the Public Architecture of Late Formative and Early Classic Jalisco. Mesoamerican Voices 1:5–22.
2009   Los Sistemas Políticos del Formativo en los Valles de Tequila, Jalisco y su Relación con la Subsistencia. *In* Las sociedades complejas del occidente de México en el mundo mesoamericano. Homenaje a Dr. Phil C. Weigand. Eduardo Williams, Lorenza López Mestas, and Rodrigo Esparza, eds. Pp. 75–95. Zamora, México: Colegio de Michoacán.

2010   Comment on Kaufmann and Justeson's "The History of the Word for Cacao in Ancient Mesoamerica." Ancient Mesoamerica 21(2):415–418.

2012   El Grillo and Epilogue: The Reestablishment of Community and Identity in Far Western Mexico. Paper presented in the symposium "Coordinate Approaches to Migrations in Epiclassic and Postclassic Mesoamerica," organized by Christopher Beekman and William R. Fowler Jr., at the 77th Annual Meeting of the Society for American Archaeology, Memphis, April 19.

Beekman, Christopher S., and Alexander F. Christensen

2003   Controlling for Doubt and Uncertainty through Multiple Lines of Evidence: A New Look at the Mesoamerican Nahua Migrations. Journal of Archaeological Method and Theory 10(2):111–164.

2011   Power, Agency, and Identity: Migration and Aftermath in the Mezquital Area of North-Central Mexico. In Rethinking Anthropological Perspectives on Migration, Graciela S. Cabana and Jeffrey J. Clark, eds. Pp. 147–171. Gainesville: University Press of Florida.

Berdan, Frances F., John K. Chance, Alan R. Sandstrom, Barbara L. Stark, James M. Taggart, and Emily Umberger

2008   Ethnic Identity in Nahua Mesoamerica: The View from Archaeology, Art History, Ethnohistory, and Contemporary Ethnography. Salt Lake City: University of Utah Press.

Berlo, Janet Catherine

1989   Early Writing in Central Mexico: In Tlilli, In Tlapalli before AD 1000. In Mesoamerica after the Decline of Teotihuacan, AD 700–900. Richard Diehl and Janet Berlo, eds. Pp. 19–48. Washington, D.C.: Dumbarton Oaks.

Bernal, Juan Pablo, Matthew Lachniet, Malcolm McCulloch, Graham Mortimer, Pedro Morales, and Edith Cienfuegos

2011   A Speleothem Record of Holocene Climate Variability from Southwestern Mexico. Quaternary Research 75:104–113.

Bourdieu, Pierre

1990   The Logic of Practice. Palo Alto: Stanford University Press.

Brambila Paz, Rosa, and Ana María Crespo

2005   Desplazamientos de poblaciones y creación de territorios en el Bajío. In Reacomodos Demográficos del Clásico al Posclásico en el Centro de México. Linda Manzanilla, ed. Pp. 155–174. México, D.F.: Instituto de Investigaciones Antropológicas, Universidad Nacional Autónoma de México.

Braniff, C. Beatriz

1972   Secuencias Arqueológicas en Guanajuato y la Cuenca de México: Intento de Correlación. In Teotihuacan: XI Mesa Redonda. Pp. 273–323. México, D.F.: Sociedad Mexicana de Antropología.

Brotherston, Gordon

1995   Painted Books from Mexico. Codices in UK Collections and the World They Represent. London: British Museum Press.

Brumfiel, Elizabeth M.

1994   Ethnic Groups and Political Development in Ancient Mexico. In Factional Competition and Political Development in the New World. Elizabeth M. Brumfiel and John E. Fox, eds. Pp. 89–102. Cambridge: Cambridge University Press.

Cárdenas García, Efraín
1999 El Bajío en el Clásico. Zamora, México: Colegio de Michoacán.

Castañeda López, Carlos, L. M. Flores, Ana María Crespo, J. A. Contreras, T. Durán, and Juan Carlos Saint Charles
1988 Interpretación de la Historia del Asentamiento en Guanajuato. *In* Primera Reunión sobre las Sociedades Prehispánicas en el Centro Occidente de México, Memoria. Pp. 321–355. México, D.F.: Centro Regional de Querétaro, Instituto Nacional de Antropología e Historia.

Castañeda López, Carlos, Beatriz Cervantes, Ana María Crespo, and Luz María Flores
1989 Poblamiento Prehispánico en el Centro-Norte de la Frontera Mesoamericana. Antropología 28:34–43.

Castañeda López, Carlos, Gabriela Zepeda García Moreno, Efraín Cárdenas García, and C. A. Torreblanca Padilla
2007 Zonas Arqueológicas de Guanajuato, Cuatro Casos: Plazuelas, Cañada de la Virgen, Peralta y El Cóporo. Guanajuato: Editorial La Rana.

Christensen, Alexander F.
1997 Cranial non-metric variation in North and Central Mexico. Anthropologischer Anzeiger 55:15–32.
2001 Anthropometric variation in west-central Mexico. Anthropologischer Anzeiger 59:97–111.

Clark, John E.
2007 Mesoamerica's First State. *In* The Political Economy of Ancient Mesoamerica. Transformations during the Formative and Classic Periods. Vernon L. Scarborough and John E. Clark, eds. Pp. 11–46. Albuquerque: University of New Mexico Press.

Conrad, Geoffrey, and Arthur Demarest
1984 Religion and Empire. Cambridge: Cambridge University Press.

Dakin, Karen, and Søren Wichmann
2000 Cacao and Chocolate. A Uto-Aztecan Perspective. Ancient Mesoamerica 11:55–75.

Dávila Garibi, Ignacio
1940 Cazcanos y Tochos. Revista Mexicana de Estudios Americanos. Tomo IV, 3:203–224.
1950 Los Cazcanes. México, D.F.: Editorial Cultura, T.G., S.A.

Elliott, Michelle, Christopher T. Fisher, Ben A. Nelson, Roberto S. Molina Garza, Shawn K. Collins, and Deborah M. Pearsall
2010 Climate, Agricultura, and Cycles of Human Occupation Over the Last 4,000 Years in Southern Zacatecas, Mexico. Quaternary Research 74:26–35.

Escobar, Jaime, Jason H. Curtis, Mark Brenner, David A. Hodell, Jonathan A. Holmes
2010 Isotope Measurements of Single Ostracod Valves and Gastropod Shells for Climate Reconstruction: Evaluation of Within-Sample Variability and Determination of Optimum Sample Size. Journal of Paleolimnology 43:921–938.

Fields, Virginia
1989   The Origins of Divine Kingship among the Lowland Classic Maya. PhD disserta-
        tion, University of Texas, Austin.
Filini, Agapi, and Efraín Cárdenas
2007   El Bajío, la cuenca de Cuitzeo y el Estado Teotihuacano. Un Estudio de Relaciones
        y Antagonismos. *In* Dinámicas culturales entre el Occidente, el centro-norte y la
        Cuenca de México, del Preclásico al Epiclásico, Brigitte Faugère, eds. Pp. 137–156.
        Zamora, México: Colegio de Michoacán, Centro de Estudios Mexicanos y Cen-
        troamericanos.
Foncerrada de Molina, Marta
1993   Cacaxtla. La Iconografía de los Olmeca-Xicalanca. México, D.F.: Universidad Na-
        cional Autónoma de México, D.F.
Fournier, Patricia, and Rocio Vargas Sanders
2002   En Busca de los "dueños del silencio": Cosmovisión y ADN Antiguo de las Po-
        blaciones Otomíes Epiclásicas de la región de Tula. Estudios de Cultura Otopame
        3:37–75.
Fowler, William R., Jr.
1989   The Cultural Evolution of Ancient Nahua Civilizations: The Pipil-Nicarao of Cen-
        tral America. Norman: University of Oklahoma Press.
Freidel, David, and Linda Schele
1988   Kingship in the Late Preclassic Maya Lowlands: The Instruments and Places of
        Ritual Power. American Anthropologist 90:547–567.
González-José, Rolando, Neus Martínez-Abadías, Antonio González-Martín, Josefina
        Bautista-Martínez, Jorge Gómez-Valdés, Mirsha Quinto, and Miguel Hernández
2007   Detection of a Population Replacement at the Classic-Postclassic Transition in
        Mexico. Proceedings of the Royal Society B 274:681–688.
Headrick, Annabeth
2002   Gardening with the Great Goddess at Teotihuacan. *In* Heart of Creation: The Me-
        soamerican World and the Legacy of Linda Schele. Andrea Stone, ed. Pp. 83–100.
        Tuscaloosa: University of Alabama Press.
Hers, Marie-Areti
1989   Los Toltecas en Tierras Chichimecas. México, D.F.: Universidad Nacional Autóno-
        ma de México, D.F.
Hirth, Kenneth G.
1989   Militarism and Social Organization at Xochicalco, Morelos. *In* Mesoamerica after
        the Decline of Teotihuacan, AD 700–900. Richard Diehl and Janet Berlo, eds. Pp.
        19–48. Washington, D.C.: Dumbarton Oaks.
2000   Archaeological Research at Xochicalco. Salt Lake City: University of Utah Press.
Hodder, Ian
1977   The Distribution of Material Culture Items in the Baringo District, Western Kenya.
        Man 12:239–269.
1979   Economic and Social Stress and Material Culture Patterning. American Antiquity
        44(3):446–453.

Hodell, David A., Mark Brenner, and Jason H. Curtis
2005   Terminal Classic Drought in the Northern Maya Lowlands Inferred from Multiple Sediment Cores in Lake Chichancanab (Mexico). Quaternary Science Reviews 24:1413–1427.

Holien, Thomas
1977   Mesoamerican Pseudo-Cloisonné and Other Decorative Investments. PhD dissertation, Department of Anthropology, Southern Illinois University, Carbondale.

Jiménez Betts, Peter
2006   La Problemática de Coyotlatelco vista desde el Noroccidente de Mesoamérica. In El Fenómeno Coyotlatelco en el Centro de México: Tiempo, Espacio y Significado. Memoria del Primer Seminario-taller sobre Problemáticas Regionales. Laura Solar V., ed. Pp. 375–392. Coordinación Nacional de Arqueología. México, D.F.: Instituto Nacional de Antropología e Historia.
2007   Alcances de la Interacción entre el Occidente y el Noroeste de Mesoamérica en el Epiclásico. In Dinámicas Culturales entre el Occidente, el Centro-Norte y la Cuenca de México, del Preclásico al Epiclásico. Brigitte Faugere, ed. Pp. 157–164. Zamora, México: Centro de Estudios Mexicanos y Centroamericanos, Colegio de Michoacán.

Jiménez Betts, Peter, and J. Andrew Darling
2000   Archaeology of Southern Zacatecas: The Malpaso, Juchipila, and Valparaíso-Bolaños Valleys. In Greater Mesoamerica: The Archaeology of West and Northwest Mexico. Michael S. Foster and Shirley Gorenstein, eds. Pp. 155–180. Salt Lake City: University of Utah Press.

Joyce, Arthur
2000   The Founding of Monte Albán. Sacred Propositions and Social Practices. In Agency in Archaeology. Marcia-Anne Dobres and John E. Robb, eds. Pp. 71–91. London: Routledge Press.

Kaufman, Terrence, and John Justeson
2007   The History of the Word for Cacao in Ancient Mesoamerica. Ancient Mesoamerica 18: 193–237.

Kelley, J. Charles
1971   Archaeology of the Northern Frontier: Zacatecas and Durango. In Handbook of Middle American Indians, vol. 11, Archaeology of Northern Mesoamerica, Part Two. Gordon Ekholm and Ignacio Bernal, eds. Pp. 768–801. Austin: University of Texas Press.

Koontz, Rex
2002   Terminal Classic Sacred Place and Factional Politics at El Tajín, Veracruz. In Heart of Creation: The Mesoamerican World and the Legacy of Linda Schele. Andrea Stone, ed. Pp. 101–117. Tuscaloosa: University of Alabama Press.
2009a   Lightning Gods and Feathered Serpents: The Public Sculpture of El Tajín. Austin: University of Texas Press.
2009b   Social Identity and Cosmology at El Tajín. In The Art of Urbanism: How Mesoamerican Kingdoms Represented Themselves in Architecture and Imagery. William L. Fash and Leonardo López Luján, eds. Pp. 260–289. Washington, D.C.: Dumbarton Oaks.

Kristan-Graham, Cynthia
1999   The Architecture of the Tula Body-Politic. In Mesoamerican Architecture as a Cultural Symbol, Jeff Karl Kowalski, ed. Pp. 162–175. New York: Oxford University Press.
2007   Structuring Identity at Tula: the Design and Symbolism of Colonnaded Halls and Sunken Spaces. In Twin Tollans: Chichen Itza, Tula, and the Epiclassic to Early Postclassic Mesoamerican World. Jeff Karl Kowalski and Cynthia Kristan-Graham, eds. Pp. 531–578. Washington, D.C.: Dumbarton Oaks.
2011   All the Earth Is a Grave: Symbolic Ancestral Burials at Tula Chico and Tula Grande. Paper presented at the 76th Annual Meeting of the Society for American Archaeology, Sacramento, March 31.
Lachniet, Matthew S., Juan Pablo Bernal, Yemane Asmerom, Victor Polyak, and Dolores Piperno
2012   A 2400 yr Mesoamerican Rainfall Reconstruction Links Climate and Cultural Change. Geology 40:259–262.
López Austin, Alfredo, and Leonardo López Luján
1999   Mito y Realidad de Zuyuá: Serpiente Emplumada y las Transformaciones Mesoamericanas del Clásico al Posclásico. México, D.F.: Colegio de México, Fondo de Cultura Económica.
McVicker, Donald
1985   The "Mayanized" Mexicans. American Antiquity 50:82–101.
Macri, Martha J.
2005   Nahua Loan Words from the Early Classic Period: Words for Cacao Preparation on a Rio Azul Ceramic Vessel. Ancient Mesoamerica 16:321–326.
Macri, Martha J., and Matthew G. Looper
2003   Nahua in Ancient Mesoamerica: Evidence from Maya Inscriptions. Ancient Mesoamerica 14:285–297.
Mastache, Alba Guadalupe, and Robert H. Cobean
1989   The Coyotlatelco Culture and the Origins of the Toltec State. In Mesoamerica after the Decline of Teotihuacan, AD 700–900. Richard Diehl and Janet Berlo, eds. Pp. 49–67. Washington, D.C.: Dumbarton Oaks.
Mastache, Alba Guadalupe, Dan M. Healan, and Robert H. Cobean
2009   Social Identity and Cosmology at El Tajín. In The Art of Urbanism: How Mesoamerican Kingdoms Represented Themselves in Architecture and Imagery. William L. Fash and Leonardo López Luján, eds. Pp. 290–328. Washington, D.C.: Dumbarton Oaks.
Mayewski, Paul A., Eelco E. Rohling, J. Curt Stager, Wibjörn Karlén, Kirk A. Maasch, L. David Meeker, Eric A. Meyerson, Francoise Gasse, Shirley van Kreveld, Karin Holmgren, Julia Lee-Thorp, Gunhild Rosqvist, Frank Rack, Michael Staubwasser, Ralph R. Schneider, and Eric J. Steig
2004   Holocene Climate Variability. Quaternary Research 62: 243–255.
Meissner, Nathan
2006   A Semiotic Approach to the Maya "Postclassic International Symbol Set." MA thesis, Department of Anthropology, Southern Illinois University, Carbondale.

Mejía, E.
2005   La Arqueología de la Sierra Gorda de Querétaro: Una Revisión. *In* Estudios Antropológicos de los Pueblos Otomíes y Chichimecas de Querétaro. M. E. Villegas Molina, ed. Pp. 146–160. México, D.F.: Instituto Nacional de Antropología e Historia.

Metcalfe, Sarah E.
2006   Late Quaternary Environments of the Northern Deserts and Central Transvolcanic Belt of Mexico. Annals of the Missouri Botanical Gardens 93:258–273.

Metcalfe, Sarah E., and Sarah J. Davies
2007   Deciphering Recent Climate Change in Central Mexican Lake Records. Climatic Change 83:169–186.

Metcalfe, Sarah E., Sarah J. Davies, John D. Braisby, Melanie J. Leng, Anthony J. Newton, Nicola L. Terrett, and Sarah L. O'Hara
2007   Long and Short-Term Change in the Pátzcuaro Basin, Central Mexico. Palaeogeography, Palaeoclimatology, Palaeoecology 247:272–295.

Migeon, Gerald, and Gregory Pereira
2007   La Secuencia Ocupacional y Cerámica del Cerro Barajas, Guanajuato, y sus Relaciones con el Centro, el Occidente y el Norte de México. *In* Dinámicas Culturales entre el Occidente, el Centro-Norte y la Cuenca de México, del Preclásico al Epiclásico. Brigitte Faugere, ed. Pp. 201–230. Zamora, México: Centro de Estudios Mexicanos y Centroamericanos, Colegio de Michoacán.

Nagao, Deborah
1989   Public Proclamation in the Art of Cacaxtla and Xochicalco. *In* Mesoamerica after the Decline of Teotihuacan, AD 700–900. Richard A. Diehl and Janet C. Berlo, eds. Pp. 83–104. Washington, D.C.: Dumbarton Oaks.

Pollard, Helen P., and Laura Cahue
1999   Mortuary Patterns of Regional Elites in the Lake Pátzcuaro Basin of Western Mexico. Latin American Antiquity 10:259–280.

Ramos de la Vega, Jorge, and Ana María Crespo
2005   Reordenamiento de los Patrones Arquitectónicos del Centro-Norte de México. Del Clásico al Epiclásico. *In* El Antiguo Occidente de México: Nuevas Perspectivas sobre el Pasado Prehispánico. Eduardo Williams, Phil C. Weigand, Lorenza López Mestas, and David C. Grove, eds. Pp. 93–106. Zamora, México: Colegio de Michoacán.

Ringle, William, Tomas Gallareta Negrón, and George J. Bey III
1998   The Return of Quetzalcoatl: Evidence for the Spread of a World Religion during the Epiclassic Period. Ancient Mesoamerica 9:183–232.

Robertson, Donald
1970   The Tulum Murals: The International Style of the Late Post-Classic. Proceedings of the XXXVIII International Congress of Americanists, Vol. II. Pp. 77–88. Stuttgart.

Schiavitti, Vincent W.
1996   Organization of the Prehispanic Suchil Mining District of Chalchihuites, Mexico, AD 400–950. PhD dissertation, Department of Anthropology, State University of New York, Buffalo.

Stahle, David W., José Villanueva Diaz, D. J. Burnette, Julian Cerano Paredes, R. R. Heim Jr., F. K. Fye, R. Acuna Soto, M. D. Therrell, M. K. Cleaveland, and D. K. Stahle
2011   Major Mesoamerican Droughts of the Past Millennium. Geophysical Research Letters 38, L05703, doi:10.1029/2010GL046472.
Stone, Tammy
2003   Social Identity and Ethnic Interaction in the Western Pueblos of the American Southwest. Journal of Archaeological Method and Theory 10:31–67.
Viramontes Anzures, Carlos
2000   De Chichimecas, Pames y Jonaces. Los Recolectores-Cazadores del Semidesierto Queretano. México, D.F.: Colección Científica, Instituto Nacional de Antropología e Historia.
Weigand, Phil C.
1982   Mining and Mineral Trade in Prehispanic Zacatecas. Anthropology 6:87–134.
Weigand, Phil C., and Acelia García de Weigand
2001   A Macroeconomic Study of the Relationships between the Ancient Cultures of the American Southwest and Mesoamerica. In The Road to Aztlan: Art from a Mythic Homeland. V. M. Fields and V. Zamudio Taylor, eds. Pp. 184–196. Los Angeles: Los Angeles County Museum of Art.
Wichmann, Søren
1998   A Conservative Look at Diffusion Involving Mixe-Zoquean Languages. In Archaeology and Language II: Correlating Archaeological and Linguistic Hypotheses. Roger Blench and Matthew Spriggs, eds. Pp. 297–323. London: Routledge.

5

The Debated Role of Migration in the Fall of Ancient Teotihuacan in Central Mexico

GEORGE L. COWGILL

Methods for Studying Ancient Migrations

Especially for the benefit of students of recent migrations, I begin with an overview of the potential of archaeology and bioarchaeology for the study of ancient migrations. I see broad areas of agreement in this volume, particularly in the chapters by Christopher Beekman (chapter 4), Catherine Hills (chapter 2), and Sonia Zakrzewski (chapter 3), even though they involve cases in different parts of the world—in western Mexico, England, and Iberia. To be sure, there are few, if any, cases where this potential has yet been fully realized, but it has often been approached, and, given adequate funding, there should soon be many more good examples.

For several decades, North American archaeologists avoided migrations in explaining sociocultural changes, in reaction to earlier uses of migration as an excessively simplistic explanation for change. But sizable ancient migrations really happened, and migration is increasingly recognized as among the plausible explanatory factors for many sociocultural changes (e.g., Anthony 1990, 2007; Burmeister 2000; Cabana and Clark 2011; Chapman and Hamerow 1997). This is not to say that migration is ever a simple process. Migrants are affected by movement; the very process of migration and exposure to different social and environmental situations is one cause of change (De León et al., chapter 7). Previous occupants of a region are rarely wholly exterminated or driven away, and complex interactions between newcomers and locals leave everyone different from before (Morrissey, chapter 9; Eder, chapter 10).

It is best if archaeology can be combined with written documents, as in Peter Heather's (2009) analysis of numerous migrations—many of them invasions—that shaped European history during the first millennium AD. But, even when written documents are unavailable, it is possible to combine multiple kinds of evidence, as argued by Christopher Beekman and Alexander Christensen (2003) and by Alison Wylie (2002:162–163). One excellent example is Scott Ortman's (2009) study of migration from the Mesa Verde area of the southwestern United States to the Rio Grande area of New Mexico, combining archaeological, linguistic, ethnographic, and environmental evidence to gain insights into the disruptions motivating the departure from the Mesa Verde area, reasons to move to the Rio Grande area, and the impacts of newcomers on previous occupants.

I frame my overview under four headings: (i) detection of a migration, (ii) dating a migration or other event, (iii) detection of disruptions and other motivations for departure from a source region, and (iv) detection of disruptions and other impacts on a receiving region.

Detection of an Ancient Migration

The most decisive evidence about ancient migrations will eventually come through bioarchaeological data, especially highly heritable skeletal and dental features that are good proxies for DNA, often available and inexpensive to measure accurately (Aubry 2009). DNA itself is expensive and requires great care to avoid contamination, but it will be increasingly valuable. At present I am cautious about interpretations based on stable isotopes of oxygen in teeth and bones (e.g., White et al. 2007), because more work needs to be done concerning possible post-deposition alterations (diagenesis), establishment of larger databases, possible effects of climatic changes, and distant water derived from streams. The situation seems somewhat better for stable isotopes of strontium, especially because it is based on unchanging local geology, and at least in the Andes it appears to give better results than oxygen (Knudson 2009). However, these stable isotope analyses are, at best, only relevant for first-generation migrants, or possibly for later generations if they made frequent visits to the home region. Stable isotopes provide no genetic information but instead provide information bearing on possible places of residence in infancy (especially through teeth that form early and thereafter do not change chemically) and late in life (especially through bones, whose composition changes throughout life in accordance with an individual's diet).

The spread of things from one region to another need not be due to a migration of people. Some things are *imports*. These usually can be identified by mere inspection by anyone deeply familiar with locally made objects, and they can always be identified by petrography, neutron analysis, and other laboratory techniques. For ceramics, clays were rarely derived from far away, and their source deposits can generally be localized to within a radius of 20 kilometers or less. Sources of obsidian artifacts, often imported from hundreds of kilometers away, are often localizable within a diameter of five kilometers or less. Imports indicate contacts, providing knowledge that can facilitate migrations, and also be models for emulation.

Inheritance refers to a novice learning how to make an object directly from a more skilled practitioner. Often the novice learns from a parent or other close relative, but learning through apprenticeship to someone else is also possible. The learning includes both unconscious and conscious practices and is at least partly what Pierre Bourdieu called *habitus*. Inheritance can occur in any material category, including that of mundane objects of little significance, and usually involves both technological and decorative styles, as Michelle Hegmon (1992, 1998) refers to them. The transfer from one region to another of subtle differences in technological style—things that few people would have noticed—is suggestive of migrants. An example of such an inconspicuous feature is faint traces of horizontal burnishing strokes on a plain ceramic vessel, versus faint traces of vertical strokes.

Emulation refers to the creation of the form by an already competent artisan, who consciously copies an object that is not part of his or her *inheritance*. Emulation in decorative style together with the persistence of a local technological style is most apt to occur in categories with salient cultural meaning, such as decorated ceramic serving wares or wares used in rituals—that is, things that everyone would have noticed. A similar outward appearance may be obtained by different means. *Emulation* may not closely copy technological style and, when a feature with a history in one region is emulated in another region, it is not diagnostic of migration. A change in local decorative style but not technological style suggests *emulation* of foreign styles considered prestigious by locals, with no migration involved.

Dating a Migration or Other Event

Archaeology is renowned for its ability to trace events as they unfold over many centuries. Less recognized is its potential to deal with episodes of relatively short duration. In the absence of calendrical inscriptions, careful excavation can often distinguish a fine sequence of superposed strata. In the absence of stratigraphic information, a sequence of brief intervals can often be established through a variety of simple or more complex mathematical methods, called seriation. But stratigraphy and seriation yield sequences rather than absolute dates that can be expressed in calendar years. To obtain absolute dates, the mainstay has been radiocarbon (C14) dating. For several reasons, C14 dates can only be expressed in terms of confidence intervals—that is, a span of years that is very likely to include the true date. Currently, in many regions, including Central and Western Mexico, 95 percent confidence intervals tend to be on the order of a century or two, which can be frustratingly imprecise, especially when one tries to relate events in one region to events in another region. However, the potential exists to obtain 95 percent confidence intervals on the order of 50 years or so, partly by obtaining larger numbers of good C14 determinations for an event or set of closely related events, but especially through Bayesian statistical methods that can systematically (rather than impressionistically) relate multiple C14 readings to one another and incorporate stratigraphy and other independent data. Zeidler et al. (1998) give an excellent example of how this process works. A 95 percent interval of a half century may seem broad to persons used to dealing with events on an annual or even a daily basis, but it is actually narrow enough to resolve many issues.

Still narrower confidence intervals can be obtained in limited regions amenable to dating by tree rings (dendrochronology), such as parts of the southwestern United States, where intervals of less than a decade have been obtained. This method works by matching sequences of broad and narrow annual growth rings, related to good or poor local conditions. So far in Mesoamerica it has only been applied to one region in Central Mexico, with a sequence back to AD 771, but additional work may carry it back further in time and/or succeed in applying it to more regions (Stahle et al. 2011).

Identification of Disruptions and Other Motivations for Departure from a Source Region

Motivations can be divided into "push" and "pull" factors. Environmental problems are often proposed as "push" factors. This possibility should always be taken seriously, but it requires careful study for confirmation, as well as consideration of alternatives (see Morrissey, chapter 9, for a modern example). We must beware of anthropologically naïve environmental scientists who tend to overemphasize environmental issues at the expense of everything else. It is also important to avoid extrapolation from regions hundreds of kilometers away. Growing "population pressure" on local resources can be a push factor, but excess population growth itself cannot be taken for granted and must be explained (Cowgill 1975). More attention needs to be given to identification of sociopolitical disruptions as causes of emigration from a source region. Evidence of increased warfare, such as destruction and desecration of monuments and other structures seems a good marker, but we need to think of signs of more subtle stresses.

Something between a push and pull factor in stimulating emigration is increasing sociopolitical centralization and control of more resources, which enables foreign conquests. This is evident in many cases where there are adequate texts, as in Europe (e.g., Heather 2009), but it needs more consideration in undocumented cases.

The most obvious pull factor is identification of an attractive target region. Inducements include perception of better environmental conditions, better economic opportunities, and/or more vulnerable target polities. Economic opportunities figure especially in movements by individuals or small groups, while perceived political vulnerability will favor organized conquests.

Identification of Disruptions and Other Impacts on a Receiving Region

Invasion and conquest are likely to produce political fragmentation in the receiving region or incorporation into an expanding empire, either of which counts as disruptive. Fragmentation will be evidenced by multiple centers instead of any single overarching center, and often by greater small-scale stylistic diversity. Provincial incorporation will often be indicated by evidence of administrative centers, structures, or practices tied to a capital in the source region. Less organized and smaller-scale migrations carried out by uncoordinated individuals or small groups may have little impact on the receiving region and be archaeologically undetectable.

A Probable Case of Migration in Central Mexico

Teotihuacan (tay-oh-tee-WAK-an) was one of the earliest and largest pre-Columbian cities in the western hemisphere (fig. 5.1, 5.3.1). It lies about 2,260 meters (7,500 feet) above sea level, in the Basin of Mexico, near present-day Mexico City (fig. 5.2). Roughly coeval with quite different early Maya centers more than 1,100 kilometers (700 miles) away, it flourished from about 100 BC until about AD 550/650, long before the Aztec Empire of the 1400s. It covered approximately 20 square kilometers (eight square miles), with an estimated population of around 80,000 to 100,000. Following the burning of its major civic-ceremonial structures, shattering of cult

Figure 5.1. An aerial view of the central part of Teotihuacan, 1965. (Photo courtesy of René Millon.)

images, and abandonment of many dwellings throughout the city some-where around AD 600 (give or take a half century), material culture in Cen-tral Mexico changed considerably. After this episode of widespread violent destruction, subsequent material culture in ceramics, stone implements, architecture, and decorative styles in the ensuing Epiclassic period (locally circa AD 600/650 to 800/850) owes little to Teotihuacan antecedents. Be-yond that, controversy reigns. Currently debated are (a) the extent to which migrants from the northwest played a role in these events and, if they did play a role, (b) what motivated their departure, (c) what the impact of their arrival in Central Mexico was, and (d) what the roles of disruptions in the source and receiving areas were. I have recently discussed these issues in more detail in a paper for specialists on Mesoamerica (Cowgill 2013). Here I add more about broad issues.

The Decline and Collapse of the Teotihuacan State

The area directly administered by the Teotihuacan state may not have ex-tended much beyond the Basin of Mexico, but Teotihuacan influences were

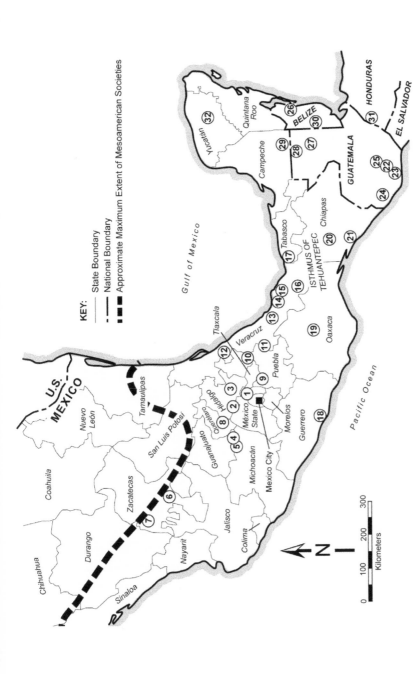

Figure 5.2. Selected archaeological sites in Mesoamerica. Sites and regions mentioned in text: Teotihuacan (1), Cuitzeo Basin (5), La Quemada (7), and sites in the Maya region (22–32).

widespread in Mesoamerica, reaching westward at least to the Cuitzeo Basin in the state of Michoacán and eastward to the Maya region (fig. 5.2). For several centuries Teotihuacan was powerful enough to discourage the growth of significant rival centers within a radius of a few hundred miles. Then, during Teotihuacan's Metepec ceramic phase, which I currently estimate to date around AD 500/550 to 600/650, the city was apparently in decline. The city's population may have shrunk by more than half, possibly even by two thirds, with population especially diminished in the outer parts of the city. Analysis of grave offerings by Martha Sempowski (1987, 1994) and spatial analyses of comprehensive surface survey (Millon 1973; Millon et al. 1973) by Ian Robertson (2005) suggest that wealth disparities were increasing. Linda Manzanilla (2006) argues that intermediate elites within the city were gaining increasing independent power and wealth, at the expense of revenues that formerly reached the state. Excavations just outside the Yayahuala multi-apartment compound (Séjourné 1966:21) found deep layers of refuse accumulating in streets, as did Rubén Cabrera and Sergio Gómez (2008:69, 71) in the La Ventilla district of the city. In that district, some streets were blocked by gates. All this evidence suggests a variety of internal problems for the state, perhaps exacerbated by administrative and ideological rigidity (Millon 1988). It is unlikely that migrants were the sole cause of the collapse of the Teotihuacan state.

There were probably no serious environmental problems within the Basin of Mexico (fig. 5.3; McClung 2009, 2012), but there may have been trouble from growing regional centers not far outside the basin, notably Xochicalco in the state of Morelos and Cacaxtla-Xochitécatl in the state of Tlaxcala (fig. 5.2). Unfortunately, chronologies are still too imprecise to tell for sure whether these centers began to rise before Teotihuacan's demise, and hence may have contributed to its decline, or if they rose only after Teotihuacan's collapse removed an obstacle to their development.

Then, around AD 600/650, dramatic events occurred at Teotihuacan. Temple pyramids, the Ciudadela complex, and other structures along the Avenue of the Dead (the central civic-ceremonial district of the city) and elsewhere were burned, and idols were demolished and their fragments scattered (Millon 1988; Martínez and Jarquín 1982; López Luján et al. 2006). Some, including Linda Manzanilla (in Soler-Arechaldi et al. 2006), argue that the burning took place somewhat earlier and that the final phase of the Teotihuacan tradition represents survivors of this catastrophe. But there is abundant evidence that considerable building took place in the civic-ceremonial center and elsewhere in the city during Teotihuacan's decline

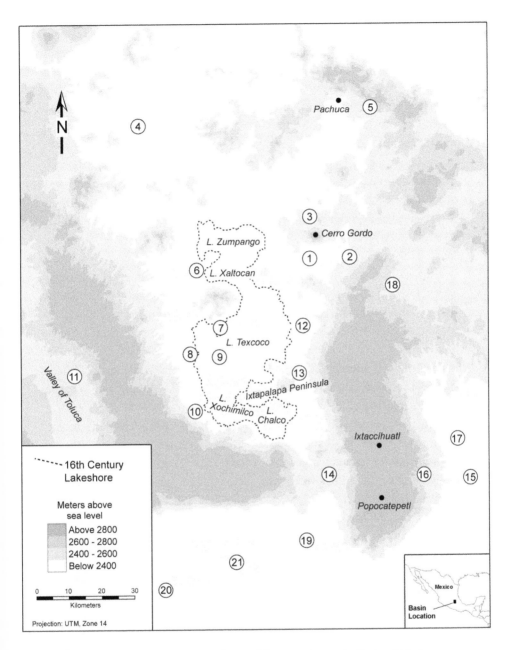

Figure 5.3. Selected archaeological sites and major lakes in and near the Basin of Mexico.

and that the episode of violence marks the collapse of the Teotihuacan state and the end of the Teotihuacan tradition (e.g., Millon 1992).

Too often, excavation techniques at Teotihuacan have left the possibility of hiatuses in occupation unclear. However, near the eastern edge of the city, a multi-apartment residential compound was abandoned and only reoccupied after an interval, by makers of a style of pottery called Coyotlatelco (Rattray 2006). Abandonment of one outlying compound could be merely part of the late Teotihuacan shrinkage of the city mentioned previously. However, in the Rancho La Ventilla district, not far from the city center, Cabrera and Gómez (2008:69, 71) found unfinished craft items and other objects left in place atop the latest Teotihuacan floor in a compound of artisans, giving them the impression that it was rapidly abandoned. At Xalla, a large civic-ceremonial complex just east of the Avenue of the Dead, a 20-centimeter layer of fine sediments introduced by wind and rain overlies evidence of burning and violent destruction of images (Leonardo López Luján, personal communication 2011). Burning and destruction of images is also seen at the Ciudadela and elsewhere along the Avenue of the Dead (López Luján et al. 2006). At Azcapotzalco, on the west side of Lake Texcoco (fig. 5.3.8), a layer interpreted as building fill by Alfred Tozzer (1921) has been reinterpreted as a destruction layer by Raúl García Chávez (1991). And, as described by Frederic Hicks (2013), there is evidence at the southeastern Basin of Mexico site of Cerro Portezuelo (fig. 5.3.13) for a significant interval of abandonment, followed by reoccupation. There are other cases where no such abandonment is reported. For example, Claudia López, Claudia Nicolás, and Linda Manzanilla (2006) report continuous occupation in underground chambers dug in Teotihuacan times to obtain building materials, a short distance east of the Pyramid of the Sun. They suggest that Epiclassic newcomers were living in marginal locations within the city before its collapse, coexisting with the previous occupants. However, much of their evidence for coexistence is based on obsidian hydration and radiocarbon dates, and I do not think they have fully taken into account the problematic character of hydration dating and the high probability that, in any sizable batch of radiocarbon dates, a few will have calibrated intercepts and even "two sigma" ranges that are well outside the true date. That is to say, the dates of ceramic complexes estimated by these methods may overlap even when the actual dates of occupations do not.

Teotihuacan soon regained its status as a populous community, but there was a very drastic shift in the districts within the former city with highest sherd densities; far more drastic than any that had occurred since the city first reached its maximum extent around AD 100 (see maps in Cowgill 2013). The Coyotlatelco spatial occupation pattern is very different from the previous pattern, and there was probably no longer a single urban center (Crider 2002; Crider et al. 2007).

The Case for Local Continuity after the Fall of Teotihuacan

In 1966, when much less was known about West Mexican cultures than is known today, James Bennyhoff (1967) believed that Epiclassic ceramics in the Basin of Mexico were largely *inherited* from Teotihuacan. He recognized that there was a pronounced change in ceramics, marked by a new phase, which he called Oxtoticpac. He saw it as "an impoverished Teotihuacán derivative, strongly influenced by Xochicalco (fig. 5.3.20), while the [ensuing] Xometla phase, as found in the Teotihuacán Valley, represents a hybrid and fusion of the altered and exhausted Teotihuacán tradition and the enigmatic Coyotlatelco culture" (Bennyhoff 1967:20–21). He felt that there were no significant displacements of the local Basin of Mexico population by massive intrusions of people until later. He thought that a few migrants probably arrived during the Epiclassic, but never in sufficient strength to alter the basic continuity of the Teotihuacan tradition (Bennyhoff 1967:21–22). René Millon agreed, distinguishing an earlier Oxtoticpac phase from later Xometla (with Coyotlatelco-style serving wares) in his chronological charts (e.g., Millon 1988:111). In the Teotihuacan Valley, this later Epiclassic subphase is well represented at the site of Xometla (fig. 5.3; Nichols and McCullough 1986).

In evaluating Bennyhoff (1967), one should remember that his mindset encouraged him to privilege inheritance from Teotihuacan wherever that was not too implausible. He never referred to any possible alternative sources for Epiclassic ceramics, and I believe that he thought of West Mexican cultures as far less developed than they are now known to have been. Nevertheless, there is a case for some degree of inheritance from Teotihuacan antecedents, though to a much lesser degree than he believed.

My views are somewhere between the polarized extremes of the late William Sanders (2006), who argued that Epiclassic society derived overwhelmingly from Teotihuacan, with little in-migration, and Evelyn Rattray (1966, 1996, 2006), who claimed that newcomers effected a complete break from Teotihuacan antecedents. Some scholars, notably Sanders, make much of alleged cultural continuity in the Basin of Mexico to argue for strong continuity in population. Many features of sixteenth-century thought and religion, such as the Storm God and the Feathered Serpent, do have very deep historical roots in Central Mexico (Carrasco et al. 2000). But many other features did not outlive the Teotihuacan state.

Yoko Sugiura (2006) is dismissive of peoples from West Mexico, describing them as marginal to Mesoamerica and on a relatively low level of sociopolitical development. Northernmost Mesoamericans in the state of Durango, north of Zacatecas, may indeed have been marginal, but this characterization hardly squares with what is now known of the variety, sophistication, and complexity of West Mexican societies further south and closer to Central Mexico, including those in the state of Guanajuato (Beekman 2010).

Patricia Fournier and Victor Bolaños (2007) also argue against any significant migration of people from West Mexico into Central Mexico during the Epiclassic, stating that current radiocarbon dates of West Mexican ceramic styles, from which Coyotlatelco styles are supposedly derived, are no earlier in West Mexico than in Central Mexico, and that the ceramic resemblances are not really that close. But they do not include any illustrations from which one could judge the degree of ceramic resemblances, and the quality of relevant dates in West Mexico is still not good enough to be decisive one way or the other. Most importantly, they do not mention the difficulties in deriving the Coyotlatelco style from Teotihuacan styles.

Persons who argue for strong ethnic continuity at Teotihuacan often do not seem to be well informed about Teotihuacan ceramics. They tend to downplay differences between ceramics before and after the city's collapse, or even ignore the issue altogether. Many Epiclassic pottery categories alleged to be derived from Teotihuacan do not in fact have convincing Teotihuacan antecedents. For example, the discussion by Margarita Gaxiola (2006) makes excellent points about the regional diversity of Epiclassic ceramics, and its likely multiple inheritances and innovations, but sees Teotihuacan influences in many examples that do not look much like anything I know of at Teotihuacan. Sugiura (2006) also tends to see more Epiclassic inheritance from Teotihuacan than I can see.

The Case for Local Discontinuity After the Fall of Teotihuacan

There are increasing indications that the Epiclassic in the Basin of Mexico can be subdivided into two ceramic phases, with the earlier phase being prior to the appearance of the well-developed Coyotlatelco style (Crider 2013). This is also the case in the Valley of Toluca just west of the Basin of Mexico (fig. 5.3; Sugiura 2006). It is natural to think that the pre-Coyotlatelco phase might have "transitional" ceramic complexes derived in large part from those of the Metepec phase of Teotihuacan. This is the way the "Oxtotipac" assemblage, found in a cave at Oxtotipac in the Teotihuacan Valley, was interpreted by William Sanders (1986, 1989, 2006). Evelyn Rattray (1966), in her major study of Coyotlatelco ceramics, was aware of the Oxtoticpac phase proposed by Sanders, Bennyhoff, and Millon, but she was skeptical of it. But in view of increasing evidence for subphases, it is now clear that Rattray was wrong when she insisted on a single Epiclassic ceramic phase. Crider (2013) takes important steps in defining subphases and identifying their spatial and temporal variants, but much more needs to be done. Among other things, it is urgent that ceramics from selected Teotihuacan Mapping Project collections with large Epiclassic sherd counts be reexamined. Stratigraphic excavations will also be critical.

Little in the early Epiclassic complexes seen at Cerro Portezuelo and elsewhere looks anything like Metepec to me. Most of the vessel forms and decorative motifs of the earlier Epiclassic and the Coyotlatelco style of the later Epiclassic serving vessels differ considerably from those of the late and terminal Teotihuacan serving ware styles. There are some elements of some Epiclassic ceramic complexes in the Basin of Mexico that appear to resemble Teotihuacan antecedents more than anything else. It has been suggested that there may be more continuity from the Teotihuacan period into the Epiclassic in utility wares than in serving and ritual wares (e.g., Gaxiola 2006). Perhaps the best candidates for such continuity are low-necked "roll-rim" ollas (large jars for storage and cooking). Some of these seem hard to tell from late Teotihuacan ollas. But other Epiclassic ollas and other utility vessels are quite different. The proportion of Epiclassic utility ware types *not* easily derivable from Teotihuacan antecedents has sometimes been overlooked, as well as the number of Teotihuacan utility forms and even whole wares that ceased to be made after the collapse of the Teotihuacan state. The great majority of Epiclassic serving wares in the Basin of Mexico do not have good Teotihuacan antecedents, although stamped decoration in some late Teotihuacan serving vessels might be a source for the stamped decoration that is more prevalent in the Epiclassic.

Ritual incense burners changed drastically at the same time that new styles of serving wares were adopted. Large composite censers, "handled covers," and the very small censers called *candeleros* disappeared, and new censers in the form of shallow bowls with tubular handles appeared. However, we should consider the possibility that there could have been an ideological, political, and even moral repudiation of things associated with the Teotihuacan state, if not with the city itself. If indeed that state collapsed largely as a result of internal tensions, it is plausible that many Epiclassic groups, even those dwelling in the ruins of the city, made a point of distancing themselves from the symbolism of that state. Identifications with the past are more likely to occur among people safely removed in time, such as the archaistic revivals created by the Aztecs (Umberger 1987; López Luján 1989), or distant in both space and time, as done by Late Classic Maya (Stone 1989).

Among decorated forms, *floreros* may be derived from Teotihuacan antecedents, but with major changes. Typical Teotihuacan *floreros* are gracile, with a long, narrow, tubular neck, a very widely flaring rim, no handles, and no supports. Several somewhat similar vessels appear in Epiclassic contexts, but they are squat and rather heavy, with a short neck, a loop handle, annular supports, and, sometimes, attached vertical fillets on the body. Very similar vessels are found in the Valley of Toluca (Sugiura 2006). To my eye, the contrast with the Teotihuacan form is pronounced, and the apparent lack of intermediate forms raises doubts about whether they were directly derived from the Teotihuacan form.

Vessels with basal overlap (sometimes called basal Z-angle) are well represented at Cerro Portezuelo in the Epiclassic phase. However, I know of no good Teotihuacan antecedent for this form. Basal overlap vessels are found at Xochicalco and other sites in Morelos (fig. 5.3.20; Cyphers 2000; Cyphers and Hirth 2000:119–120), estimated to date AD 650–800.

Some Epiclassic vessels have a very distinctive style of angular narrow-line incising in still-plastic clay, enclosing areas filled with numerous punctate dots, with both finer and coarser variants. These probably began in early Epiclassic times, before Coyotlatelco. There is no Teotihuacan antecedent for this vessel form or decorative style. Its source is mysterious.

Ceramic figurines show some continuity with Teotihuacan antecedents. Warren Barbour (1987, 1998) reports that certain late Teotihuacan forms, "half-conicals" and "thrones," continue into the Epiclassic phase, though they are generally of inferior technical quality. The disappearance of other figurine types, such as "portraits," seems understandable, since "portraits" probably represent Teotihuacan soldiers. But the elaborate mold-made half-conicals and thrones are heavily laden with meaning. Annabeth Headrick (2007) proposes that they represent deceased Teotihuacan elites. If so, their continuation seems to mark an especially strong identification with the collapsed Teotihuacan state, or at least its elite ritual. But they generally have blurred features. I wonder if they were made from worn Metepec molds by artisans who perhaps did not understand their original meanings.

Zachary Nelson's (2009) discussion of a Coyotlatelco phase lithic workshop at Teotihuacan illustrates large corner-notched projectile points that are very different from the stemmed points typical of earlier periods at Teotihuacan. David Carballo (2011) notes that corner-notched points are characteristic of the Epiclassic phase elsewhere in Central Mexico. It seems highly unlikely that a drastic change in lithic style would occur simply by emulation at the same time that drastic changes occur in ceramic styles. I think it is further evidence in support of a significant migration.

Western Mexico as a Source of Migrants

To what extent are the new styles most plausibly derived from antecedents outside Teotihuacan? Western and northwestern Mexico is a vast part of Mesoamerica, with many distinct regions (fig. 5.2). Ceramic traditions are varied, and their complex interrelations are not well understood, and their chronological uncertainties have been troubling (Beekman 2010; Beekman and Christensen 2011).

Critical here is the degree of continuity or discontinuity in technological style, especially in things that can be detected by a keen eye that have little effect on the general appearance of objects. If the changes are in outward appearances but not in technological style, it suggests they were *emulations* of foreign styles, made by Teotihuacan descendants, as I explained earlier. If these hard-to-see technological styles also change, it suggests newcomers. Unfortunately, I know of no studies that have made the kind of comparisons needed to distinguish inheritance of a foreign style (indicative of newcomers) from emulations (more ambiguous). From illustrations alone, it is usually impossible to distinguish inheritances from emulations. Nevertheless, in view of the difficulties in deriving Central Mexican Epiclassic ceramics from local antecedents, ceramic traditions in parts of western Mexico, especially from the Bajío region in eastern Guanajuato (fig. 5.2), have long been considered by some as likely sources for many features of Epiclassic ceramics in the Basin of Mexico. More distant regions, to the west around Guadalajara in the state of Jalisco or to the north around La Quemada in Zacatecas (fig. 5.2), are much less likely sources.

In the central Mexican region around Tula, about 60 kilometers north-northwest of Teotihuacan (figs. 5.2 and 5.3.4), there had been a number of Teotihuacan settlements. Probably as early as the 500s, new kinds of ceramics appeared in the Tula area, believed by many to have been carried by newcomers from within or near the Bajío, (e.g., Cobean and Mastache 1989; Mastache et al. 2002; Healan 2012). Recent comparative work by Christine Hernandez and Dan Healan (2012), based on examination of objects rather than reliance on illustrations, makes a strong case for a specific region around Ucareo, just east of the Cuitzeo Basin (fig. 5.2), where ceramics show striking similarities to the new ceramic forms that began to appear in Central Mexico around AD 500. Beekman (chapter 4) sees small groups trickling eastward into the Tula region, in contrast to organized conquests emanating from the Bajío westward into what is now the state of Jalisco. This far-western region had never been part of the Teotihuacan sphere. Although it had distinctive cultures of its own, it was perhaps more vulnerable to conquest than was Teotihuacan before its decline. One can speculate that less organized migrants were drifting into the Tula region at a time when Teotihuacan had declined enough to have lost control of that region, but while it was still strong enough to not be itself an attractive target for invasion.

The site of Tula Chico has been thought to have been still too small at this time to have had much influence in the Basin of Mexico. However, recent work suggests that Tula Chico may have been larger than was thought (Suárez Cortés et al. 2007). In the ensuing Early Postclassic period (circa AD 800/850 to 1100/1200), Tula grew into the capital of a sizable regional state.

Why Knowing the Principal Language of Teotihuacan Is Important

The indigenous languages of Mesoamerica are very diverse, belonging to a number of unrelated families. The dominant language of the Aztecs, Nahuatl, belongs to the Uto-Aztecan family. Linguists agree that its homeland was somewhere northwest of Central Mexico, although just where is debated. They also agree that Nahuatl was widely spoken in Central Mexico by no later than AD 900, and probably somewhat earlier, but many scholars argue that it was prominent much earlier, and in fact was the dominant language of Teotihuacan. If so, this linguistic continuity would weaken the case for significant Epiclassic migration into Central Mexico, although it does not decisively refute it, since migrants may have spoken a slightly different dialect of Nahuatl. On the other hand, if the dominant language of Teotihuacan was unrelated to Nahuatl, it would strengthen the case for a significant migration of Nahuatl speakers at or around the time of the collapse of the Teotihuacan state. Unfortunately, evidence about the language of Teotihuacan is currently highly controversial (e.g., Hill 2012), so the matter remains unresolved. Further research may settle the issue before long.

Motivations for Migrants

If migrants from within or near the Bajío were important, what were likely push and pull factors? Evidence for drought at this time in West or Central Mexico is mixed. Michelle Elliott (2007) finds no evidence for drought in the Malpaso Valley in the state of Zacatecas before the 1500s. Emily Mc-Clung (2009, 2012) sees no significant Epiclassic climate change in the Teotihuacan Valley. Lachniet et al. (2012) see evidence of a megadrought that culminated around AD 770 in the state of Oaxaca, about 200 miles south of the Basin of Mexico. But one cannot extrapolate from one region to other regions hundreds of kilometers away. In the Bajío, pollen cores point to drought. However, it seems that aridity only gradually increased and extreme conditions prevailed only after about AD 800, in the Early Postclassic phase, when sedentary agriculture nearly disappeared in large parts of western Mexico (Beekman, chapter 4). In general, environmental evidence for severe drought seems about two centuries later than the Epiclassic migrations. In any case, sudden severe droughts are more apt to produce refugees than conquerors, as in the US dust bowl of the 1930s or the West African Sahel in the 1970s. Even though many parts of Western Mexico supported sizable farming populations during the Epiclassic phase, the Basin of Mexico may well have been perceived as a richer environment, which may have been a pull factor for potential migrants.

Peter Heather (2009) argues that the reason that the Romans in the first century AD did not extend their empire east of the Rhine was because the region had so little to offer them, rather than because of effective resistance (the Germanic annihilation of three Roman legions in AD 7 was a fluke, not repeated). By the 400s, peoples east of the Rhine had developed very much stronger polities, largely because of wealth acquired through interactions with the Roman state, and this, rather than any marked weakening of Rome itself, was what made possible devastating conquests of key Imperial provinces, notably western north Africa, by "barbarians." Did the Teotihuacan state have any comparable effect in West Mexico, helping to bring about the rise of stronger polities that, eventually, played a large role in Teotihuacan's destruction? At present, the evidence does not suggest this, but I do not think the possibility has been considered, and it is worth investigating. Or could it be that Teotihuacan's impacts closer to home led to the rise of polities like Xochicalco, weakening the Teotihuacan state and leaving it vulnerable to West Mexican invaders? This is another topic for further research, including better chronologies for these sites, hopefully by methods such as

Bayesian analysis of multiple calibrated radiocarbon dates, along the lines pioneered for Mesoamerica by Beramendi-Orosco et al. (2009).

Impacts of Migrants

If there were large migrations, did migrants arrive as conquerors, playing a major role in the collapse of the Teotihuacan state (possibly in collusion with elements within that state), or only as fillers of a vacuum left by self-destruction of the Teotihuacan state? At the moment, neither possibility can be ruled out, but I lean toward the former. Violent conquests are well documented around the world in cases where we have written evidence. Teotihuacan certainly appears to have been in a weakened condition in its last century. Perhaps less organized early migrants who moved into the Tula region paved the way for a more organized conquest of Teotihuacan later. Possibly smallish West Mexican polities formed an alliance to topple their large neighbor to the east. Here is another topic for research. Central Mexican inheritances from two or more West Mexican sources would suggest such an alliance.

Beekman (chapter 4) suggests that Epiclassic political fragmentation in central Mexico led to competition by rulers to attract followers by means of religious innovations marked by intensified traffic in exotic preciosities. I am not sure that the traffic in preciosities increased, and if it did, it may have been due more to a general Mesoamerican increase in commerce, perhaps less restricted by political controls than before (as suggested by Blanton et al. 1993), and I suspect that, at least for farmers, the promise of lightly taxed land would have meant more than new religion. Nevertheless, Beekman's suggestions offer new lines of research to see if Epiclassic polities were more egalitarian than before. Did standards of living for commoners improve? Household economies should be explored along the lines suggested by Earle and Smith (2012).

In some discussions of the Epiclassic there seems to be an unstated assumption that descendants of the city of Teotihuacan could not have just become archaeologically invisible. It is assumed that whether they mostly stayed in place or mostly emigrated, they must have left traces of themselves *somewhere*. This has been referred to as a "billiard ball" model, in which ethnic groups are discrete, tightly bound, and durable. This assumption is unwarranted. In terms of sheer biological survival, besides the likelihood that the city's population dwindled considerably in its final century, it is conceivable that a high proportion of the remainder lost their lives through outright slaughter, and possibly from other factors such as famine.

However, one should remember that an annual excess of only one percent in deaths over births will cut a population in half in only 70 years. But, even with a high rate of survival, many of Teotihuacan's descendants may have changed their cultural identity within a generation or two and ceased to produce objects related to the Teotihuacan tradition, thereby becoming untraceable on the basis of material culture. This is especially so because survivors who migrated out probably moved in small groups. It cannot be assumed that they moved in organized mass migrations. And, as Beekman points out in chapter 4, migrants departing in small groups are hard to detect archaeologically. I postulate that at least some of the in-migrants from the west moved in organized groups and had good reasons for maintaining enough of their former identities to be detectable in archaeological data, whereas refugees from Teotihuacan were less detectable.

A major theme of the recent volume on ethnic identity by Berdan et al. (2008) is its complexity and volatility in Postclassic and present-day Mexico. They suggest that it may have been more fixed in strong states such as Teotihuacan, but less so in times of political instability. The Epiclassic phase assuredly counts as a time of instability. Teotihuacan dissidents may have made a point of distancing themselves from the collapsed state, while supporters may have seen little to gain by drawing attention to their connection. We cannot assume that Teotihuacan survivors are necessarily to be identified by their ceramics or anything else, except perhaps genetic markers.

Summary

Epiclassic materials at Teotihuacan and elsewhere in Central Mexico provide less evidence of inheritance from Teotihuacan than is often claimed or assumed. Some elements of some Epiclassic ceramic complexes may derive from Teotihuacan antecedents, but the proportion of new elements is large. This does not, by itself, demonstrate beyond all reasonable doubt the arrival of substantial numbers of newcomers, but it lends additional support to that scenario, which is also suggested by biological and lithic evidence, and by hiatuses in occupation in some Teotihuacan structures reoccupied in the Epiclassic phase. These newcomers apparently interacted in complex ways with Teotihuacan survivors, leading to ceramic complexes and other cultural features that included both emulation and inheritance from multiple antecedents. Ethnic identities probably shifted and may have been rapidly redefined.

Acknowledgments

I am indebted to all of my fellow workshop participants, especially Chris Beekman, for their lively discussions and insights. Shearon Vaughn produced figures 5.2 and 5.3.

References Cited

Anthony, David W.
1990   Migration in Archaeology: The Baby and the Bathwater. American Anthropologist 92(4):895–914.
2007   The Horse, the Wheel, and Language: How Bronze-Age Riders from the Eurasian Steppes Shaped the Modern World. Princeton: Princeton University Press.
Aubry, Brian Scott
2009   Population Structure and Interregional Interaction in Pre-Hispanic Mesoamerica: A Biodistance Study. PhD dissertation, Department of Anthropology, Ohio State University, Columbus.
Barbour, Warren D.
1987   Ceramic Figurines from Oxtoticpac. In The Toltec Period Occupation of the Valley: Part 2—Surface Survey and Special Studies. William T. Sanders, ed. Pp. 697–754. University Park: Department of Anthropology, Pennsylvania State University.
1998   The Figurine Chronology of Teotihuacan, Mexico. In Los Ritmos de Cambio en Teotihuacan: Reflexiones y Discusiones de Su Cronología. Rosa Brambila and Rubén Cabrera, eds. Pp. 243–353. Mexico City: Instituto Nacional de Antropología e Historia.
Beekman, Christopher S.
2010   Recent Research in Western Mexican Archaeology. Journal of Archaeological Research 18:41–109.
Beekman, Christopher S., and Alexander F. Christensen
2003   Controlling for Doubt and Uncertainty Through Multiple Lines of Evidence: A New Look at the Mesoamerican Nahua Migrations. Journal of Archaeological Method and Theory 10(2):111–164.
2011   Power, Agency, and Identity: Migration and Aftermath in the Mezquital Area of North-Central Mexico. In Rethinking Anthropological Perspectives on Migration. Graciela S. Cabana and Jeffery J. Clark, eds. Pp. 147–171. Gainesville: University Press of Florida.
Bennyhoff, James A.
1967   Continuity and Change in the Teotihuacan Ceramic Tradition. In Teotihuacan: Onceava Mesa Redonda. Pp. 19–29. Mexico City: Sociedad Mexicana de Antropología.
Beramendi-Orosco, Laura E., Galia González-Hernández, Jaime Urrutia-Fucugauchi, Linda R. Manzanilla, Ana M. Soler-Arechalde, Avto Goguitchaishvili, and Nick Jarboe
2009   High-Resolution Chronology for the Mesoamerican Urban Center of Teotihuacan

Derived from Bayesian Statistics of Radiocarbon and Archaeological Data. Quaternary Research 71:99–107.

Berdan, Frances F., John K. Chance, Alan R. Sandstrom, Barbara L. Stark, James M. Taggart, and Emily Umberger
2008   Ethnic Identity in Nahua Mesoamerica: The View from Archaeology, Art History, Ethnohistory, and Contemporary Ethnography. Salt Lake City: University of Utah Press.

Blanton, Richard E., Stephen A. Kowalewski, Gary M. Feinman, and Laura M. Finsten
1993   Ancient Mesoamerica (2nd edition). Cambridge: Cambridge University Press.

Burmeister, Stefan
2000   Archaeology and Migration: Approaches to an Archaeological Proof of Migration. Current Anthropology 41(4):539–567.

Cabana, Graciela S., and Jeffery J. Clark, eds.
2011   Rethinking Anthropological Perspectives on Migration. Gainesville: University Press of Florida.

Cabrera Castro, Rubén, and Sergio Gómez Chávez
2008   La Ventilla: A Model for a Barrio in the Urban Structure of Teotihuacan. In Urbanism in Mesoamerica/El Urbanismo en Mesoamérica, vol. 2. Alba Guadalupe Mastache, Robert H. Cobean, Á. García Cook, and Kenneth G. Hirth, eds. Pp. 37–83. Mexico City and University Park: Instituto Nacional de Antropología e Historia and Pennsylvania State University.

Carballo, David M.
2011   Obsidian and the Teotihuacan State: Weaponry and Ritual Production at the Moon Pyramid/La obsidian y el Estado Teotihuacano: La Producción Militar y Ritual en la Pirámide de la Luna. Pittsburgh and Mexico City: University of Pittsburgh Center for Comparative Archaeology and the Instituto de Investigaciones Antropológicas, Universidad Nacional Autónoma de México.

Carrasco, Davíd, Lindsay Jones, and Scott Sessions, eds.
2000   Mesoamerica's Classic Heritage: From Teotihuacan to the Aztecs. Boulder: University Press of Colorado.

Chapman, John, and Helena Hamerow, eds.
1997   Migrations and Invasions in Archaeological Explanation. British Archaeological Reports International Series, 664. Oxford: Archaeopress.

Cobean, Robert H., and Alba Guadalupe Mastache
1989   The Late Classic and Early Postclassic Chronology of the Tula Region. In Tula of the Toltecs: Excavation and Survey. Dan M. Healan, ed. Pp. 34–48. Iowa City: University of Iowa Press.

Cowgill, George L.
1975   On Causes and Consequences of Ancient and Modern Population Changes. American Anthropologist 77:505–525.
2013   Possible Migrations and Shifting Identities in the Central Mexican Epiclassic. Ancient Mesoamerica 24(1):131–149.

Crider, Destiny L.
2002   Coyotlatelco Phase Community Structure at Teotihuacan. MA paper, Department of Anthropology, Arizona State University, Tempe.

2013   Shifting Alliances: Epiclassic and Early Postclassic Interactions at Cerro Portezu-
        elo. Ancient Mesoamerica 24(1):107–130.
Crider, Destiny, Deborah L. Nichols, Hector Neff, and Michael D. Glascock
2007   In the Aftermath of Teotihuacan: Epiclassic Pottery Production and Distribution
        in the Teotihuacan Valley, Mexico. Latin American Antiquity 18(2):123–143.
Cyphers, Ann
2000   Cultural Identity and Inter-Regional Interaction during the Gobernador Phase:
        A Ceramic Perspective. In Archaeological Research at Xochicalco, Vol. Two: The
        Xochicalco Mapping Project. Kenneth G. Hirth, ed. Pp. 11–16. Salt Lake City: Uni-
        versity of Utah Press.
Cyphers, Ann, and Kenneth G. Hirth
2000   Ceramics of Western Morelos: The Cañada through Gobernador Phases at Xochi-
        calco. In Archaeological Research at Xochicalco, Vol. Two: The Xochicalco Map-
        ping Project. Kenneth G. Hirth, ed. Pp. 102–135. Salt Lake City: University of Utah
        Press.
Earle, Timothy, and Michael E. Smith
2012   Household Economies Under the Aztec and Inka Empires: A Comparison. In The
        Comparative Archaeology of Civilizations. Michael E. Smith, ed. Pp. 238–284.
        New York: Cambridge University Press.
Elliott, Michelle
2007   Human Occupation and Landscape Change in the Malpaso Valley, Zacatecas,
        Mexico. PhD dissertation, School of Human Evolution and Social Change, Ari-
        zona State University, Tempe.
Fournier, Patricia, and Victor H. Bolaños
2007   The Epiclassic in the Tula Region Beyond Tula Chico. In Twin Tollans: Chichén
        Itzá, Tula, and the Epiclassic to Early Postclassic Mesoamerican World. Jeff Karl
        Kowalski and Cynthia Kristan-Graham, eds. Pp. 480–529. Washington, D.C.:
        Dumbarton Oaks.
García Chávez, Raúl E.
1991   Desarrollo Cultural en Azcapotzalco y el Área Suroccidental de la Cuenca de
        México, desde el Preclásico Medio hasta el Epiclásico. Mexico City: Escuela Na-
        cional de Antropología e Historia.
Gaxiola González, Margarita
2006   Tradición y Estilo en el Estudio de la Variabilidad cerámica del Epiclásico en el
        Centro de México. In El fenómeno Coyotlatelco en el centro de México: tiempo,
        espacio y significado. Laura Solar Valverde, ed. Pp. 31–54. Mexico City: Instituto
        Nacional de Antropología e Historia.
Headrick, Annabeth
2007   The Teotihuacan Trinity: Reconstructing the Sociopolitical Structure of an An-
        cient Mesoamerican City. Austin: University of Texas Press.
Healan, Dan M.
2012   The Archaeology of Tula, Hidalgo, Mexico. Journal of Archaeological Research
        20(1):53–115.
Heather, Peter
2009   Empires and Barbarians: The Fall of Rome and the Birth of Europe. Oxford: Ox-
        ford University Press.

Hegmon, Michelle

1992   Archaeological Research on Style. Annual Review of Anthropology 21:517–536.

1998   Technology, Style, and Social Practices: Archaeological Approaches. *In* The Archaeology of Social Boundaries. Miriam T. Stark, ed. Pp. 264–279. Washington, D.C.: Smithsonian Institution Press.

Hernandez, Christine L., and Dan M. Healan

2012   The Role of Migration in Shaping Trans-Regional Interaction in Post-Classic Central and Near West Mexico. Paper presented at the Annual Meeting of the Society for American Archaeology, Memphis.

Hicks, Frederic

2013   The Architectural Features of Cerro Portezuelo. Ancient Mesoamerica 24(1):73–85.

Hill, Jane H.

2012   How Mesoamerican Are the Nahua Languages? Paper presented at the Annual Meeting of the Society for American Archaeology, Memphis.

Kaufman, Terrence, and John Justeson

2007   The History of the Word for Cacao in Ancient Mesoamerica. Ancient Mesoamerica 18(2):193–237.

Knudson, Kelly J.

2009   Oxygen Isotope Analysis in a Land of Environmental Extremes: The Complexities of Isotopic Work in the Andes. International Journal of Osteoarchaeology 19:171–191.

Lachniet, Matthew S., Juan Pablo Bernal, Yemane Asmerom, Victor Polyak, and Dolores Piperno

2012   A 2,400 Yr Mesoamerican Rainfall Reconstruction Links Climate and Cultural Change. Geology 40:259–262.

López Luján, Leonardo

1989   La Recuperación Mexica del Pasado Teotihuacano. Mexico City: Instituto Nacional de Antropología e Historia.

López Luján, Leonardo, Laura Filloy Nadal, Barbara W. Fash, William L. Fash, and Pilar Hernández

2006   The Destruction of Images in Teotihuacan: Anthropomorphic Sculpture, Elite Cults, and the End of a Civilization. RES: Anthropology and Aesthetics 49/50:13–39.

López Pérez, Claudia, Claudia Nicolás Careta, and Linda Manzanilla Naim

2006   Atributos Morfológicos y Estilísticos de la Cerámica Coyotlatelco en el Centro Ceremonial de Teotihuacan. *In* El fenómeno Coyotlatelco en el Centro de México: Tiempo, Espacio y Significado. Laura Solar Valverde, ed. Pp. 216–230. Mexico City: Instituto Nacional de Antropología e Historia.

Manzanilla, Linda

2006   Estados Corporativos Arcaicos: Organizaciones de Excepción en Escenarios Excluyentes. Cuicuilco 13(36): 3–45.

Martínez Vargas, Enrique, and Ana María Jarquín Pacheco

1982   Arquitectura y Sistemas Constructivos de la Fachada posterior de la Ciudadela: Analisis Preliminar. *In* Teotihuacan 80–82: Primeros Resultados, Rubén Cabrera Castro, Ignacio Rodríguez García, and Noel Morelos García, coordinators. Pp. 41–47. Mexico City: Instituto Nacional de Antropología e Historia.

Mastache, Alba Guadalupe, Robert H. Cobean, and Dan M. Healan
2002   Ancient Tollan: Tula and the Toltec Heartland. Boulder: University Press of Colorado.

McClung de Tapia, Emily
2009   Los Ecosistemas del Valle de Teotihuacan a lo Largo de su Historia. *In* Teotihuacan: Ciudad de los Dioses. Pp. 36–45. Mexico City: Instituto Nacional de Antropología e Historia.
2012   Silent Hazards, Invisible Risks: Prehispanic Erosion in the Teotihuacan Valley, Central Mexico. *In* Surviving Sudden Environmental Change. Jago Cooper and Payson Sheets, eds. Pp. 143–165. Boulder: University Press of Colorado.

Millon, René
1973   The Teotihuacán Map. Part One: Text. Austin: University of Texas Press.
1988   The Last Years of Teotihuacan Dominance. *In* The Collapse of Ancient States and Civilizations. N. Yoffee and G. L. Cowgill, eds. Pp. 102–164. Tucson: University of Arizona Press.
1992   Teotihuacan Studies: From 1950 to 1990 and Beyond. *In* Art, Ideology, and the City of Teotihuacan. Janet Catherine Berlo, ed. Pp. 339–429. Washington, D.C.: Dumbarton Oaks.

Millon, René, R. Bruce Drewitt, and George L. Cowgill
1973   The Teotihuacán Map. Part Two: Maps. Austin: University of Texas Press.

Nelson, Zachary
2009   Obsidian Biface Production at Teotihuacan: Reexamining a Coyotlatelco Phase Workshop from Hacienda Metepec. Ancient Mesoamerica 20(1):149–162.

Nichols, Deborah L., and John McCullough
1986   Excavations at Xometla (TT-21). *In* The Teotihuacan Valley Project—Final Report Vol. IV: The Toltec Occupation of the Valley. William T. Sanders, ed. Pp. 53–194. University Park: Pennsylvania State University.

Ortman, Scott G.
2009   Genes, Language and Culture in Tewa Ethnogenesis, AD 1150–1400. PhD dissertation, School of Human Evolution and Social Change, Arizona State University, Tempe.

Price, T. Douglas, Linda Manzanilla, and William D. Middleton
2000   Immigration and the Ancient City of Teotihuacan in Mexico: A Study Using Strontium Isotope Ratios in Human Bone and Teeth. Journal of Archaeological Science 27:903–913.

Rattray, Evelyn Childs
1966   An Archaeological and Stylistic Study of Coyotlatelco Pottery. Mesoamerican Notes 7–8:87–211. Mexico City: Department of Anthropology, University of the Americas.
1996   A Regional Perspective on the Epiclassic Period in Central Mexico. *In* Arqueología Mesoamericana: Homenaje a William T. Sanders. Alba Guadalupe Mastache, Jeffrey R. Parsons, Robert S. Santley, and Mari Carmen Serra Puche, eds. Pp. 213–231. Mexico City: Instituto Nacional de Antropología e Historia.
2006   El Epiclásico de Teotihuacan y Azcapotzalco. *In* El Fenómeno Coyotlatelco en el

Centro de México: Tiempo, Espacio y Significado. Laura Solar Valverde, ed. Pp. 201–214. Mexico City: Instituto Nacional de Antropología e Historia.

Robertson, Ian G.

2005   Patrones Diacrónicos en la Constitución Social de los Vecindarios Teotihuacanos. *In* Arquitectura y Urbanismo: Pasado y Presente de los Espacios en Teotihuacan: Memoria de la Tercera Mesa Redonda de Teotihuacan. Maria Elena Ruiz Gallut and Jesús Torres Peralta, eds. Pp. 277–294. Mexico City: Instituto Nacional de Antropología e Historia.

Sanders, William T.

1986   Ceramic Chronology. *In* The Teotihuacan Valley Final Report: 4. The Toltec Period Occupation of the Valley: Part 1—Excavations and Ceramics. William T. Sanders, ed. Pp. 367–373. University Park: Department of Anthropology, Pennsylvania State University.

1989   The Epiclassic as a Stage in Mesoamerican Prehistory: An Evaluation. *In* Mesoamerica After the Decline of Teotihuacan: AD 700–900. Richard A. Diehl and Janet C. Berlo, eds. Pp. 211–218. Washington, D.C.: Dumbarton Oaks.

2006   Late Xolalpan-Metepec/Oxtotipac-Coyotlatelco; Ethnic Succession or Changing Patterns of Political Economy: A Reevaluation. *In* El fenómeno Coyotlatelco en el centro de México: tiempo, espacio y significado. Laura Solar Valverde, ed. Pp. 183–200. Mexico City: Instituto Nacional de Antropología e Historia.

Séjourné, Laurette

1966   Arqueología de Teotihuacan: La Cerámica. Mexico City: Fondo de Cultura Económica.

Sempowski, Martha L.

1987   Differential Mortuary Treatment: Its Implications for Social Status at Three Residential Compounds in Teotihuacan, Mexico. *In* Teotihuacan: Nuevos Datos, Nuevas Síntesis, Nuevos Problemas. Emily McClung de Tapia and Evelyn Childs Rattray, eds. Pp. 115–131. Mexico City: Universidad Nacional Autónoma de México.

1994   Mortuary Practices at Teotihuacan. *In* Mortuary Practices and Skeletal Remains at Teotihuacan. Martha L. Sempowski and Michael W. Spence. Pp. 1–314. Salt Lake City: University of Utah Press.

Soler-Arechaldi, Ana M., F. Sánchez, M. Rodríguez, C. Caballero-Miranda, Avto Goguitchaishvili, Jaime Urrutia-Fucugauchi, Linda Manzanilla, and D. H. Tarling

2006   Archaeomagnetic Investigation of Oriented Pre-Columbian Lime-Plasters from Teotihuacan, Mesoamerica. Earth Planets Space 58:1–7.

Stahle, David W., José Villanueva Díaz, D. J. Burnette, Julian Cerano Paredes, R. R. Heim Jr., F. K. Fye, R. Acuna Soto, M. D. Therrell, M. K. Cleaveland, and D. K. Stahle

2011   Major Mesoamerican Droughts of the Past Millennium. Geophysical Research Letters 38(5):L0573, doi:10.1029/2010GL046472.

Stone, Andrea

1989   Disconnection, Foreign Insignia, and Political Expansion: Teotihuacan and the Warrior Stelae of Piedras Negras. *In* Mesoamerica After the Decline of Teotihuacan: AD 700–900. Richard A. Diehl and Janet C. Berlo, eds. Pp. 153–172. Washington, D.C.: Dumbarton Oaks.

Suárez Cortés, María Elena, Dan M. Healan, and Robert H. Cobean
2007   Los orígenes de la Dinastía real de Tula: Excavaciones Recientes en Tula Chico. Arqueología Mexicana 25(85):48–50.
Sugiura Yamamoto, Yoko
2006   ¿Cambio Gradual o Discontinuidad en la Cerámica?: Discusión Acerca del Paso del Clásico al Epiclásico, Visto desde el Valle de Toluca. In El fenómeno Coyotlatelco en el centro de México: tiempo, espacio y significado. Laura Solar Valverde, ed. Pp. 128–162. Mexico City: Instituto Nacional de Antropología e Historia.
Tozzer, Alfred M.
1921   Excavation of a Site at Santiago Ahuitzotla, D. F. Mexico. Smithsonian Institution, Bureau of American Ethnology, Bulletin 74. Washington, D.C.: Government Printing Office.
Umberger, Emily
1987   Antiques, Revivals, and References to the Past in Aztec Art. RES: Anthropology and Aesthetics 13:61–105.
White, Christine D., T. Douglas Price, and Fred J. Longstaffe
2007   Residential Histories of the Human Sacrifices at the Moon Pyramid, Teotihuacan: Evidence from Oxygen and Strontium Isotopes. Ancient Mesoamerica 19(1):159–172.
Wylie, Alison
2002   Thinking from Things: Essays in the Philosophy of Archaeology. Berkeley: University of California Press.
Zeidler, James A., Caitlin E. Buck, and Clifford D. Litton
1998   Integration of Archaeological Phase Information and Radiocarbon Results from the Jama River Valley, Ecuador: A Bayesian Approach. Latin American Antiquity 9(2):160–179.

6

Migration as a Response to Environmental and Political Disruption

The Middle Horizon and Late Intermediate Periods in the South-Central Andes

KELLY J. KNUDSON AND CHRISTINA TORRES-ROUFF

There is a growing body of archaeological literature on migration and residential mobility—and its political and environmental context—in the south-central Andes between AD 500 and 1400. Given the political and environmental upheaval seen around AD 1100, the south-central Andean region is an ideal area to investigate the long-term human responses to political collapse and environmental change. Here, we investigate the role of environmental and political disruption on migration patterns in the south-central Andes during the Middle Horizon (ca. AD 500–1100) and Late Intermediate (circa AD 1100–1400) Period. We focus on the San Pedro de Atacama oases of northern Chile's Atacama Desert (figure 6.1). Located in one of the driest deserts in the world, the oases have been home to vibrant and populous communities for thousands of years (Berenguer et al. 1988; Núñez et al., 2002, 2010). Importantly, inhabitants of the oases articulated with larger, expansive states, such as the Middle Horizon Tiwanaku polity and the later Inka Empire (ca. AD 1400–1532), and also played important roles in the large llama caravans that moved people and goods across the Atacama Desert and the Andes (Torres and Conklin 1995; Torres-Rouff 2008). During the centuries covered by our study, life in the oases was impacted by the decline of the Tiwanaku polity in Bolivia (see overviews in Janusek 2008; Kolata 1993; Stanish 2003), as well as a severe drought (Betancourt et al. 2000; Erickson 1999; Grootes et al. 1989; Ortloff and Kolata 1993; Thompson et al. 1985; Williams 2002). By examining residential mo-

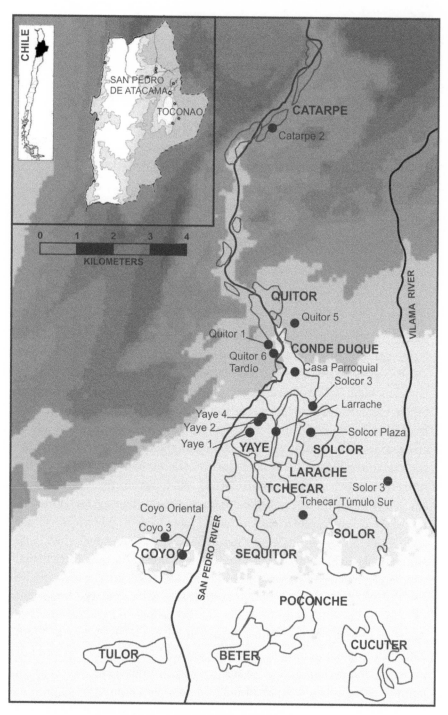

Figure 6.1. Map of the study area in the south-central Andes.

bility in the oases before and after AD 1100, we investigate migration in the region as a possible response to environmental and political disruption.

We first briefly discuss our approach to migrations and disruptions, defining the terms used and contextualizing our work in the Andean literature on migration. We then introduce the bioarchaeological and biogeochemical methods we use to identify residential mobility and migration in the oases. Utilizing biogeochemical and bioarchaeological data, we then discuss migration in the Middle Horizon and Late Intermediate Period, both before and after the political and environmental disruptions around AD 1100. We conclude with a discussion of the long-term human responses to political and environmental disruptions in the San Pedro de Atacama oases and the implications for a broader understanding of the relationships between disruptions and migrations in the present and past.

Theoretical and Methodological Background

Migrations and Disruptions: An Introduction

In the Andes, there is a long history of scholarship on population movement, including various types of short- and long-term migrations. For example, both seasonal transhumance and the human movement that accompanies short-term and very long camelid caravans are important ways that humans moved in the Andean past and present (e.g., Dillehay and Núñez 1988; Knudson et al. 2012; Kuznar 1995; Lynch 1989; Nielsen 2001; Stanish et al. 2010). In addition, some communities in the Andes were organized into "vertical archipelagos," in which individuals from one community established multiethnic settlements in different ecozones to gain access to a wider variety of resources (Murra 1972, 1985a, 1985b; Pease 1985; Stanish 1989; Van Buren 1996). In this chapter, however, we focus on migration, which we define as a one-way change in residence from one site or region to another site or region perceived as different by the individuals moving (Knudson 2011), across significant cultural, political and/or environmental boundaries (Tsuda et al., chapter 1). Here, we use residential relocation and residential mobility to refer more generally to changes in an individual's long-term place of residence. Therefore, migration is distinct from residential relocation or residential mobility, in that migration occurs across significant cultural, political, and/or environmental boundaries. We define boundaries as divisions between different cultural, political, environmental, or linguistic areas (see Tsuda et al., chapter 1). In order to attempt to understand the environmental boundaries that may have been useful in the Andean past, we use Quechua geographic terms (Pulgar Vidal 1981), including *puna* for the high-altitude zone above 4,800 meters above sea level. Finally, we define a disruption as something causing substantial interruption of accustomed activities and having a significant structural impact on a society (see Tsuda et al., chapter 1).

Identifying Paleomobility and Past Migrations through Biogeochemistry and Bioarchaeology

Studies of migration in the past have traditionally been hampered by difficulties in identifying the movement of individuals, as opposed to the movement of artifacts (see discussions in Anthony 1990, 1992; Burmeister 2000). However, in the last 20 years, archaeological studies using biogeochemistry have been used to identify movement between different geographic or environmental zones in the individuals themselves through isotopic analyses of archaeological tooth enamel and bone. Since radiogenic strontium isotope data ($^{87}Sr/^{86}Sr$) varies geologically, these data can be used to examine paleomobility in archaeological human remains (see discussions in Bentley 2006; Knudson et al. 2010; Slovak and Paytan 2011). Briefly, during enamel and bone formation in the first and last years of life, bioavailable strontium is incorporated into human tissues, where it substitutes for calcium in tooth enamel and bone. If "local" strontium is imbibed and/or consumed, the $^{87}Sr/^{86}Sr$ values in an individual's tooth enamel and bone will reflect the geologic region or regions in which that individual lived during enamel and bone formation. Since enamel does not incorporate strontium after it forms, $^{87}Sr/^{86}Sr$ values in an individual's tooth enamel will reflect dietary strontium sources, and place of residence, in the early years of life. In contrast, bone remodels throughout an individual's lifetime, so that $^{87}Sr/^{86}Sr$ values in bone reflect dietary strontium, and place of residence, in the later years of life. Finally, we note that, worldwide, $^{87}Sr/^{86}Sr$ values range from approximately $^{87}Sr/^{86}Sr=0.704$ to $^{87}Sr/^{86}Sr=0.720$ (Bentley 2006), so that differences in the third or fourth decimal place are typically used to identify movement in the past (see discussions in Bentley 2006; Knudson et al. 2010; Slovak and Paytan 2011).

Other isotope systems can identify movement between environmental zones. For example, light stable oxygen isotope values ($\delta^{18}O$) in precipitation vary according to environmental factors, such as distance from the ocean and elevation (Gat 1996; Knudson 2009).[1] Oxygen isotope values in an individual's tooth enamel and bone will reflect the oxygen isotope values in the water imbibed during enamel and bone formation, thereby reflecting residence. However, we note that many variables affect $\delta^{18}O$ values in the environment, such as mixing of water from different sources and breast-feeding and weaning in the human body (Knudson 2009).

We also consider calculations of biodistance based on nonmetric cranial traits as another means of assessing patterns of migration, by way of deter-mining biological affinity and diversity. Nonmetric traits are minor discrete morphological features that can be readily observed and scored (on either a presence/absence basis or using a graded scale) during macroscopic analysis of skeletal remains. Analyses of these suites of traits have been employed in biodistance and evolutionary studies in physical anthropology with success since at least the late 1950s (Berry and Berry 1967; Saunders 1989; Sjøvold 1973, 1977). More specifically, bioarchaeologists frequently use these traits, which display high heritability, to assess biological relation-ships or patterns of genetic relatedness in archaeological populations (e.g., Blom 2005; Sutter and Mertz 2004). As such, they provide a nice comple-ment to biogeochemical studies. In contrast to paleomobility studies using biogeochemistry, studies of genetic relatedness, such as those using an-cient or modern DNA or the cranial nonmetric traits considered here, can elucidate the relationships between different populations. However, these analyses generally cannot determine the direction of population move-ment, a characteristic of radiogenic and stable isotope analyses. Therefore, combining multiple lines of evidence to understand paleomobility and past migrations is ideal.

Case Study: Environmental and Political Disruptions in the South-Central Andes

Introduction to the Study Area: San Pedro de Atacama During the Middle Horizon and Late Intermediate Periods

During the Andean Middle Horizon, the inhabitants of the San Pedro de Atacama oases maintained economic relationships with the Tiwanaku pol-ity, which had its capital site of Tiwanaku located in the Lake Titicaca Ba-sin of Bolivia (see overviews in Janusek 2008; Kolata 1993; Stanish 2003). Tiwanaku-style textiles, ceramics, and snuffing paraphernalia for the in-halation of hallucinogens (figure 6.2) are present in burials in numerous Middle Horizon period cemeteries (Oakland Rodman 1992; Stovel 2001; Torres 1987; Torres-Rouff 2008). There is also material-culture evidence

Figure 6.2. Middle Horizon period snuff tray carved with Tiwanaku iconography interred with individual 107 from the Solcor-3 cemetery. (Photo by Christina Torres-Rouff.)

for ties with other parts of the south-central Andes, such as northwestern Argentina and other parts of northern Chile, in both the Middle Horizon and the subsequent Late Intermediate Period (Conklin and Conklin 2007). During the Late Intermediate Period, however, the Tiwanaku polity declined in population, and Tiwanaku-affiliated sites throughout the south-central Andes were abandoned or transformed (see overviews in Goldstein 2005; Kolata 1993; Stanish 2003). In the San Pedro de Atacama oases, there are changes in the settlement patterns, indicating that populations were consolidating into larger settlements and building fortified sites, perhaps for safety (Llagostera and Costa 1999).

The political changes at the end of the Middle Horizon coincided with severe environmental decline. Based on archaeological data and paleoclimatological data from the Quelccaya ice core, there was a severe drought around AD 1100–1200 (Betancourt et al. 2000; Erickson 1999; Grootes et al. 1989; Ortloff and Kolata 1993; Thompson et al. 1985; Williams 2002). The consolidation of settlements in the Late Intermediate Period in the San Pedro de Atacama oases adds support to the idea of large-scale climate change. Together, these data concerning political and ecological shifts lead us to characterize the transition between the Middle Horizon and the Late Intermediate Period as a time of disruption. We focus here on the use of biogeochemistry and bioarchaeology as a means of assessing migration during and around this disruption.

Migration and Paleomobility During the Middle Horizon and Late Intermediate Periods: Biogeochemical Data and Interpretations

During the Middle Horizon, and before the political and environmental disruptions of approximately AD 1100, biogeochemical data from radiogenic strontium isotope analysis show that the inhabitants of the San Pedro de Atacama oases generally lived in the oases or the surrounding geological zone during the first and last years of life (Knudson 2008). More specifically, for all samples from individuals in Middle Horizon San Pedro de Atacama cemeteries, mean enamel and bone data are $^{87}Sr/^{86}Sr=0.70834\pm0.00172$ (2σ, n=273). The mean radiogenic strontium isotope data for each cemetery in use during the Middle Horizon are reported in table 6.1.

However, during the Middle Horizon, there are also a number of individuals who lived elsewhere in the south-central Andes during enamel formation in the first years of life and/or bone formation in the last years of life. Generally, a "local" range for $^{87}Sr/^{86}Sr$ values is defined as the mean of modern or archaeological baseline faunal data plus or minus two standard

Table 6.1. Comparison of mean radiogenic strontium isotope values from San Pedro de Atacama cemeteries included in this study

Site	$^{87}Sr/^{86}Sr$	Standard Deviation (2σ)	Number of Samples
MIDDLE HORIZON			
Casa Parroquial	0.70835	0.00175	36
Coyo Oriental	0.70771	0.00024	17
Coyo-3	0.70765	0.00023	18
Larache	0.70986	0.00335	38
Quitor-5	0.70790	0.00049	29
Solcor Plaza	0.70837	0.00123	16
Solcor-3	0.70820	0.00077	40
Solor-3	0.70864	0.00205	20
Tchecar Túmulo Sur	0.70796	0.00072	59
LATE INTERMEDIATE PERIOD			
Catarpe-2	0.70771	0.00009	19
Quitor-1	0.70755	0.00067	11
Quitor-6 Tardio	0.70776	0.00007	7
Yaye-1	0.70769	0.00005	4
Yaye-2	0.70776	0.00025	7
Yaye-4	0.70781	0.00007	4

deviations (Bentley et al. 2004; Evans and Tatham 2004; Price et al. 2002). Using this definition, the "local" range in the San Pedro de Atacama oases has been defined as $^{87}Sr/^{86}Sr=0.7074–0.7079$ (Knudson and Price 2007). We interpret individuals with enamel or bone $^{87}Sr/^{86}Sr$ values higher or lower than the "local" range of $^{87}Sr/^{86}Sr=0.7074–0.7079$ as likely to have resided in a different geologic zone during enamel or bone formation. The diversity of $^{87}Sr/^{86}Sr$ values implies that individuals were moving from a wide variety of regions within the south-central Andes and were not simply migrants from the Lake Titicaca Basin, where the site of Tiwanaku is located. Interestingly, the presence of migrants from outside of San Pedro de Atacama varies by cemetery, with cemeteries such as Larache and Solor-3 showing greater diversity of geographic origins (table 6.1).

During the subsequent Late Intermediate Period, there are not as many available mortuary contexts in San Pedro de Atacama. However, the Late Intermediate Period cemeteries included in this study are generally similar to the earlier Middle Horizon contexts in terms of paleomobility. During the Late Intermediate Period, all enamel and bone samples collected from

San Pedro de Atacama exhibit $^{87}Sr/^{86}Sr=0.70770\pm0.00033$ (2σ, n=52 (see mean data for each cemetery in table 6.1). As in the Middle Horizon, most individuals buried in Late Intermediate Period contexts lived in or around San Pedro de Atacama during their first and last years of life. However, the lack of diversity of radiogenic strontium isotope values, both between and within Late Intermediate Period sites, implies that there were fewer migrants present during the Late Intermediate Period in San Pedro de Atacama. In other words, during the Late Intermediate Period, there were fewer individuals with enamel or bone $^{87}Sr/^{86}Sr$ values higher or lower than the "local" range of $^{87}Sr/^{86}Sr=0.7074$–0.7079, when compared to the earlier Middle Horizon period.

In addition to the radiogenic strontium isotope data discussed previously, stable oxygen isotope data are also available for some of the individuals buried in Late Intermediate Period contexts. All Late Intermediate Period enamel and bone samples collected from San Pedro de Atacama exhibit $\delta^{18}O_{carbonate(VPDB)}= -5.0‰\pm2.6‰$ (2σ, n=15). Using published conversion equations (Coplen et al. 1983; Iacumin et al. 1996; Longinelli 1984; Luz et al. 1984), the oxygen isotope value obtained from an enamel or bone sample ($\delta^{18}O_{carbonate(VPDB)}$) can be mathematically converted into the oxygen isotope value in the drinking water that the individual would have consumed ($\delta^{18}O_{drinking\ water(VSMOW)}$). Oxygen isotope values in drinking water that an individual imbibed can then be compared to oxygen isotope values observed in water sources in the region, such as rivers and springs, as a way to determine if that individual was drinking "local" water, or if she or he moved from a region with different water sources.

When $\delta^{18}O_{carbonate(VPDB)}$ values from all Late Intermediate Period enamel and bone samples are converted into $\delta^{18}O_{drinking\ water(VSMOW)}$ values (Coplen et al. 1983; Iacumin et al. 1996; Longinelli 1984; Luz et al. 1984), mean $\delta^{18}O_{drinking\ water(VSMOW)}= -9.5‰\pm4.1‰$ (2σ, n=15) for individuals buried in Late Intermediate Period contexts in San Pedro de Atacama. Although we note that converting carbonate data into drinking water values has disadvantages and can introduce error (Pollard et al. 2011), here we compare expected drinking water values with observed groundwater and precipitation values in the environment as a preliminary means of investigating geographic origin. In the Andes, oxygen isotope values in precipitation and groundwater range from $\delta^{18}O_{surface\ water(VSMOW)}= -3.3‰$ on the coast to $\delta^{18}O_{surface\ water(VSMOW)}= -17.6‰$ in high-altitude Lake Titicaca (Knudson 2009). Based on $\delta^{18}O_{drinking\ water(VSMOW)}$ values from Late Intermediate Period contexts in San Pedro de Atacama, most individuals were "local" and were likely not migrants from other environmental zones characterized by much lower or higher oxygen isotope values.

Finally, in the neighboring Loa River Valley, individuals buried at Caspana exhibit mean $^{87}Sr/^{86}Sr=0.707715\pm0.00038$ (n=31, 2σ), and individuals buried at the smaller cemetery of Toconce exhibit $^{87}Sr/^{86}Sr=0.707725\pm0.00002$ (n=3, 2σ). All Late Intermediate Period enamel and bone samples collected from the Loa River Valley exhibit mean $\delta^{18}O_{carbonate(VPDB)}= -4.6\pm1.7$ (2σ, n=18). When the data are converted to expected drinking water values (Coplen et al. 1983; Iacumin et al. 1996; Longinelli 1984; Luz et al. 1984), the Loa River Valley enamel and bone samples exhibit mean $\delta^{18}O_{drinking\ water(VSMOW)}= -8.1\pm2.7$ (2σ, n=18). In the Loa River Valley, there is no clear evidence for in-migration from the Lake Titicaca Basin or from other areas.

Migration and Paleomobility During the Middle Horizon and Late Intermediate Periods: Bioarchaeological Data and Interpretations

Exploring patterns of biodistance, which are estimates of biological relatedness, in the San Pedro de Atacama populations should allow us to see moments of greater population diversity. Here, we consider 23 cranial nonmetric traits in a sample of 834 individuals from the two periods. Biodistances derived from nonmetric cranial traits were calculated using C.A.B. Smith's Mean Measure of Divergence (MMD; following Sjøvold 1977), which is used to calculate the degree of dissimilarity between a priori groups using the relative frequency of expression of the traits observed in each group. Each biodistance comparison between the groups in question was computed using the full suite of traits observed in the remains (all-trait analysis). Significance of the MMD between cemeteries was obtained by comparing the MMD to the variance between cemeteries, following Sjøvold (1977). Distances were considered significant ($p<0.05$) if they were higher than two times the observed variance. To represent the relationship between series graphically, the matrix of MMD between pairs of cemeteries was included in a Multidimensional Scaling analysis (MDS; figure 6.3), which represents the most meaningful dimensions of the differences between series, given by any distance matrix (Hair et al. 2010). In our cases, specifically, MDS allows for the visualization of the biological affinities between each pair of series, in relation to all other cemeteries included. MDS was performed with the complete matrix of pairwise MMDs in Statistica 7 (Statsoft, Inc). Loa River sites are not included in this analysis.

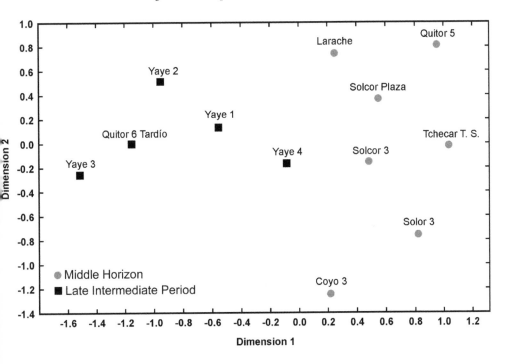

Figure 6.3. Multidimensional scaling plot of Mean Measure of Divergence (biological distance) between cemeteries. Middle Horizon (MH) sites are indicated with a circle, while Late Intermediate Period (LIP) sites are marked with a square. Note the dispersion of MH sites and the clustering of LIP ones, which parallels the significant differences seen between many of the MH sites.

The MMD values demonstrate a greater degree of diversity in Middle Horizon sites, while the Late Intermediate Period sites are more similar among themselves. Of the Middle Horizon cemeteries, Solcor Plaza shows the least difference from other sites. It should be mentioned that this site stands out as one of the most insular of the Middle Horizon sites analyzed here, with very little material evidence of interaction with other groups (Nado et al. 2012; Torres-Rouff 2011). In contrast, Quitor 5 and Larache are significantly different from nearly all others in MMD analysis 2 and, for Larache at least, there is evidence of an abundance of foreign goods compared to the other sites. The MMD and MDS suggest that biological diversity was diminished in the later period, following a period of more genetic variation during the Middle Horizon.

Changes in Mobility Patterns After Environmental and Political Disruptions

The bioarchaeological data indicate that there was an increase in genetic diversity in the Atacameño population in the Middle Horizon, a pattern also documented through craniometric studies (Varela and Cocilovo 2000). However, that diversity was reduced in the subsequent Late Intermediate Period, possibly due to a lack of new genetic diversity in the form of decreased population movement and the assimilation of the already extant diversity from the Middle Horizon. The interregional exchange networks used by Atacameños and the Tiwanaku as well as the numerous smaller groups that occupied the Atacama Desert and Andean foothills during the Middle Horizon likely promoted population movement along with the movement of material goods. The Late Intermediate Period witnessed serious political and ecological upheaval that seems to have led to a reduction in the number of people moving into the oases.

Following this tumultuous period, it is quite interesting that there was no large-scale in-migration into the oases during the Late Intermediate Period. The lack of a large number of immigrants moving into San Pedro de Atacama is also seen in data on cranial vault modification, a deliberate and permanent alteration to infant head shape reflecting an individual's ethnic group. In San Pedro de Atacama, these head shapes become more homogenous during the Late Intermediate Period, which also suggests less social diversity (Torres-Rouff 2009). Our data indicate that the Middle Horizon, which is the period associated archaeologically with prosperity and calm, has more movement and diversity than the subsequent Late Intermediate Period, which is the period that underwent significant disruptions.

A Comparison of Mobility Patterns After Environmental and Political Disruptions

We had initially hypothesized that a disruptive long-term drought in the south-central Andes between AD 1100 and 1200 would have caused individuals from the *altiplano* and the Lake Titicaca Basin to move into the relatively wet and productive oases of the San Pedro de Atacama Desert, as has been seen in other regions in the past and present (e.g., Beekman, chapter 4; Morrissey, chapter 9). For example, in Mesoamerica, disruption caused by a long-term drought was likely at least part of the impetus for migration from northwestern Mexico into central Mexico (Beekman, chapter 4). The decline of Teotihuacan in Mesoamerica is associated with substantial migration and more, not less, movement of people (Beekman, chapter 4; Cowgill, chapter 5). However, in San Pedro de Atacama, and the south-central Andes more generally, there is less, not more, evidence for increased mobility during and after a long-term drought in the region. Like Morrissey (chapter 9) has argued based on studies of contemporary migrants in highland Ethiopia (Morrissey, chapter 9), we encourage scholars to test directly the effects of environmental disruptions on migration, rather than assuming that environmental stress, such as drought, automatically leads to migration.

In the south-central Andes, the environmental disruptions cannot be separated from the political disruptions that occurred at the same time, and both disruptions are, of course, interrelated. However, rather than political disruption in the neighboring highlands causing migration into the San Pedro de Atacama oases, we see the opposite pattern. Migration from the Lake Titicaca Basin was actually more common during the Middle Horizon, when the Tiwanaku polity based in the Lake Titicaca Basin was stable and powerful. The Middle Horizon period was characterized by large social and economic networks, which may have promoted migration and resulted in individuals from different parts of the south-central Andes being buried in San Pedro de Atacama cemeteries. During the subsequent Late Intermediate Period, political disruptions and the decline of the Tiwanaku polity impeded movement from the Lake Titicaca Basin and other regions as these social and economic networks contracted. In the south-central Andes, therefore, the decline of the Tiwanaku polity led to disruptions in the social networks that reduced migration. In contrast, the decline of Teotihuacan in Mesoamerica is associated with substantial migration and increased movement of people (Beekman, chapter 4; Cowgill, chapter 5).

Conclusion

While it is possible, and in some cases likely, for disruption to cause population movement (e.g., Beekman, chapter 4; Cowgill, chapter 5), our data suggest that the tumult associated with the transition between the Middle Horizon and Late Intermediate Period did not cause large-scale population shifts in the San Pedro de Atacama oases. In contrast, what had been potentially regular and visible migration and interregional movements in the Middle Horizon was greatly reduced in the subsequent Late Intermediate Period, a period characterized by political and environmental disruption. In concert with the broader spread of foreign material and the exchange networks promoted by Tiwanaku, our data support the idea that the Middle Horizon saw more population movement, while the Late Intermediate Period was a time of more insularity as the wide-ranging social and economic networks facilitated by the Tiwanaku polity declined. The importance of social networks in enabling migration has been well documented in modern migration studies (see discussions in Brettell 2000; Tsuda 2011). It is likely that networks had a similarly central role in past migrations as well. During and after environmental and political disruptions and the resulting changes in social and economic networks in the south-central Andes, Atacameños perhaps chose to stay put and tie their success to local endeavors as a means of surviving and possibly even prospering during the Late Intermediate Period. Like Morrissey (chapter 9), we argue that human responses to environmental disruptions vary, and may or may not include migration from one environmental zone to another, presumably less affected, zone. We hope that this case study has demonstrated the variable human responses to both environmental and political disruptions and the complex relationship between disruptions and migrations in the past.

Acknowledgments

The research presented here would not have been possible without generous funding from the National Science Foundation (BCS-0721388 and BCS-0721229), the American Association for the Advancement of Science, Colorado College, the Institute for Social Science Research (ASU), and the School of Human Evolution and Social Change (ASU). We also thank the personnel at the Archaeological Chemistry Laboratory (ASU), the W. M. Keck Foundation Laboratory for Environmental Biogeochemistry (ASU), and the Instituto de Investigaciones Arqueológicas y Museo in San Pedro de Atacama, particularly Mark Hubbe. Finally, the first author would also like to thank the organizers and participants in the Disruptions as a Cause and Consequence of Migration in Human History Workshop, held May 3–6, 2012, for stimulating discussions.

Notes

1. We define $\delta^{18}O$ as $\delta^{18}O = ([^{18}Osample/^{18}Ostandard]-1) \times 1{,}000$. Standards utilized and types of materials sampled are listed as subscripts.

References Cited

Anthony, David W.
1990   Migration in Archaeology: The Baby and the Bathwater. American Anthropologist 92:895–914.
1992   The Bath Refilled: Migration in Archaeology Again. American Anthropologist 94:174–176.

Bentley, R. Alexander
2006   Strontium Isotopes from the Earth to the Archaeological Skeleton: A Review. Journal of Archaeological Method and Theory 13(3):135–187.

Bentley, R. Alexander, T. Douglas Price, and Elisabeth Stephan
2004   Determining the "Local" $^{87}Sr/^{86}Sr$ Range for Archaeological Skeletons: A Case Study from Neolithic Europe. Journal of Archaeological Science 31:365–375.

Berenguer, José, Alvaro Roman, Angel Deza, and Agustín Llagostera
1988   Testing a Cultural Sequence for the Atacama Desert. Current Anthropology 29(2):341–346.

Berry, A. Caroline, and R. J. Berry
1967   Epigenetic Variation in the Human Cranium. Journal of Anatomy 101(2):361–379.

Betancourt, J. L., C. Latorre, J. A. Rech, J. Quade, and K. A. Rylander
2000   A 22,000-Year Record of Monsoonal Precipitation from Northern Chile's Atacama Desert. Science 289(5484):1542–1546.

Blom, Deborah E.
2005   Embodying Borders: Human Body Modification and Diversity in Tiwanaku Society. Journal of Anthropological Archaeology 24(1):1–24.

Brettell, Caroline B.
2000   Theorizing Migration in Anthropology: The Social Construction of Networks, Identities, Communities, and Globalscapes. In Migration Theory: Talking Across Disciplines. Caroline B. Brettell and James F. Hollifield, eds. Pp. 97–136. London: Routledge.

Burmeister, Stefan
2000   Archaeology and Migration: Approaches to an Archaeological Proof of Migration. Current Anthropology 41(4):539–567.

Conklin, William J., and Barbara Mallon Conklin
2007   An Aguada Textile in an Atacamenian Context. Andean Past 8:407–448.

Coplen, Tyler B., Carol Kendall, and Jessica Hopple
1983   Comparison of Stable Isotope Reference Samples. Nature 302(5905):236–238.

Dillehay, Tom D., and Lautaro Núñez A.
1988   Camelids, Caravans, and Complex Societies in the South-Central Andes. In Recent Studies in Precolumbian Archaeology. Nicholas J. Saunders and Olivier de Montmollin, eds. Pp. 603–634. British Archaeological Reports International Series, 421. Oxford: BAR.

Erickson, Clark L.
1999   Neo-Environmental Determinism and Agrarian 'Collapse' in Andean Prehistory. Antiquity 73:634–642.

Evans, J. A., and S. Tatham

2004   Defining "Local Signature" in Terms of Sr Isotope Composition Using a Tenth-
        to Twelfth-Century Anglo-Saxon Population Living on a Jurassic Clay-Carbonate
        Terrain, Rutland, England. *In* Forensic Geoscience: Principles, Techniques and
        Applications. K. Pye and D. J. Croft, eds. Pp. 237–248. Geological Society Special
        Publication 232. London: Geological Society.

Gat, J. R.

1996   Oxygen and Hydrogen Isotopes in the Hydrologic Cycle. Annual Review of Earth
        and Planetary Sciences 24(1):225–262.

Goldstein, Paul S.

2005   Andean Diaspora: The Tiwanaku Colonies and the Origins of South American
        Empire. Gainesville: University Press of Florida.

Grootes, P. M., M. Stuiver, L. G. Thompson, and E. Mosley-Thompson

1989   Oxygen Isotope Changes in Tropical Ice, Quelccaya, Peru. Journal of Geophysical
        Research 94(D1):1187–1194.

Hair, Joseph F., Rolph E. Anderson, Ronald L. Tatham, and William C. Black

2010   Multivariate Data Analysis. New York: Prentice Hall.

Iacumin, P., H. Bocherens, A. Mariotti, and A. Longinelli

1996   Oxygen Isotope Analyses of Co-Existing Carbonate and Phosphate in Biogenic
        Apatite: A Way to Monitor Diagenetic Alteration of Bone Phosphate? Earth and
        Planetary Science Letters 142:1–6.

Janusek, John Wayne

2008   Ancient Tiwanaku. Cambridge: Cambridge University Press.

Knudson, Kelly J.

2008   Tiwanaku Influence in the South Central Andes: Strontium Isotope Analysis and
        Middle Horizon Migration. Latin American Antiquity 19(1):3–23.

2009   Oxygen Isotope Analysis in a Land of Environmental Extremes: The Complexi-
        ties of Isotopic Work in the Andes. International Journal of Osteoarchaeology
        19(2):171–191.

2011   Identifying Archaeological Human Migration Using Biogeochemistry: Case Stud-
        ies from the South Central Andes. *In* Rethinking Anthropological Perspectives on
        Migration. Graciela S. Cabana and Jefferey J. Clark, eds. Pp. 231–247. Tallahassee:
        University Press of Florida.

Knudson, Kelly J., William J. Pestle, Christina Torres-Rouff, and Gonzalo Pimentel

2012   Assessing the Life History of an Andean Traveler through Biogeochemistry: Stable
        and Radiogenic Isotope Analyses of Archaeological Human Remains from North-
        ern Chile. International Journal of Osteoarchaeology 22(4):435–451.

Knudson, Kelly J., and T. Douglas Price

2007   Utility of Multiple Chemical Techniques in Archaeological Residential Mobility
        Studies: Case Studies from Tiwanaku- and Chiribaya-Affiliated Sites in the Andes.
        American Journal of Physical Anthropology 132(1):25–39.

Knudson, Kelly J., Hope M. Williams, Jane E. Buikstra, Paula Tomczak, Gwyneth Gordon,
        and Ariel D. Anbar

2010   Introducing $\delta^{88/86}$Sr Analysis in Archaeology: A Demonstration of the Utility of

Strontium Isotope Fractionation in Paleodietary Studies. Journal of Archaeological Science 27(9):2352–2364.

Kolata, Alan L.
1993   The Tiwanaku: Portrait of an Andean Civilization. Oxford: Blackwell.

Kuznar, Lawrence A.
1995   Awatimarka: The Ethnoarchaeology of an Andean Herding Community. New York: Harcourt Brace College Publishers.

Llagostera, Agustín, and María Antonietta Costa
1999   Patrones de Asentamiento en la Epoca Agroalfarera de San Pedro de Atacama (Norte de Chile). Estudios Atacameños 17:175–206.

Longinelli, Antonio
1984   Oxygen Isotopes in Mammal Bone Phosphate: A New Tool for Paleohydrological and Paleoclimatological Research? Geochimica et Cosmochimica Acta 48:385–390.

Luz, Boaz, Yehoshua Kolodny, and Michal Horowitz
1984   Fractionation of Oxygen Isotopes between Mammalian Bone-Phosphate and Environmental Drinking Water. Geochimica et Cosmochimica Acta 48:1689–1693.

Lynch, Thomas F.
1989   Regional Interactions, Transhumance, and Verticality: Archaeology Use of Zonal Complementarity in Peru and Northern Chile. Michigan Discussions in Anthropology 8:1–11.

Murra, John V.
1972   El 'control vertical' de un máximo de pisos ecológicos en la economía de las sociedades Andinas. In Visita de la Provincia de Leon de Huanuco en 1562. Vol. 2. John V. Murra, ed. Pp. 429–476. Huanuco: Universidad Nacional Hermilio Valdizan.
1985a   "El Archipielago Vertical" Revisited. In Andean Ecology and Civilization: An Interdisciplinary Perspective on Andean Ecological Complementarity. Shozo Masuda, Izumi Shimada, and Craig Morris, eds. Pp. 3–14. Tokyo: University of Tokyo Press.
1985b   The Limits and Limitations of the "Vertical Archipelago" in the Andes. In Andean Ecology and Complementarity. Shozo Masuda, Izumi Shimada, and Craig Morris, eds. Pp. 15–20. Tokyo: University of Tokyo Press.

Nado, Kristin L., Sara J. Marsteller, Laura M. King, Blair M. Daverman, Christina Torres-Rouff, and Kelly J. Knudson
2012   Examining Local Social Identities through Patterns of Biological and Cultural Variation in the Solcor Ayllu, San Pedro de Atacama. Chungará 44(2):341–357.

Nielsen, Axel E.
2001   Ethnoarchaeological Perspectives on Caravan Trade in the South-Central Andes. In Ethnoarchaeology of Andean South America: Contributions to Archaeological Method and Theory. Lawrence A. Kuznar, ed. Pp. 163–201. Ann Arbor: International Monographs in Prehistory.

Núñez, Lautaro, Martin Grosjean, and Isabel Cartajena
2002   Human Occupations and Climate Change in the Puna de Atacama, Chile. Science 298:821–824.

2010   Sequential Analysis of Human Occupation Patterns and Resource Use in the Ata-
        cama Desert. Chungará 42(2):363–392.

Oakland Rodman, Amy
1992   Textiles and Ethnicity: Tiwanaku in San Pedro de Atacama, North Chile. Latin
        American Antiquity 3(4):316–340.

Ortloff, Charles R., and Alan L. Kolata
1993   Climate and Collapse: Agro-Ecological Perspectives on the Decline of the Tiwan-
        aku State. Journal of Archaeological Science 20:195–221.

Pease, Franklin G. Y.
1985   Cases and Variations of Verticality in the Southern Andes. *In* Andean Ecology and
        Civilization. Shozo Masuda, Izumi Shimada, and Craig Morris, eds. Pp. 185–231.
        Tokyo: University of Tokyo Press.

Pollard, A. M., M. Pellegrini, and J. A. Lee-Thorp
2011   Technical Note: Some Observations on the Conversion of Dental Enamel $\delta^{18}O_p$
        Values to $\delta^{18}O_w$ to Determine Human Mobility. American Journal of Physical An-
        thropology 145(3):499–504.

Price, T. Douglas, James H. Burton, and R. Alexander Bentley
2002   The Characterization of Biologically Available Strontium Isotope Ratios for the
        Study of Prehistoric Migration. Archaeometry 44(1):117–136.

Pulgar Vidal, Javier
1981   Geografia del Peru: Las ocho regiones naturales del Peru. Lima, Peru: Editorial
        Universo S.A.

Saunders, Shelly R.
1989   Nonmetric Skeletal Variation. *In* Reconstruction of Life from the Skeleton. Mehm-
        etY. Işcan and Kenneth A. R. Kennedy, eds. Pp. 95–108. New York: Liss.

Sjøvold, T.
1973   The Occurrence of Minor Non-Metrical Variants in the Skeleton and Their Quan-
        titative Treatment for Population Comparisons. Homo 24:204–233.
1977   Nonmetrical Divergence between Skeletal Populations: The Theoretical Founda-
        tion and Biological Importance of C.A.B. Smith's Mean Measure of Divergence.
        Ossa 4 (Supplement 1):1–133.

Slovak, Nicole M., and Adina Paytan
2011   Applications of Sr Isotopes in Archaeology. *In* Handbook of Environmental Iso-
        tope Geochemistry, Vol. 2. Mark Baskaran, ed. Pp. 743–768. New York: Springer.

Stanish, Charles
1989   Household Archaeology: Testing Models of Zonal Complementarity in the South
        Central Andes. American Anthropologist 91:7–24.
2003   Ancient Titicaca: The Evolution of Complex Society in Southern Peru and North-
        ern Bolivia. Berkeley: University of California Press.

Stanish, Charles, Edmundo de la Vega, Michael Moseley, Patrick Ryan Williams, Cecilia
        Chavez J., Benjamin Vining, and Karl LaFavre
2010   Tiwanaku Trade Patterns in Southern Peru. Journal of Anthropological Archaeol-
        ogy 29(4):524–532.

Stovel, Emily M.

2001   Patrones funerarios de San Pedro de Atacama y el problema de la presencia de los contextos tiwanaku. Boletín de Arqueología PUCP 5:375–398.

Sutter, Richard C., and Lisa Mertz

2004   Nonmetric Cranial Trait Variation and Prehistoric Biocultural Change in the Azapa Valley, Chile. American Journal of Physical Anthropology 123(2):130–145.

Thompson, L. G., E. Mosley-Thompson, J. F. Bolzan, and B. R. Koci

1985   A 1500-Year Record of Tropical Precipitation in Ice Cores from the Quelccaya Ice Cap, Peru. Science 229(4717):971–973.

Torres, Constantino M.

1987   The Iconography of the Prehispanic Snuff Trays from San Pedro de Atacama, Northern Chile. Andean Past 1:191–245.

Torres, Constantino M., and William J. Conklin

1995   Exploring the San Pedro de Atacama/Tiwanaku Relationship. In Andean Art: Visual Expression and Its Relation to Andean Beliefs and Values. Penny Dransart, ed. Pp. 78–108. Aldershot: Avebury.

Torres-Rouff, Christina

2008   The Influence of Tiwanaku on Life in the Chilean Atacama: Mortuary and Bodily Perspectives. American Anthropologist 110(3):325–337.

2009   The Bodily Expression of Ethnic Identity: Head Shaping in the Chilean Atacama. In Bioarchaeology and Identity in the Americas. Kelly J. Knudson and Christopher M. Stojanowski, eds. Pp. 212–277. Gainesville: University Press of Florida.

2011   Hiding Inequality Beneath Prosperity: Patterns of Cranial Injury in Middle Period San Pedro de Atacama, Northern Chile. American Journal of Physical Anthropology 146(1):28–37.

Tsuda, Takeyuki

2011   Modern Perspectives on Ancient Migrations. In Rethinking Anthropological Perspectives on Migration. Graciela S. Cabana and Jeffery Clark, eds. Pp. 313–338. Gainesville: University Press of Florida.

Van Buren, Mary

1996   Rethinking the Vertical Archipelago: Ethnicity, Exchange, and History in the South Central Andes. American Anthropologist 98(2):328–351.

Varela, Hector Hugo, and Jose Alberto Cocilovo

2000   Structure of the Prehistoric Population of San Pedro de Atacama. Current Anthropology 41(1):125–132.

Williams, Patrick Ryan

2002   Rethinking Disaster-Induced Collapse in the Demise of the Andean Highland States: Wari and Tiwanaku. World Archaeology 33(3):361–374.

III

MODERN PERSPECTIVES

7

"Disruption," Use Wear, and Migrant Habitus in the Sonoran Desert

JASON DE LEÓN, CAMERON GOKEE, AND ANNA FORRINGER-BEAL

Undocumented immigration and drug smuggling operations have deleterious effects on the fragile landscape of the Sonoran Desert. Unauthorized automobile, bicycle, and foot travel create trails and roads throughout this landscape that are continually used for illegal purposes. Vehicles and bicycles used in these illegal activities are often abandoned in the desert if they . . . become disabled. . . . Trash left by undocumented immigrants (UDIs) is another all-too-common problem. Groups . . . often move en masse through Arizona's borderlands leaving trash along their routes and also in great concentrations at "lay up" sites where they rest or wait for rides.

United States Bureau of Land Management (2009:1)

Mexico is a DUMP and [Mexicans] turn anywhere they go into a dump, starting in our deserts, and then the communities they settle.

Huffington Post online comment, January 17, 2012

We walked for five days. . . . We ran out of food and spent the last two days without anything to eat. . . . I got very sick from walking so far. My blood pressure dropped very low while I was trying to climb out of a wash. . . . We ran out of water but were able to find a cattle tank. . . . The water was very dirty, but we drank it anyway. . . . We ended up throwing away our backpacks and our extra clothes on the fourth day. We put all our water into one backpack and took turns carrying it for a few hours at a time. . . . In the end I think we walked more than 60 miles. This was my fifth time trying to cross the desert, and I finally made it. . . . I keep this backpack as a memento of that last trip.

Victor, 43-year-old Mexican migrant

Since the mid-1990s, the U.S. Border Patrol has employed an enforcement strategy along the southern border known as "Prevention through Deterrence" (PTD; United States Government Accountability Office 1997:64–65). The basis of this policy revolves around placing heightened security infrastructure in unauthorized crossing areas surrounding urban ports of entry with the goal of directing undocumented migration toward remote

Table 7.1. U.S. Border Patrol apprehensions, 2000–2012, based on data from www.cbp.gov

Southern Border Sectors	2000	2001	2002	2003	2004
San Diego, CA	151,681	110,075	100,681	111,515	138,608
El Centro, CA	238,126	172,852	108,273	92,099	74,467
Yuma, AZ	108,747	78,385	42,654	56,638	98,060
Tucson, AZ	**616,346**	**449,675**	**333,648**	**347,263**	**491,771**
El Paso, TX	115,696	112,857	94,154	88,816	104,399
Big Bend (formerly Marfa, TX)	13,689	12,087	11,392	10,319	10,530
Del Rio, TX	157,178	104,875	66,985	50,145	53,794
Laredo, TX	108,973	87,068	82,095	70,521	74,706
Rio Grande Valley, TX	133,243	107,844	89,927	77,749	92,947
Total Number of Southwest Apprehensions	1,643,679	1,235,718	929,809	905,065	1,139,282

Southern Border Sectors	2000	2001	2002	2003	2004
San Diego, CA	0.09	0.09	0.11	0.12	0.12
El Centro, CA	0.14	0.14	0.12	0.10	0.07
Yuma, AZ	0.07	0.06	0.05	0.06	0.09
Tucson, AZ	**0.37**	**0.36**	**0.36**	**0.38**	**0.43**
El Paso, TX	0.07	0.09	0.10	0.10	0.09
Big Bend (formerly Marfa, TX)	0.01	0.01	0.01	0.01	0.01
Del Rio, TX	0.10	0.08	0.07	0.06	0.05
Laredo, TX	0.07	0.07	0.09	0.08	0.07
Rio Grande Valley, TX	0.08	0.09	0.10	0.09	0.08
Total Percentage of Southwest Apprehensions	1.00	1.00	1.00	1.00	1.00

border regions, such as the Sonora Desert of Arizona, where security is less intense but crossing conditions are more difficult (Cornelius 2001; Nevins 2002; Dunn 2009). For over a decade, Arizona has been the busiest crossing point along the southern border (table 7.1). Those passing through this region must walk for long distances (e.g., upward of 70 miles) and often for several days. In addition, migrants must negotiate an inhospitable landscape characterized by extreme environmental conditions (e.g., summer temperatures often exceeding 100 degrees Fahrenheit and winter temperatures that can reach freezing), rugged terrain, border bandits who rob and assault people, and *coyotes* (human smugglers) who may aban-

2005	2006	2007	2008	2009	2010	2011	2012
126,909	142,122	152,459	162,392	118,712	68,565	42,447	28,461
55,726	61,469	55,881	40,962	33,520	32,562	30,191	23,916
138,438	118,537	37,994	8,363	6,952	7,116	5,833	6,500
439,090	**392,104**	**378,323**	**317,709**	**241,667**	**212,202**	**123,285**	**120,000**
122,689	122,261	75,464	30,310	14,998	12,251	10,345	9,678
10,536	7,517	5,537	5,390	6,357	5,288	4,036	3,964
68,510	42,634	22,919	20,761	17,082	14,694	16,144	21,720
75,342	74,843	56,715	43,659	40,571	35,287	36,053	44,872
134,188	110,531	73,430	75,476	60,992	59,766	59,243	97,762
1,171,428	1,072,018	858,722	705,022	540,851	447,731	327,577	356,873

2005	2006	2007	2008	2009	2010	2011	2,012
0.11	0.13	0.18	0.23	0.22	0.15	0.13	0.08
0.05	0.06	0.07	0.06	0.06	0.07	0.09	0.07
0.12	0.11	0.04	0.01	0.01	0.02	0.02	0.02
0.37	**0.37**	**0.44**	**0.45**	**0.45**	**0.47**	**0.38**	**0.34**
0.10	0.11	0.09	0.04	0.03	0.03	0.03	0.03
0.01	0.01	0.01	0.01	0.01	0.01	0.01	0.01
0.06	0.04	0.03	0.03	0.03	0.03	0.05	0.06
0.06	0.07	0.07	0.06	0.08	0.08	0.11	0.13
0.11	0.10	0.09	0.11	0.11	0.13	0.18	0.27
1.00	1.00	1.00	1.00	1.00	1.00	1.00	1.00

don clients in the desert. People must also evade border patrol agents, who use sophisticated ground and aerial surveillance technology to detect and capture those entering the country illegally. A growing body of research has shown that while PTD essentially has failed to deter migration (e.g., Cornelius and Salehyan 2007), it has succeeded in shaping border crossing into a well-organized, dangerous, and violent social process with a unique set of material culture and technologies (De León 2012). In response to PTD, the human smuggling industry in Mexico has grown to deal with the influx of migrants to the region. The Mexican town of Altar (see figure 7.1 for a map of all locations mentioned), which is just south of the Arizona

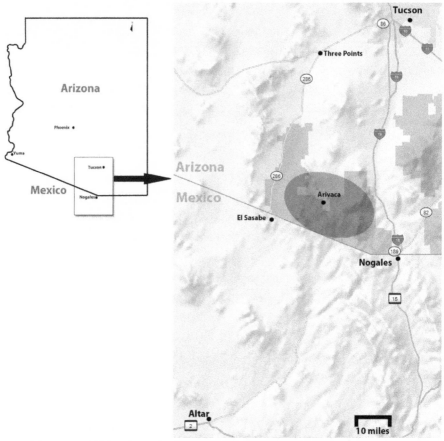

Figure 7.1. Map of the study area, showing major towns and cities mentioned in the text. The gray rectangle areas designate national forest and federal nature reserve lands. The shaded circle around the town of Arivaca represents the approximate boundaries of the archaeological survey area.

desert, has since become a major staging area for hundreds of thousands of border crossers who arrive each year. Subsequently, smugglers, vendors, and local manufacturers now capitalize on people who need guide services, temporary housing, food, and equipment. The goods associated with border crossing include camouflage and dark-colored clothing, specialized water bottles, first-aid supplies (e.g., gauze, muscle cream, pain relievers), high-salt-content foods, hydration beverages, religious paraphernalia (e.g., prayer cards), and many other items (figure 7.2). During the migration process, border crossers often eat, sleep, change clothes, and leave many of these aforementioned items at temporary campsites, which we refer to as *migrant stations* (figure 7.3).

Figure 7.2. Typical items carried by migrants. *A*, Energy and hydration beverages. *B*, 500-milliliter and one-liter water bottles. *C*, Standard white one-gallon bottle. *D*, White bottle that has been painted black for camouflage. *E*, Water bottle made from black plastic. *F*, Super glue used for shoe repairs. *G*, Pain medication and ointments for muscle aches. *H*, Foot powder. *I*, Pocket mirror used to signal for help. *J*, Gauze used for injuries. *K*, Typical foods that people bring with them on trips.

The theme of this edited volume is to explore how the concept of *disruption* can be a useful framework for bridging past and present analyses of migration. As the quotations at the beginning of this chapter suggest, there are two contrasting narratives that have tended to characterize undocumented migration in the Sonoran Desert as disruptive. The first (and most dominant) one is that Latino border crossers are unhygienic (i.e., culturally inferior) invaders who wreak havoc on the natural environment through damage caused by foot traffic, illegal roads, and littering (Meierotto 2012; Sundberg 2008) before eventually disrupting the American communities in which they settle. As Meierotto (chapter 8) points out, opponents of unauthorized immigration have tended to exaggerate the disruptive effect that water bottles and backpacks have on the desert, while ignoring the long-term and more damaging impacts of U.S. Border Patrol surveillance strategies (also see De León et al. in press). As Tsuda (chapter 11) demonstrates, despite evidence that Mexican and Asian immigrants have entered the United States for the last several decades in roughly equal numbers, the prevailing anti-immigrant narrative has focused on the perceived social, economic, and environmental disruptions created by "invading" Mexicans

Figure 7.3. Migrant stations. *A*, Resting at a migrant station. *B*, Over the course of repeated use, migrant stations can develop into sizable archaeological sites.

and others from Latin America. While concern about the environmental impact of Latino border crossers is primarily a late-twentieth-century phenomenon (Hill 2006), the characterization of Mexicans as "filthy" builds on long-standing racist stereotypes that date to at least the turn of the twentieth century (Romo 2005:235–240).

The second, less popular narrative associated with desert crossings is that the things left behind by migrants are the material evidence of the physically and emotionally disruptive journeys that millions have undertaken since the start of PTD in order to join the undocumented American labor force. For some, the stories of hardship, such as the one told by Victor in the opening pages of this chapter, are archaeologically visible in the many empty water bottles, food wrappers, and broken-down shoes found in the desert. Given the five million people apprehended by the U.S. Border Patrol in Arizona since 2000 (table 7.1), it is safe to say that desert migration is now a well-established social process for a large population of working-class Latinos. Because of the clandestine nature of crossing the border and the marginal social position that the undocumented occupy in American society, these objects found in the desert can often tell stories that those who left them behind cannot. Thus, a detailed study of the material traces of migration may help demystify, historicize, and humanize this process. While we are hesitant to use the blanket term "garbage" in reference to the diverse things that border crossers leave behind (sometimes unintentionally), we agree with Rathje and Murphy (2001:11) that, "If our garbage, in the eyes of the future, is destined to hold a key to the past, then surely it already holds a key to the present." As migration researchers, we find this second narrative more compelling than the first. Our position, however, is a minority one. The tendency, even among those with more sensitivity toward understanding the complexities of undocumented migration, has generally been to deploy the terms "garbage" and "trash" uncritically when referring to migrant objects (Sundberg 2008:882–883). We argue that this one-sided interpretation fails to recognize how the things that people leave in the desert can be interrogated to better understand many elements of the crossing process, including how individuals prepare for and experience this often traumatic event.

In this chapter, we draw on data from the Undocumented Migration Project (UMP), a long-term anthropological study of the social process of border crossing between Latin America and the United States that has (until recently) focused largely on people crossing from Sonora, Mexico, into southern Arizona (see De León 2015). One aspect of the UMP involves employing archaeological techniques to recover and analyze the many objects that people leave behind in the desert to better understand the connection between migrant material culture and specific components of border crossing, including the techniques used to clandestinely traverse the desert, the socioeconomic system that structures the process, and the suffering and violence experienced by participants.

In this context, an archaeological approach allows for the collection of new types of data on migration that can be integrated into the UMP's overarching ethnographic narrative. Instead of focusing on migrant-sending and -receiving communities (a theme that unites many of the chapters in this volume), here we explore the concept of disruption in a slightly different manner. By focusing on the materiality of contemporary border crossings, we (1) explore some of the physical disruptions that people experience individually and collectively during attempts to cross the desert, (2) highlight how the crossing process has created a new context-specific form of *habitus* (i.e., the set of learned perspectives, tastes, and dispositions people use to orient themselves in their relations with people and objects [Bourdieu 1977]), (3) illustrate how the techniques that people rely on to cross the desert (and the corresponding physical pain of each of them) are often reflected materially through used and discarded objects, and (4) argue that the things left in the desert are not "trash" but, instead, are complex artifacts for which study may improve our understanding of the routinized and widespread forms of suffering that many experience en route. Borrowing and expanding upon the archaeological concept of *use wear* (i.e., modifications made to objects as a result of being employed in specific tasks), we demonstrate how an analysis of the worn and deposited items in the desert can illuminate the shared system of crossing techniques, as well as the intimate and often painful relationships between people's bodies and the tools on which they rely. First, we briefly discuss our methods and data. This is followed by an outline of our theoretical approach to migrant habitus, techniques of the body, and use wear. We then describe different forms of use wear found on migrant artifacts. Finally, we present data from a migrant station that has been destroyed by desert conservation efforts and discuss the immediate and long-term implications of treating these artifacts as garbage.

The bulk of the ethnographic and archaeological data presented here were collected between 2009 and 2012. Our ethnographic work took place in the Mexican towns of Nogales and Altar. Semi-structured and informal interviews were conducted in Spanish with hundreds of migrants either before crossing or immediately following deportation. Interviews took place on the streets of Nogales, in humanitarian shelters, in parks and restaurants frequented by migrants, and in front of a government aid office where recent deportees seek assistance. Individuals interviewed were men and women between the ages of 18 and 70 and included Mexican citizens and non-Mexican nationals. All university protocols were followed in the recruitment of interviewees, and informed consent was obtained in all cases. Interviews, which ranged from short conversations (approximately 15 minutes) to multiple hour-long sessions, were recorded by taking handwritten notes, using a digital recorder, or both. These data were then transcribed and coded for major themes. In addition, hundreds of hours of observational data on the day-to-day experiences of deported people in Nogales were also collected. In 2009 several migrants were given disposable cameras and asked to photograph their crossing experiences for anonymous publication (for a similar project, see Adler et al. [2007]), some of which are included here. The archaeological data come from surveys and detailed studies of trails and migrant stations conducted in the deserts northwest of Nogales during the summers of 2009, 2010, and 2012.

Migration-Specific Habitus and Body Techniques

Recent research on "undocumented" people around the globe has shown similarities in the types of habitus and physical and mental stresses associated with this juridical status. Ethnographic and historical analyses of the lives of undocumented people have demonstrated that the themes of social and economic inequality, racism, and exposure to state-crafted violence characterize the experiences of this population across recent time and space (e.g., Chavez 1998; Darling 2009; Hernández 2010; Lucht 2012; Talavera et al. 2010; Willen 2007). In his analysis of Mexicans undertaking border crossings in south Texas, David Spener (2009) discusses how the physical act of undocumented migration is partially shaped by the habitus associated with membership in a marginalized and impoverished social group. He argues that several generations of migration experience has led to the development of a form of *migration-specific habitus* that predisposes working-class Latinos to tolerate abnormal levels of misery and death during this process (Spener 2009:227). This can include walking across rugged terrain with minimal supplies, expecting to get assaulted by bandits, and assuming that your guide will rob or swindle you at some point. Migrants are often socialized through communication networks and information-sharing about the crossing process, as well as through popular culture and media that warn of the dangers and misery that typically accompany each trip. Spener (2009:227) notes that the poor living conditions associated with the Mexican working class mean that their lives are often character-ized by inadequacies related to income, health care, diet, sanitation, water supply, and security. Subsequently, "migrants learn to expect and then bear the bad conditions as a matter of course in their lives, including as they make . . . efforts to improve their condition by heading north."

Although Spener is referring specifically to Latinos undertaking cross-ings in south Texas, we posit that migration-specific habitus can be identi-fied in other contemporary migration contexts. For example, in his discus-sion of West African migrants crossing the Sahara and the Mediterranean en route to Italy, Hans Lucht (2012:119–176) highlights the many dangers that people face, including dying of thirst in the desert, being robbed or murdered by bandits, and drowning at sea. The descriptions of the Sahara migration process that Lucht recorded are quite similar to narratives from the Sonoran Desert, such as the one in the opening of this chapter. In an in-terview with Lucht, a West African migrant named Louis describes a typi-cal Sahara crossing experience: "There's nothing there, no living things. You have your food and water in your bag, and if you run short, it's a problem. The sun too, it's very hot; you have to drink all the time, and soon your water is finished. The journey is three to four days, walking, so it's very dangerous. People used to die on that route" (Lucht 2012:170). The West African journey to Europe is longer and more extreme than the Sonoran example we highlight here. There are, however, obvious parallels in both the types of experiences people have and the expectations of the trip that they have developed over the last decade. Although he does not use the term "migration-specific habitus," the following assessment by Lucht of how West Africans view the migration process mirrors the work of Spener. "In general, the . . . migrants seem well informed beforehand about the dangers of the trans-Saharan migration and the risky sea voyage to Europe; they are aware of the risk of drowning at sea, of dying of thirst and exhaus-tion in the desert, and of getting killed by armed robbers. In fact, once the decision to emigrate has been made, some migrants appear almost eager to force the issue of whether they'll live or die, leaving, as they say, the de-cision up to God, as if death would be a kind of liberation from the slow but inevitable 'death' of modern African village life. To be sure, this all-or-nothing attitude is quite typical of migrant interviews, concerning the risk of illegal immigration" (Lucht 2012:173).

Building on Spener (2009), we contend that different migration contexts (e.g., the Sahara Desert, the Sonoran Desert) and the associated crossing strategies employed in those situations create unique migration-specific habituses. The form of migration-specific habitus that is found in the Sonoran Desert involves particular body techniques coupled with routinized physical trauma and suffering (e.g., blisters, exhaustion, dehydration) that over the last ten years have developed into a taken-for-granted or expected component of the process. The physical disruptions that border crossers experience are often visible in the archaeological fingerprint of this phenomenon (i.e., in the objects left behind that many have come to dismiss as "trash").

Those crossing the Sonoran Desert rely on a suite of specialized goods, as well as techniques that are often learned en route and practiced over the course of several attempts. These behaviors, which include learning what to bring, how to effectively and clandestinely move across the landscape, how to conserve water, and how to handle physical strain, fall under what Singer and Massey call *migration-specific capital* (1998:569). As people accrue this capital, such as knowledge about where, when, and how to cross, they increase their likelihood of success (Singer and Massey 1998:569) and their tolerance for the process (Spener 2009; Parks et al. 2009). The body techniques (Mauss 2006:77–95) that are learned en route are both unique to the desert-crossing context and shaped by a complex network that includes border enforcement, the environment, migrant material culture, smugglers, and other factors. During these crossings, individuals acquire knowledge about the desert, border patrol, and the limits of their own bodies. In addition, crossers learn how to make do with the limited tool kit at their disposal, including adapting their body techniques and ways of being to adjust to material and technological constraints. As Downey (2007) has shown in his study of contestants in Ultimate Fighting Championships, physical techniques are less conservative than we think and can be collectively, intentionally, and systematically learned and refined in order to adjust to material constraints (e.g., clothing style) and better accomplish set tasks (e.g., defeating an opponent). In the case of border crossings, there are unique techniques of the body that people adopt over the course of multiple crossing attempts, and these techniques are often influenced by the tools (and their functional limitations) that migrants rely on. Moreover, these behaviors are identifiable in the form of habitual wear patterns on objects.

Use Wear

Archaeologists have long recognized that use-wear patterns (i.e., modifications made to objects as a result of being employed in specific tasks) on
artifacts can be helpful for inferring how items were utilized by ancient
people (e.g., Hayden 1977) and also provide insight into broader social
phenomena, such as exchange patterns (e.g., Hirth 2000) and subsistence
practices (e.g., Stafford and Stafford 1983; see review in Odell 2001). Our
contention is that, in the rare instances where archaeologists can successfully identify the material traces of the physical act of migration, use wear
may also be a helpful analytical framework for documenting how people
experienced this process. This is especially true on occasions where migration was forced, violent, or traumatic, and here we highlight a few provoca-
tive examples.

Historical archaeologists studying nineteenth-century migrations have
successfully identified remnants of the Oregon Trail that connected the
midwestern United States to the Pacific Coast (e.g., Tveskov et al. 2001),
as well as the many routes, forts, and campsites associated with the tragic
displacement of thousands of Cherokee during the 1830s (e.g., Riggs and
Greene 2006). In the case of westward expansion, broken wagon hardware
and worn-out oxen shoes speak to the difficulty of these journeys and are
the "trademark ferrous relics scattered along, and used to identify, vestiges
of the Overland Emigrant Trail" (Dixon 2011:114). While archaeologists have
tended to interpret worn-out horseshoes and abandoned-wagon artifacts
as evidence that a trail is simply present (Tveskov et al. 2001:22), more detailed studies of what these abandoned items individually and collectively
may represent in terms of the phenomenology of difficult migrations could
be a new avenue of research. Riggs and Greene's (2006) excellent summary
of the material evidence for the Trail of Tears in North Carolina highlights
a number of sites associated with the forced removal of indigenous people.
Future use-wear analyses of Cherokee artifacts found along this trail could
potentially shed new light on the harsh conditions people experienced, as
well as the specific strategies of survival that were used. Narratives of those
who lived through the Trail of Tears suggest that objects associated with
this event may have wear patterns that hint at both desperation and the
structure of social life in adverse conditions. For example, Cherokee survi-
vor Rebecca Neugin remembers her family having to hunt for food during
periodic stops in the migration and also having to share cooking vessels
with less fortunate families: "My father had a wagon pulled by two spans of

oxen to haul us in. Eight of my brothers and sisters and two or three widow women and children rode with us. . . . My father and mother walked all the way also. The people got so tired of eating salt pork on the journey that my father would walk through the woods as we traveled, hunting for turkey and deer which he brought into camp to feed us. Camp was usually made at some place where water was to be had and when we stopped and prepared to cook our food, other emigrants who had been driven from their homes without opportunity to secure cooking utensils came to our camp to use our pots and kettles" (Neugin 1978:176 [quoted by Thornton 1984:291]).

One of the most (in)famous historical examples of a migration rife with suffering and trauma is the Donner Party Expedition of 1846–47, whereby a group of emigrants headed for California became trapped for the winter in the Sierra Nevada Mountains and eventually resorted to cannibalism to survive. The specific sites where people took shelter that winter have been the focus of much historical curiosity, looting, and archaeological research since the late nineteenth century (Hardesty 2011). Although the Donner Party survivors and their rescuers commented on the cannibalism that they either participated in or observed that winter, there has never been direct archaeological or osteological evidence of this practice found at any of the identified sites (Robbins Schug et al. 2011). However, recent analyses of faunal remains from the Donner family campsite at Alder Creek show potential for understanding how the desperation of this group was reflected in their cooking practices and wear patterns seen on bone. "The Alder Creek inhabitants consumed domestic and wild animals, including cattle, horses, deer, rodent-size creatures, and a dog. What makes these bones unique, however, is the butchering and processing pattern: they were cooked to the point of near-incineration, they were cut up into tiny pieces, and they revealed evidence of pot polish, a condition indicating that bones have been boiled to extract grease. Such intensive processing suggests that someone at the Alder Creek site was attempting to obtain trace nutrients from minute bits of bone" (Dixon 2011:114). These few examples suggest that a use-wear approach could potentially shed new light on how people experienced historic migrations.

Archaeologists have made great strides in studies of use wear over the last several decades, but this work has had little influence on those studying contemporary material culture or modern migration. Nevertheless, ethnographic research on materiality has increasingly focused on the intimate relationship between the body and objects (e.g., Banerjee and Miller 2003; Entwistle 2000; Norris 2004:62–63) and some have sought to understand what the biological substances absorbed by things (often through repeated use) can tell us about cultural processes and experience. Here we highlight a few key examples that have informed this study of use wear.

In a 1993 essay on mourning, Peter Stallybrass writes about the way that the jacket of a deceased friend haunted him through the traces of the former owner manifested as permanent wrinkles, stains, and smells embedded in the fabric. For Stallybrass (1993:36–37), garments can capture the imprints (e.g., gestures) of those who once wore them. The traces of these former owners can be experienced by others at multisensory levels, including touch, smell, and sight. While Stallybrass focused on the unique biographies of individual items, Catherine Allerton's (2007:25) work among the Mangarrai of Indonesia demonstrates how somatic and phenomenological approaches to everyday classes of items such as sarongs can help us understand broad-scale patterns of use and "multi-sensory means of being in the world." For Allerton (2007:30), sarongs "inculcate certain bodily habits and dispositions" and through prolonged use they absorb many bodily substances that connect them to their owners and help shape the biographies of these objects (Kopytoff 1986). Allerton's nuanced study provides insight into how use wear on clothing reflects many Manggarai cultural practices associated with gender and age, as well as the ways that the sights and smells of objects can bring us closer to understanding people's everyday ways of being. Combined, Stallybrass and Allerton help us appreciate the importance of both the individual and collective traces of humanity embedded in well-worn items.

As people move across the U.S.-Mexico geopolitical boundary (and subsequent vast desert), disruption is felt at the level of the individual's body in the form of corporeal (and often psychological) pain and suffering. By looking closer at materials that have been written off by many as "trash," we posit that evidence of some of the routinized physical and emotional disruptions experienced by migrants can be identified. The use-wear approach outlined here seeks to (1) illuminate the experiences of individual border crossers evidenced on objects; (2) incorporate individual desert experiences into a broader framework that improves our understanding of shared techniques of the body and collective suffering; and (3) move beyond viewing migrant artifacts as merely refuse.

Migrant Techniques and Use Wear

Traditional archaeological studies of use wear have tended to focus on understanding how the function of an object can be inferred from analyses of patterns of wear, with little emphasis on body techniques. Our approach seeks to show the intimate connection between people and objects and how this relationship can leave traces that, when analyzed, can open up new understandings of crossing techniques and migrant ways of being in the desert. Compared to most archaeological approaches, we define use wear more broadly to encompass both the modifications made to the physical structure of an artifact as well as objects that have been emptied of their contents and in essence "used up." Admittedly, this wider definition conflates the concepts of use wear, consumption, and deposition. Still, because we are focused on contemporary, often observable behavior, we are less constrained by the limitations of inference that characterize more traditional archaeological studies. Below we describe three different forms of use wear (wear patterns, biological traces, and modifications).

Wear Patterns

We define *wear patterns* as modifications made to objects resulting from their employment in tasks or activities for which they were intentionally designed. Here we briefly describe wear patterns on two classes of artifacts: shoes and water bottles. Migrants who walk long distances commonly suffer from friction blisters (subdermal pockets of fluid caused by forceful rubbing) on their feet. These painful injuries are caused by poorly conditioned feet, ill-fitting shoes and socks, improper footwear, heat, and moisture, all of which are typical conditions for border crossers. People attempt to combat blisters by carrying foot powder, extra socks, and bandages (figure 7.2, H and J). Despite these preventative measures, blisters are usually caused by poorly fitting or cheaply manufactured shoes, a person's failure to recognize and adequately treat the early stages of a blister, unhygienic desert conditions that can lead to infection, and a general inability to rest one's feet for any significant period of time. Many of the shoes recovered in the desert show signs of intense walking in the form of worn-out treads, shredded uppers, or soles with holes worn completely through (figure 7.4). Holes are often created by the persistent rubbing of feet against the shoe bottom during long-distance hiking over rough terrain in shoddy footwear. This repeated motion typically leads to the formation of blisters (figure 7.5). A 33-year-old migrant named Felipe comments on how unsuitable shoes

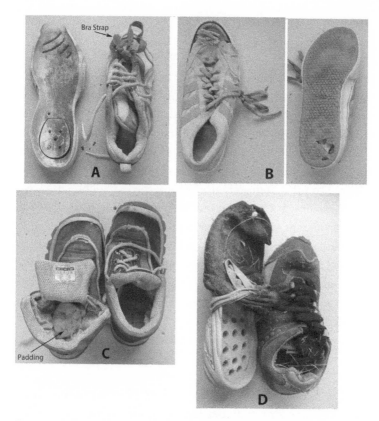

Figure 7.4. Use wear on shoes. *A*, A woman's shoe with the sole separated from the upper. Someone attempted to reattach the sole using a bra strap. *B*, A shoe with a hole worn through the sole and the upper toe section torn open. *C*, A shoe with a maxi pad inserted into the heel area as padding against blisters. *D*, A shoe with the sole separated from the upper, showing where someone has attempted to reattach it using cloth strips and a sock. The shoe is also riddled with cactus spines.

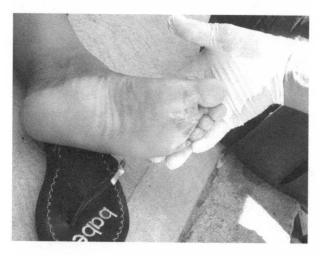

Figure 7.5. A woman's blistered foot.

can lead to other types of injuries: "Sometimes you can walk in the shade and it isn't so bad. Inside the arroyos [washes], you can find shade. The risks in those places are the rocks. Some of these rocks are very sharp and you are going up and down the mountain climbing all over these rocks. . . . Up and down. Up and down. The mountains are all the same, and that is how the coyote takes you . . . People bring their walking shoes, but not shoes for mountain climbing! They end up climbing all over rocks. People in Converse [sneakers] try to mountain climb! They end up stepping on sharp rocks and getting stuck by cholla [cactus] in the feet and legs." In this quotation, Felipe highlights both the activities that injure feet and the decisions that people must make in regard to hiking strategies. A person has to decide whether to hike on flat terrain, where you expose yourself more directly to the sun (and border patrol), or to walk in shaded arroyos, where the rocky ground can injure your ill-equipped feet.

The many water and beverage bottles found in the desert are another class of objects that show an interesting wear pattern. On a general level, these empty containers suggest that their previous owners consumed all of the liquid contents and thus had no more need for the receptacle. However, several related factors must be considered in the interpretation of these discarded items. First, many of them are small, ranging from 500 milliliters to 1.5 liters (figures 7.2 B–E, 7.6), and these sizes suggest that people were underprepared for long-distance hiking, especially in the summer, when average daily consumption of water can be upward of 6 liters (De León 2012:485). Second, finding these discarded bottles in areas nowhere near additional water sources or roads suggests that their owners were unable to conserve their supply and ran out in an inopportune place. A lack of water leads many to suffer from hyperthermia, as a 36-year-old migrant named Raúl describes: "I thought I was going to die out there . . . I couldn't take it. My heart was pounding and I started to see things. I was delirious. I was hallucinating. I was looking at the trees, but I was seeing houses and cities all around me . . . I would stop and take a small drink of water, but five minutes later I would see things again . . . I only brought a gallon of water with me." In this all-too-common scenario, Raúl must ration the water in his bottle. Most do not carry more than two gallons of water for each trip, and the practice of taking small drinks for conservation purposes is widespread. The following excerpt is from a conversation with a migrant named Enrique an hour before entering the desert: "I've lived in the U.S. for the last 14 years and was deported here [to Sonora] last week . . . I'm going to try and cross the desert tonight . . . I'm bringing one gallon of water. I know it

Figure 7.6. Bottles recovered from a migrant station. This sample suggests that many people carry bottles that are less than one gallon in size.

is not enough, but water is really heavy. I can't carry more than one gallon. Look at my bag [points to a small duffel bag] . . . I don't want to drink too much water before I leave . . . I don't want to get a cramp . . . I just take little sips of my bottle and hope that I find more water along the way if I run out."

Raúl and Enrique describe a water consumption technique where one drinks to combat the effects of the sun, but the sips must be small to both prevent cramping and conserve a limited supply. Enrique has not attempted a border crossing in many years, but he is familiar with this technique and will attempt to reproduce it. Both men discuss packing only a one-gallon bottle, which suggests that they have little choice but to use this strategy if they want to succeed. Carrying an insufficient amount of water typically is linked to a person's (1) physical inability to transport a heavy load (partially influenced by backpack size), (2) underestimation of what an adequate supply of water is, and/or (3) inability to purchase extra water. Both the many interviews conducted with migrants regarding dehydration-related injuries and the overwhelming number of small empty bottles found in the desert suggest that this practice of conservation is a difficult technique to maintain, especially during the summer months. Those who run out of water may replenish their supply at bacteria-laden tanks used for watering livestock if they are "lucky" enough to encounter one. The consumption of cattle tank water is visible archaeologically via recovered bottles refilled with green liquid. Many remarked that drinking this water causes illness and increased dehydration: "We crossed with another man who was 62 years old. He couldn't handle it. He drank some water from a cattle tank that made him sick. Well, we all drank it, but he got an infection. The water had little animals swimming in it, but we were so thirsty . . . He started vomiting and had diarrhea, so we took him back into Mexico" (Andres, 43-year-old migrant).

The practice of water conservation, which forces people to deprive themselves even when they are thirsty, can be thought of as a strategy that both keeps the body minimally hydrated and prevents someone from having to drink from cattle tanks. Drinking techniques are thus simultaneously used to conserve liquid, combat hyperthermia, and avoid having to imbibe unclean water. Empty bottles and those found refilled with filthy water suggest a failure to practice this technique successfully. Given that people accumulate crossing knowledge after multiple attempts (Singer and Massey 1998), some may learn this drinking strategy after failing to ration fluids during previous crossings.

Biological Traces

Desert hikes are physically challenging and often lead to the formation of biological residues on clothes and objects. We refer to these as *biological traces*, and they include sweat, urine, feces, menstrual blood, skin, and hair. Many of the better-preserved archaeological items bear these marks of human activity, including salt-encrusted sweat stains on shirts and backpack straps, socks and bandages soiled by blood-filled blisters (figure 7.7 A), and urine-drenched clothes (figure 7.7 B) resulting from loss of bladder control related to physiological stress associated with hyperthermia. Most biological traces are visible, but some are only identified through odor. Aromas provide a different type of somatic insight that may not be visible with other forms of use wear. For example, many migrants have to wear the same clothes for several days, including while they walk in the desert, sit in federal detention, and when they are deported back to Mexico. In one migrant shelter in Nogales, people must place their shoes in giant trash bags that are sealed at night to contain the overwhelmingly foul odor that is created after several days of desert walking (figure 7.7 C). Some have highlighted the way that smells embedded in worn clothes can induce memories of deceased individuals (Stallybrass 1993:37) or bring comfort (Allerton 2007:35). In the context of border crossing, the pungent aromas of sweat, feces, and urine conjure up images of physical pain, discomfort, suffering, and incarceration.

A

B

C

Figure 7.7. *A*, Soiled gauze and a used foot brace. *B*, A female child's urine-soaked jeans. *C*, Migrant shoes that are kept in a trash bag in a shelter in Mexico to control the pungent odor of these items.

Modifications

Both before and during a crossing event, people may make alterations to items to improve their function, repair damage, or add some additional use or level of meaning. We refer to these adjustments as *modifications* and highlight three examples (personalizing, repairing, and repurposing). It is common to see shoes, backpacks, and other objects that have been personalized with handwritten messages intended to inspire or protect the wearer. For example, in figure 7.8, people write farewell messages on the backpacks of migrants preparing to undertake a crossing. Another common modification involves repairing broken items. Clothes and backpacks that break in transit often show sewn holes, mended straps, and other types of jury-rigging (also see Spener [2010:17, 20–22]). Shoes tend to be the items most commonly in need of mending, and recovered footwear exhibit a wide range of repairs and modifications, including re-glued soles, uppers re-stitched to the sole, and added internal padding (figure 7.4 C). The maintenance on some shoes suggests desperation. For example, figure 7.4 A shows a common repair on a woman's shoe where the upper com-

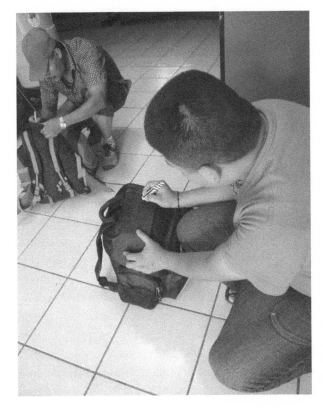

Figure 7.8. Writing farewell messages on the backpacks of people preparing to cross the border.

pletely separated from the sole and the user attempted to reconnect them using a bra strap. A final type of modification involves repurposing items for a different use. Although border crossers prepare by bringing an assortment of food, clothing, and first-aid materials, issues often arise that require ad hoc ingenuity. Some people find that they are unable to carry a heavy water bottle over long distances and fashion handles for these items using backpack straps or materials found in nature (e.g., a tree branch). It is also common to find bottles with cloth covers constructed out of pant legs or T-shirts. These modifications typically have to do with mitigating the discomfort associated with carrying particular objects. However, in some cases, objects have been repurposed for emergencies. In the summer of 2010 we recovered a sweatshirt that had been attached to a stick with twine and was likely used as a flag by someone trying to signal for help.

What Little Remains

What is Arizona Border Trash? Border trash refers to items discarded by persons involved in illegal immigration such as plastic containers, clothing, backpacks, foodstuffs, vehicles, bicycles and paper. It can also consist of human waste and sometimes medical products.

https://www.azbordertrash.gov/about.html

540 tons (1,080,887 pounds) of trash removed

Fiscal year 2011 total for cleanup conducted by Bureau of Land Management's Southern Arizona Project to Mitigate Environmental Damages Resulting from Illegal Immigration

A great deal of anthropological attention has been paid to why people migrate and how immigrants impact receiving communities. Considerably less work has focused on the physical act of migration. The dearth of ethnographic research on this particular phenomenon is understandable given that many modern migrations are conducted clandestinely (often illegally), making direct observation both difficult and ethically questionable. Archaeologists have also tended to avoid studying the act of migrating, because these moments are ephemeral, rapid, and often poorly preserved in the material record. In the second part of this chapter, we briefly return to the conflicting narratives regarding whether migrant objects are "trash" to be disposed of or artifacts to be studied. The tendency to view Latino migrants as a source of environmental disruption means that desert conservationists rarely think critically about the implications of characterizing the things people leave behind as garbage or the potential damage that is done to the archaeological record when migrant stations are "cleaned up." Here

A   B

Figure 7.9. BK-03. *A*, Before cleanup. *B*, After cleanup.

we highlight how treating migrant objects as refuse has the potential to both silence the narratives of border crossers and prevent future archaeological analyses of this process.

During the 2009 field season, a large migrant station (known as BK-03) was identified and mapped, and a small sample of artifacts was collected (figure 7.9 A). The site measured approximately 170 meters in length and had an area of 3,243 square meters. In 2010, we returned to BK-03 to conduct a more detailed survey, only to discover that most of the material had been taken away by an unknown conservation group (figure 7.9 B). The removal of migrant objects from the desert by federal, state, and private conservation groups has been ongoing since at least 2002 (see http://www.blm.gov/az/st/en/info/newsroom/undocumented_aliens.html) and, because of these efforts, we predict that most archaeological evidence of this process eventually will be erased. Still, when visiting BK-03 in 2010, it was observed that while all of the large objects had been taken away, many smaller artifacts ("microfacts") were still visible on the surface (also see

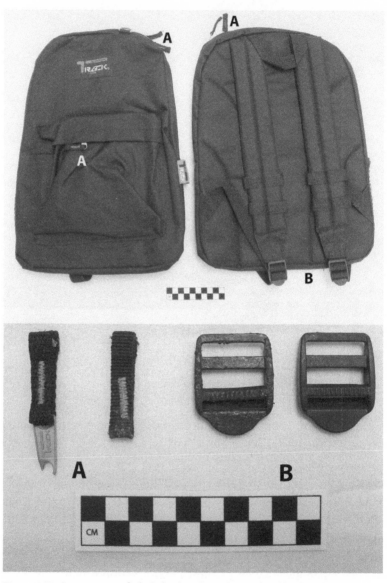

Figure 7.10. Comparison of whole backpacks with recovered backpack components from BK-03. One Track brand backpack has three zippers (labeled *A*)
and two black strap clips (labeled *B*), and a minimum number of once-present
backpacks can be calculated based on the total number of these items recovered.
These zippers and clips are distinguishable from other backpack brands based on
characteristics such as labels, size, shape, and profile.

Schiffer's discussion of "residual primary refuse" [1987:62]). In 2010, we systematically collected all remaining objects from BK-03, and Forringer-Beal analyzed this material in 2011.

The microfacts recovered from BK-03 consisted of small overlooked items (e.g., coins, thread), fragments of broken objects (e.g., lotion bottles, glass jars), and whole pieces of larger items (e.g., a shoelace, a shirt sleeve, backpack strap buckles). In order to investigate how these materials may relate to the relative numbers of artifacts present at a site prior to cleanup or after years of natural erosion, it was necessary to convert microfact frequencies into a Minimum Number of Individuals (MNI) by adapting an analytical strategy developed for similarly fragmented archaeofaunal remains (Reitz and Wing 1999:194–199). Backpacks, for example, were represented in the material assemblage from BK-03 by some 112 microfacts, including strap holders, zippers, plastic clips, and denim cloth fragments. By comparing differences, such as ridging, impression dots, lip shape, and the body shape of these items in reference to a comparative collection (figure 7.10), we determined that a minimum of 17 backpacks could have accounted for all such microfacts present at the site (table 7.2). This count is striking given that it initially was estimated that, prior to cleanup, BK-03 had more than 600 backpacks. Similarly, we calculated MNI for non-fragmented artifacts, such as processed-food cans, lids, and pull tabs. While the total count of all such artifacts was 142, we found that 29 of the lids and five pull tabs could potentially be matched with cans to generate an MNI of 108. Moreover, MNI also helped to reduce the estimated frequencies of cloth, plastic, and metal microfacts that we could not attribute to a major artifact category.

Although most items from BK-03 had been removed prior to a detailed inventory by the UMP, four other migrant stations of similar size, setting, and distance from the U.S.-Mexico border document the range of variability in artifact proportions across relatively undisturbed surface assemblages (table 7.2). As might be expected, microfacts do appear to underrepresent the numbers of larger items, such as backpacks, clothing, and beverage containers typically found at migrant stations. Whereas backpacks and beverage containers comprise 7–19 percent and 8–15 percent, respectively, of the assemblages at the four inventoried sites, the MNI from these same items only accounts for four and three percent of these artifact categories at BK-03. The proportion of clothing from BK-03 (20 percent) is only slightly less than the low range found at inventoried sites (25–40 percent), and may actually fall within this range if unidentifiable cloth fragments could be attributed confidently to clothing, rather than backpacks or utility items.

Table 7.2. Comparison of artifact counts at BK-03 and comparable sites

| Artifact Category/Type | Cleaned-Up Site | | | | |
| | BK-03 (2010) | | | BBR-01 | |
	N	MNI	Site % (MNI)	N	Site %
Backpacks	**112**	**17**	**3.67%**	**178**	**18.78%**
Whole	-	-	0.00%	124	13.08%
Fragment	112	17	3.67%	54	5.70%
Clothing	**133**	**92**	**19.87%**	**375**	**39.56%**
Hat/Accessories	19	19	4.10%	23	2.43%
Shirt	15	12	2.59%	135	14.24%
Pants	45	23	4.97%	68	7.17%
Undergarment	6	6	1.30%	62	6.54%
Sock	30	30	6.48%	68	7.17%
Shoe	2	2	0.43%	19	2.00%
Fragment	16	16	3.46%	0	0.00%
Beverage Containers	**16**	**15**	**3.24%**	**75**	**7.91%**
Water	3	3	0.65%	36	3.80%
Electrolyte	4	4	0.86%	15	1.58%
Energy Drink	-	-	0.00%	2	0.21%
Dairy/Juice/Soft Drink	2	2	0.43%	9	0.95%
Unknown Cap/Fragment	7	6	1.30%	13	1.37%
Food Containers	**166**	**130**	**28.08%**	**33**	**3.48%**
Can, Protein	23	23	4.97%	7	0.74%
Can, Other/Unknown	12	12	2.59%	26	2.74%
Can, Lid/Pull Tab	107	73	15.77%	0	0.00%
Plastic Food Wrapper	19	17	3.67%	0	0.00%
Condiment Jar	5	5	1.08%	0	0.00%
Utility Items	**47**	**31**	**6.70%**	**67**	**7.07%**
First Aid	**39**	**32**	**6.91%**	**32**	**3.38%**
Hygiene/Cosmetics	**108**	**82**	**17.71%**	**187**	**19.73%**
Personal/Recreational Item	**16**	**16**	**3.46%**	**1**	**0.11%**
Border Patrol Hand Restraint	**10**	**10**	**2.16%**	**0**	**0.00%**
Unidentifiable Fragments	**48**	**38**	**8.21%**	**-**	**0.00%**
Cloth	26	16	3.46%	-	0.00%
Plastic/Other	22	22	4.76%	-	0.00%
Total	**695**	**463**	**100.00%**	**948**	**100.00%**

BW (2012)		CW-01		EV		Range
N	Site %	N	Site %	N	Site %	Site %
54	7.15%	190	11.28%	45	11.03%	7.2–18.8%
50	6.62%	190	11.28%	45	11.03%	6.6–13.1%
4	0.53%	-	0.00%	-	0.00%	0.0–5.7%
208	27.55%	665	39.49%	130	31.86%	25.0–39.6%
13	1.72%	44	2.61%	6	1.47%	1.5–2.6%
61	8.08%	163	9.68%	39	9.56%	8.1–14.2%
37	4.90%	96	5.70%	19	4.66%	4.7–7.2%
22	2.91%	125	7.42%	14	3.43%	2.9–7.4%
55	7.28%	204	12.11%	45	11.03%	7.2–12.1%
8	1.06%	21	1.25%	7	1.72%	1.1–3.4%
12	1.59%	12	0.71%	0	0.00%	0.0–1.2%
100	13.25%	259	15.38%	53	12.99%	7.9–15.4%
65	8.61%	177	10.51%	37	9.07%	3.8–10.5%
23	3.05%	46	2.73%	9	2.21%	1.6–3.8%
7	0.93%	11	0.65%	1	0.25%	0.2–1.1%
2	0.26%	24	1.43%	6	1.47%	0.3–1.5%
3	0.40%	1	0.06%	0	0.00%	0.0–3.0%
177	23.44%	92	5.46%	17	4.17%	3.5–13.3%
21	2.78%	18	1.07%	9	2.21%	0.7–3.4%
132	17.48%	72	4.28%	8	1.96%	2.0–4.3%
4	0.53%	0	0.00%	0	0.00%	0.0–0.3%
19	2.52%	2	0.12%	0	0.00%	0.0–7.0%
1	0.13%	0	0.00%	0	0.00%	0.0–0.3%
83	10.99%	126	7.48%	49	12.01%	7.1–12.0%
27	3.58%	52	3.09%	44	10.78%	3.1–10.8%
95	12.58%	289	17.16%	68	16.67%	16.7–23.4%
11	1.46%	11	0.65%	2	0.49%	0.1–1.0%
0	0.00%	0	0.00%	0	0.00%	-
-	0.00%	-	0.00%	-	0.00%	-
-	0.00%	-	0.00%	-	0.00%	-
-	0.00%	-	0.00%	-	0.00%	-
755	100.00%	1684	100.00%	408	100.00%	-

Conversely, the microfact assemblage from BK-03 seems to overestimate the number of small personal and recreational items (e.g., coins, jewelry, small toys) and lids from cans of processed food. In all likelihood, the disparities across these artifact assemblages result from the preferential selection of larger, whole objects as "trash" for removal during site cleanup (Schiffer 1987:62-63)—a strategy that negatively impacts the potential to view use wear on these same large objects that are often intimately associated with the body and the reproduction of habitus during migration.

Although our data are still preliminary, we anticipate that future interpretations of microfacts from BK-03 and other sites will benefit from time-dependent models of natural and cultural transformation processes developed from the assemblages of the several dozen migrant stations thus far documented by UMP, particularly sites such as BW that we collected in 2010 and re-collected in 2012. By developing such models, we hope to establish a framework for reconstructing the types of material culture carried and consumed by undocumented migrants across the Sonoran Desert—both today as cleanup efforts continually silence the contemporary archaeological record, and in the future as erosion by wind, water, sunlight, and sand work ultimately to reduce all migrant stations into microfacts. Regardless of the ultimate source of artifact loss and decomposition, the fragility of migrant material culture and the ephemerality of border crossing sites mean that the potential to study use wear, and the associated disruption of the daily lives of migrants, may be short-lived. It is imperative to collect and preserve a portion of these artifacts as a chapter of American history on par with other important historic migrations.

Conclusion

Drawing on the work of Galtung (1969) and Farmer (2004), some scholars have used the concept of *structural violence* (i.e., violence that is exerted systematically and indirectly by social structures toward particular groups of people) to explain the connections between federal border enforcement practices and the embodied experiences of migrants (Nevins 2005; Slack and Whiteford 2011). One understudied element of the structural violence that occurs in the Sonoran Desert is the systematic erasure of the archaeological evidence of this highly politicized social process. As Paul Farmer (2004:308) notes: "Erasing history is perhaps the most common explanatory sleight-of-hand relied upon by the architects of structural violence. Erasure or distortion of history is part of the process of desocialization necessary for the emergence of hegemonic accounts of what happened and why."

It would be too simplistic (and unfair) to label all desert conservation groups "architects of structural violence." We do, however, see their often uncritical removal of migrant items and the discourse they employ to talk about these objects to be symptomatic of the American public's general lack of understanding or appreciation regarding the connections among border enforcement strategies, migration patterns, embodied forms of suffering that border crossers systematically experience, and the historical record of this clandestine process. Those who have recently picked up the cause of environmental protection in a thinly veiled attempt to hide their xeno-phobia (e.g., Banks 2009) are using the lens of anti-immigrant vitriol to color how objects found in the desert are to be interpreted. They are also actively contributing to the distortion of the public's understanding of what this process is actually like. We acknowledge that all archaeological inter-pretations are political, including ours and those we disagree with. Still, to view migrant material culture simplistically as disruptive trash is prob-lematic given that it allows for the erasure of the historical evidence of the movement of millions of border crossers who run the geopolitical gauntlet known as the Sonoran Desert in order to enter the U.S. labor market. At the current rate of "cleanup," there may soon be no archaeological record left to debate.

In this chapter we have critiqued the dominant narrative that character-izes migrant artifacts as "trash" and attempted to show that a more nuanced ethnographic-archaeological appreciation and analysis of these items can provide new insight into the border-crossing process, the techniques and embodied experiences of crossers, and the ephemeral nature of the ar-chaeological record of undocumented migration. Moreover, there is strong evidence to suggest that over the last two decades, Latino border crossers have developed a form of migration-specific habitus unique to the Sonoran Desert. This habitus involves a disposition toward (or acceptance of) the many forms of physical and emotional disruption that migrants experience en route. This habitus is also visible in the routinized techniques people use to cross the desert, the objects they rely on during this process, and the use-wear patterns that crossing behaviors leave on objects. Use wear is a pro-ductive analytical approach that allows for the illumination of disruptions felt by border crossers, both individually and collectively. This framework can potentially be employed to better understand other contemporary and historic migrations that leave an archaeological footprint. Finally, we have shown that the dominant narrative that writes off migrant material culture as trash is a way to silence or ignore what these objects can tell us about many aspects of border crossing, including how material culture articulates with immigration enforcement, new forms of migrant habitus, and the political economy of undocumented migration that connects labor markets in Mexico and the United States. The material fingerprint of practically all ancient and modern migrations is minor, if not invisible. The erasure of the recent historical evidence of Latino migrants by conservation efforts has short-term consequences for how we understand this ongoing social process and potentially damaging impacts on the ability of future archaeologists to study this phenomenon.

Acknowledgments

Parts of this research were funded by the National Science Foundation (award No. 0939554), the University of Washington's Royalty Research Fund, University of Michigan, and the Institute for Field Research. We wish to thank the many residents of Arivaca who supported us while we did archaeological fieldwork and all of the students who participated in the 2009, 2010, and 2012 field seasons. This work would not have been possible without the help and trust of the many people we have met along the border who have graciously shared their migration stories. Although we cannot name them here, we have tried to repay their generosity by doing our best to document accurately what they experience on a daily basis.

Note

Epigraph: All names are pseudonyms.

References Cited

Adler, Rudy, Victoria Criado, and Brett Huneycutt
2007   Border Film Project: Photos by Migrants & Minutemen on the U.S.-Mexico Border. New York: Abrams.
Allerton, Catherine
2007   The Secret Life of Sarongs: Manggarai Textiles as Super-Skins. Journal of Material Culture 12(1): 22–46.
Banerjee, Mukulika, and Daniel Miller
2003   The Sari. Oxford: Berg Publishers.

Banks, Leo W.
2009   Trashing Arizona: Illegal Immigrants Dump Tons of Waste in the Wilderness Every Day—and It's Devastating the Environment. Tucson Weekly, April 2, 2009. http://www.tucsonweekly.com/tucson/trashing-arizona/Content?oid=1168857, accessed March 20, 2012.
Bourdieu, Pierre
1977   Outline of a Theory of Practice. Cambridge: Cambridge University Press.
Broyles, Bill, and Mark Haynes
2010   Desert Duty: On the Line with U.S. Border Patrol. Austin: University of Texas Press.
Chavez, Leo R.
1998   Shadowed Lives: Undocumented Immigrants in American Society. 2nd edition. Fort Worth: Wadsworth.
Cornelius, Wayne A.
2001   Death at the Border: Efficacy and Unintended Consequences of US Immigration Control Policy. Population and Development Review 27(4): 661–685.
Cornelius, Wayne A., and Idean Salehyan
2007   Does Border Enforcement Deter Unauthorized Immigration? The Case of Mexican Migration to the United States of America. Regulation & Governance 1(2):139–153.
Darling, Jonathan
2009   Becoming Bare Life: Asylum, Hospitality, and the Politics of Encampment. *Environment and Planning D: Society and Space* 27(4):649–665.
De León, Jason
2012   "Better To Be Hot Than Caught": Excavating the Conflicting Roles of Migrant Material Culture. American Anthropologist 114(3):477–495.
2015   The Land of Open Graves: Living and Dying on the Migrant Trail. Berkeley: University of California Press.
De León, Jason, Cameron Gokee, and Ashley Schubert
In Press   "By the Time I Get to Arizona": Citizenship, Materiality, and Contested Identities along the U.S.-Mexico Border. Anthropological Quarterly.
Dixon, Kelly J.
2011   An Archaeology of Despair. *In* An Archaeology of Desperation: Exploring the Donner Party's Alder Creek Camp. Kelly J. Dixon, Julie M. Schablitsky, and Shannon A. Novak, eds. Pp. 101–131. Norman: University of Oklahoma Press.
Downey, Greg
2007   Producing Pain: Techniques and Technologies in No-Holds-Barred Fighting. Social Studies of Science 37(2):201–226.
Dunn, Timothy J.
2009   Blockading the Border and Human Rights: The El Paso Operation that Remade Immigration Enforcement. Austin: University of Texas Press.
Entwistle, Joanne
2000   Fashion and the Fleshy Body: Dress as Embodied Practice. Fashion Theory 4(3):323–347.
Farmer, Paul
2004   An Anthropology of Structural Violence. Current Anthropology 45(3):305–325.

Galtung, Johan
1969   Violence, Peace, and Peace Research. Journal of Peace Research 6(3):167–191.
Hardesty, Donald L.
2011   Historical Perspectives on the Archaeology of the Donner Party. *In* An Archae-
        ology of Desperation: Exploring the Donner Party's Alder Creek Camp. Kelly J.
        Dixon, Julie M. Schablitsky, and Shannon A. Novak, eds. Pp. 89–100. Norman:
        University of Oklahoma Press.
Hayden, Brian, ed.
1977   Lithic Use-Wear Analysis. New York: Academic Press.
Heyman, Josiah McC.
1995   Putting Power in the Anthropology of Bureaucracy: The Immigration and Natu-
        ralization Service at the Mexico-United States Border. Current Anthropology
        36(2):261–287.
Hernández, Kelly Lytle
2010   Migra!: A History of the U.S. Border Patrol. Berkeley: University of California
        Press.
Hill, Sarah
2006   Purity and Danger on the U.S.-Mexico Border, 1991–1994. South Atlantic Quar-
        terly 105(4):777–799.
Hirth, Kenneth G.
2000   Ancient Urbanism at Xochicalco. The Evolution and Organization of a Prehispanic
        Society. Salt Lake City: University of Utah Press.
Holmes, Seth M.
2007   "Oaxacans Like to Work Bent Over": The Naturalization of Social Suffering among
        Berry Farm Workers. International Migration 45(3):39–68.
Kopytoff, Igor
1986   The Cultural Biography of Things: Commoditization as Process. *In* The Social Life
        of Things: Commodities in Cultural Perpsective. Arjun Appadurai, ed. Pp. 64–91.
        Cambridge: Cambridge University Press.
Lucht, Hans
2012   Darkness Before Daybreak: African Migrants Living on the Margins in Southern
        Italy Today. Berkeley: University of California Press.
Mauss, Marcel
2006   Techniques, Technology and Civilisation. Nathan Schlanger, ed. New York: Dur-
        kheim Press/Berghahn Books.
Meierotto, Lisa
2012   The Blame Game on the Border: Perceptions of Environmental Degradation on the
        United States–Mexico Border. Human Organization 71(1):11–21.
Neugin, Rebecca
1978   Memories of the Trail. Journal of Cherokee Studies 3 (special issue):176.
Nevins, Joseph
2002   Operation Gatekeeper: The Rise of the "Illegal Alien" and the Making of the U.S.-
        Mexico Boundary. New York: Routledge.
2005   A Beating Worse than Death: Imagining and Contesting Violence in the U.S.-
        Mexico Borderlands. AmeriQuests 2(1):1–25.

Norris, Lucy
2004   Shedding Skins: The Materiality of Divestment in India. Journal of Material Culture 9(1):59–71.
Odell, George H.
2001   Stone Tool Research at the End of the Millennium: Classification, Function, and Behavior. Journal of Archaeological Research 9(1):45–100.
Parks, Kristen, Gabriel Lozada, Miguel Mendoza, and Lourdes García Santos
2009   Strategies for Success: Border Crossing in an Era of Heightened Security. In Migration from the Mexican Mixteca: A Transnational Community in Oaxaca and California. Wayne Cornelius, David Fitzgerald, Jorge Hernández-Díaz, and Scott Borger, eds. Pp. 31–61. San Diego: Center for Comparative Immigration Studies.
Rathje, William, and Cullen Murphy
2001   Rubbish!: The Archaeology of Garbage. Tucson: University of Arizona Press.
Reitz, Elizabeth J., and Elizabeth S. Wing
1999   Zooarchaeology. Cambridge and New York: Cambridge University Press.
Riggs, Brett, and Lance Greene
2006   The Cherokee Trail of Tears in North Carolina: An Inventory of Trail Resources in Cherokee, Clay, Graham, Macon, and Swain Counties. Revised Report Submitted to the National Park Service, Trail of Tears National Historic Trail, Santa Fe, New Mexico. University of North Carolina Research Laboratories of Archaeology and the Trail of Tears Association, North Carolina Chapter.
Robbins Schug, Gwen, and Kelsey Gray, with Guy L. Tasa, Ryne Danielson, and Matt Irish
2011   What Remains: Species Identification and Bone Histology. In An Archaeology of Desperation: Exploring the Donner Party's Alder Creek Camp. Kelly J. Dixon, Julie M. Schablitsky, and Shannon A. Novak, eds. Pp. 163–183. Norman: University of Oklahoma Press.
Romo, David
2005   Ringside Seat to a Revolution: An Underground Cultural History of El Paso and Juárez: 1893–1923. El Paso: Cinco Puntos Press.
Schiffer, Michael
1987   Formation Processes of the Archaeological Record. Albuquerque: University of New Mexico Press.
Singer, Audrey, and Douglas S. Massey
1998   The Social Process of Undocumented Border Crossing Among Mexican Migrants. International Migration Review 32(3):561–592.
Slack, Jeremy, and Scott Whiteford
2011   Violence and Migration on the Arizona-Sonora Border. Human Organization 70(1):11–21.
Spener, David
2009   Clandestine Crossings: Migrants and Coyotes on the Texas-Mexico Border. Ithaca: Cornell University Press.
2010   Movidas Rascuaches: Strategies of Migrant Resistance at the U.S.-Mexico Border. Aztlán: A Journal of Chicano Studies 35(2): 9–36.

Stafford, C. Russell, and Barbara D. Stafford
1983   The Functional Hypothesis: A Formal Approach to Use-Wear Experiments and Settlement-Subsistence. Journal of Anthropological Research 39(4):351–375.
Stallybrass, Peter
1993   Worn Worlds: Clothes, Mourning, and the Life of Things. Yale Review 81:35–50.
Sundberg, Juanita
2008   'Trash-Talk' and the Production of Quotidian Geopolitical Boundaries in the USA-Mexico Borderlands. Social & Cultural Geography 9(8):871–890.
Talavera, Victor, Guillermina Gina Núñez-Mchiri, and Josiah Heyman
2010   Deportation in the U.S.-Mexico Borderlands: Anticipation, Experience, and Memory. In The Deportation Regime: Sovereignty, Space, and the Freedom of Movement. Nicholas De Genova and Nathalie Peutz, eds. Pp. 166–195. Durham: Duke University Press.
Thornton, Russell
1984   Cherokee Population Losses during the Trail of Tears: A New Perspective and a New Estimate. Ethnohistory 31(4):289–300.
Tveskov, Mark, Kelly Derr, Nicole Norris, and Richard Silva
2001   Archaeological Investigations of the Siskiyou Trail Cascade-Siskiyou National Monument, Jackson County, Oregon: A Report to the U.S. Department of the Interior Bureau of Land Management Medford District Office.
United States Bureau of Land Management (BLM)
2009   The Southern Arizona Project to Mitigate Damages Resulting from Illegal Immigration and Smuggling: Fiscal Year 2009 End-of-Year Summary. http://www.blm.gov/pgdata/etc/medialib/blm/az/pdfs/undoc_aliens.Par.0977.File.dat/09-report.pdf, accessed December 6, 2012.
United States Government Accountability Office
1997   Report to the Committee on the Judiciary, U.S. Senate and the Committee on the Judiciary, House of Representatives, Illegal Immigration: Southwest Border Strategy Results Inconclusive; More Evaluation Needed. http://www.gao.gov/archive/1998/gg98021.pdf, accessed March 1, 2011.
Willen, Sarah S.
2007   Toward a Critical Phenomenology of "Illegality": State Power, Criminalization, and Abjectivity among Undocumented Migrant Workers in Tel Aviv, Israel. International Migration 45(3):8–38.

8

Environmental Disruption as a Consequence of Human Migration

The Case of the U.S.-Mexico Border

LISA MEIEROTTO

This chapter considers human migration, as well as political/military responses to migration, as a factor in environmental disruption and degradation on the United States–Mexico border. The specific focus is the impact of human migration compounded with the increasing presence of Homeland Security on wilderness and protected areas in southern Arizona. In particular, I focus on contemporary environmental problems connected to human migration through Cabeza Prieta National Wildlife Refuge. Cabeza Prieta is the third-largest wildlife refuge in the United States and shares more than 50 contiguous miles with the Mexican border. The refuge has suffered significant environmental degradation in recent years as a direct result of human migration and U.S. immigration policy.

In the U.S.-Mexico border region, environmental disruption is intricately connected to social, political and economic disruptions. In this chapter, I discuss how perceptions of environmental degradation are shaped and influenced by wider social and cultural beliefs and, in particular, ways in which ideas about race and ethnicity shape our perceptions of the extent of environmental degradation resulting from human migration. I argue that negative environmental perceptions of migration are both caused by and contribute to beliefs about people of Mexican origin as environmentally threatening and invasive. Through an analysis of the causes and perceptions of environmental degradation currently manifesting on the U.S.-Mexico border, we gain insight into the politics and social tensions present in contemporary immigration debates and conflicts. First, before examining the contemporary environmental situation on the border, it is important to begin with a thorough evaluation of the environmental history of the region to offer a more balanced and broader perspective on the long-term process of human migration through the American Southwest.

Section One: An Environmental History of Migration through Arizona's Borderlands

For thousands of years, humans have migrated across the U.S.-Mexico border region. Tracing human-environment interactions through time reveals a fascinating pattern of movement and change combined with a trend toward ever-increasing human influence on the land, air, and water. This section utilizes an environmental history approach to examine the history of human-environment interactions in the borderlands. Environmental history is "ideally situated to bind together approaches from the natural sciences, social sciences, and history in non-deterministic accounts of change" (Sorlin and Warde 2007:118). By beginning with the environmental history of the area under study, the groundwork is laid to develop an analytical framework that straddles social science, natural science, and the humanities to analyze drivers and consequences of human migration.

History can be told from any number of different angles and perspectives. Social and environmental history, however, cannot be recounted independently of one another. The interrelationship of the two is especially apparent in a place like the Sonoran Desert, where climatic extremes have shaped both the human use of the land and the actual physical and biological attributes of the environment. Thus, the first section of this chapter focuses on three waves of migration and transitory interaction with the landscape in the space that is now Cabeza Prieta.

1. Native Americans—subsistence and migration
2. Europeans and gold rush—Cabeza Prieta as travel corridor
3. Mexicans—origin, northward-bound migration

The First Migrants: Native Americans

The area of land that now encompasses Cabeza Prieta is often referred to as the Papagueria Desert region. The refuge lies in the westernmost portion of the Papagueria region, which extends from the Gila River in Arizona to the Gulf of California, and is the hottest and driest portion of the region. This area is an incredibly harsh and difficult environment for human existence. There is an ever-looming scarcity of water. In spite of the natural challenges of living in the region, the Western Papagueria has a rich archaeological record (Altschul and Rankin 2008), suggesting a long history of human-environment interaction. The story of human presence in the region is fairly typical of human occupation throughout the Southwest. There are more than 30 documented archaeological sites on the wildlife refuge, and some of the more recent sites are quite spectacular, with impressive rock art. It is not uncommon for a visitor to the refuge to stumble upon pot shards or other artifacts while visiting Cabeza Prieta.

While it is unlikely that there were past permanent settlements in the area that is now Cabeza Prieta, Native Americans have lived there, in small numbers and often in a transitory manner, for thousands of years. Archaeological evidence suggests that humans were present as far back as 12,000 years ago (Ahlstrom 2001). Climatic conditions at the beginning of human occupation were likely very different from what we see now but, for at least the past 9,000 years, the environment has been characterized by water scarcity and extreme heat (Ahlstrom 2001:7).

The people most closely associated with the area today are the Tohono O'odham. They are likely descendants of the Papago, or Desert People. The people living in the exact area that is Cabeza Prieta immediately prior to European contact were known as the "sand people,"[1] a small band of nomadic people probably only numbering around 150 (Byran in Hackenberg 1964). They did not practice agriculture, instead relying on hunting and gathering, especially of desert roots, edible beans, and seeds. They would travel as far as the Sea of Cortez to the south and traded regionally with other people. Agriculture was more likely to be utilized as a subsistence strategy in the surrounding areas by other Papago tribes.

Today the Tohono O'odham are closely associated with the Papagueria region. They have a rich and vibrant culture that mirrors and exemplifies their desert existence. However, during the early 1900s, most of these people migrated into U.S. towns and villages in search of economic and educational opportunities (out of a total population of 10,000–15,000). Tohono O'odham people continue to fight today for the right to move freely between the two countries, and to be exempted of the obligation of citizenship in either place. Historically they were able to move freely, but over the past hundred years they have faced ever-increasing restriction on their travel and traditional migratory paths.

The Second Migrants: Post-European Context

Throughout each of the various phases of Native American presence in the region, trade, exchange, and migration were common. Many archaeological sites on the refuge can be defined as "fragile pattern areas" (United States Department of Interior 1976:38), meaning that there is not much depth of accumulation of artifacts or cultural debris—further supporting the argument that this area was never permanently occupied but was part of a travel path. The area was likely used for resource extraction or perhaps ceremonial purposes, but it never hosted any large, permanent settlements. Of course, the nature of human-environment relations changed dramatically with the arrival and increasing impact of Europeans, emanating from both the eastern and southern portions of the continent. Similar to Native Americans, very few people of European descent ever settled in the area that is now Cabeza Prieta. While there were a few ranching/homesteading endeavors, for the most part, the landscape is simply too harsh, there is too little water, and it is too hot much of the year. However, the area has long been used as a migration route (or, as it is more commonly termed when referencing people of European descent, a "travel corridor").

The Camino del Diablo has long been a popular migration and travel route from Mexico to California. Translated literally as the "Road of the Devil" and more commonly as the "Devil's Highway," this popular travel route was known first and foremost for the adversity it presented to its travelers, and countless numbers of European, Mexican, and American travelers died due to exposure, extreme heat, and lack of water. The road runs nearly the total length of the refuge, from east to west just north of the Mexican border. It is dry and dusty, and it is as dangerous a place today as it ever was. Initially an east-west migration route for wildlife, such as bighorn sheep, the road was also traveled by the Hohokam and later the Papago Indians on their traditional migration paths. The first documented trip by a European on the Camino del Diablo occurred in 1540 by the Spanish missionary Melchor Diaz. Diaz was appointed directly by Coronado to command Spanish forces in Sonora, and he traveled across Cabeza Prieta utilizing its natural waterholes. Later, in the late 1600s, another Spanish explorer, Padre Kino, traveled through and mapped much of the area, including the Camino del Diablo (Simmons 1964:22).

After Padre Kino's explorations, additional Spanish missionaries came into the area, but they were met with resistance among Native Americans. It was not until the California gold rush of the 1850s that the Camino del

Diablo began to see extensive traffic. Europeans, Americans, and Mexicans traveled the nearly waterless route in an attempt to shorten the length of the trip to California. It is through the demise of some four hundred gold seekers during this time period that the road earned its designation as a place of death. Urrea (2005:11) describes the history of the road: "It was still little more than a rough dirt trail—it is still a rough dirt trail—but it was slyly posing as a handy southern route through Arizona. White Arizonans and Texans hove to and dragged their wagons. Thousands of travelers went into the desert, and piles of human bones revealed where many of them fell. Though the bones are gone, wagon ruts can still be found, and near these ruts, piles of stone still hide the remains of those who fell."

After the gold rush of the 1850s and until the 1990s, travel through the area was not extensive, and no permanent settlements were developed. There were a few attempts at cattle grazing. In the area that is now Cabeza Prieta, however, grazing did not flourish as it did elsewhere in the Southwest. During this time, the town of Ajo (where the Cabeza Prieta visitor center is located) grew as the copper mine flourished, but the deserts around town remained isolated but for the few remaining Tohono O'odham, who had mostly settled in the nearby reservation. Tourism began to increase as parks and other protected areas were designated throughout the region, but most areas were hard to reach and without provisions. Cementing the perception that Cabeza Prieta is about as far from humanity as one can get, the refuge was reportedly chosen as the burial grounds for the well-known wilderness advocate and misanthrope Edward Abbey. While this description of the early human and cultural history of the area may seem terse, the reality is that human interaction with this land has been limited. Early human visitors and the occasional settler left a very light footprint in comparison to the very visible presence of modern-day humans.

The Third Wave: Migration from Mexico

The range of official estimates of the number of undocumented border crossers varies dramatically depending on the organization and political affiliation of the estimator. One estimate is that in the early 2000s about 500,000 individuals entered the country each year without documentation, (Hanson 2009:12). The number of undocumented entrants rose steadily throughout the 1990s but tapered off slightly after September 11, 2001.[2] It is not fully understood to what extent the numbers have declined as a result of increased border protection—fewer attempted crossings, or more broadly the economic situation in the United States. Since the 1990s, most undocumented migrants have crossed through rural desert regions and, in particular, into Arizona, where large expanses of wilderness and isolation offer cover for people seeking to enter the country without documentation.

There is a long history of a northward flow of people from Mexico to the United States. Spanish explorers traveled north to explore and Spanish missionaries traveled north to save souls. Since the 1900s, however, those most likely to move northward out of Mexico have been farmers and agricultural workers seeking employment in the United States. During the 1940s, when the Bracero Program was enacted, it became legal to bring Mexican workers into the country for short-term jobs in fields where there was a labor shortage. But this program was short-lived (1942–64), and in the absence of a contemporary farmworker program, many individuals from Mexico and Central America pursue undocumented employment and thus cross the border illegally.

Arizona has not always been on the front line in border crossing. Changes to federal immigration policy in the 1990s had a substantial influence on where people choose to cross the border. Through a series of militaristic-sounding campaigns, a radical shift took place in the way the southern border was policed by American forces. "Hold-the-Line," "Operation Gatekeeper," "Operation Safeguard," "Operation Jumpstart," and "Operation Rio Grande" are the catchy names that convey changes in immigration policy throughout the 1990s. These programs relied on tactics like "prevention-through-deterrence" and "concentrated border enforcement" (Cornelius 2001:662–663) to deter undocumented entry at popular urban crossing areas. Fences were built and the number of agents was increased at notorious border-crossing spots in urban areas like San Diego and El Paso. The goal in increasing the presence of border patrol agents and using sophisticated new technologies, was to elevate apprehensions and thereby deter potential entrants in the future. Likewise, the assumption was that undocumented entry would decrease because the rest of the border was so inhospitable and dangerous that few people would attempt to cross in more remote regions. Unfortunately, this strategy backfired, as migrants funneled to remote areas, unprepared for extreme weather conditions and without sufficient water for their long trek. "Many migrants suffer severe dehydration and heat exhaustion as a result of attempting to cross the desert where temperatures can exceed 115 degrees in the summer" (U.S. GAO 2006:9; see also De León et al., chapter 7).

There are no reliable statistics on the annual number of migrant deaths associated with crossing the border, but it is evident that the number has increased and that most are due to environmental factors like heat, dehydration, and exposure (Cornelius 2001:669–670). Amnesty International estimated that migrant fatalities rose 500 percent after changes in immigration policies (cited in Camacho 2006:835), due to stricter U.S. border policing and the expansion of organized crime in the border region. There is also no evidence that the shift in border enforcement policy has led to a long-term reduction in illegal migration (Davila et al. 2002). Many of the migrant deaths occur in Arizona. The number of apprehensions on the Arizona portion of the border increased 351 percent between 1994 and 2000 (Cornelius 2001:667).

In the most notorious example of the dangers of desert crossing, in May 2001, a group of migrants entered the boundaries of Cabeza Prieta. The migrants suffered raging heat and no water and eventually were abandoned by their guide. Twelve members of the original group survived and were rescued by border patrol, but 14 men died. The group was totally unprepared for the crossing: they carried insufficient water and no maps or survival supplies. When their guide became disoriented, he abandoned them, and they wandered for days in the desert before their bodies—some dead and some alive—were discovered by border patrol (Urrea 2005). This incident resulted in the single-largest number of deaths since immigration law changed in the early 1990s. The story of the group is now a part of local folklore and has received national and international press coverage.

People continue to make the journey today, crossing the Sonoran Desert as people have done for thousands of years and likely will continue to do for many years to come. Migration tends to ebb and flow with the American economy and to a lesser extent in response to U.S. immigration policy. Migration today is taking on new shapes and strategies (see De León et al., chapter 7), but the physical reality of the lack of water, extreme heat, and isolation affects humans today in the same way it has affected humans in the area for thousands of years—it is a difficult place for human survival.

Section Two: Environmental Disruption from Human Migration and Responses to Migration in Cabeza Prieta National Wildlife Refuge

Changes to U.S. immigration policy in the 1990s resulted in increasing levels of undocumented border-crossing and smuggling across Arizona's desert wilderness (Cornelius 2001; Martínez 2006; Nevins 2002; Regan 2010). In the 1990s, as urban crossing points were closed down by border patrol, immigrants and smugglers were forced to develop new migration routes.

The Sonoran Desert in Arizona provided a large wilderness expanse of land ideal for escaping detection or apprehension by border patrol. While the original intent of the so-called "prevention through deterrence" policy was to discourage undocumented immigration across the U.S.-Mexico border, the actual effect of the policy has been only a modest reduction in border crossings (which may simply be a direct result of the declining American economy) and an overall increase in number of deaths on routes through dangerous deserts.

While the effects of immigration policy on migration patterns have been well documented, the environmental repercussions of shifting migration are less understood. What we do know is that, as immigration and smuggling activities increased in the Sonoran Desert, there was a corresponding increase in the number of border patrol agents and infrastructure in the region. After the terrorist acts of September 11, 2001, security measures on the U.S.-Mexican border accelerated with the creation of the Department of Homeland Security (Chavez 2008; Urban 2008). A relationship exists between the evolution of immigration policy and increasing human impact on the Sonoran Desert.

Several national and state parks have been impacted severely by immigration policy. One of these areas is Cabeza Prieta National Wildlife Refuge (CPNWR), one of 300 wildlife refuges nationwide and a nationally designated wilderness area in Arizona that shares 56 contiguous miles with the Mexican border. Cabeza Prieta, Spanish for "dark head," derives its name from a dark-colored mountain in the western part of the refuge. Established in 1939 for the protection and management of desert resources, Cabeza Prieta is the third-largest wildlife refuge in the continental United States, with 860,010 acres. A national park and the Tohono O'odham Nation are located to the east of the refuge, the massive Goldwater Air Force range lies to its west, and Mexico to the south.

Due to immigration policy changes over the last two decades, Cabeza Prieta has been greatly affected by both migration and Homeland Security. Estimates of the number of migrants crossing the area vary, with the highest suggesting that 4,000 to 6,000 crossings occurred each month between April and June in the early 2000s (Slown 2003). There was a slight decline in the number of undocumented crossings in the region in the early 2000s corresponding with the economic recession in the United States, but the number is on the rise again since 2011 (Nwosu et al. 2014). As a direct result of undocumented immigration, the landscape has suffered from concomitant increasing vehicular traffic (Meierotto 2012:13; United States Department of Interior, 2011). The impact is especially pronounced in off-road wilderness areas.

Some argue that Cabeza Prieta National Wildlife Refuge is one of the most environmentally degraded wilderness areas in the United States (Lusk 2008; Public Employees for Environmental Responsibility 2008; Wilderness Society 2008). Ideally, a federally designated wilderness area should be protected from most human impact, and especially untouched by motorized vehicles. At Cabeza Prieta, however, a large number of vehicles regularly traverse the wilderness landscape. Vehicles might carry bighorn sheep hunters, biologists studying endangered Sonoran pronghorn, Air Force personnel conducting training exercises, hikers and adventurers exploring the Camino del Diablo, and, of course, migrants and Homeland Security forces.

Refuge staff, border patrol agents, and recreational visitors all attest to the fact that increases in traffic (both vehicular and foot) in recent years are undeniable and are creating long-term environmental damage. Research conducted by refuge staff claims that over 8,000 miles of vehicle trails now scar the landscape (United States Department of Interior 2011). Who the primary underlying drivers of this degradation are, however, is a subject of great controversy. Blame for environmental degradation tends to be assigned in one of two directions: one perspective is that migrants and smugglers are destroying the environment. Another perspective is that, border patrol (i.e., Homeland Security) is to blame for the worst assaults on nature. Accusations abound, with fingers pointing at different groups who access the refuge (Shifting perceptions of blame for environmental degradation are explained in greater detail in Meierotto 2012).

The media tends to focus on the environmental impact of migrants. However, based on my own observations during fieldwork, I found that the environmental impact of U.S. Border Patrol was at least as significant, if not greater, than the impact of border crossers, recreationalists, or the military (Meierotto 2012). The following section summarizes the general environmental impact of migration and U.S. Border Patrol.

2.2. Environmental Impacts of Migration

Large-scale migration affects environmental conservation on a global scale (Brechin et al. 2003; Homer-Dixon 1999; Pirages and DeGeest 2004). It is estimated that up to 300 million people migrate across international borders each year (Oglethorpe et al. 2007). Environmental disruption can occur in multiple ways. For example, disruptive migration can arise at the origin site through the loss of local place-based knowledge, at the destination site through increases in population, and along the migration corridor itself (Oglethorpe et al. 2007). Migration frequently disrupts the environment by affecting biodiversity, by contributing to habitat loss and fragmentation, pollution, the spread of invasive species, and the loss of indigenous species and genetic diversity (Oglethorpe et al. 2007). Four general categories of negative environmental impacts from migration have been itemized by The International Symposium on the Environmental Impacts Resulting from Mass Migrations. These include: (1) direct damage to ecosystems (i.e., from roads), (2) indirect impact on local markets and prices (i.e., enforcement costs), (3) indirect effects on environmental health conditions (i.e., human waste), and (4) political impacts (i.e., tensions between local residents and migrants (adapted from McIntyre and Weeks 2002).

Popular media and policymakers have noticed the environmental disruption caused by human migration in southern Arizona (e.g., Clarke 2006). However, the story in the popular media tends to reinforce the popular perception that migrants and smugglers are the primary drivers of environmental disruption (e.g., Fox News 2008; Nealson 2009). The media story is predictable: "dirty" migrants are viewed as depositing food, human waste, and plastic water jugs in environmentally fragile areas (see De León et al., chapter 7, for examples). While migrants are often blamed for environmental degradation on the border in both the mainstream media and among local residents, the impact of garbage (primarily plastic bottles, discarded clothing, backpacks, and food) on plant and animal life in border-area conservation sites has not been calculated empirically. Instead, an a priori assumption is that illegal immigrants cause significant environmental damage in wilderness areas (e.g., McIntyre and Weeks 2002:393). My own research suggests that the perception of migrant garbage degrading the environment at Cabeza Prieta is exaggerated (Meierotto 2012).

In contrast to media portrayals, many local people and conservation experts attribute a large part of the environmental damage along the border to Homeland Security and post-1990 immigration policies (Meierotto 2012:15). Border patrol is identified as a perpetrator of environmental degradation and reduces recreational visitors' wilderness experience. Homeland Security vehicles and helicopters are almost always visible, day and night and in the most remote of locations. Even with the advanced remote surveillance systems (like helicopters and drones) in place, Homeland Security predominately operates out of vehicles, which is a major cause of environmental disruption throughout the region.

Section Three: Linking Environmental Degradation with Social Perceptions

The overemphasis on the environmental impact of undocumented migrants at Cabeza Prieta (as opposed to that of border patrol) has much to do with social perceptions of Mexican-origin migrants (see also Tsuda, chapter 11, and Maupin, chapter 12). To summarize, the multiple ways in which people assign responsibility for environmental disruption are embedded in broader social and political systems (Meierotto 2012). One important question is, why has environmental degradation at the U.S.-Mexico border emphasized trash rather than illegal roads? Part of the explanation is the stereotype of "the 'dirty Mexican'" prevalent in popular American culture (Sundberg 2008:877), as well as the more general negative perception of Mexican-origin immigrants in American society (Meirotto 2012:18). Negative perceptions are illustrated through popular Latino metaphors such as the "Mexican as invader" or "Mexican as degrader" (Santa Ana 2002:8). Framing the discourse of Mexican immigration as invasive immediately inspires a discourse of disruption.

An overemphasis on the disruptive nature of illegal immigrants shifts the discussion to migrant activities rather than to border and immigration policies (Sundberg 2008:874). Stories depicting discarded water bottles, clothing, and other personal belongings left behind at unsanitary camping spots are retold in the popular media, portraying undocumented Mexican migrants as invaders disrupting pristine wilderness. This "trash-talk," however, relates as much to issues of social identity, class, and race as it does to environmental degradation (Sundberg 2008). This discourse is inherently influenced by preexisting cultural beliefs about the disruptive effects of human migration, although human migration in this region has a long history.

Perceptions of Mexican immigration into the United States are often alarmist (Chavez 2001). When the discussion is framed as the border region suffering from a Mexican invasion, it shifts the conversation away from the environmental impact of Homeland Security. In actuality, the construction of fences and walls and the buildup of border patrol helped create the concept of the "illegal" Mexican migrant (Nevins (2002). In other words, immigration policy helped create the very problem (i.e., illegal immigration) that it is now fighting.

This "blame game" over environmental degradation has created an "unintended feedback mechanism" in border policies that "contributes to a persistent escalation in damage and tension" that is not unique to environmentally centered issues (Meierotto 2012:19). Perceptions of environmentally disruptive migration propels border and immigration policies and in specific and predictable directions through the "primacy of images and symbols for state actors engaged in border management" (Andreas 2009:9). The prioritization of a focus on migrant disruption is illustrative of the "greening of hate" phenomenon (Hartmann 2004) and the "Latino Threat Narrative" (Chavez 2008:3).

Conclusion

Environmental disruption occurs in Cabeza Prieta through both the processes of migration and the response to that migration via Homeland Security. Perceptions of the impact of the disruption vary culturally, nationally, and politically. Digging deeper in time and considering the broader history of the refuge, a more complex historical narrative is unveiled. One theme that arises when one looks at the environmental history of Cabeza Prieta is that it is inherently a transitory space, whether one is looking at the natural gradient from east to west, the migratory paths of wildlife, or the movement of humans across the area throughout the ages. It is ironic, given the current political trend protesting the passage of humans from Mexico north through the area, that one of the most accepted theories of past human occupation suggests that the Hohokam in the region arrived from what is now Mexico thousands of years ago! This history of mobility, migration, and transition creates a powerful juxtaposition with the concept of what is now Cabeza Prieta—a bounded, stable area whose very conception was designed to protect and prohibit entrance and exit (for example, the entrance of humans and the exit of endangered species.)

The most recent political and social effects of immigration and the militarization of the border, in addition to being embedded in larger historical processes, are also impacting the natural environment, creating a new dialectic linking environment and cultural and political processes (Meierotto 2014). As a telling example, environmental effects of the new fences being constructed along the border are already being felt. During summer 2008, there were several strong monsoon rainstorms—not unusually strong, but with a significant amount of rainfall. New reports were published sporadically that revealed unforeseen environmental consequences of the fences. Because floodwaters in the region typically flow on a north-south gradient, when the runoff during the monsoons began, water quickly ran into the fence, which acted as a barrier as it filled with debris and rapidly accumulating water. An article in the local newspaper, *Ajo Copper News*, titled "New Pedestrian Fence Caused Flooding at Lukeville Port" (August 20, 2008), describes how "grates along the bottom of the pedestrian fence quickly plugged with debris and floodwater began moving laterally along the fence, then pooling as if behind a dam." Several homes and businesses on the border sustained significant damage.

The story of these floods has become a part of the most recent chapter of the environmental history of Cabeza Prieta and the U.S.-Mexico border. The occurrence of the floods highlights the fact that one cannot separate the social from the natural world. Human actions take place within and are a part of the broader physical environment, and the physical environment is constantly being affected by human social actions, manifesting itself in phenomena like climate change, increased flooding on the border, and widespread environmental degradation. Migration is but one human action that offers a valuable perspective for considering the human/nature relationship, especially in terms of environmental disruption.

Notes

1. Also referred to as the Hia C'ed O'odham.

2. In recent years the severe decline in the U.S. economy has resulted in decreasing numbers of people crossing the border.

References Cited

Ahlstrom, Richard, ed.
2001   A Cultural Resources Overview and Assessment for the Cabeza Prieta National Wildlife Refuge. Tucson: SWCA Cultural Resources Report.
Altschul, Jeffrey H., and Adrianne G. Rankin, eds.
2008   Fragile Patterns: The Archaeology of the Western *Papagueria*. Tucson: SRI Press.
Andreas, Peter
2009   Border Games: Policing the U.S.-Mexico Divide. 2nd edition. Ithaca: Cornell University Press.
Annerino, John
1999   Dead in Their Tracks: Crossing America's Desert Borderlands. New York: Four Walls Eight Windows.
USA Today
2007   "Chertoff Defends Southwest Border Fence." USA Today, Posted 10/1/2007. http://www.usatoday.com/news/washington/2007-10-01-chertoff-fence_N.htm, accessed December 7, 2011.

Brechin, Steven R., Peter R. Wilshusen, Crystal L. Fortwangler, and Patrick C. West, eds.
2003   Contested Nature: Promoting International Biodiversity with Social Justice in the Twenty-first Century. Albany: State University of New York Press.

Camacho, Alicia Schmidt
2006   Migrant Melancholia: Emergent Discourses of Mexican Migrant Traffic in Transnational Space. South Atlantic Quarterly 105:4.

Chavez, Leo R.
2001   Covering Immigration: Popular Images and the Politics of the Nation. Berkeley: University of California Press.
2008   The Latino Threat: Constructing Immigrants, Citizens, and the Nation. Stanford: Stanford University Press.

Clarke, Chris
2006   The Battered Border: Immigration Policy Sacrifices Arizona's Wildernesss. Earth Island Journal, Autumn 2006. http://www.earthisland.org/journal/index.php/eij/article/the_battered_border, accessed October 20, 2010.

Cornelius, Wayne A.
2001   Death at the Border: Efficacy and Unintended Consequences of US Immigration Control Policy. Population and Development Review 27(4):661–685.

Cronon, William, ed.
1996   Uncommon Ground: Rethinking the Human Place in Nature. New York: W.W. Norton.

Davila, Alberto, José A. Pagán, and Gökçe Soydemir
2002   The Short-Term and Long-Term Deterrence Effects of INS Border and Interior Enforcement on Undocumented Immigration. Journal of Economic Behavior & Organization 49(4):459–547.

Donnan, Hastings, and Thomas M. Wilson, eds.
2010   Borderlands: Ethnographic Approaches to Security, Power, and Identity. Lanham, MD: University Press of America.

Douglas, Mary
1966   Purity and Danger: An Analysis of the Concepts of Pollution and Taboo. London: Routledge and Kegan Paul.

Ferguson, Kathryn, Norma A. Price, and Ted Parks
2010   Crossing With the Virgin: Stories From the Migrant Trail. Tucson: University of Arizona Press.

Fox News
2008   Groups Struggle to Clean Up Mess Illegal Immigrants Leave Behind. http://www.foxnews.com/story/0,2933,354398,00.html, accessed December 7, 2011.

Gauthier, Melissa
2010   Researching the Border's Economic Underworld: The 'Fayuca Hormiga' in the US-Mexico Borderlands. In Borderlands: Ethnographic Approaches to Security, Power, and Identity. Hastings Donnan and Thomas M. Wilson, eds. Pp. 53–72. Lanham, MD: University Press of America.

Hackenberg, Robert
1964   Aboriginal Land Use and Occupancy of the Papago Indians. In Papago Indians. D.A. Horr, ed. New York: Garland Publishing.

Hanson, Gordon
2009   The Economics and Policy of Illegal Immigration in the United States. Migration and Policy Institute, December 2009.

Hartmann, Betsy
2004   Conserving Racism: The Greening of Hate at Home and Abroad. DifferenTakes: A Publication of the Population and Development Program at Hampshire College, No. 27. http://popdev.hampshire.edu/sites/default/files/uploads/u4763/DT%20 27%20-%20Hartmann.pdf, accessed June 11, 2014.

Hill, Sarah
2006   Purity and Danger on the U.S.-Mexico Border, 1991–1994. South Atlantic Quarterly 105(4):777–800.

Homer-Dixon, Thomas F.
1999   Environment, Scarcity, and Violence. Princeton, NJ: Princeton University Press.

Kenworthy, Tom
2006   New Outlaws Plague Arizona's Desert Refuges. USA Today (McLean, VA), August 22. http://www.usatoday.com/news/nation/2006-08-22-parks-borders_x.htm, accessed December 7, 2011.

Kosek, Jake
2006   Understories: The Political Life of Forests in Northern New Mexico. Durham, NC: Duke University Press.

Kraly, Ellen Percy
1995   U.S. Immigration and the Environment: Scientific Research and Analytic Issues. Research Paper. Washington, D.C.: U.S. Commission on Immigration Reform.

Lacey, Marc
2010   Water Drops for Migrants: Kindness, or Offense? New York Times, September 27, p. A10. http://www.nytimes.com/2010/09/27/us/27water.html?_r=3&ref=global-home, accessed December 7, 2011.

Maril, Robert Lee
2004   Patrolling Chaos: The U.S. Border Patrol in Deep South Texas. Lubbock: Texas Tech University Press.

Martínez, Oscar J.
2006   Troublesome Border. Tucson: University of Arizona Press.

McCombs, Brady
2009   Death Count Rises With Border Restrictions. Officials: Crossers Now Trek Farther to Dodge Security. Arizona Daily Star, May 17. http://azstarnet.com/news/local/border/article_5eafc47d-9751-54db-80f6-b76fd195df42.html, accessed December 7, 2011.

McIntyre, David L., and John R. Weeks
2002   Environmental Impacts of Illegal Immigration on the Cleveland National Forest in California. The Professional Geographer 54(3):392–405.

Meierotto, Lisa
2012   The Blame Game on the Border: Perceptions of Environmental Degradation on the United States–Mexico Border. Human Organization 71(1):11–21.

2014   A Disciplined Space: The Co-evolution of Conservation and Militarization on the US-Mexico Border." Anthropology Quarterly, Special Collection: Hybrid Landscapes: Science, Conservation, and the Production of Nature 87(3):637–664.

Nash, Roderick
1973   Wilderness and the American Mind. New Haven: Yale University Press.
Nealson, Christina
2009   Garbage Grows Well on the Border. High Country News (Paonia, CO), April 30. http://www.hcn.org/wotr/garbage-grows-well-on-the-border, accessed December 7, 2011.
Nevins, Joseph
2002   Operation Gatekeeper: The Rise of the "Illegal Alien" and the Making of the U.S.-Mexico Boundary. New York: Routledge.
Nuñez-Neto, Blas, and Michael John Garcia
2007   Border Security: Barriers Along the U.S. International Border. Washington, D.C.: Congressional Research Service.
Nwosu, Chiamaka, Jeanne Batalova, and Gregory Auclair
2014   Frequently Requested Statistics on Immigrants and Immigration in the United States. Migration Policy Institute. http://www.migrationpolicy.org/article/frequently -requested-statistics-immigrants-and-immigration-united-states#9, accessed November 25, 2014.
Oglethorpe, Judy, Jenny Ericson, Richard E. Bilsborrow, and Janet Edmond
2007   People on the Move: Reducing the Impact of Human Migration on Biodiversity. Washington, D.C.: World Wildlife Fund and Conservation International Foundation.
Peluso, Nancy Lee
1996   Fruit Trees and Family Trees in an Anthropogenic Forest: Ethics of Access, Property Zones, and Environmental Change in Indonesia. Comparative Studies in Society and History 38(3):510–548.
Peluso, Nancy Lee, and Michael Watts, eds.
2001   Violent Environments. Ithaca: Cornell University Press
Pinkerton, James
2008   Hispanics Hold 52 Percent of Border Patrol Jobs. Houston Chronicle, December 29. http://www.chron.com/disp/story.mpl/front/6184818.html, accessed May 15, 2011.
Pirages, Dennis Clark, and Theresa Manley DeGeest
2004   Ecological Security: An Evolutionary Perspective on Globalization. Lanham, MD: Rowman & Littlefield.
Public Employees for Environmental Responsibility
2008   America's Ten Most Imperiled Wildlife Refuges. May 22. http://www.peer.org/news/news-releases/2008/05/22/america%E2%80%99s-ten-most-imperiled-wildlife-refuges/, accessed June 11, 2014.
Pulido, Laura
1996   Environmentalism and Economic Justice: Two Chicano Struggles in the Southwest. Tucson: University of Arizona Press.
Regan, Margaret
2010   The Death of Josseline: Immigration Stories from the Arizona-Mexico Borderlands. Boston: Beacon Press.

Santa Ana, Otto
2002   Brown Tide Rising: Metaphors of Latinos in Contemporary American Public Discourse. Austin: University of Texas Press.
Simmons, Norman
1964   Exploring La Cabeza Prieta. Desert Magazine (May):22–23.
Slown, John
2003   Taking Refuge. United States Fish and Wildlife Service. http://www.fws.gov/south west/refuges/Plan/docs/refuges.pdf, accessed June 11, 2014.
Sorlin, Sverker, and Paul Warde
2007   The Problem of Environmental History: A Re-Reading of the Field. Environmental History 12(January):107–130.
Stoller, Ann Laura
2008   Imperial Debris: Reflections on Ruins and Ruination. Cultural Anthropology 23(2):191–219.
Sundberg, Juanita
2008   'Trash-Talk' and the Production of Quotidian Geopolitical Boundaries in the USA-Mexico Borderlands. Social & Cultural Geography 9(8):871–890.
Sundberg, Juanita, and Bonnie Kaserman
2007   Cactus Carvings and Desert Defecations: Embodying Representations of Border Crossings in Protected Areas on the Mexico–United States Border. Environment and Planning D: Society and Space 25(4):727–744.
United States Department of the Interior
2011   Cabeza Prieta National Wildlife Refuge: Vehicle Trails Associated with Illegal Border Activities on Cabeza Prieta National Wildlife Refuge–July 2011. http://re wilding.org/rewildit/images/Cabeza-Prieta-Vehicle-Trails_2011July.pdf, accessed November 25, 2014.
1976   Proposed Cabeza Prieta Wilderness Area Arizona. Washington, D.C.: United States Department of the Interior.
United States Fish and Wildlife Service
2010   Compatibility Determination Construction of a Communication Tower Cabeza Prieta National Wildlife Refuge. http://www.fws.gov/southwest/refuges/arizona/cabeza/docs/CPNWR.FinalCD.SBInetTower189.pdf, accessed April 28, 2011.
United States Government Accountability Office (U.S. GAO)
2006   Illegal Immigration: Border-Crossing Deaths Have Doubled Since 1995: Border Patrol's Efforts to Prevent Deaths Have Not Been Fully Evaluated. GAO-06-770. Washington, D.C.: U.S. Government Accountability Office.
Urban, Jessica LeAnn
2008   Nation, Immigration, and Environmental Security. New York: Palgrave MacMillan.
Urrea, Luis Alberto
2005   The Devil's Highway: A True Story. New York: Back Bay Books.
Wilderness Society
2008   Cabeza Prieta National Wildlife Refuge: A Landscape Under Assault. Washington, D.C.: Wilderness Society.

9

Rethinking "Causation" and "Disruption"

The Environment-Migration Nexus in Northern Ethiopia

JAMES MORRISSEY

This chapter interrogates the usefulness of linking disruption and causation in analyses of mobility. To do so, it explores the contemporary work linking environmental change to migration that has sprung up as a result of concern about the future impacts that climate change might have on settlement patterns, as well as on human and national security. The intention of this comparison is to highlight how work on the environment-migration nexus has evolved from viewing climate change as a significant disruption in an otherwise stable system of community livelihoods (and thus a cause of migration) to one in which the interactions between climate change and the context in which such change occurs are considered most important in explaining mobility. The aim of the chapter is thus to ensure that the lessons learned in contemporary studies of environmental change and migration might be understood by archaeological scholars, so that more accurate pictures of historical mobility might be generated.

The chapter begins with an introduction to the literature linking climate change and migration, most notably through the notion of an "environmental refugee." It then moves on to clarify some conceptual/terminological issues before describing the findings of contemporary works on the relationship between environmental change and migration. The central message here is that different forms of (non)mobility manifest under the different contexts in which environmental stress occurs. A particular case study from northern Ethiopia is described, in which the role of environmental stress in mobility decisions is made clear. Next, the important role that non-environmental factors play in this process is considered, while, at the same time, illuminating a conceptual framework for making sense of the interaction between environmental and non-environmental factors in mobility decisions, taken in a context of environmental stress. The chapter closes with a discussion of what such a case means for conceiving of disruption as a cause of migration.

Climate Change as a Disruption and Cause of Migration?

Early, hypothetical work on the relationship between potential future climate change and human migration invoked a logic that mirrored the sentiments of the workshop from which this collection stems. It posited that climate change would act as a disruption to the "normal" state of society, undermining livelihoods and generating impacts so profound that they would force people to leave their places of permanent residence en masse (Jacobson 1988; Myers 1993, 2002; Myers and Kent 1995; Westing 1992, 1994). From such logic was spawned the notion of an "environmental refugee," which persists in the contemporary popular discourse but has been largely dismissed in the academic literature.

As will be discussed later, much of the reason for dismissing the idea of an "environmental refugee" is that one cannot meaningfully conceive of the environment as "causing" migration.[1] As such, in order to engage with the focus of this collection, this chapter explores the limitations of viewing *disruption* as a *cause* of migration.

Writing on "environmental refugees" flourished throughout the 1990s and 2000s. This focus was spurred, on the one hand, by growing concern over continued inaction on limiting greenhouse gas emissions (as well as other perceived environmental problems) and, on the other, by concern about the proliferation of increasingly restrictive policies and popular sentiment toward issues of asylum and migration (Morrissey 2009, 2012). In the former case, the hope was that the threat of hundreds of millions of asylum seekers and migrants would galvanize the polities of industrialized economies to move on decarbonizing. In the latter case, there was concern that the presentation of migrants and asylum seekers as a "problem" would further undermine the effective rights of migrants and asylum seekers.

Within the debate over the appropriate means for representing this relationship, proponents of the "environmental refugee" found their position bolstered by archaeological and paleoclimatological work that highlighted strong temporal correlations between shifts in population distributions[2] and historic changes in climate[3] (Fang and Liu 1992; Huang et al. 2003; Tyson et al. 2002; Verschuren et al. 2000). In spite of such evidence, on the other side of the debate, critics of the "environmental refugee" pointed out that despite proponents forecasting hundreds of millions of environmental refugees by 2050, as well as claiming that there were in existence between 10 and 20 million environmental refugees today (Jacobson 1988; Myers and Kent 1995), no one had been able to identify clearly someone who had moved for reasons of environmental stress alone (Black 2001). As a result, significant effort has been expended attempting to document people moving (or not) in response to environmental change, in the hope that the notion of an "environmental refugee" (or a host of other labels [Renaud et al. 2007, 2011]) could either be substantiated or refuted (Morrissey 2012).

Such studies, examining contemporary migrations and their relationship to environmental change, have proven to be the mainstay of empirical work on the environment-migration nexus. As such, they provide an important departure point for examining the complexities of the relationship between environmental change and migration. Prior to discussing them, for the sake of clarity, some issues of conception and terminology are worth a brief mention.

Studying the Environment-Migration Nexus

First, regarding conception, because of issues surrounding the definition of change (over what length of time does variability have to occur in order for it to be meaningfully thought of as "change"?), as well as the probabilistic nature of the climate system (wherein any weather event can occur under any set of average climatic conditions, with the likelihood of different events simply taking on different probabilities), researchers have taken to exploring the potential impacts of climate change in an analogous fashion. This has meant focusing on processes of environmental stress[4] (whether or not they have their origins in processes of anthropogenic climate change) whose impacts are analogous to those expected to accompany future climate change. Such an approach has been thought of as meaningful for exploring the relationship between environmental stress and human migration.

Second, on a similar conceptual note, due to the arbitrary distinction between movement and migration (how far does someone have to move, and for how long do they have to remain there, in order to be considered a "migrant"?), I will, in my discussion of the literature and Ethiopian case study, refer to "mobility," rather than "migration." Such an approach is thought to be the best way to account accurately for the multitude of distinctions (in time and space) that are made in the different studies.

Turning then to the empirical literature on the topic, the most notable feature of the environment-migration nexus is that, while many studies have found evidence of a meaningful relationship between environmental stress and human mobility (Afifi 2011; Apeldoorn 1981; Barrios et al. 2006; Carr 2005; de Haan et al. 2002; Doevenspeck 2011; Ezra 2001; Ezra and Kiros 2001; Findley 1994; Gila et al. 2011; Gray 2011; Gray and Mueller 2012; Hampshire 2002; Haug 2002; Kidane 1989; Morrissey 2012; Mortimore 1989; Pedersen 1995; Sporton et al. 1999; Stal 2011; Wouterse and van den Berg 2004), a great deal of variety remains across the different studies in terms of what that relationship looks like. For example, Mortimore (1989), Findley (1994), Hampshire (2002), and Wouterse and van den Berg (2004) all find that droughts in the Sahel have resulted in *temporary* mobility strategies. On the other hand, Apeldoorn (1981) and McLeman et al. (2008) cite cases of drought, in both Oklahoma and the Sahel, as generating *permanent* changes in settlement. Similarly, while some studies have linked drought to *long-distance* movements (Apeldoorn 1981; Bassett and Turner 2007; Hampshire 2002; McLeman et al. 2008), others have been shown to result in *shorter distance, cyclical* moves (Findley 1994; Hampshire 2002; Mortimore 1989; Wouterse and van den Berg 2004). An even more complex picture emerges when one understands that a drought event can sometimes generate movement among individuals, whereas others compel entire households to move (de Bruijn and van Dijk 2003).

Beyond simple differences in the nature of movement, however, empirical work on the subject has found that, in a single community, under the same conditions of environmental stress, individuals and households experience a differing propensity to move. In this regard, Wouterse and van den Berg (2004), McLeman and Smit (2006), Findley (1994), Hampshire (2002), Hampshire and Randall (1999), and Morrissey (2012) have all described cases in which some people leave while others remain behind. Further complicating this picture, McLeman et al. (2008) have documented changes in mobility strategies among the same communities, under the same conditions of environmental stress, simply in response to changes in the political leadership of the country.

Notably, the findings described previously (which provide evidence of a link between environmental change and mobility, while, at the same time, highlighting the multiple forms that (im)mobility can take across time and space) hold across both social contexts and types of environmental stress. This means that while the propensity to move in a context of environmental stress appears to be differentiated in terms of both macro-scale variables,

such as gender (Afifi 2011; Carr 2005; de Haan et al. 2002; Gray and Mueller 2012; Hampshire 2002; Sporton et al. 1999), class (Ezra and Kiros 2001;
Gray and Mueller 2012; Hampshire 2002; Pedersen 1995), and ethnicity
(de Haan et al. 2002; Pedersen 1995), and micro-scale variables, such as
a household or individual's relative position in a community (Gray 2011;
Gray and Mueller 2012; Hampshire 2002; Morrissey 2012), such differentia-
tion persists across a range of environmental stresses. These include both
slow- and rapid-onset events, such as flooding (Haque and Zaman 1989;
Kayastha and Yadava 1985; Lein 2000; Zaman 1991), tropical storms and
tornadoes (Belcher and Bates 1983; Frey and Singer 2006; Paul 2005; Smith
et al. 2006), and sea-level rise (Gibbons and Nicholls 2006).

Such a variety of mobility responses can only be explained if we acknowledge that it is not environmental stress that determines mobility—
either in terms of its occurrence or its particular manifestation. Instead,
given the clear linkages between environmental stress and mobility, and
the variety of (im)mobility responses that manifest, it must be that while
environmental stress is important in shaping mobility strategies, the relationship between environmental stress and mobility is also heavily mediated by a host of non-environmental variables that constitute the context in
which such stress occurs. As such, any attempt at understanding mobility
decisions and their relationship with environmental stress requires an account of how that experience of stress interacts with non-environmental,
contextual factors to shape particular mobility decisions among particular
households or individuals.

With that in mind, this chapter now turns to a detailed account of a
particular case linking environmental stress and mobility in the northeastern highlands of Ethiopia. In so doing, it explores the complexity of the
relationship(s) and therefore highlights the limitations of simply invok-
ing "disruption" and "causation" in discussions of migration. In addition, it
seeks to outline something of a conceptual framework that can be used to
make sense of the complex interactions between environmental and non-
environmental variables, in the hope that the dynamics of both contemporary and historical migrations might be better understood.

Environmental Stress and Mobility in Highland Ethiopia

The work informing this account comes from two periods of fieldwork in
northern Ethiopia, one in 2009 and the other in 2011–2012. The 2009 work
consisted of eight months of fieldwork, conducted across two regions of

the country. The first of these was in the northernmost region, in the Tigray National Regional State (NRS), while the second was in the Amhara NRS, located just south of Tigray. In both cases, the work entailed the study of two urban areas, in which migrants who had left the rural areas were interviewed using a semi-structured interview format. This was followed by a number of livelihood assessments (again making predominant use of semi-structured interviews) among farmers, who had decided to remain in the rural areas. In both cases, the work was conducted on the edge of the eastern escarpment of the country. Notably, the Amhara field sites had a greater variation in altitude between sending and receiving areas, going from around 3,000–3,500 meters on the rural plateau to between 2,000 and 2,500 meters in the town. The difference in Tigray was only about 500 meters.

The second period of fieldwork consisted of three months of work, this time only in the Amhara NRS, using one of the same urban field sites as the previous study but a different rural field site. In total, in excess of four hundred interviews were conducted over the course of the two visits.

Livelihoods, Stresses, and Mobility

Rural, highland livelihoods in Ethiopia revolve around small-scale mixed, rain-fed subsistence agriculture. The dominant environmental stresses consist of worsening rainfall—reduced total rains that start later, end sooner, fall harder, and, while falling in a more clearly defined period, have an increasingly variable date of onset. At the Amhara field site, this early cessation of the rains results in an increased exposure to frost that occurs at the high altitudes, following the rains as the skies clear and radiative cooling dominates nighttime conditions. In addition, livelihood security is undermined by the impacts of hail, wind, losses of topsoil, and reductions in soil fertility. Such features affect livelihood security, reducing the agricultural production of a single household, as well as its access to grazing.

While respondents described hail and wind events as having been fairly stable through time, they reported that worsening rainfall conditions (and resultant frosts in Amhara) have been affecting agriculture in the area for the last 20 to 25 years. In addition, severe drought conditions have affected the study areas for the last four to six years. Accounts of these longer-term trends are corroborated in the empirical literature on rainfall change in Ethiopia (Rosell 2011; Rosell and Holmer 2007; Verdin et al. 2005), while the variability (in both time and space) of highland rainfall is well established (Bewket and Conway 2007; Cheung et al. 2008; Verdin et al. 2005).

Conditions of contemporary drought were evident to the researcher and simultaneously supported in accounts from local administrators and the media (BBC 2009). Claims of the worsening soil conditions are also supported by the academic literature (Holden and Yohannes 2002; Hurni 1983; Keeley and Scoones 2000; Nyssen et al. 2004).

Such stresses are thought to be suitable analogies for the impacts expected to accompany climate change in Africa, which include decreases in the availability of (agriculturally) unconstrained, prime land, decreases in cereal production (Boko et al. 2007; Fischer et al. 2005; Schlenker and Lobell 2010), increases in rainfall variability (Boko et al. 2007; Fischer et al. 2005; Goodes 2011; Stern 2007), and the occurrence of drought (Field et al. 2012; Goodes 2011).

With this context in mind, accounts of environmental stress impacting mobility decisions were apparent for migrants and farmers alike. Such stresses manifest in both acute and chronic conditions of livelihood insecurity and prosperity. In terms of acute stresses, migrants described leaving the rural areas in response to some drought-specific event, such as acute food insecurity, or the loss of a household member to illness, thought to be induced by a lack of food caused by the drought.

Regarding generalized impoverishment, migrants described leaving the rural areas due to the low productivity of the land or the poor productivity of the soil. They also described leaving in order to escape what they perceived to be the interminable conditions of "hunger" or "poverty" in the rural areas that had been caused by the general conditions of agricultural decline. Such dynamics are exemplified in excerpts from a number of migrant interviews:

> "I left [rural area] because the life there is too hard" (Murt[5] 2009).
> "Weldiya is better than [rural area] . . . there it is the same food every day and old clothes" (Filike 2009).
> "I had to leave [rural area] because of the poverty that is always there" (Bosana 2009).

Notable in these accounts is that, although they cite issues of low productivity, hunger, and poverty, migrants and farmers alike appeared well aware of the linkages between such conditions and their experience of environmental stress. The following account from a migrant, Arhet, is illustrative in this regard:

Interviewer: Why did you decide to leave [rural area] and come to Kone[6]?

Respondent: I left because of the low production.

Interviewer: Why was the production bad in [rural area]?

Respondent: The production was going down in [rural area] for a long time. It was caused by the frost, hail and drought and because my cattle had died.

Interviewer: What happened to your cattle? What killed them?

Respondent: My cattle died because of the lack of grazing, and disease.

(Arhet 2009)

Important in these accounts of generalized decline were descriptions of how migration manifests as a response when processes of gradual decline were punctuated by particular shocks. Such cases would include either particularly severe combinations of stress, such as the complete failure of a harvest, owing to the combined impacts of drought, frost, hail, and pests, or to gradual decline in wealth, resulting in discrete changes in livelihood sustainability. The most common account of this sort was gradual decline in wealth resulting in the sale of the last productive head of cattle—a circumstance that would mean that the household would likely have to sharecrop their land and thereby halve their already meager income. In all of these accounts, evidence of the central role that environmental stress played in people's mobility decision was the fact that many said that they would return to the rural areas if the rains improved.

These accounts show clear linkages between environmental stress, livelihood (in)security, and mobility. They are the sorts of accounts that have been hypothesized in concerns about the impacts of climate change on mobility and have been documented elsewhere in studies seeking to highlight these linkages. They, thus, in a fashion akin to the focus of this collection, present as the type of argument that views environmental stress as a *disruptive* force in established livelihoods and thus a *cause* of migration.

Given the findings of other studies described previously, however, as well as the focus of this chapter, it should not be surprising to hear my claim that such an account does not provide a complete picture of the factors shaping mobility in Ethiopia. This is the case for a number of reasons.

1. Mobility is not driven solely by environmental stress. A variety of other structural factors also shape livelihood insecurity in Ethiopia and therefore contribute to the imperative to move.

2. Environmental stress does not occur in a contextless vacuum. Rather, particular features exist that, first, leave households vulnerable to environmental stress, and second, make mobility a more or less suitable strategy for responding to that stress.

3. Tied into the fact that migration might prove to be a more or less suitable livelihood response to environmental stress is the fact that a host of non-environmental factors undermine the effectiveness of moving as a means for households to secure their livelihoods. As such, many households do not move and instead instigate a number of non-mobility responses in order to deal with the impacts of environmental stress.

In the following section, I seek to highlight the operation of these factors in the Ethiopian case before asking what their existence and operation might mean for our understanding of "causation" and the usefulness of "disruption" as a heuristic for interrogating mobility.

Other Factors at the Environment-Migration Nexus

Beginning with an account of factors other than environmental stress that drive migration, it is clear, even in the briefest accounts from migrants, that issues of land play a central role, in combination with environmental stress. Land in Ethiopia is currently owned entirely by the state, with citizens only being granted usufruct rights and having no ability to transfer privately such rights completely. As a result, the Ethiopian government has had to undertake periodic centralized redistributions of the land so as to allow new households access to the land required to sustain themselves. This process was first implemented by the Derg government when it overthrew the Imperial regime in 1975 and replaced the existing feudal form of land tenure in the country. The current government chose to maintain this arrangement when it came to power in 1992–1994 and, thus, has had to maintain the practice of periodic redistribution.

The implications of such decisions over land policy have been multiple; however, there are two that are worth focusing on here. The first is that the ongoing redistribution of a finite amount of land to an increasingly large population has rendered landholdings in the populous north very small. In this regard, landholdings are now so small that interviews revealed how households in the north of the country are only able to grow enough food to feed themselves for around four to eight months of the year—even with good rainfall. This, in turn, has led the government to place a moratorium on any further redistributions of land, as to do so would render the sustenance of established livelihoods impossible.

As a result, land and the particular tenure relations around it act in two important ways to increase the imperative to move under conditions of environmental stress. First, they act to reduce the harvest and grazing available to each household. In this regard, they interact with environmental stress in what could be considered a "directly additive fashion" (see Morrissey 2013), for a more detailed account of the framework from which these terms and concepts are derived) in that they generate a stress on livelihoods that is the same as that generated by the environmental stress itself: in this case, a reduction in household production. Such a case is captured in the following account:

> Interviewer: Why did you come to Weldiya?
> Respondent: I came to get another income.
> Interviewer: Why did you need another income?
> Respondent: Because of the bad rainfall . . . this is the third year that the spring rains have failed and the summer rains have also been getting worse. . . .
> Interviewer: Have you had to move away from your land before this?
> Respondent: No. Before this, my land [soil] was in better condition.
> Interviewer: What happened to the soil on your land?
> Respondent: My land has gotten smaller with my family getting bigger. This means that I can't leave the soil without crops and so the soil has gotten weaker.
>
> (Yimam 2009)

Second, the lack of any ability to acquire more land leaves this state of impoverished landholding intractable or, in the case of individuals too young to have received land in the last redistribution, in a state of permanent landlessness. In this regard, land tenure interacts with environmental stress in an "indirect, additive" fashion (Morrissey 2013). It is "additive" because it adds to the imperative to move but "indirect" because that imperative is not the same as that generated by the experience of environmental stress. As such, one might think of such a context as adding to the imperative to move generated (in part) by environmental stress by reducing the opportunity cost of remaining in the rural areas. The operation of such an indirect additive effect is captured in the following account:

> Interviewer: Why did you decide to leave [rural area] and come to Weldiya?
> Respondent: I came to find work.
> Interviewer: Why did you need work, why could you not work in [rural area]?
> Respondent: There is no work in the rural areas. At most there is work for one season for temporary manual labor.
> Interviewer: How had you been surviving in the rural areas [before coming to Weldiya]? Why could you not keep doing this?
> Respondent: We had been living on our parents' land, but we could not keep doing this because of the frost, which was getting worse. This meant that there was not enough to eat.
> Interviewer: Why did you have to be on your parents' land?
> Respondent: I had no land of my own.
>
> (Merikane 2011)

In addition to issues of land, a second overwhelmingly common explanation provided by migrants in their description of why they came to the towns pertained to their desire to attend school. In order to disentangle the relationship among schooling, mobility, and environmental stress, first one needs to appreciate the manner in which worsening environmental conditions have acted to place a premium on schooling and, second, how schooling is accessed in Ethiopia.

Regarding environmental stress placing a premium on schooling, interviews with school-going migrants revealed that, with agricultural livelihoods being rendered interminably poor, getting an education presented itself as a central means for securing one's future livelihood. In terms of how education is accessed, one needs to understand both that some basic material wealth is required for children to attend school (exercise books must be purchased, and the household has to be able to forgo the potential labor that children provide in the home), and that the Ethiopian government has chosen to situate its schools in urban areas. Regarding the former, migrants described how worsening agricultural conditions had meant that parents could no longer afford to send their children to school. As a result, young migrants had come to town hoping to find work to support their education. Regarding the latter, because it is predominantly the case that there are no senior-level high schools in the rural areas, people wanting to pursue their education have to come to Weldiya in order to do so. The following interview excerpts capture these dynamic interactions, highlighting how environmental stress places a premium on education and how this premium necessitates migration in order to access schooling, both geographically and monetarily:

Interviewer: Why did you choose to leave [rural area] and come to Weldiya?

Respondent: . . . I came for schooling.

. . .

Interviewer: Why did you want to go to school and not stay in [rural area] and work on the land?

Respondent: First I learned up to grade 8, but when I reached grade 8, I realized that I have to continue to grade 9,[7] because if I stop at grade 8 I will have to be a farmer. I didn't want to be a farmer, at that time, because there is no water, at all, there [in rural area], so I can't grow [anything].

Interviewer: So it's good to grow [food] if there is water in [rural area]?

Respondent: It is good only if there is water. Because of this [there being no water], I wanted to continue to grade 9.

Interviewer: You say there is not enough water in [rural area]. Is the problem rainfall or irrigation?

Respondent: You can see: it is raining today. This rain also harms the harvest.[8] Mostly, there is one summer rain in [rural area], so the rain is not enough.

. . .

Interviewer: Are lots of people leaving [rural area]?

Respondent: Yes. The young people who fail to pass their grade 12, they will leave.

Interviewer: And they will also leave because they don't want to be farmers due to the water problems? Or why do you think they will leave?

Respondent: What you do in the rural areas and what you get is not good. It is not balanced. So people are discouraged and they leave the area. There is an easier way to live in the towns.

(Habtam 2011)

Interviewer: Why did you choose to leave [rural area] and come to Weldiya?

Respondent: I left so that I could live with my aunt and continue my schooling.

Interviewer: Why couldn't you continue your schooling in [rural area], with your parents?

Respondent: My parents' income was too low there, and they could not support me at school.

Interviewer: What was wrong, why couldn't they support you?

Respondent: My parents have no cattle; they only have one horse and so have to share animals with other people just to plow the land.

Interviewer: Why do your parents have so few cattle now?

Respondent: It is because the rains now come at the wrong time. So there is no grain from the harvest and no money to buy cattle.

Interviewer: When did you decide to leave [rural area]?

Respondent: I left three months ago, because I was at school until June. Then, when my parents told me that they could not afford schoolbooks and uniforms for the next year, I left after hearing that my aunt was looking for help in her house.

(Adelo 2011)

These accounts highlight an important interaction among environmental stress, non-environmental, contextual factors, and mobility dynamics. Notably, we see that while environmental stress generates an imperative to get an education, so as to ensure a sustainable livelihood in the future, it is the non-environmental factor (locating schools in the urban areas) that results in mobility as a response. As such, one has to understand that the Ethiopian government's decision as to where to locate resources has made mobility a particularly viable response to dealing with environmental stress. Such interactions between environmental and non-environmental factors in mobility decisions, undertaken in a context of environmental stress, can be conceived of as "enabling effects" (Morrissey 2013), as they enable migration as a particularly viable livelihood strategy in a context of environmental stress.

The account describing the role of education in mobility decisions points to another interactive effect that operates in addition to the "additive" and "enabling effects" already described. Such an effect pertains to the macro-level context in which livelihoods are situated. In northern Ethiopia, such a context is responsible both for making livelihoods vulnerable to changes in rainfall in the first place and for making education a necessary asset for competing in the contemporary urban marketplace. I have, elsewhere, termed the role of such factors "vulnerability effects" (Morrissey 2013).

Vulnerability effects mediate the impact(s) of environmental stress on livelihood security and thereby shape the imperative to move—into other livelihoods—in response. They are distinguishable from additive effects in that they have no impact on the imperative to move. Instead, they simply provide a context in which the experience of environmental stress can produce a particularly strong imperative to move. While "vulnerability effects" are certainly central to understanding the relationship between environmental change and mobility (some authors [e.g., Lonergan 1998 and Black 2001] have considered them to be the most important explanatory variables), it should also be acknowledged that tracing all of the processes involved in constructing vulnerability (Wisner et al. 2004) is certainly a daunting task.

While these effects highlight features, beyond the disruptive impacts of environmental stress, that contribute to mobility as a strategy enacted in a context of such stress, it also needs to be understood that a multitude of non-environmental factors act to undermine the imperative to move. The interactions of such features can meaningfully be captured in the notion of "barrier effects" (Morrissey 2013), which present as non-environmental factors acting to undermine the likelihood of mobility being pursued as a livelihood response in a context of environmental stress.

From the previously detailed accounts of "additive," "vulnerability," and "enabling effects," one can imagine how "barrier effects" could constitute any non-environmental, or contextual, factor(s) that: (i) reduces the imperative to move (i.e., the opposite of an "additive effect"[9]), (ii) undermines vulnerability to environmental stress (i.e., the opposite of a "vulnerability effect"), or (iii) acts to decrease the viability of mobility as a response to environmental stress (i.e., the opposite of an "enabling effect").

Regarding the first of such effects, food aid is a good example. In the case of Ethiopia, food aid clearly acts to undermine the impacts of reduced productivity and, as such, undermines the imperative to move in a context of environmental stress. This was made clear in the accounts of farmers who, when asked what they would do if things continued to get worse, said that they would move "when the food runs out." Since food aid prevents or delays this from happening, even in a context of localized environmental stress, it is clear that such aid undermines the imperative to move created (in part) by the environmental stress.

Beyond food aid, one might consider a number of other factors that act in the opposite direction of the effects already described. For example, one could see attempts by NGOs and the Ethiopian government to encourage water-harvesting strategies as being the opposite of "vulnerability effects." This is because they undermine vulnerability to water stress among rain-fed agricultural livelihoods and thereby reduce the imperative to move that is created by worsening rainfall conditions. Similarly, one could see the policy, in Ethiopia, by which food aid is only made available to households living in the rural areas as the opposite of an "enabling effect," because it results in mobility presenting as a particularly poor strategy for households reliant on food aid, as moving to the towns would undermine their access to it.

In addition to barrier effects operating in the opposite fashion of the other effects, already described, such effects can also act in a multitude of ways that have not yet been described. Exemplary in this regard are accounts from farmers explaining their decision not to move due to the high costs of living, as well as the difficulty of finding work, and the insecure nature of that work, in the towns. Such concerns were particularly pronounced among both individuals with dependents and the elderly. Among individuals with dependents, it was the cost of living in the towns that made clothing and feeding an entire household prohibitively expensive in comparison to the rural areas, where goods are cheaper and children can more readily contribute productive household labor through tasks such as fetching water and tending cattle. Among the elderly, the concern was that they would not be able to compete for manual-labor jobs against younger, stronger individuals, whom employers tended to favor.

Attachment to land, which was closely linked to health concerns, also presented as an important barrier effect, with respondents describing how they had no intention of migrating, as they wanted to live and die on the land of their ancestors. They also described the highlands as being clean and having good water, and being places where nobody was ever sick. Particularly important in this regard at the Amhara field site was a concern over the health implications (most notably around contracting malaria[10]) of moving to the hotter climates at lower altitudes.

When discussing barrier effects such as these, it becomes important to understand that they do not manifest simply to make moving more difficult, with only a limited effect or no effect on actual mobility decisions. In many cases, farmers described how the problems of finding work and food, their fears of contracting a serious illness, and their desire to be on the highlands where they have spent most of their lives meant that they would not migrate regardless of how dire the situation in the sending region became. Most illustrative of the important role played by barrier effects were the accounts of farmers that they would prefer dying in the rural areas to migrating out of them:

> Interviewer: What will you do if things continue to get worse?
> Respondent: . . . I will die here.
> Interviewer: Why would you do that? Why wouldn't you leave?
> Respondent: I am not willing to leave my birthplace.
>
> (Aduna 2011)

> Interviewer: Have you experienced any shocks or stresses lately?
> Respondent: Every year is a problem, there is nothing special about this year. I have to stay here with my children, but I want to leave.
>
> (Mulu 2011)

Having now highlighted how the relationship between environmental stress and mobility in Ethiopia is heavily mediated by a host of non-environmental factors, and having placed those factors within a conceptual framework of different effects, I turn to discuss what the operation of such effects means for conceiving of migration as a "cause" of "disruption."

The Role of Non-Environmental Factors: Rethinking Causation and Disruption

By highlighting the central role of context, the previous account of mobility in the northern highlands of Ethiopia warns against simplistic Rube Goldberg conceptions of causation in which relationships are linear, direct, and simply chronological. In so doing, it queries our focus on disruption. To make these implications clear, we must first take the notion of "causation."

Simplistic linear accounts of causation seek to relate one event to another by way of a "causal chain." Under such a conception, the central idea is that events are linked to one another in chronological order. As such, one can understand the relation of one event to another by altering events that occur earlier in a sequence and examining the impact of such alterations on subsequent outcomes. Should an outcome persist, regardless of how an earlier event is amended, one may conclude that there is no relationship between the observed events.

Because environment-society relationships are incredibly complex, laboratory tests in which one can control all the variables other than those of interest are hard to construct. As a result, inquiries into the relationship between biophysical and social processes have had to rely on counterfactual thought experiments to test for causative relationships[11] (Walters and Vayda 2009). In this approach, causation is explored by comparing an observed case of interactions with a hypothetical case in which the elements of interest are removed from the interaction. If the outcome remains plausible in both cases, then the feature that was omitted in the hypothetical case is thought to have no relationship to the outcome being observed. Applying this approach, the question "does environmental stress cause migration?" could be explored by asking if the cases of mobility described in the highlands of Ethiopia can be explained in the absence of environmental stress. From the previous accounts, which documented clear linkages between changes in rainfall, decreases in harvests, and people's decision to move for reasons of impoverishment, it would seem hard to imagine patterns of rural-urban migration looking the same in the absence of environmental stresses. As such, using the logic described, one could claim that mobility at the field sites is *caused* by environmental stress.

Such an argument falls apart, however, when we acknowledge the role of other, non-environmental factors that add to the imperative to move, mediate the degree to which mobility is a more or less viable response to environmental stress, create the conditions by which environmental stress generates impoverishment in the first place, and even undermine, altogether, the imperative to move that is generated by environmental stress. Thinking again about the Ethiopian case then, as much as we might say that we cannot see migration patterns looking the same in the absence of environmental stress, can we see them looking the same in a context of irrigated agriculture, ample food aid, and larger landholdings? Can we see them looking the same if educational facilities were equally available in the rural areas as they are in the towns?

How then do we conceive of causation in migration? Does environmental stress cause migration, or is it the state of landholdings? Is it the lack of rain or the lack of irrigation? Is it the frost or the lack of food aid? There are clearly no answers to these questions, because they are asking the wrong thing. For the question is not *does environmental change/stress cause migration*? Rather, it is *what is the role played by environmental stress in mobility decisions*? Only by reframing the question in these terms can we appreciate that it is the *interaction* of environmental and non-environmental factors that results in migration under conditions of environmental stress. What we should be interested in when explaining the relationship between environmental change and migration is the nature of these interactions. For it is only through such an approach that we are able to render intelligible the role of environmental stress in mobility decisions and thereby understand the *causes* of mobility. What such conclusions possibly suggest is the need for a rethinking of our notion of causation in discussions of the impact of environmental stress. Perhaps we would be better off replacing it with a more sophisticated and nuanced language that can accommodate "multiple drivers" of migration and (to borrow from the language of the medical sciences) account for the multiple "risk factors"[12] in migration or "necessary and/or (in)sufficient" conditions for movement.

This discussion, problematizing linear notions of causation, in turn, raises questions about the usefulness of "disruption" as a meaningful heuristic for apprehending mobility. As was made clear previously, the impact of environmental stress—that can be (and has been) conceived of as a specific disruption—on mobility could only be rendered intelligible through an exploration of how it interacted with other non-environmental factors that also shape livelihoods, such as land tenure, food aid, etc. In this regard, an important feature of the Ethiopian case is that one cannot conceive of such non-environmental factors as existing by default, or constituting some natural, apolitical state resulting from an absence of "development." For as was mentioned in the case of a reliance on rain-fed agriculture, we have to appreciate the social construction of risk (Wisner et al. 2004) and, thus, of these conditions that predispose livelihoods to the impacts of environmental stress and migration.

In this regard, while a complete account of the political and economic forces shaping all of the features of rural livelihoods in Ethiopia is beyond the scope of this chapter, the case of land tenure and food aid, briefly discussed herein, is illustrative because the Ethiopian state has chosen to maintain ownership of all of the land in the country and to distribute all of the food aid. While the exact intentions behind this decision are hard to know for sure, there can be no doubt that, in a country wherein the vast majority of the population remains reliant on agrarian livelihoods that are not sufficient to sustain themselves, control of the country's land and the means for distributing food aid is an incredibly empowering position. The relevance of such factors is evident when one considers that Ethiopia is considered to have a highly centralized and coercive form of government, in which democratic institutions are severely compromised.

As such, the context in which environmental stress operates needs to be seen as a particular outcome of structures of power, rather than an inevitable preindustrial state. Similarly, issues of disruption need to be seen in context, and the structures shaping that context need to be acknowledged, rather than taken for granted. The danger here is that the very notion of "disruption" connotes some form of a normalized state of affairs—that which is being disrupted. Since this work has shown both that such a state of affairs is not normal or inevitable and that such conditions play as large a role in accounting for mobility decisions as the disruptive influence of environmental stress does, the notion of disruption as a cause and consequence of migration could be particularly misleading because it runs the risk of biasing explanations of mobility in the direction of the variable that the researcher considers to be "disruptive."

Discussion and Conclusion

This chapter has sought to problematize the notion of "disruption" as a meaningful avenue for exploring causes and consequences of migration. To do so, it has examined contemporary work on the environment-migration nexus in which environmental stress (as part of a growing concern over the implications of climate change for human mobility and well-being) has often been understood as a disruptive variable in an otherwise stable and secure livelihood context. Specifically, this chapter has explored the empirical literature on the topic to highlight the degree to which environmental stress is mediated by the context in which it occurs and thus has differential implications for mobility in different contexts. Following from this, this chapter explored the specific case of Ethiopia, highlighting how the impacts of environmental stress on mobility can only be rendered intelligible through an account of how they interact with other non-environmental, contextual factors.

Such an account raises problems with both a focus on singular disruptive events and causal outcomes, as it suggests that instead we need to see disruptions in context if we are to make sense of their impact on mobility. Additionally, such an account raises questions about the usefulness of "disruption" at all. For not only does the notion problematically conceive of migration as some form of aberration from the norm (Bakewell 2008), it also biases our explanation toward what we view to be disruptive, by the manner in which such an approach necessarily constructs the context in which it occurs as natural/inevitable or stable. What this chapter shows, however, is the extent to which such important contextual factors are not natural or inevitable but rather the product of particular forms of social organization in which power is embedded.

What then does this mean for work on migration, both archaeological and contemporary? In both cases, it appears to suggest that when migration is thought to be linked to a particular disruption, that disruption needs to be seen in context and, as such, some significant focus needs to fall on understanding which contextual factors matter and why. Such a protocol presents a daunting challenge to archaeological accounts, which do not have the luxury that contemporary studies permit in being able to, with relative simplicity, investigate the particular formations of power that shape access to the goods that make mobility a more or less viable/desirable livelihood strategy. That said, contemporary work certainly can inform archaeological endeavors by highlighting features that appear to make important contributions to mobility responses in different contexts. In this regard, something along the lines of the "effects" framework (Morrissey 2013) described here could prove a useful starting point for orienting archaeological investigation.

Notes

1. There have been other objections to the use of the term "environmental refugee" too, most notably that the 1951 Convention pertaining to the status of refugees makes no mention of the term "environment," thereby rendering the term legally meaningless.

2. These were measured using methods such as historical reports (Fang and Liu 1992) and archaeological evidence (Huang et al. 2003; Tyson et al. 2002).

3. These were observed through phonological phenomena and long human records (Fang and Liu 1992; Verschuren et al. 2000), as well as soil analysis (Huang et al. 2003).

4. Note here that the notion of "environmental stress" is understood to be *only* a stress in context (Bassett 1988; Robbins 2004). Thus, such a conception appreciates that the changes in the biophysical environment, described here, could manifest not as stresses, but as opportunities in other contexts (technical, social, political). In fact it is an explicit aim of this chapter to account for such context—see the section on vulnerability effects.

5. All names used in this chapter are pseudonyms.

6. "Kone" was one of the urban field sites involved in the study. It is located in the North Wollo region of the Amhara National Regional State.

7. Most rural areas in northern Ethiopia do not have educational facilities for students beyond grade 8.

8. At the time of the interview, it was raining, which was highly unseasonal for that time of year. Such rains, late in the harvest season, can knock the seed from the plant and also delay harvesting, making threshing and storage impossible and causing the harvest to rot.

9. One might reasonably term such effects "subtractive effects." However, since there is

no equivalent term for factors opposing "vulnerability" and "enabling effects," and for the sake of simplicity, such additional jargon will be avoided in this chapter.

10. Malaria is occasionally experienced farther down the escarpment but is endemic in the eastern lowlands of the country. It does not exist on the highland plateau in Amhara.

11. It is worth noting that it might be possible to model these hypothetical cases through agent-based models. At the moment, however, there does not appear to be any such means of modeling such complex interactions.

12. Note that the term "risk factors" is potentially problematic for the manner in which it invokes a discourse of risk as negative (such as risk factors for cancer or heart disease) and, therefore, mobility as negative or as an aberration. In fact, there is a host of important work that sees migration as a potentially important and valuable means for responding to livelihood insecurity, and documents it as an established component of many livelihoods. All that I am suggesting here is that more nuanced accounts of causation, such as those captured in the notion of "risk factors," are necessary for understanding the environment-migration nexus.

References Cited

Adelo
2011   Weldiya Interview Respondent 31. Interview conducted on December 9.
Aduna
2011   Waro Interview Respondent 15. Interview conducted on December 22.
Afifi, Tamer
2011   Economic or Environmental Migration? The Push Factors in Niger. International Migration 49(s1):e95–e124. doi:10.1111/j.1468-2435.2010.00644.x.
Apeldoorn, G. Jan van
1981   Perspectives on Drought and Famine in Nigeria. London: George Allen & Unwin.
Arhet
2009   Kone Interview Respondent 26. Interview conducted on September 2.
Bakewell, Oliver
2008   'Keeping Them in Their Place': The Ambivalent Relationship Between Development and Migration in Africa. Third World Quarterly 29(7):1341–1358.
Barrios, Salvador, Luisito Bertinelli, and Eric Strobl
2006   Climatic Change and Rural-Urban Migration: The Case of Sub-Saharan Africa. Journal of Urban Economics 60(3):357–371.
Bassett, Thomas J.
1988   The Political Ecology of Peasant-Herder Conflicts in the Northern Ivory Coast. Annals of the Association of American Geographers 78(3):453–472.
Bassett, Thomas J., and Matthew D. Turner
2007   Sudden Shift or Migratory Drift? FulBe Herd Movements to the Sudano-Guinean Region of West Africa. Human Ecology 35(1):33–49.
BBC
2009   Drought Brings Fresh Fear to Ethiopia. http://news.bbc.co.uk/2/hi/africa/8319342.stm, accessed June 13, 2014.

Belcher, John C., and Frederick L. Bates
1983   Aftermath of Natural Disasters: Coping Through Residential Mobility. Disasters 7(2):118–128.
Bewket, Woldeamlak, and Declan Conway
2007   A Note on the Temporal and Spatial Variability of Rainfall in the Drought-Prone Amhara Region of Ethiopia. International Journal of Climatology 27(11):1467–1477.
Black, Richard
2001   Environmental Refugees: Myth or Reality? Working Paper. Geneva: United Nations High Commissioner for Refugees.
Boko, M., I. Niang, A. Nyong, C. Vogel, A. Githeko, M. Medany, B. Osman-Elasha, R. Tabo, and P. Yanda
2007   Africa. In Climate Change 2007: Impacts, Adaptation and Vulnerability. Martin Parry, Osvaldo Canziani, Jean Palutikof, Paul van der Linden, and Clair Hanson, eds. Pp. 433–467. Contribution of Working Group II to the Fourth Assessment Report of the Intergovernmental Panel on Climate Change. Cambridge: Cambridge University Press.
Bosana
2009   Weldiya Interview Respondent 35. Interview conducted on August 18.
Carr, Edward R.
2005   Placing the Environment in Migration: Environment, Economy, and Power in Ghana's Central Region. Environment and Planning A 37(5):925–946.
Cheung, Wing H., Gariel B. Senay, and Ashbindu Singh
2008   Trends and Spatial Distribution of Annual and Seasonal Rainfall in Ethiopia. International Journal of Climatology 28(13):1723–1734.
de Bruijn, Mirjam, and Han van Dijk
2003   Changing Population Mobility in West Africa: Fulbe Pastoralists in Central and South Mali. African Affairs 102(407):285–307.
de Haan, Arjan, Karen Brock, and Ngolo Coulibaly
2002   Migration, Livelihoods and Institutions: Contrasting Patterns of Migration in Mali. Journal of Development Studies 38(5):37–58.
Doevenspeck, Martin
2011   The Thin Line Between Choice and Flight: Environment and Migration in Rural Benin. International Migration 49(s1):e50–e68. doi:10.1111/j.1468-2435.2010.00632.x.
Ezra, Markos
2001   Demographic Responses to Environmental Stress in the Drought- and Famine-Prone Areas of Northern Ethiopia. International Journal of Population Geography 7(4):259–279.
Ezra, Markos, and Gebre-Egziabher Kiros
2001   Rural Out-Migration in the Drought Prone Areas of Ethiopia: A Multilevel Analysis. International Migration Review 35(3):749–771.
Fang, Jin-Qi, and Guo Liu
1992   Relationship Between Climatic Change and the Nomadic Southward Migrations in Eastern Asia During Historical Times. Climatic Change 22(2):151–169.

Field, Christopher B., Vicente Barros, Thomas F. Stocker, Dahe Qin, David J. Dokken, Kristie L. Ebi, Michael D. Mastrandrea, Katharine J. Mach, Gian-Kasper Plattner, Simon K. Allen, Melinda Tignor, and Pauline M. Midgley, eds.

2012 Managing the Risks of Extreme Events and Disasters to Advance Climate Change Adaptation. A Special Report of the Intergovernmental Panel on Climate Change. Cambridge: Cambridge University Press.

Filike

2009 Weldiya Interview Respondent 21. Interview conducted August 14.

Findley, Sally E.

1994 Does Drought Increase Migration? A Study of Migration from Rural Mali During the 1983–1985 Drought. International Migration Review 28(3):539–553.

Fischer, Günter, Mahendra Shah, Francesco N. Tubiello, and Harrij van Velhuizen

2005 Socio-economic and Climate Change Impacts on Agriculture: An Integrated Assessment, 1990–2080. Philosophical Transactions of the Royal Society B: Biological Sciences 360(1463):2076–2083.

Frey, William H., and Audrey Singer

2006 Katrina and Rita Impacts on Gulf Coast Populations: First Census Findings. Metropolitan Policy Program. Washington, D.C.: The Brookings Institution.

Gibbons, Sheila J. Arenstam, and Robert J. Nicholls

2006 Island Abandonment and Sea-Level Rise: An Historical Analog from the Chesapeake Bay, USA. Global Environmental Change 16(1):40–47.

Gila, Oscar Alvarez, Ana Ugalde Zaratiegui, De Maturana Diéguez, and Virginia López

2011 Western Sahara: Migration, Exile and Environment. International Migration 49(s1):e146–e163. doi:10.1111/j.1468-2435.2010.00665.x.

Goodes, C.

2011 How Is the Frequency, Location and Severity of Extreme Events Likely to Change Up to 2060? Migration and Climate Change. London: Government Foresight Project.

Gray, Clark

2011 Soil Quality and Human Migration in Kenya and Uganda. Global Environmental Change 21(2):421–430.

Gray, Clark, and Valerie Mueller

2012 Drought and Population Mobility in Rural Ethiopia. World Development 40(1):134–145.

Habtam

2011 Weldiya Interview Respondent 22. Interview conducted on November 24.

Hampshire, Kate

2002 Fulani on the Move: Seasonal Economic Migration in the Sahel as a Social Process. Journal of Development Studies 38(5):15–36.

Hampshire, K., and S. Randall

1999 Seasonal Labour Migration Strategies in the Sahel: Coping with Poverty or Optimising Security? International Journal of Population Geography 5:367–385.

Haque, C. E., and M. Q. Zaman

1989 Coping with Riverbank Erosion Hazard and Displacement in Bangladesh: Survival Strategies and Adjustment. Disasters 13(4):300–314.

Haug, Ruth
2002   Forced Migration, Processes of Return and Livelihood Construction Among Pastoralists in Northern Sudan. Disasters 26(1):70–84.
Holden, Stein, and Hailu Yohannes
2002   Land Redistribution, Tenure Insecurity, and Intensity of Production: A Study of Farm Households in Southern Ethiopia. Land Economics 78(4):573–590.
Huang, Chun Chang, Shichao Zhao, Jiangli Pang, Qunying Zhou, Shue Chen, Pinghua Li, Longjiang Mao, and Min Ding
2003   Climatic Aridity and the Relocations of the Zhou Culture in the Southern Loess Plateau of China. Climatic Change 61:361–378.
Hurni, Hans
1983   Soil Erosion and Soil Formation in Agricultural Ecosystems: Ethiopia and Northern Thailand. Mountain Research and Development, 3(2):131–142.
Islam, M.
1992   Natural Calamities and Environmental Refugees in Bangladesh. Refuge 12(1):5–10.
Jacobson, Jodi L.
1988   Environmental Refugees: A Yardstick of Habitability. Worldwatch Paper, 86. Washington, D.C.: Worldwatch Institute.
Kayastha, S. L, and R. P. Yadava
1985   Flood Induced Population Migration in India: A Case Study of Ghaghara Zone. In Population, Redistribution and Development in South Asia. Leszek A. Kosiński, and K. Maudood Elahi, eds. Pp. 79–88. Dordrecht: D. Reidel.
Keeley, James, and Ian Scoones
2000   Knowledge, Power and Politics: The Environmental Policy-Making Process in Ethiopia. The Journal of Modern African Studies 38(1):89–120.
Kidane, Asmerom
1989   Demographic Consequences of the 1984–1985 Ethiopian Famine. Demography 26(3):515–522.
Lein, Haakron
2000   Hazards and "Forced" Migration in Bangladesh. Norsk Geografisk Tidsskrift (Norwegian Journal of Geography) 54(3):122–127.
Lonergan, S.
1998   The Role of Environmental Degradation in Population Displacement. Environmental Change and Security Project Report, no. 4: 5–15.
McLeman, Robert, and Barry Smit
2007   Migration as an Adaptation to Climate Change. Climatic Change 76:31–53.
McLeman, Robert, Dick Mayo, Earl Strebeck, and Barry Smit
2008   Drought Adaptation in Rural Eastern Oklahoma in the 1930s: Lessons for Climate Change Adaptation Research. Mitigation and Adaptation Strategies for Global Change 13(4):379–400.
Merikane
2011   Weldiya Interview Respondent 33. Interview conducted on December 9.
Morrissey, James
2009   Environmental Change and Forced Migration: A State of the Art Review. Refugee Studies Centre. Oxford: University of Oxford.

2012   Contextualising Links Between Mobility and Environmental Stress in Northern Ethiopia. *In* Climate Change and Human Mobility: Global Challenges to the Social Sciences. Kirsten Hastrup and Karen Fog Olwig, eds. Pp. 110–146. Cambridge: Cambridge University Press.

Morrissey, James William

2013   Understanding the Relationship between Environmental Change and Migration: The Development of an Effects Framework Based on the Case of Northern Ethiopia. Global Environmental Change 23(6): 1501–1510. doi:10.1016/j.gloenvcha.2013.07.021

Mortimore, Michael

1989   Adapting to Drought: Farmers, Famines, and Desertification in West Africa. Cambridge: Cambridge University Press.

Mulu

2011   Waro Interview Respondent 5. Interview conducted on December 19.

Murt

2009   Wukro Interview Respondent 20. Interview conducted on May 15.

Myers, Norman

1993   Environmental Refugees in a Globally Warmed World. BioScience 43(11):752–761.

2002   Environmental Refugees: A Growing Phenomenon of the 21st Century. Philosophical Transactions of the Royal Society B: Biological Sciences 357(1420):609–613.

Myers, Norman, and J. Kent

1995   Environmental Exodus: An Emergent Crisis in the Global Arena. Washington D.C.: Climate Institute.

Nyssen, Jan, Mitiku Haile, Jan Moeyersons, Jean Poesen, and Jozef Deckers

2004   Environmental Policy in Ethiopia: A Rejoinder to Keeley and Scoones. Journal of Modern African Studies 42(1):137–147.

Otunnu, O.

1992   Environmental Refugees in Sub-Saharan Africa: Causes and Effects. Refuge 12(1):11–14.

Paul, Bimal Kanti

2005   Evidence Against Disaster-Induced Migration: The 2004 Tornado in North-Central Bangladesh. Disasters 29(4):370–385.

Pedersen, Jon

1995   Drought, Migration and Population Growth in the Sahel: The Case of the Malian Gourma: 1900–1991. Population Studies 49(1):111–126.

Renaud, Fabrice G., Janos Bogardi, Olivia Dun, and Koko Warner

2007   Control, Adapt or Flee: How to Face Environmental Migration? InterSecTions 5:1–44.

Renaud, Fabrice G., Olivia Dun, Koko Warner, and Janos Bogardi

2011   A Decision Framework for Environmentally Induced Migration. International Migration 49 (S1):e5–e29.

Robbins, Paul

2004   Political Ecology: A Critical Introduction. Malden, MA: Blackwell.

Rosell, Staffan
2011   Regional Perspective on Rainfall Change and Variability in the Central Highlands of Ethiopia, 1978–2007. Applied Geography 31:329–338.
Rosell, Staffan, and Björn Holmer
2007   Rainfall Change and Its Implications for Belg Harvest in South Wollo, Ethiopia. Geografiska Annaler. Series A, Physical Geography 89(4):287–299.
Schlenker, Wolfram, and David B. Lobell
2010   Robust Negative Impacts of Climate Change on African Agriculture. Environmental Research Letters 5(1):1–8.
Smith, V. Kerry, Jared C. Carbone, Jaren C. Pope, Daniel G. Hallstrom, and Michael E. Darden
2006   Adjusting to Natural Disasters. Journal of Risk and Uncertainty 33(1–2):37–54.
Sporton, Deborah, David S. G. Thomas, and Jean Morrison
1999   Outcomes of Social and Environmental Change in the Kalahari of Botswana: The Role of Migration. Journal of Southern African Studies 25(3):441–459.
Stal, Marc
2011   Flooding and Relocation: The Zambezi River Valley in Mozambique. International Migration 49(S1):e125–e145.
Stern, Nicholas
2007   The Economics of Climate Change: The Stern Review. Cambridge: Cambridge University Press.
Tyson, P. D., J. Lee-Thorp, K. Holmgren, and J. F. Thackeray
2002   Changing Gradients of Climate Change in Southern Africa During the Past Millennium: Implications for Population Movements. Climatic Change 52:129–135.
Verdin, James, Chris Funk, Gabriel Senay, and Richard Choularton
2005   Climate Science and Famine Early Warning. Philosophical Transactions of the Royal Society B: Biological Sciences 360(1463):2155–2168.
Verschuren, Dirk, Kathleen R. Laird, and Brian F. Cumming
2000   Rainfall and Drought in Equatorial East Africa During the Past 1,100 Years. Nature 403(6768):410–414.
Walters, Bradley, and Andrew Vayda
2009   Event Ecology, Causal Historical Analysis, and Human-Environment Research. Annals of the Association of American Geographers 99(3):534–553.
Westing, Arthur H.
1992   Environmental Refugees: A Growing Category of Displaced Persons. Environmental Conservation 19(3):201–207.
1994   Population, Desertification, and Migration. Environmental Conservation 21(2):110–114.
Wisner, Ben, Piers Blaikie, Terry Cannon, and Ian Davis
2004   At Risk: Natural Hazards, People's Vulnerability and Disasters. 2nd edition. London: Routledge.
Wouterse, F. S., and M. M. van den Berg
2004   Migration for Survival or Accumulation: Evidence from Burkina Faso. In Agricultural Development and Rural Poverty Under Globalization: Asymmetric Processes

and Differentiated Outcomes. Proceedings of the 85th Seminar of the European Association of Agricultural Economists. Wageningen UR.

Yimam

2009   Weldiya Interview Respondent 23. Interview conducted on August 14.

Zaman, M. Q.

1991   The Displaced Poor and Resettlement Policies in Bangladesh. Disasters 15(2):117–125.

10

Migration and Disruption on Palawan Island, the Philippines

A Comparison of Two Cases

JAMES F. EDER

In this chapter I draw on my ethnographic research in the Philippines, which has broadly concerned the impact of development and change on the various indigenous, migrant, and migrant-origin inhabitants of Palawan Island. More particularly, I use two strands of this research that I have not previously attempted to compare but which I will here draw into a single frame of reference, that of migration and disruption.

The first strand of the research concerns the environmental degradation and cultural dislocation that has attended the agricultural settlement of Palawan's forested uplands. Here my focus has been on changes in land use and in household economic strategies over time, and on the implications of these changes for natural resource management policies and for the livelihoods and well-being of indigenous upland residents. The second strand concerns ethnic differences, Islamic consciousness, and Muslim-Christian relations in those regions of Palawan inhabited by its Muslim minority population. Here my focus has been on how significant differences in length of residence and sense of place, in how Islam is known and practiced, and in the acceptance of the Philippine state and associated institutions of power crosscut ethnic boundaries and make both ethnic and religious labels of limited predictive value.

Stated in this fashion, these two strands of my research indeed seem very different and appear to share little more than the same geographical setting. But each has centrally involved migration from one part of the Philippines to another, and each has centrally involved, on the receiving end, consider-

able environmental, social, and political disruption. And, while I will draw
primarily here on my own observations in Palawan, parallels to each process are found throughout the Philippines, for agricultural migrants from
densely populated lowland regions continue to fill in present-day upland
land frontiers, and Muslim migrants from the southern Philippines continue to flow into the nation's northern regions, particularly its cities.

It is the disruptive consequences that have attended these two population movements that are the focus of this chapter. Like Takeyuki Tsuda,
who, in chapter 11, similarly compares two migrant groups to the same
host society, I attempt to determine if something useful can be said about
these two cases of migration together, beyond enumeration of how each has
proved disruptive in its own way. Like other contributors to this volume, I
have sometimes found our effort to draw our many disparate projects into
a common framework to be a challenging one. As one long accustomed to
the language of case studies and who otherwise works close to the ground,
I felt that for me best to engage the themes of this volume, it made sense
to see what I might be able to accomplish by first bringing together two of
the cases of migration and disruption with which I was most familiar—
cases that I have heretofore approached in different frames and for different
purposes.

I begin with a brief description of Palawan Island and the national and
global processes of change that have led to its settlement by migrants from
throughout the Philippines. I give particular attention to the two streams
of migrants of greatest interest here: the land-seeking agricultural settlers
from Luzon and the Visayan Island region who have flooded into Palawan's hilly interior regions since the 1930s, and the various Muslim peoples
who, beginning in the 1970s, have migrated from their ethnic homelands
in southern Palawan, Mindanao, and Sulu to settle in the towns and fishing villages of northern Palawan. Drawing on the project framework that
contributors to this volume developed beforehand (chapter 1), I then systematically compare these two migrations, discussing in detail both similarities and differences, and seek an answer to the question *which of these
migrations proved more disruptive, and why?*

This comparison leads me to two principal conclusions. The first concerns the difference between objective measurement of the disruptions
that attend migration and the perception of those disruptions by the host
population. I argue that while the impact of agricultural migration on both
society and the environment has been the most disruptive in objective reality—based on such criteria as numbers of migrants, duration of settlement,

degradation of forest cover, and loss of biodiversity—the more recent and smaller numbers of Muslim migrants are *perceived* as being more disruptive, due to their greater cultural, religious, and political differences from the host population.

My second principal conclusion is that the notion of disruption is inexorably linked to the notion of transformation. While not all migratory disruptions lead to societal transformations, over the longer term some of them do, and the linkage between the notions is hence worthy of attention. I show that while the two cases of disruptive migrations considered here have both transformed the social orders of their respective host regions, the resulting "transformations" have been of a different order. Drawing on the notion of societal resilience to help account for this difference, I argue that the social-ecological systems of the coasts and towns proved more resilient to shocks and other perturbations than did those of Palawan's uplands. I then argue that despite the widespread perception that Muslim migrants are more disruptive, Muslim migration has in fact only transformed the surface features of recipient communities and towns, leaving their more fundamental structures intact. In contrast, agricultural migration to Palawan's interior regions has fundamentally reworked both upland ecology and the lives of indigenous peoples, to the great detriment of both.

Migration, Disruption, and Palawan Island

Palawan Island, located in the southwestern part of the Philippines, is the fourth-largest island in the Philippines and the largest of the 1,768 islands forming Palawan Province. The island is long and narrow, extending 425 kilometers from northeast to southwest and varying in width from about 40 to only 5 kilometers. The total area is 1.2 million hectares, most of it mountainous or hilly upland.

For the social scientists who study Palawan, as well as for millions of Filipinos, Palawan is special, both as a place and for its people. The story of Palawan the place has been well told; briefly, it is a place of immense biological significance and stunning natural beauty. Its mountains hold some of the most extensive stands of tropical forest in the Philippines; along its coasts are outstanding beaches and coral reefs and about a third of the nation's remaining mangroves. Palawan's geographical position on the edge of the Sunda Shelf is associated with flora and fauna that are predominantly Bornean or even unique in character. Examples include the Palawan mouse deer, the Palawan bearcat, and the Palawan peacock pheasant. One measure of the special import of Palawan's environment is the presence of eight protected areas, intended to conserve high-value, biodiverse landscapes.

The story of Palawan's people has been less well told, in good part for the simple reason that so many different peoples are found there. Indeed, Palawan's ethnolinguistic diversity is also among its most striking attributes; more languages are spoken in the home there than in any other province in the Philippines. The basic outlines of this diversity, however, are well established. Palawan is home to a number of indigenous peoples: the Palawan, traditionally shifting cultivators inhabiting the foothills and mountains in the south; the Tagbanua, a name shared by several culturally distinct groups of shifting cultivators and fishers that variously inhabit the riverbanks and valleys of the central mountains, the Malampaya Sound region, and the Calamianes Islands; and the Batak, forest foragers and shifting cultivators inhabiting the north-central part of Palawan. In addition, also considered indigenous under a broader understanding of the term are the Molbog, an Islamized population native to Balabac Island, as well as the Cuyonon, the Agutaynen, the Cagayanin, and the Calamiane, all Hispanicized peoples native to the small islands lying north and east of Palawan Island. And Palawan has also become home to a bewildering array of migrants and people of differing origins. Many are recent arrivals, while many others have themselves lived in Palawan for generations. These migrants and migrant-origin peoples includes Christians from Luzon and the Visayas; Muslims from Mindanao and Sulu; and even indigenous people from various parts of the nation. All of these peoples have figured prominently in the story of Palawan past and present.

For analytical purposes, migrants to Palawan may be separated into various "streams," two of which are of particular interest here. The first such stream has consisted of the movement of rural peoples originating from the lowlands of Luzon and the Visayan Islands, in the northern and central Philippines, first to settle along Palawan's coasts and then, later, its forested uplands and other interior regions. This migration has been in turn wrapped up with the larger story of the agricultural settlement of Palawan Island and, ultimately, the agricultural settlement of the upland Philippines generally. In 1903, the total population of Palawan was only about 35 thousand persons, many of whom resided on Cuyo and the province's other outer islands, whereas by 2010 the region's population was nearly one million persons, most of whom resided on Palawan Island (NSO 2010). What brought about this dramatic increase in Palawan's population? The short answer is that over the years and particularly after World War II, Palawan's land and other resources have not only attracted the attention of logging, mining, and other corporate business interests (other significant players in Palawan's drama, which I will mention only in passing here); they have also beckoned ordinary settlers and other migrants from throughout the Philippines.

Myriad national and global processes of change underlie migration and agricultural settlement in the Philippines. Again, though, very briefly, such population movement, now nearly a century old in Palawan and older still elsewhere in the Philippines, has unfolded as people—mostly poor people—have sought to escape overcrowding and attendant scarcity of land and other resources in long-settled "homelands," such as Panay in the central Philippines and the Ilocos coast of northern Luzon, by emigrating to less settled areas that offer more economic promise. Seen more critically, Philippine land frontiers have historically served as a politically convenient "safety valve" to relieve some of the socioeconomic and political pressures caused by government inability or unwillingness to undertake meaningful land reform programs or to resolve other agrarian problems in densely populated regions where land ownership is concentrated in relatively few hands (Eder and Fernandez 1996:9). Resource depletion and other livelihood-related environmental issues thus have figured prominently in the decisions of individuals and households to migrate. But, with the proviso that I did not specifically research the matter in migrant donor regions, I agree with James Morrissey (chapter 9) that the role of environmental stress in migrant mobility is usually mediated by a variety of non-environmental, contextual factors (e.g., by the presence or absence of military oppression or social unrest). It would hence be simplistic and misleading to characterize Palawan's agricultural settlers solely as environmental migrants or environmental refugees.

With the passage of time, the frontier regions thus "opened" in the Philippines by each new wave of land-seeking migrants have been increasingly remote in nature, but the same general process has remained at work, both in Palawan's uplands and on its coasts. A few intrepid settlers lead the way but are soon followed by others, typically kin, who provide reciprocal assistance and support; over time, information networks are established and patterns of "chain" migration emerge, whereby those who go ahead "sponsor" those who follow (Chaiken 1994; Seki 2000).

As with central Luzon, the Cagayan Valley, and Mindanao before it, too, the settlement of Palawan has transformed the island's ecology and had a corrosive and enduring impact on its indigenous peoples, consequences that have long been a major theme in Palawan studies (see, e.g., Dressler 2009; Eder 1987, 2009; Lopez 1987; McDermott 2000). The most profound environmental impacts on the island itself have been the removal of a considerable portion of the island's primary forest cover and the erosion of biodiversity in the remaining areas of forest due to excessive harvesting of tree resins, rattans, and other non-timber forest products (Eder and Fernandez 1996). In the island's coastal zone, these impacts have been matched by the relentless depletion of fish stocks and by the destruction of coral reefs, mangrove forests and sea grass beds due to overfishing and blast fishing, cyanide, and other forms of illegal fishing (Austin 2003; Eder 2009).

The consequences of in-migration for Palawan's indigenous peoples have been equally severe. These consequences have included population decline; loss of ancestral lands and livelihoods; erosion of social institutions and cultural traditions; and political-economic subordination to wider Philippine society and to the Philippine state (Dressler 2009; Eder 1987; Novellino 1998). These processes are being resisted in various ways, and, here and there, bright spots of ethnic and cultural survival may be found. But the outcome for many local groups of Batak, Tagbanua, and Palawan has been extensive acculturation and a debilitating sort of reverse assimilation into migrant society.

The second stream of migrants has been composed of various Muslim peoples emanating from Mindanao and the Sulu zone in the southern Philippines. As with the first stream of migrants, Muslim settlement of Palawan has been wrapped up with a larger, national-level story. There are about three and a half to five million Muslims in the Philippines, making up about five percent of the total national population. They belong to about a dozen ethnolinguistic groups, each with a home region in some part of Mindanao Island or the Sulu Archipelago, known collectively as the "Muslim South" (Watanabe 2008:289). Also known as "Moros," Muslim Filipinos have long been a disesteemed minority and posed seemingly intractable governance problems for the Philippine state, particularly after the intensification of the Moro separatist movement during the 1970s. One of the major outcomes of the long-standing armed conflict between the government of the Philippines and the various Muslim groups fighting for independence or regional autonomy in the south (particularly the Moro National Liberation Front and the Moro Islamic Liberation Front) has been the movement of Muslim peoples from their ethnic homelands in the south to Manila and other northern cities and towns. For example, an estimated 120,000 Muslims, mostly of recent arrival, today form communities in various parts of metropolitan Manila (Watanabe 2008:289).

Although little is known about them either historically or anthropologically, about 75 thousand to 100 thousand Muslims today reside in Palawan, mostly in the southern part of Palawan Island and on Balabac Island. Palawan's Muslims vary widely in geographical origin, ethnic group membership, political orientation, and livelihood, making it difficult to characterize the population as a whole. Compared to the Muslim-inhabited parts of the southern Philippines, however, Palawan is distinctive because most Muslims—like most Christians—are of migrant origin. In Balabac are found the Molbog, an indigenous group of Muslims, but far more numerous are the Tausug, Jama Mapun, and other Muslim inhabitants who originated in Mindanao or Sulu but have made Palawan their home. Some are recent arrivals, but others have lived in Palawan for generations and can trace their presence to the centuries-old incorporation of Palawan into the Sultanate of Sulu, whose representatives governed in southern Palawan by the eighteenth century (Warren 1981:136–138).

In recent decades, Muslims have begun to settle in northern Palawan, either by moving northward from the southern part of the island or by direct migration from Mindanao or Sulu. In the early 1980s, the first mosque was established in Puerto Princesa City; six more have since appeared. Most migrant and migrant-origin Muslims in Palawan have not settled in the uplands but are instead either found in the towns (where they characteristically work as market vendors, merchants, or civil servants), along the coasts (where they engage in fishing), or on the coastal plains (where they engage in coconut farming and other forms of permanent-field agriculture). Despite their many differences in geographical origins, ethnic group membership, religious beliefs, and present livelihoods, migrants to Palawan from the Muslim south share with migrants from the Christian north the same general desires to escape social unrest and to improve their economic well-being (Eder 2010).

As with lowland settlement of the uplands, Muslim settlement in the north has also brought disruptive consequences. The earlier-noted long-standing Muslim territorial claims in southern Palawan resurfaced during the 1970s and 1980s with a series of "incidents" involving armed confrontations between the Philippine military and elements of the Moro National Liberation Front, which was then actively fighting in Mindanao and Sulu for the creation of an independent Muslim homeland. More recently, Muslim territorial claims have been expressed with the hotly contested inclusion of Palawan in a 1989 plebiscite and a 2001 referendum to establish the boundaries of the Autonomous Region of Muslim Mindanao (ARMM), and then again in a vote on a proposal (later withdrawn) to establish a Bangsamoro Juridical Entity (BJE). All three efforts were defeated in Palawan, and Palawan's Muslim population was itself divided on the issues. But many non-Muslims in Palawan felt threatened by the repeated efforts of Muslim political leaders based elsewhere to assert territorial claims to Palawan that the majority of its residents felt were tenuous at best, and the third proposal in particular prompted a number of peaceful public demonstrations.

Beyond these military and political conflicts, the growing Muslim presence in Palawan has been accompanied by widespread accusations that Muslims are disproportionately involved in various illegal activities, including the sale of smuggled and counterfeit goods in the marketplace and the use of blast fishing and other environmentally destructive methods in the coastal zone. Also contributing a measure of social and political disruption, in Palawan and beyond, have been land disputes framed as religious struggles (Watanabe 2008), tensions and compromises in the legal system involving Muslim and non-Muslim litigants and defendants, the efforts of some Muslim migrants to establish madrassas, and the opposition of some non-Muslims to the construction of mosques in their neighborhoods. These and other developments in parts of the Philippines that have historically lacked a Muslim presence have significant challenged the Philippine state's ability to serve the needs of increasingly multicultural local populations.

In view of the highly charged and at times violent nature of Muslim-Christian relations elsewhere in the Philippines and the world, I want to emphasize that social relations between Muslims and non-Muslims in Palawan are almost entirely peaceable. Yes, there have indeed been disruptive consequences of Muslim migration and settlement in northern Palawan, but with rare exception Palawan has escaped the chronic and debilitating conflict and unrest found in Mindanao and elsewhere in the southern Philippines, and most Muslims in Palawan have assimilated into the host society in important ways.

The Two Cases Compared

These two migrant streams have much in common. Both involve boundary crossing; in each case, migrants crossed from a part of the Philippines that they had long inhabited to a part they had not. Both have occurred over a period of decades. Both are composed of ethnically diverse peoples who may variously be labeled as settlers, commoners, or refugees. Both are composed of migrants bent on improving their household well-being by escaping resource depletion or social unrest and intending to remain permanently in their new locale. And, of greatest interest here, both streams of migrants have had significant and disruptive consequences on the receiving end.

To be sure, these two migrant streams also differ in important ways. First, while both kinds of migrants have crossed significant geographical and cultural boundaries, agricultural migrants to the uplands have also crossed a significant ecological boundary. Second, agricultural settlement of the nation's uplands has almost entirely involved rural-to-rural migration, while Muslim migrants are of both rural and urban origin and select both rural and urban destinations. Third is a difference in scale, both temporal and demographic. Migration from the Philippine lowlands to the nation's uplands has been going for more than a century and involved hundreds of thousands of settlers; migration from the Muslim south began in earnest during the 1970s and has involved tens of thousands of migrants. Further, while both migrant streams have resulted in "assimilation" on the receiving end, migrant-origin settlers in the uplands are today in most places dominant numerically, socially, and culturally, and it is into their culture that indigenous peoples have had to assimilate, whereas Muslim migrants to the historically Christian north remain a minority, and their assimilation remains a work in progress. Finally, and considered in greater detail later, are differences in the precise *kinds* of disruptions that the two streams of migrants have caused.

More can be said, of course, about what these two cases have in common or about how they differ. Here, however, trusting that I have at least established the dimensions of their comparability, I will turn to a more systematic effort to compare—and to make some low-level generalizations about—the disruptions that each stream of migrants has caused. In what immediate ways are these two cases similar? Beginning with some close-to-the-ground observations, I find the notion that migrants pose "threats" of various kinds to be attractive, given that the notion of threat has both objective and subjective dimensions, and threats are commonly thought of as prompting responses, which I believe also merit attention. I also find useful the following typology, slightly revised from this volume's conceptual framework (Tsuda et al., chapter 1), as a way to categorize these threats:

1. Threats to the environment. Both migrations are visibly associated with the erosion of biodiversity in Palawan, whether in the uplands or in the coastal zone. (In both cases, other actors have also been involved, and there is scholarly, political, and public disagreement over which ones are most to blame; see below.) Loss of forest and coastal resources in Palawan and elsewhere in the Philippines has commanded the attention of foreign and local scholars, international and local NGOs, and various Philippine government agencies. These individuals and groups see such migration-related loss as a threat to the long-term environmental well-being of the nation.

2. Threats to state authority and control. Both migrations have tested the ability of the Philippine state to control a variety of illegal behaviors, including unauthorized forest cutting, the use of illegal fishing methods, and the sale of smuggled or counterfeit goods. In its inconsistent policy efforts to address these threats, the state has oscillated between various compromises with migrants and "crackdowns" on their misbehavior (e.g., arrests by forest guards, marketplace raids, and the like).

3. Threats to local lives and livelihoods. Both migrations have undermined the traditional livelihoods of many local residents, particularly the poorer ones, in part due to the sheer numbers of migrants and the resulting overpopulation in relation to available natural resources and economic opportunities. Further, the introduction of "unfair competition," whether in the forest, the ocean, or the marketplace, and whether from those engaged in illegal behavior or from those with more social capital or political clout, all threaten the well-being of both indigenous and migrant-origin peoples who were there before and who played by conventional rules.

So far, I have shown that the disruptions that both streams of migration have entailed can indeed be viewed in a common frame, but the effort has not proven particularly satisfying. Part of the reason lies in the significant differences, noted earlier, in the precise disruptions—or the precise threats, to the environment, to state authority, and to local lives—that each migration has caused.

The migration of lowland settlers to the Philippine uplands has had profound consequences on the environment and on indigenous peoples, and it has sparked vigorous political action, characteristically led by (but not limited to) "environmentalist" NGOs, to protect the forest that remains and to defend the interests of its indigenous residents. The activities of NGOs have in turn greatly influenced the conduct of electoral politics and helped to transform environmental governance in the Philippines. Nonetheless, it is my impression that the general Philippine public does not care about the consequences of the settlement of the nation's uplands by migrant lowlanders. For most ordinary people—and I am admittedly painting with a broad brush here—it is the inevitable outcome of population growth and development and is, at worst, the "price of progress."

The migration of Muslims to the Philippine north has lacked environmental, demographic, and cultural consequences of similar scale. But, on the other hand, it has attracted at least as much public notice, in good part because the consequences are experienced in more densely populated areas. In Puerto Princesa City, for example, the construction of seven mosques, the Department of Education's implementation of Arabic-language and Islamic-values instruction in the public schools, and the opening of a Kuwait-funded Islamic Studies Center are all recent and highly visible reminders of the different concerns of a growing Muslim minority population. More generally, Muslim migration to historically Christian regions in the Philippines is also seen as an unwelcome reminder of the long-standing militarization of the conflict in the south and, for many people, it calls to mind an association (whether warranted or not) of Muslims with lawbreaking and troublemaking.

Further, such "troubles" as Muslims are involved with are more likely to get in the news and in ways that *worry* people than, say, do the forest clearance and biodiversity loss attributable to agricultural settlement—processes that are also well known but not worrisome in the same fashion. For example, when the aforementioned Islamic Studies Center was closed, following a military raid prompted by allegations (which turned out to have been greatly overblown) that it had become a training ground for terrorists, the news dominated talk radio and public conversation for several days, for what it might augur for public safety. Again, when the Muslim Association of Puerto Princesa City held an election to choose its president, and the ethnic rivalry between the two candidates (a Tausug and a Maranao) threatened to turn violent, the occasion was cited by non-Muslims as one more affirmation of the reputation of Muslims as quarrelsome and quick to anger. In short, unlike their agricultural migrant counterparts, Muslim migrants arrive with a considerable amount of reputational baggage that worsens their image in the public eye and ensures that even if they collectively cause no more "trouble" than their non-Muslim counterparts, the troubles that they do cause will receive a disproportionate amount of public attention.

Discussion

Given these contrasts, I find it difficult to compare even these two relatively similar migrations, according to the scale or type of disruptions that each has caused. Returning, however, to the earlier typology of threats posed by migrants of both kinds, for all three types—threats to the environment; threats to state authority and control; and threats to local lives and livelihoods—the agricultural migrants have been the more disruptive. Collectively, they have been responsible for far more environmental degradation than have Muslim migrants. Further, the sheer numbers of agricultural migrants and their sometimes prodigal use of natural resources have undermined the livelihoods of indigenous and other local peoples, and preoccupied government authorities, to a far greater degree than have their Muslim counterparts. These observations are consistent with the emphasis in our project framework on the scale, duration, and frequency of migration. On these variables, agricultural migration would be expected to have been the more disruptive of the two; agricultural migrants have arrived in far greater numbers than Muslim migrants, and agricultural migration has occurred over a far broader area and longer period of time.

This comparison looks different, however, when we turn to a further variable included in our project framework (chapter 1): the type of migrant. By this variable—which must be seen in the context of the nature of the receiving society—Muslim migrants would appear to more disruptive than their agricultural (and non-Muslim) counterparts, due to their greater social, cultural, and religious differences from the host population. Certainly I have the impression from conversations with longtime Palawan residents that Muslim migration is concerning, in ways that agricultural migration is not. Unfortunately I have only fragmentary observations to support this point and lack the kind of data needed to evidence it satisfactorily; e.g., data from the mass media, on the relative amounts of newspaper space or radio airtime dedicated to each type of migration, or data on the relative amounts of time dedicated to discussion of each type of migration by various provincial and municipal legislative bodies. So, for now, the point remains only that, an impression.

An alternative is to stand back from these two cases and move to a higher level of abstraction or generalization. With an eye toward the possible applicability and relevance of my findings to other cases of disruptive migration, two things about these two cases stand out.

The first is that both cases involve some tension and distance between objectively measurable disruptions (or at least of disruptions as understood by the social scientist observer) and subjectively understood disruptions (i.e., disruptions as experienced by the hosts). There may be more salutary ways to express this thought, but what I have in mind here are local claims about the allegedly disruptive effects of migration that run the gamut from notions about national identity and religion in the public sphere to inflammatory newspaper headlines and rumor-mongering. It may be argued that the perception of disruption is what it is all about, in much the same fashion that race and racial differences in America matter in ways that go far beyond the biological reality or objective measurability of these traits. But the facts remain that (a) some disruptions are more objectively measurable than others, and (b) objectively measurable or not, all disruptions are subject to discursive representation (and misrepresentation). The chapters in this volume by Jason de León et al. (chapter 7), Lisa Meierotto (chapter 8), Takeyuki Tsuda (chapter 11), and Jonathan Maupin (chapter 12) all similarly emphasize perceptual issues and together illustrate the crucial importance of understanding how migrant disruptions are subjectively experienced by differently positioned members of the host society.

What sort of opportunity this observation offers for comparative study remains to be developed further, but in modern societies (and perhaps earlier ones as well), state-sponsored and other hegemonic discourses play a crucial role in shaping public perceptions of the disruptions that attend migration. Thus, with respect to ecological change in the Philippine uplands, migrant-shifting cultivators are still routinely villainized through the use of such pejorative terms as "squatter" or "slash-and-burn farmer," whereas the Philippine state long allowed and even encouraged commercial logging, and agribusiness plantation development (currently a major driver of landscape change in the uplands) is currently given a free pass. Forsyth and Walker (2008) have shown how, in official and alternative discourses of economic development, the Hmong, the Karen, and the other peoples living in Thailand's uplands are typically (and simplistically) cast as either guardians or destroyers of forest resources, often depending on their ethnicity. In a similar vein, Sturgeon (2005) has shown how processes of state formation, construction of ethnic identity, and regional security concerns have contributed to different outcomes for Akha and their forests in China and Thailand, with Chinese Akha portrayed as citizens and grain producers and Akha in Thailand viewed as "non-Thai" forest destroyers. Granted, these various peoples are not uniformly "migrants"—the Akha are residents of China but viewed as migrants in Thailand—but both cases illustrate the powerful role of hegemonic discourses in shaping public perceptions of whether the presence of a particular people is "disruptive" or not, with even the degree to which a particular people are "migrants" itself subject to discursive representation.

Again, and turning to Muslim migration to the north, most Christian Filipinos discount or remain ignorant of the resentment that Philippine Muslims have about how their religion, history, and contemporary concerns are represented in the national educational system and in the media. This resentment continues to color their social and political relations with non-Muslims and with the Philippine state. As a small but revealing example, several years ago, following an armed confrontation in Mindanao between a group of MNLF soldiers and the Philippine military, the headline in Manila newspapers was along the lines of "MNLF Rebels Kidnap a Busload of Passengers and Only Release Them Following Hours of Intense Negotiations." What had actually happened, however—at least according to a Muslim source—was that, in preparation for the expected confrontation, the MNLF soldiers had, in the interest of avoiding civilian casualties, blockaded the highway along which the confrontation was to take place and advised the bus driver (and other civilian vehicles) that, for everyone's safety, it would be best to delay his trip until the conclusion of the incident and getting the all-clear signal. While the MNLF fighters involved in this incident were not themselves migrants, "news" accounts of this sort follow Philippine Muslims wherever they go and help to delegitimize their concerns in the eyes of the majority population.

A second aspect of my comparison that also stands out in broader view is how "disruption" in each case has imperceptibly graded into something we might call "transformation." For most people, and again painting with a broad brush, life goes on, post-disruption. True, the trees may be gone and the fish may be fewer than before, many indigenous people in the mountains may have lost their ancestral lands and no longer engage in shamanistic rituals, and a mosque may now stand down the street in the city. But as these circumstances become the new normal, new livelihoods emerge and new cultural understandings come into being. Whether these new ways serve as well as the old ways is of course debatable—and, for many, they clearly do not—but at some point the notion of disruption becomes progressively less apt to characterize the changes brought by migration.

To be sure, the notion of transformation has its own problems, and just as there are different kinds of disruptions, there are different kinds of transformations. And of course some migrant disruptions do not result in anything we would wish to consider a transformation but instead lead, more simply and with the passage of time, to the return of the previous status quo—the old normal. But in the two cases considered here, both agricultural migration to the uplands and Muslim migration to the north have, in the process of resulting in some degree of assimilation of migrants into their hosts' culture, arguably led to the emergence of a new social order—i.e., to a transformation—on the migrant-receiving end. In the first case, the transformed social order has emerged largely on the terms of the migrant population, whereas in the second case, the transformed order has emerged largely on the terms of the host population, but in wider perspective the outcomes have been the same.

Why do some disruptions attending migration lead back to the "old normal," while others lead on to a "new normal"? This question suggests that there may some value in pursuing the notion of transformation as well as the notion of disruption in relation to migration, a task for which the related notion of resilience is useful. Resilience is often understood as the ability of a social-ecological system (or, more simply, a society) to withstand shocks and other perturbations without altering its basic foundation—i.e., without fundamental structural change (Carpenter et al. 2001; Gunderson and Holling 2002; Walker et al. 2006). Pinchon (2011) has recently explored the relationship between the resilience of social-ecological systems and the potentially transformative consequences of shocks (i.e., disruptions) to those systems. Pinchon studied the social changes taking place among small-scale wild-capture fishermen in Chile, who have seen their generations-old profession give way, in the face of the loss of sea tenure and the decline of the fishery, to wage labor in the salmon aquaculture industry. Granted, the disruption in this case was not caused by in-migration but instead by other factors; there are some important parallels, including the loss of a traditional occupation and sense of identity—losses that can also be among migration's disruptions.

Employing several well-established questionnaires, including the Satisfaction with Life Scale, to measure perceived well-being, Pinchon concludes that the change from being hunters (i.e., capture fishers) to farmers (i.e., aquaculturalists), while an adaptation to the changes taking place, has actually been "more of a transformation, which is still considered an element of resilience provided that original structures are maintained" (Pinchon 2011:203). The dispossessed fishermen who had joined the aquaculture cooperatives indeed showed characteristics of resilience, for "even though they had structurally changed their occupation, basic elements of their foundation persist, such as autonomy, use of pre-existing knowledge, and the maintenance of social networks" (Pinchon 2011:205).

Returning to the two cases of migration considered here, both resulted in transformations of the former social-ecological system. But the outcome each case has been different in a way that Pinchon's (2011) use of the notion of resilience helps clarify. Muslim migration to the coasts and towns of northern Palawan has resulted in a surface transformation of those areas—visible in the construction of mosques, new styles of public dress, changes in the school curriculum to accommodate Muslim concerns and sensibilities, and the like—but it has left the "fundamental structure" of the migrant-receiving society largely intact, due to the considerable resilience of the latter. While many factors in turn determine a society's resilience to migratory and other systemic disruptions, two singled out in this volume's introduction are particularly relevant to Palawan's coasts and urban centers. First, by comparison with similar regions elsewhere in the Philippines, these are relatively prosperous areas that offer a variety of economic opportunities to successive waves of new migrants. Second, the considerable pre-existing social and cultural diversity of Palawan has made it relatively easy for new migrants—including Muslim migrants—to find ethnic niches and communities in which they can develop a sense of belonging. Further, not only were Palawan's coasts and towns long inhabited by ethnically diverse, migrant-origin peoples from throughout the Philippines well in advance of the arrival of Muslim migrants, but prior religious diversity has likely enhanced resilience as well. Catholics in Palawan have long since been joined by followers of numerous Protestant and other religious denominations, some of which were introduced from abroad (e.g., Baha'i; Latter Day Saints) and some of which were homegrown. On this diverse religious map, Islam has relatively easily been accommodated as simply one more religion.

In contrast, agricultural migration to Palawan's uplands has pretty much swept away the old order, basic structures and all. There, agricultural migrants, often in conjunction with commercial loggers, have been collectively responsible for a fundamental ecological transformation: the conversion of much of the island's onetime tropical forest landscape into an agricultural one. The social-ecological systems of Palawan's indigenous peoples proved insufficiently resilient to withstand or reorganize in the face of this change. Over time, the cumulative consequences of agricultural migration undermined the forest-based livelihoods of indigenous peoples without providing satisfactory replacements and, crucially, eroded their economic, social, and political autonomy as well. Unlike the Chile case considered previously, where "basic cultural and community structures" were maintained (Pinchon 2011:207), here such structures were not maintained. Far from resulting only in a "surface transformation," then, agricultural migration has fundamentally changed the region's ecology and social and economic life. In short, the "new normal" that has taken hold in Palawan's uplands as a result of agricultural migration really is new.

Summary and Conclusion

In this chapter, I have compared the disruptions that have attended two migrant streams to Palawan Island from elsewhere in the Philippines. The first stream, which I have termed "agricultural migrants," consists of land-seeking settlers from Luzon and the Visayan Islands who, beginning in the 1930s, have established farmsteads in Palawan's interior and upland regions, removing in the process much of the island's tropical forest cover and displacing many of its indigenous peoples. The second stream consists of Muslim migrants, who, since the 1970s, have left their ancestral homelands in southern Palawan and elsewhere in the southern Philippines and established themselves on the coasts and in the urban centers of northern Palawan.

By such objective criteria as scale, duration, and frequency, agricultural migration to Palawan has been by far the larger of the two migrations; agricultural migrants have been far more numerous than Muslim migrants, and their migration has occurred over a far broader area and longer period of time. Again, by such objective criteria as the amount of environmental damage, the challenges to state authority and control and the consequences for the lives and livelihoods of indigenous peoples, this stream of migrants has—not surprisingly—proven the more disruptive of the two. But a closer look at the characteristics of the migrants themselves—a further criterion appropriately employed to compare migrations and their consequences— suggests that there is more to the story. Muslim migrants differ ethnically, religiously, and politically from their non-Muslim hosts. Further, they have been preceded in northern Palawan by a certain amount of "reputational baggage" that identifies Muslims with the armed conflict that plagues some parts of the southern Philippines and views them as given to law-breaking and troublemaking. In short, Muslim migration is worrisome in ways that agricultural migration is not. This finding suggests that studies of the disruptions that migrants cause in receiving societies should attend to the local *perceptions* of these disruptions and to the manifold influences on those perceptions—influences that in the case of Philippine Muslims include how their history and present circumstances and concerns are represented by the national media, in the national educational system, and by state authorities.

A final concern of the chapter has been with the transformative consequences that some migration-induced disruptions hold for their host societies. What may initially be seen or experienced as a disruption may, over time, become something more akin to a transformation—and to the emergence of what I have here termed a "new normal." Such was the case with both migrant streams considered here. In the case of agricultural migration, however, the transformed social order emerged largely on the terms of the migrants themselves, whereas in the case of Muslim migration, the transformed order has emerged largely on the terms of the host population. Further, not all disruption-induced "transformations" are alike. Making use of the notion of social-ecological resilience, I argue that the considerable resilience of coastal and urban society in the face of Muslim migration has left the fundamental structures of the host society largely intact, despite various surface transformations that have resulted from that migration. In contrast, whatever resilience resided in the social and ecological systems of Palawan's uplands was eventually overwhelmed by the sheer scale of agricultural migration, which over time has fundamentally reworked upland ecology and economic and social life.

References Cited

Austin, Rebecca L.
2003   Environmental Movements and Fisherfolk Participation on a Coastal Frontier, Palawan Island, Philippines. Ph.D. dissertation, Department of Anthropology, University of Georgia.
Carpenter, Steve R., Brian Walker, J. Marty Anderies, and Nick Abel
2001   From Metaphor to Measurement: Resilience of What to What? Ecosystems 4(8):941–944.

Chaiken, Miriam
1994   Economic Strategies and Success on the Philippine Frontier. Research in Economic Anthropology 15:277–305.
Dressler, Wolfram
2009   Old Thoughts in New Ideas: State Conservation Measures, Development and Livelihood on Palawan Island. Quezon City, Philippines: Ateneo de Manila University Press.
Eder, James F.
1987   On the Road to Tribal Extinction: Depopulation, Deculturation, and Adaptive Well-being among the Batak of the Philippines. Berkeley: University of California Press.
2009   Migrants to the Coasts: Livelihood, Resource Management, and Global Change in the Philippines. Belmont, CA: Cengage Learning.
2010   Ethnic Differences, Islamic Consciousness, and Muslim Social Integration in the Philippines. Journal of Muslim Minority Affairs 30:317–332.
Eder, James F., and Janet O. Fernandez, eds.
1996   Palawan at the Crossroads: Development and the Environment on a Philippine Frontier. Quezon City, Philippines: Ateneo de Manila University Press.
Forsyth, Tim, and Andrew Walker
2008   Forest Guardians, Forest Destroyers: The Politics of Environmental Knowledge in Northern Thailand. Seattle: University of Washington Press.
Gunderson, Lance H., and Crawford S. Holling, eds.
2002   Panarchy: Understanding Transformations in Human and Natural Systems. Washington, D.C.: Island Press.
Lopez, Maria Elena
1987   The Politics of Land at Risk in a Philippine Frontier. *In* Lands at Risk in the Third World: Local-Level Perspectives. Peter D. Little and Michael Horowitz, eds. Pp. 230–248. Boulder, CO: Westview Press.
McDermott, Melanie Hughes
2000   Boundaries and Pathways: Indigenous Identity, Ancestral Domain, and Forest Use in Palawan, the Philippines. Ph.D. dissertation, Department of Wildland Resource Science, University of California, Berkeley.
National Statistics Office (NSO)
2010   Census of the Philippines. Manila: Government Printing Office.
Novellino, Dario
1998   Sacrificing People for Trees: The Cultural Cost of Forest Conservation on Palawan Island (Philippines). Indigenous Affairs 4:5–14.
Pinchon, Ana
2011   Sea Hunters or Sea Farmers? Transitions in Chilean Fisheries. Human Organization 70(2):200–209.
Seki, Koki
2000   Wherever the Waves Shall Carry Us: Historical Development of a Visayan Fisherfolk's Livelihood Strategies. Philippine Quarterly of Culture and Society 28(2):133–157.

Sturgeon, Janet C.
2005   Border Landscapes: The Politics of Akha Land Use in China and Thailand. Seattle: University of Washington Press.
Walker, Brian, Lance Gunderson, Ann Kinzig, Carl Folke, Steve Carpenter, and Lisen Schultz
2006   A Handful of Heuristics and Some Propositions for Understanding Resilience in Social-Ecological Systems. Ecology and Society 11(1):13.
Warren, James Francis
1981   The Sulu Zone 1768–1898: The Dynamics of External Trade, Slavery, and Ethnicity in the Transformation of a Southeast Asian Maritime State. Singapore: Singapore University Press.
Watanabe, Akiko
2008   Representing Muslimness: Strategic Essentialism in a Land Dispute in Metro Manila. Philippine Studies 56:285–311.

11

Unequal in the Court of Public Opinion

Mexican and Asian Immigrant Disruptions in the United States

TAKEYUKI TSUDA

It is undeniable that certain immigrant groups have had a more disruptive impact on the host society than others. While the degree of disruption caused by a specific immigrant group can be assessed by examining its various economic, social, political, and ethnic impacts, the disruptive consequences of immigration are also a matter of public social perception. If the host society does not perceive an immigrant group as that disruptive, the amount of sociopolitical and ethnic upheaval associated with it may be mitigated and reduced. On the other hand, even if an immigrant group is not that disruptive, it may become so if the host society perceives it as disruptive, leading to various types of social conflicts. This chapter addresses the disconnect between public perceptions of immigrants and their actual disruptive impact and, therefore, is similar to those by Eder (chapter 10), Maupin (chapter 12), and Meierotto (chapter 8) in this volume.

Why Is Mexican Immigration Seen as More Disruptive Than Asian Immigration?

Although public opinion toward immigrants in the United States generally has been unfavorable, especially since the 1990s (see Espenshade and Hempstead 1996:535–541), certain immigrant groups have always been viewed more positively than others. German immigrants were favored over the Irish in the nineteenth century. In the early twentieth century, northern and western Europeans were preferred to southern and eastern European immigrants, who were seen as both culturally and racially inferior (Dinnerstein and Reimers 2009). Today, the American public clearly favors Asian over Hispanic immigrants.

It is quite remarkable that current negative public sentiment toward immigrants is directed almost entirely at Hispanics (namely, Mexicans), and Asian immigrants are rarely the target of any anti-immigrant wrath. As a result, the public's anti-immigrant sentiment is mainly an anti-Hispanic one (Cornelius 2002:174). Anti-immigrant websites and literature focus almost exclusively on Mexicans and Hispanics (when specific immigrant groups are mentioned) and blame them for a wide range of problems, including taking jobs away from Americans and lowering their wages; increasing crime and poverty; refusing to assimilate; overburdening public services, social welfare, education, and health-care systems; and taking over the American Southwest. Anti-immigrant websites, such as the Federation for American Immigration Reform (FAIR; www.fairus.org), U.S. Border Control (www.usbc.org), and www.usillegalaliens.com rarely mention Asian immigrants when they complain about the perceived negative consequences of immigration.

Likewise, prominent anti-immigrant books, such as Peter Brimelow's 1995 *Alien Nation: Common Sense About America's Immigration Disaster*, Samuel Huntington's 2004 (b; see also 2004a) *Who Are We?: The Challenges to America's National Identity*, and Patrick Buchanan's 2006 *State of Emergency: The Third World Invasion and Conquest of America* hardly ever specifically refer to Asian immigrants. When they are mentioned, it is quite brief and often in a positive[1] (or at least non-negative) context, with any negative comments usually referring to poorer Southeast Asian immigrants. Likewise, analyses of nativism and negative public opinion by scholars toward specific immigrant groups focus exclusively on Mexican and Hispanic immigrants (e.g., see Chavez 1997, 2001, 2008; Cornelius 2002; Perea 1997; cf. Johnson 1997; Sanchez 1997). Therefore, it is not surprising that local laws enacted by state legislatures in response to anti-immigrant public sentiment have also primarily been directed at Mexican immigrants, including legislation that authorizes local police to question and detain illegal immigrants, bans bilingual education and declares English the country's official language, and prohibits undocumented immigrants from obtaining driver's licenses, in-state university tuition, social services, and other public services (see Esbenshade et al. 2010:269–273; Johnson 1997; Tatalovich 1997; Waslin 2010).

Public opinion polls have shown consistently that the American public prefers Asian to Hispanic immigrants by a significant margin. According to Cornelius (2002:174), surveys since 1965 show that the public ranks Latin American immigrants (especially Mexicans) near the bottom, with Europeans at the top and Asians in the middle (see also Deaux 2006:70). Questions from Gallup polls in the 1980s and 2000s about whether the United States has too many immigrants from specific regions of the world indicate that Europeans are the most preferred, with Asians in second place and Latin Americans in last place (Gallup poll June 2006; Lapinski et al. 1997:364–365). Similar results were reported in 2000 polling data (see Alba et al. 2005:911). In a 1993 Gallup poll, which asked respondents whether immigrants from various countries benefit the United States or create problems, Mexicans received significantly lower ratings than the Chinese, Koreans, and Vietnamese, who were in turn rated lower than the Irish and Poles (Lapinski et al. 1997:366–367). Another poll showed that Americans have significantly more negative views of the characteristics of Latin American immigrants compared to Asian immigrants (Espenshade and Hempstead 1996:540).[2]

What accounts for this difference in public opinion toward these two different immigrant groups? Why are Hispanics (and specifically Mexicans), the target of virtually all anti-immigrant public opinion and sentiment? The American public has a significantly more negative view of Mexicans and Hispanics compared to Asian immigrants for a number of rather apparent reasons. The former are seen as much more socially, economically, and culturally disruptive for the host country because of their perceived size, their status as predominantly illegal and unskilled immigrant workers, and their greater cultural differences due to a perceived unwillingness to assimilate. By contrast, Asians are seen as a smaller immigrant group that is legal, highly skilled, and better-integrated in American society because of socioeconomic mobility and cultural assimilation.

However, I also argue in this chapter that such perceptions of these two immigrant groups are quite problematic and that the public understanding of the disruptive effects of Mexican immigration seems to be exaggerated. In fact, the relative absence of negative public sentiment toward Asian immigrants has partly masked the extent to which they may be more socially and economically disruptive than commonly thought. Not only are the sizes and duration of the Mexican and Asian immigrant flow roughly equivalent, the public discourse on immigrant illegality focuses exclusively on the clandestine Mexican border crosser while ignoring the substantial numbers of illegal Asian visa overstayers. In addition, highly skilled and professional Asian immigrants are more likely to have a negative economic impact on American workers than unskilled Mexican immigrants, who fill jobs that are shunned by native workers. The apparently lower rates of cultural assimilation among Mexican immigrants are a product of structural barriers more than a simple unwillingness to assimilate.

Nonetheless, such disparities in public perceptions of these two immigrant groups have had serious consequences. Negative public perceptions of Mexican immigrants have exacerbated their disruptive impact, leading to increased political controversy and ethnic tension within the host society, and the strong public backlash against them has led to a prominent nationwide anti-immigrant movement. This backlash, in turn, has had disruptive impacts on the Mexican immigrants themselves, subjecting them to considerably more ethnic prejudice and discrimination, violence, and hate crimes than Asian immigrants.[3] In addition, the federal government has cracked down on undocumented Mexican immigrants in response to the public demand that they stop illegal immigration, and numerous state governments have passed their own anti-immigrant and immigration-control measures (e.g., see Cornelius 2005; Nevins 2002; Varsanyi 2010). As a result, Mexican immigrants have suffered harsh and disruptive apprehension and deportation measures, police harassment, and the loss of basic public and social services and rights. Because Asian immigrants have not been subject to a concerted anti-immigrant backlash, in contrast to the Mexicans, they have mostly escaped its disruptive consequences.

Demographics and Duration of Immigration Flows

The simplest explanation for why Mexican immigrants are viewed as so disruptive and controversial is simply because they are by far the largest immigrant group in the United States. The Pew Research Center's 2006 poll indicates that more than half of Americans grossly overestimate the number of immigrants in the United States (by a factor of two or greater), and one of the main complaints is that the country has too many of them (especially Mexicans), as indicated on anti-immigrant websites and literature (e.g., see Brimelow 1995:ch. 2; Huntington 2004a). Studies have shown that the perceived size of an immigrant group is correlated with negative attitudes toward it (namely, a desire to impose numerical restrictions on the group; Alba et al. 2005:911; Schneider 2008).[4]

According to 2010 Census Bureau data, the number of Mexican immigrants reached 11.7 million, or 29 percent of the total U.S. immigrant population of 39.95 million. This figure is over five times the population of the second-largest immigrant group, the Chinese, which numbers only 2.17 million (the third-largest immigrant group is Filipinos, at 1.78 million). Nonetheless, although the population of immigrants from any given Asian country is comparatively small, the total number of immigrants from *all* Asian countries has now grown to 11.28 million (28 percent of the total immigrant population), which is roughly equivalent to the number of Mexican immigrants in the United States. It is only when other Spanish-speaking Latin American immigrants are added to the Mexican population that the total number of Hispanic immigrants becomes 18.8 million, or 47 percent of the total immigrant population. However, these immigrants from other Latin American countries are usually not subject to significant anti-immigrant vitriol, which is primarily directed at Mexicans.

Therefore, from a purely demographic standpoint, there is no real reason why Mexican immigration should be viewed as more disruptive than Asian immigration. Nonetheless, the American public probably overestimates the size of the Mexican immigrant population in relation to other immigrant groups, and probably relatively few are aware that it is essentially the same size as the Asian immigrant population. Also, the public is less likely to tolerate the large number of Mexican immigrants because they come from only one country, whereas Asian immigrants come from numerous different countries, each of which constitutes only a relatively small amount of the total immigrant flow.

In addition to its size, the duration and persistence of the Mexican migration flow is often mentioned by anti-immigrant writers as a major reason why they feel it threatens the United States (e.g., see Huntington 2004a:33–36). However, the Asian immigrant flow resembles the Mexican immigrant flow in duration as well. Mexican immigration to the United States began in the early twentieth century, increased considerably after the 1970s, and shows no signs of abating, because economic disparities between Mexico and the United States, as well as transborder social networks between the two countries that enable migration, will continue to persist for the foreseeable future. Asian immigration began in the mid-nineteenth century (earlier than Mexican immigration) with Chinese and Japanese immigration;[5] it also increased considerably after the 1970s and will continue to increase into the distant future, despite the continued economic development of countries such as China and India.

Mexican versus Asian Illegality

Since neither demographics nor duration fully account for why the public believes that Mexican immigration is more controversial and disruptive, we must look at other characteristics of the two migrant flows. Mexican immigration is viewed by the American public as disruptive because it mainly consists of illegal immigrants and unskilled immigrants, who are seen as having a more negative impact on the host society and its economy than Asian immigrants, who are generally regarded as legal and highly skilled/professional immigrants. In other words, the *composition* of the two migrant groups explains differences in public opinion toward them, more than their sheer size and persistence (see also Brader et al. 2008). However, these divergent public perceptions of Mexican and Asian immigrants are also problematic.

Public Attitudes toward Illegal Immigrants

Public opinion polls indicate that Americans are not necessarily intolerant toward immigration in general. Unlike Europeans, Americans do not rank immigration among the top political issues about which they are concerned. For instance, in a June 2010 Gallup poll, respondents ranked immigration seventh, after the economy, unemployment/jobs, natural-disaster relief, dissatisfaction with government, health care, and the federal deficit. Gallup polls since 2002 indicate that, generally, 52 to 67 percent of Americans believe that immigration is a good thing for the country, and only 31 to 42 percent believe that it is a bad thing for the country, although larger percentages of the public (31 to 58 percent) believe that immigration levels should be decreased.[6] Likewise, in an April 2010 CBS/New York Times poll, 49 percent of respondents felt that immigration contributes to the country and only 31 percent felt that it causes problems. At worst, public opinion toward immigration can most aptly be characterized as ambivalent (Cornelius 2002).

It is quite clear that most of the public's anti-immigrant sentiment is directed not at general or legal immigrants, but at illegal immigrants (see also Fetzer 2000:93–95, Muller 1997:115). This distinction is shown not only on nativist websites and writings,[7] but in public opinion polling data as well. According to various recent polls, 85 to 93 percent of respondents felt that illegal immigration was either a "very serious" or "somewhat serious" problem, with only a few percent indicating that is it not a problem (AP-Univision poll May 2010, CBS News poll August 2010, New York Times/

CBS News poll May 2006, Quinnipiac University poll May 2010). According to a June 2010 Gallup poll, respondents ranked illegal immigration as one of the greatest threats to the future well-being of the United States, after the federal debt, unemployment, terrorism, and health-care costs, with 64 percent claiming that it is an "extremely/very serious" threat.[8]

Undocumented immigrants are perceived as very disruptive for American society because the public greatly overestimates their number. Although the estimated 11.2 million unauthorized immigrants[9] comprise only 28 percent of the total U.S. immigration population of close to 40 million, 44 percent of Americans believe that *most* immigrants in the United States are illegal (Pew Research Center poll 2006) and another eight percent believe that half of all immigrants are illegal.[10] In a 2007 Arizona State University (ASU) Institute for Social Science Research (ISSR) poll, 84 percent of respondents living in the Southwest greatly overestimated the percentage of *total residents* in their state who are undocumented immigrants. In fact, 52 percent of respondents believed that 25 percent or more of their state's population consisted of illegal immigrants (in Arizona, for example, it is only six percent). A May 2010 CNN/Opinion Research Corporation poll shows that 76 percent of respondents want the number of illegal immigrants reduced (in contrast to only 31 to 58 percent of people who feel that immigration levels in general should be reduced, as noted previously). Over three quarters of the American public believe that the country is not doing enough to keep illegal immigrants from entering (ABC News/Washington Post poll April 2007, April 2009, June 2010), and a majority want more fences to be built and more U.S. Border Patrol and National Guard deployed at the US-Mexican border (ABC News/Washington Post poll June 2010; CNN/Opinion Research Corporation poll July 2010; Rasmussen poll March 2010, May 2010). Fifty-eight to 70 percent of Americans favor laws such as Arizona's SB 1070 that require local police to question and detain individuals that they suspect of being in the country illegally (Pew Research Center poll 2010; Rasmussen poll April 2010; Washington Post/ABC poll June 2010).

Undocumented immigrants are the target of the public's wrath not only because they are perceived as lawbreakers who have violated the country's immigration laws and national sovereignty, but because they are often perceived as a disruptive burden and threat to the host society (see also Espenshade and Calhoun 1993; Nevins 2002:11, 114). A majority of the American public believes that undocumented immigrants hurt American society (AP-Univision poll May 2010; Ipsos/McClatchy poll May 2010). Although the public generally believes that they take low-paying jobs that Americans do not want (AP-Univision poll May 2010; Gallup Poll June 2008), 53 percent are "very concerned" that they cause employers to pay lower wages to American workers (Gallup poll May 2010).[11] Most of the public also feels that undocumented immigrants are an economic burden on taxpayers because they use government services like public education and health care (Rasmussen poll March 2010; Gallup poll June 2010). Sixty-one percent of the public believes that there would be less poverty in the country if immigration laws were enforced (Rasmussen poll April 2011), and 43 percent cite terrorism and increased crime as their biggest concerns about illegal immigration (Pew Research Center poll 2006). According to a Southwest poll conducted by the ASU ISSR in 2007, 30 percent of respondents felt that undocumented immigrants commit more crimes than legal immigrants.

The American public undoubtedly views Mexican immigrants as more disruptive than Asian immigrants because they are predominantly seen as illegal immigrants, whereas Asians are not. On anti-immigrant websites and books, illegal immigration is automatically equated with Mexican or Hispanic immigration (e.g., see Brimelow 1995; Buchanan 2006; Huntington 2004b; www.fairus.org; www.usbc.org; www.usillegalaliens.com). As Samuel Huntington (2004a:34) claims, "Illegal entry into the United States is overwhelmingly a post-1965 and Mexican phenomenon." It is also quite apparent that the various state laws cracking down on illegal immigration, such as Arizona's SB 1070, are directed against Mexican and Latino immigrants and not illegal Asian immigrants. As Adalberto Aguirre (2004) notes, Asian immigrants are never racially profiled as potential illegal immigrants, whereas the practice is quite common among Mexican immigrants and even Mexican Americans (see also Waslin 2010:106).

Because the public overestimates the number of illegal immigrants in general and believes that most of them are Mexican, the perception of the number of unauthorized Mexican immigrants and their disruptive impact is exaggerated. Mexicans are indeed a majority (58 percent) of the unauthorized immigrant population of 11.2 million (Passel and Cohn 2011:11). However, the approximately 6.5 million undocumented Mexican immigrants comprise only 16 percent of the total immigrant population in the United States. Although the public undoubtedly believes that the vast majority of Mexican immigrants are in the United States illegally, only 55 percent of them are actually undocumented, which means that 45 percent of them are legal immigrants.

Meanwhile, the American public generally ignores the illegal Asian immigrant population, despite the fact that it is substantial. There are an estimated 1.3 million unauthorized Asian immigrants, which is 11 percent of the total illegal immigrant population in the United States (Passel and Cohn 2011:11). In fact, four of the top ten countries that send undocumented immigrants to the United States are Asian (Philippines, India, Korea, and China; Hoefer et al. 2010).

The Social Construction of Immigrant Illegality

In addition to their smaller numbers, unauthorized Asian immigrants are not regarded as disruptive by the public because of the way in which immigrant illegality is socially constructed. It is important to remember that the illegal immigrant is not simply an official and objective legal status. It is mainly a social construct based on prevailing public images and discourses of what the typical illegal immigrant looks like, which leads to the greater illegalization of certain types of unauthorized immigrants over others.

In the United States, the dominant and quintessential public image of the illegal immigrant is the Mexican who clandestinely crossed the U.S.-Mexican border, a social construction that emerged in the first half of the twentieth century and has recently become stronger in the public consciousness (Chavez 2008:24–25; Nevins 2002:111–118). Unauthorized immigrants who fit this racialized profile of the Latino border crosser are viewed by the public as disruptive and forced to bear the full brunt of their illegality. As a result, they are constantly subject to the state's immigration enforcement efforts (apprehension at the border, employer raids and deportation, interrogation and detention by local law enforcement officers, etc.).

By contrast, unauthorized immigrants who do not conform to this dominant image of illegality tend to escape public surveillance and state enforcement, including the estimated 500,000 illegal European and Canadian immigrants who constitute four percent of the total unauthorized immigrant population (Passel and Cohn 2011:11) and the approximately 1.3 million illegal Asian immigrants. Not only do these immigrants not fit the racial profile of Latino illegality, they also differ from the prevalent image of the illegal border crosser. Instead, the vast majority of them are visa overstayers who enter the United States legally with short-term (usually tourist) visas but remain and work illegally in the country after their visas expire. Although the public believes that most illegal immigrants are clandestine border crossers, they are estimated to make up only 55 percent of the total unauthorized immigrant population, with the remaining 45 percent consisting of visa overstayers (Pew Hispanic Center Fact Sheet, May 22, 2006, http://pewhispanic.org/files/factsheets/19.pdf). Not surprisingly, only about 16 percent of undocumented Mexican immigrants are visa overstayers, whereas an estimated 91 percent of unauthorized immigrants from countries outside of Mexico and Central America overstay their visas (Pew Hispanic Center Fact Sheet, May 22, 2006).

Despite the fact that almost half of all illegal immigrants are visa overstayers, they are hardly noticed by the public and mass media, whose attention is focused on the hordes of Mexicans thought to be swarming across the US-Mexican border. For instance, of the 68,300 articles published in the *New York Times* since 1990 about illegal immigration in the United States, only 286 of them refer to visa overstayers. Similar results are found on other newspaper websites. Public opinion polls often contain questions about various means to reduce illegal immigration (more border patrol agents, more border fences and fortifications, tougher employer sanctions, a database of eligible workers, national or employment ID cards, mass deportation, etc.), but never mention cracking down on visa overstayers. Neither do anti-immigrant websites or nativist writings about illegal immigration, which only complain about the out-of-control U.S.-Mexican border.[12] In addition to the public's general lack of knowledge about illegal visa overstayers, they are not as controversial as the Mexican border crosser because they initially met the criteria for legal entry into the United States.

Since visa overstayers simply are not part of the public consciousness about immigrant illegality and therefore are not seen as disruptive, the government makes no serious effort to apprehend and deport them, in contrast to the billions of dollars it spends annually on apprehending illegal Mexican immigrants (both at the southern border and those residing in the United States). For instance, in 2004, the U.S. Border Patrol and Immigration and Customs Enforcement apprehended 1,142,807 undocumented Mexican immigrants (Office of Immigration Statistics 2004:156), whereas only 671 total visa overstayers were apprehended by the government (and only 87 of them were actually deported [Department of Homeland Security 2005:17]). In fact, as of 2011, the U.S. government had yet to implement a reliable system to track visa overstayers and had no way of determining whether foreign nationals admitted on temporary visas actually leave the country.

Therefore, the United States has a two-tiered system of illegality in which the clandestine Mexican border crosser is illegalized to a greater extent than the Asian (or white European/Canadian) visa overstayer and seen as much more disruptive. While it is clear that illegality is produced by immigration law (e.g., De Genova 2002: 423–431), its actual social consequences depend on prevailing public images and stereotypes about the typical illegal immigrant. Although undocumented Mexican border crossers are actually only about 14 percent of the total immigrant population, because they epitomize immigrant illegality in the public mind, they have been subject to a disproportionate amount of public controversy and ire and forced to suffer the full disruptive consequences of their illegality. Meanwhile, Asian visa overstayers are hardly noticed by the public and are left alone by the government, although they are just as illegal as Mexican border crossers.

Unskilled versus Skilled Immigrants

The public also perceives Mexican immigrants as disruptive because they are seen as predominantly poor, less educated, and unskilled immigrant workers who have a negative impact on the economy. By contrast, Asian immigrants are seen as highly skilled/professional immigrants who contribute their knowledge and skills to the economy and increase America's technological and scientific competitiveness. According to the U.S. Census Bureau's 2010 American Community Survey, only 20 percent of Mexican immigrants are doing management, business, science, and sales/office jobs, in contrast to 71 percent of East Asian immigrants and 59 percent of Southeast Asian immigrants. These differences show how the composition of the Mexican and Asian immigrant flows has a strong influence on public perceptions of their respective disruptive impact.

The strong public preference for highly skilled over unskilled immigrants is quite apparent in opinion polls (see also Brader et al. 2008). According to one survey, more than 60 percent of respondents were opposed to increases in low-skilled immigrants, whereas only 40 percent were opposed to increases in highly skilled immigrants, and over 35 percent actually approved of such increases (Hainmueller and Hiscox 2010:62). In a Southwest poll conducted by the ASU ISSR in 2007, 71 percent of respondents felt that highly skilled and professional immigrants bring much-needed skills and expertise and help fill labor shortages in knowledge industries, and 64 percent felt that they help maintain U.S. leadership in science and technology. Highly skilled immigrants are also seen as making greater fiscal contributions to the government (through taxes) than they consume in government services (Hainmueller and Hiscox 2010:79). Although the U.S. government has long imposed restrictions on unskilled immigrants, it has welcomed highly skilled, non-Latino immigrants (Cornelius 2002:166; Usdansky and Espenshade 2001).

Asian immigrants definitely benefit from such positive public attitudes toward highly skilled and professional immigrants. In the ASU ISSR poll, 65 percent of respondents approved of highly skilled immigration from developing Asian countries. According to one survey, 71 percent of white Americans had a favorable opinion of the contributions of skilled Asian immigrants (He 2002:13). In fact, Hispanic Americans had more positive perceptions of the contributions of skilled Asian immigrants than skilled European immigrants.

It is clear that, overall, Asian immigrants have considerably higher educational and socioeconomic status compared to Mexican immigrants. According to the U.S. Census Bureau's 2010 American Community Survey, 28 percent of Asian immigrants over 25 years of age have bachelor's degrees, compared to only 3.9 percent of Mexican immigrants, and 20 percent of them have graduate or professional degrees, compared to only 1.4 percent of their Mexican counterparts. Likewise, median household income for Asian immigrants is $63,777, whereas it is only $35,254 for Mexicans. The relatively high socioeconomic status of Asian immigrants and the resulting social mobility of their Asian American descendants have led to the stereotype that they are overachieving, hardworking model minorities who are academically and socioeconomically successful. By contrast, Mexican immigrants experience low rates of economic mobility over time, a trend that persists among their Mexican American descendants (e.g., see Borjas and Katz 2007; Telles and Ortiz 2008; Vigdor 2008). The poverty rate among Mexican immigrants is 28 percent, compared to 14 percent for their Asian counterparts.

Undoubtedly, the public views poor, less educated, and unskilled Mexican immigrants as more economically disruptive than wealthier, well-educated Asian immigrants because they increase overall poverty, overburden social welfare and public services, and take jobs away from American workers. However, the general assumption that Mexican immigrants are a fiscal burden to the U.S. government is problematic. Although a National Research Council study found that low-skill immigrants from Latin America in California cost more in terms of public benefits and services than they contributed to the federal government in taxes in 1994–1995 (Smith and Edmonston 1997:293), the long-term fiscal impact of immigrants in general (most of whom are unskilled) is positive (see also Lee and Miller 2000). Over their lifetimes, immigrant households pay $80,000 more in taxes than they receive in government benefits and services (Smith and Edmonston 1997:351).[13] In fact, undocumented immigrants contribute $7 billion in Social Security payroll taxes each year, even though they cannot claim the benefits (Capps and Fix 2005).

In addition, it is important to remember that not all Asian immigrants are socioeconomically successful model minorities. In contrast to East Asian immigrants, substantially fewer Southeast Asian immigrants from Vietnam, Laos, and Cambodia (who initially came to the United States as refugees from poorer, sometimes peasant backgrounds) are in high-skill or white-collar jobs. They have significantly lower education rates and median household incomes (US Census Bureau's American Community Survey 2010) and high rates of poverty and welfare usage (Camarota 2007:21). As a result, some of them have become welfare dependent.

Although the public often perceives unskilled Mexican immigrants as taking jobs away from native workers and lowering their wages, economists generally agree that immigrants actually have little to no impact on the wages and employment of American workers (Card 2005; Fix and Passel 1994:47–49; Smith and Edmonston 1997:236–237; cf. Borjas 2005),[14] undoubtedly because most immigrants fill manual, low-wage jobs at the bottom of a segmented labor market that Americans do not want to perform. One study shows that even if undocumented immigrants were eliminated from the workforce, unemployed native workers (who have higher educational and skill levels) would simply not take their jobs (Jaeger 2006). In fact, opinion polls indicate that the public itself is not sure whether unskilled immigrants have a disruptive impact on the American labor market. When polls ask respondents whether immigrants take jobs away from Americans, a strong majority of respondents say that they do (see Lapinski et al. 1997:370).[15] However, when respondents are asked if immigrants take jobs Americans *don't want* or take jobs away from Americans, a majority feel that they take jobs Americans don't want (see Lapinski et al. 1997:371; Pew Research Center March 2006).

In contrast to unskilled immigrants, the public generally approves of highly skilled immigrants and does not seem to perceive them as the source of much labor market disruption (see Hainmueller and Hiscox 2010). In fact, only 35 percent of respondents in the ASU ISSR poll expressed concern that highly skilled and professional immigrants take jobs away from skilled American workers. As noted previously, only a minority of respondents in one survey opposed increases in skilled immigrants and over one third was actually supportive (Hainmueller and Hiscox 2010:62). However, in an October 2011 Washington Post/Bloomberg News poll, 59 percent of respondents were opposed to increasing the number of visas for highly skilled immigrant workers because U.S. companies claim that they cannot find enough highly skilled American workers. But even in this poll, 31 percent supported increases in the number of highly skilled immigrants.

Although it is quite clear that unskilled immigrant workers performing undesirable, low-paying jobs do not compete with American workers, highly skilled immigrants are hired for well-paid, high-tech, IT, and professional jobs that native workers also desire. As a result, the possibility that such immigrants compete with American workers and have a disruptive impact on their employment prospects and wages is stronger. Highly skilled immigrant workers generally earn less than native highly skilled workers because they are often hired on temporary H-1B visas and must stay with the same employer if they wish to obtain permanent residence, making them more willing to endure lower wages and poorer working conditions. They are also less likely to receive full benefit packages (Gurcak et al. 2001; Usdansky and Espenshade 2001). As a result, U.S. high-tech employers may be more willing to hire them over native workers, causing them to displace American high-tech workers. Although high-tech firms constantly claim that they are forced to hire immigrants because there is a shortage of qualified American IT workers (and not because immigrants are cheaper to employ), many economists are skeptical, because there is little evidence of upward pressures on wages that such shortages would cause (Cornelius and Espenshade 2001:8–9; Lowell 2001:149). In fact, there is evidence that highly skilled immigrant workers are depressing wages for native IT workers, even though the effect seems relatively small (Borjas 2005; Gurcak et al. 2001:61–62). The general conclusion seems to be that some harm is being done to American workers (Gurcak et al. 2001:61–62). As a result, although general public opinion is favorable toward highly skilled and professional immigrants, native high-tech workers and those with graduate degrees are less supportive and are more likely to view them as displacing American workers (He 2002:13).

Ethnic Differences and Cultural Assimilation

The last factor that must always be considered when assessing the potentially disruptive impact of immigrants is ethnicity. Immigrants who are more ethnically different from the majority host population are generally considered to be more disruptive and threatening than those who are similar (see also Deaux 2006:76; Sniderman et al. 2004). This perception is one reason why host governments in other countries have had ethnic preference policies that prioritize immigrants who are ethnically related to the host population, usually drawing from the country's pool of diasporic descendants born abroad (Joppke 2005; Tsuda 2009).

It is quite apparent that American anti-immigrant sentiment is not only based on the perceived negative economic and fiscal consequences of immigration but its ethnically disruptive impact as well (see Cornelius 2002). In fact, Samuel Huntington (2004a), the most prominent anti-immigrant scholar, argues that Americans should be more concerned about the negative cultural consequences of immigration than its economic costs and warns that the ethnic differences of immigrants threaten the core Anglo-Protestant culture that is the foundation of the American nation. In fact, nativist feelings are often a type of cultural nationalism based on an intense opposition to the cultural foreignness and ethnic differences of immigrants (e.g., see Nevins 2002:97; Sanchez 1997:1020). As a result, the perceived cultural threat of particular immigrant groups can be a more significant determinant of public opinion than their presumed disruptive impact on the economy or public safety (Fetzer 2000:107; Schneider 2007; Sniderman et al. 2004). In fact, public opinion polls from the Pew Research Center from 2004 to 2010 show that close to half of Americans believe that growing numbers of immigrants threaten traditional American customs and values. One third of the respondents to a 1986 opinion poll cited the negative cultural traits of immigrants as the biggest problem associated with immigration (Espenshade and Hempstead 1996:540).

From the perspective of ethnicity, one would expect Mexican immigrants to be perceived as less controversial and disruptive than Asian immigrants. Racially, most Mexicans are mestizos, a mixture of Spanish and indigenous ancestry, and are therefore technically closer to majority white Americans of European descent than Asian immigrants. Mexicans are also culturally more similar to mainstream Americans than Asians. Not only do both Mexicans and white Americans come from countries that were initially colonized by Europeans, they share a similar religious background (Christianity/Catholicism), and Spanish as a European language is closer to English than Asian languages. In fact, in the latter half of the nineteenth century, Mexicans living in the southwestern United States who were incorporated into the country after the Mexican-American War were favored and treated much better than Chinese immigrants, because they were perceived as much more ethnically similar to European Americans. As a result, they were exempted from the anti-miscegenation laws of the time and were classified as "white" for legal purposes in California (Almaguer 1994).

Despite their apparently greater racial and cultural similarities to Americans, Mexican immigrants today are no longer ethnically favored compared to Asian immigrants. Because of their lower immigrant and often undocumented status, they are often ethnically stereotyped as poor, uneducated, and illegal, as well as dirty, noisy, and lazy—cultural characteristics that are disapproved as not compatible with American values and therefore disruptive. In fact, some nativist websites and writers portray Mexicans as culturally prone to crime, welfare dependence, mistreatment and violence against women, and illegitimate births (e.g., Brimelow 1995; www.usillegalaliens.com). In general, immigrant groups like Mexicans that are perceived to be more demographically, economically, and socially threatening will be subject to more negative ethnic stereotyping (see, for example, Stephan et al. 1999) and thus be seen as more culturally disruptive (see also Eder, chapter 10, for another example). By contrast, because of their legal and higher socioeconomic status, Asian immigrants are often ethnically stereotyped in positive ways as hardworking, intelligent, socially mobile, and law-abiding model minorities. Although some of these images are based on global ethnic stereotypes about Asians, they are generally regarded as desirable cultural qualities that are similar to those expected of model American citizens (e.g., see Ong 1996).

Public perceptions of the culturally disruptive nature of immigrants also depend heavily on their level of cultural assimilation. Regardless of their actual cultural differences, immigrants who assimilate and become similar to the host society will be regarded as much less disruptive than those who do not and remain culturally different. In a 2006 Center for Immigration Studies poll, the failure of immigrants to assimilate to American culture was cited by respondents as the second-biggest concern about immigration (the first was the burden immigrants place on taxpayers). A March 2006 Pew Research Center poll found that 44 percent of Americans felt that immigrants today are less willing to adapt to American customs, compared to immigrants from the early 1900s, and 58 percent felt that immigrants do not learn English fast enough. Close to 50 percent said that immigrants "keep to themselves and don't try to fit in."

The primary reason that Mexicans are seen as culturally more disruptive than Asian immigrants is because they are regarded as immigrants who do not (or refuse to) assimilate. Therefore, even though they may share a European colonial cultural legacy with Americans, their apparent unwillingness to assimilate culturally makes them appear more ethnically different than Asians and therefore a greater disruptive cultural threat and target for public hostility. This perception is exacerbated by the excessively large number of Mexicans that the public believes resides in the United States (although their population is roughly equivalent to that of Asian immigrants, as noted earlier). According to Samuel Huntington (2004a), Latinos are a major threat to American culture and national unity because of their large numbers and their failure to assimilate.

Not only are Mexican immigrants of lower socioeconomic status than Asian immigrants, and experience less social mobility, they seem to show lower rates of cultural assimilation over time, which is usually measured by the level of English proficiency (see, e.g., Myers and Pitkin 2010:18). U.S. Census Bureau statistics (2010 American Community Survey) indicate that 72 percent of Mexican immigrants speak English less than very well, whereas this is the case for only 47 percent of Asians. Eleven percent of Asian immigrant households speak only English at home, in contrast to 3.2 percent of Mexican immigrant households. In fact, U.S.-born Mexican American descendants also seem to retain their native language much more than Asian Americans. Their cultural assimilation is gradual over the generations and slower than it is for European Americans (Telles and Ortiz 2008:16, 187).

Nonetheless, it is quite difficult to make generalizations about the relative rates of cultural assimilation of different immigrant groups. With the exception of language proficiency, cultural assimilation is extremely difficult to measure (compared to socioeconomic, educational, or civic assimilation) since it involves defining the normative cultural characteristics of both immigrant and majority host cultures, which cannot be done without resorting to highly problematic and simplistic stereotypes. As a result, in addition to language, indices such as intermarriage rates and ethnic identification are often used to assess levels of cultural assimilation.

According to the assimilation indices used in one study (Vigdor 2008), Asian immigrants show high levels of economic and civic assimilation, but Chinese and Indian immigrants were actually lower on cultural assimilation than Mexicans (although Korean, Filipino, and Vietnamese immigrants were higher). In fact, although Mexican immigrants had very low rates of economic and civic assimilation, their rates of cultural assimilation were comparable to other immigrant groups. Another study (Wong-Rieger and Quintana 1987) found that Southeast Asian immigrants were less culturally assimilated than Hispanics and had a stronger ethnic identification and social orientation.

Even if Mexican immigrants are indeed less culturally assimilated than Asian immigrants, it is important to remember that this situation is not the result of their sheer refusal to assimilate, but structural barriers that they often cannot control. Most Mexican immigrants work in unskilled jobs where their coworkers are primarily other Mexicans, and they tend to live in poorer immigrant enclave communities where they interact mainly with compatriots in Spanish and do not have much interaction with mainstream Americans. Their children also grow up in these immigrant neighborhoods and are often primarily exposed to other Latino children in local schools. Also, because Mexican immigrants are less educated, perform low-paid jobs at the bottom of the U.S. labor market, and face significant discrimination, it is more difficult for them to become socioeconomically mobile and enter mainstream American society. By contrast, Asian immigrants tend to be more culturally assimilated because of their greater exposure to mainstream American society and culture. A majority of them perform highly skilled and professional jobs with other Americans and live primarily in middle-class suburban neighborhoods instead of in isolated immigrant enclaves. A number of them are highly educated and already proficient in English when they arrive in the United States.

Although differential rates of immigrant assimilation are difficult to gauge, and the reasons can mainly be attributed to larger structural forces in society rather than a simple unwillingness to assimilate, Mexicans are often stereotyped by the public as an unassimilated immigrant group that is unwilling or unable to give up its foreign culture and language and become part of the national community (Cornelius 2002:177–179; Chavez 2008:2, 22). Because of their large numbers and regional concentration in the Southwest, they are seen as a threat to American cultural identity and national unity that can ultimately fragment the nation into separate ethnic regions. Such exaggerated perceptions of the culturally disruptive impact of Mexican immigration are quite prevalent on nativist websites and literature. Not only are Mexicans seen as culturally dividing the American nation, they are literally portrayed as invading and reconquering the American Southwest and creating a politically and culturally separate Hispanic region (Chavez 2008:26–40; see, for example, Brimelow 1995:194–195, 218–219; Buchanan 2006; Huntington 2004a, 2004b).

Conclusion: From Immigrant Disruption to Transformation?

When it comes to their disruptive impact, not all immigrant groups are equal in the court of public opinion. Certain immigrant groups are negatively stereotyped as a threat to the host society because of their perceived size, composition, and cultural differences, whereas others seem to escape public controversy and hostility. Mexicans are widely regarded as much more disruptive than Asians because they are seen as an excessively large group of illegal, unskilled immigrants who retain their ethnic differences instead of culturally assimilating. Therefore, in addition to infringing on the country's territorial sovereignty, Mexicans are more likely to be seen as increasing poverty and crime, becoming a public fiscal burden, having an adverse effect on native workers, and threatening the cultural integrity of the nation. By contrast, Asian immigrants are perceived as legal, highly skilled, and professional immigrants who not only contribute their human capital to the American economy but are model minorities who are more culturally compatible with middle-class American values.

There is often a disconnect between the degree of disruption an immigrant group actually causes and the host society's perception of its disruptive impact. Although the size and duration of the Mexican and Asian immigrant flows are roughly equivalent, it is the Mexicans who are "invading" the United States. Because unauthorized Asian immigrants enter legally and simply overstay their visas, their disruptive illegality is ignored by the public and government officials, whereas the illegality of the "clandestine" Mexican border crosser is made highly visible and subject to public backlashes and harsh government enforcement. Although Asian immigrant engineers and IT workers are much more likely to economically compete with American workers, it is the unskilled Mexican gardener or janitor who is "taking our jobs," lowering American wages, and overburdening social welfare systems and public services. Likewise, the public also seems to have an exaggerated perception of the disruptive cultural consequences of Mexican migration.

Regardless of their distorted nature, such public perceptions and attitudes must be taken into account when assessing the relative amount of disruption caused by different immigrant groups. Even though a particular immigrant group may not be that disruptive, if the public feels threatened by it, the disruptive impact of the group is likely to be magnified, resulting in ethnic tension, political controversy, and anti-immigrant public backlashes. Attitudes toward immigration in this sense become a self-fulfilling prophecy. If the public is convinced that an immigrant group is disruptive, it will indeed become so because of the negative public response to it. Negative public opinion is also disruptive for the immigrant group itself, as it becomes the target of public hostility and racism and is subject to harsh government enforcement measures and crackdowns.

Even in a multiethnic country like the United States that ostensibly cherishes diversity and difference, immigrant groups seem to be judged by whether they fit dominant conceptions of the American nation. It may be true that inclusion in the national community is no longer restricted to one racial or ethnic group. However, in the popular imagination, mainstream America consists of educated, English-speaking, economically self-sufficient, and law-abiding citizens living in middle-class suburban communities. Despite their foreign origins and ethnic differences, Asian immigrants appear to share such social qualities that are approved by the American public and are therefore not regarded as socially disruptive. Because Mexican immigrants to not fit this dominant narrative of the American nation, their differences are perceived as a social threat, and the important contributions that they make to the United States are not sufficiently recognized. Therefore, the amount of public controversy generated by specific immigrant groups reveals much about a country's national self-image.

Although immigrant groups like Mexicans that introduce significant ethnic, cultural, and social differences to the host country may initially be regarded as disruptive to the prevailing status quo, they are also more likely to have a transformative impact over time. In other words, their differences may eventually be incorporated as part of the accustomed activities of the host society, leading to a new and stable status quo. By contrast, immigrant groups that are regarded as more similar and compatible with American cultural standards and lifestyles, such as Asians, may be seen as less disruptive, but they are also less likely to be transformative over time and, instead, simply reinforce the status quo.

Undoubtedly, it is difficult to predict the long-term impact of an immigrant group. However, the history of immigration to the United States contains examples of many immigrant groups that were initially viewed as quite disruptive but eventually became incorporated into the mainstream fabric of a transformed American society. The Irish, who arrived in large numbers in the nineteenth century, were initially seen as both culturally disruptive, because they were Catholics and not Anglo Protestants, and socially disruptive because of their poverty, lack of education, and proclivity for fighting and urban unrest. The massive waves of southern and eastern European immigrants in the late nineteenth and early twentieth centuries were also perceived as very disruptive, not only because of their cultural differences and low socioeconomic status but also because they were not seen as really white, but members of an inferior, darker race. Nonetheless, these initially disruptive immigrant groups eventually became incorporated into majority white American society. This is partly because they became culturally assimilated and socioeconomically mobile over time, joining the American middle class and reinforcing the prevailing status quo. However, they also transformed mainstream American society in the process by expanding its religious and racial boundaries, thereby producing a new status quo. As a result, mainstream American religion today includes Catholicism and not just Protestantism, and the majority white ethnic group includes those of southern and eastern European (and Jewish) descent and not just Anglos.

Like their European immigrant predecessors, Mexican immigrants may also transform our understandings of mainstream American society in the future. Their descendants will eventually become assimilated to mainstream American culture and a number of them will become upwardly mobile, becoming part of the middle class. At the same time, they may also transform the racial boundaries of majority American society to include those of darker complexion and not simply those who are considered "white." In addition, it is becoming increasing clear that not all Mexican Americans are joining the American middle class, and that they are experiencing lower rates of socioeconomic mobility across the generations (Telles and Ortiz 2008), especially compared to Asian Americans. Some have become trapped in a cycle of poverty from one generation to the next. This situation, however, is reflective of a broader change in American society, which is increasingly characterized by socioeconomic inequality between rich and poor. As a result, Mexican immigration may be contributing to an eventual transformation of America from a more egalitarian society where the majority considers itself middle class to a much more socioeconomically polarized society where widening gaps between rich and poor become the new norm. Although such an eventual outcome may be less desirable, transformations do not always entail positive changes. In this manner, today's disruptive immigrants can eventually become part of tomorrow's status quo.

Notes

1. For example, Buchanan (2006) notes that Asians have a lower rate of welfare use and crime than whites, excel academically, and attain high educational levels.

2. Only one polling organization (the Pew Research Center 2007) has shown that the public's view of Latin American immigrants is positive and not significantly different from Asians. However, their 2006 poll indicates that Americans have a much more favorable view of Asian than Latin American immigrants in terms of work ethic, school achievement, welfare use, and crime rates.

3. According to a 2007 Gallup poll, 72 percent of Americans are satisfied with the treatment of Asian minorities in the United States, whereas only 57 percent are satisfied with the treatment of Hispanics.

4. However, at the local community or municipal level, larger concentrations of immigrants do not necessarily produce stronger anti-immigrant attitudes (Hood and Morris 1997), except when local economic conditions are poor (Hjerm 2009). This may be because actual contact with immigrants in local communities reduces majority prejudice toward them (Hood and Morris 1997:315).

5. There was also limited Filipino and Indian immigration to the United States at this time.

6. See http://www.gallup.com/poll/141560/Amid-Immigration-Debate-Americans-Views-Ease-Slightly.aspx.

7. There are some nativist organizations and writers, such as the Federation for American Immigration Reform and Peter Brimelow (1995:4–5), who wish to reduce both legal and illegal immigration.

8. Illegal immigration essentially was tied with the decision to have U.S. troops in Iraq/Afghanistan (with 65 percent claiming it was an extremely/very serious threat). However, this issue has likely receded in importance since June 2010.

9. This March 2010 estimate is from the Pew Hispanic Center (2011), which provides one of the most reliable estimates of the unauthorized immigrant population.

10. In 1993, 68 percent of Americans thought that most immigrants were illegal (Lapinski et al. 1997).

11. The few labor market studies of undocumented immigrants that have been conducted find that they have no discernible effect on native workers and may actually increase labor market opportunities (Fix and Passel 1994).

12. Among all the anti-immigrant books and websites that I perused, only the FAIR website explicitly mentions visa overstayers.

13. This figure includes the taxes that the descendants of immigrants in these households pay over their lifetimes (since they make a significant positive contribution to the fiscal impact for immigrants).

14. There is some evidence that immigrants may hurt the employment of less skilled native workers, especially in areas where they are highly concentrated.

15. Most respondents in these polls are most likely assuming that "immigrants" refers to unskilled immigrants, who make up the majority of the immigrant populace and is the dominant image most people have when they think of immigrants.

References Cited

Aguirre Jr., Adalberto
2004   Profiling Mexican American Identity: Issues and Concerns. American Behavioral Scientist 47(7):928–942.
Alba, Richard, Rubén G. Rumbaut, and Karen Marotz
2005   A Distorted Nation: Perceptions of Racial/Ethnic Group Sizes and Attitudes Toward Immigrants and Other Minorities. Social Forces 84(2):901–919.
Almaguer, Tomás
1994   Racial Fault Lines: The Historial Origins of White Supremacy in California. Berkeley: University of California Press.
Borjas, George J.
2005   The Labor-Market Impact of High-Skill Immigration. The American Economic Review 95(2):56–60.
Borjas, George J., and Lawrence F. Katz
2007   The Evolution of the Mexican-Born Workforce in the United States. In Mexican Immigration to the United States. George Borjas, ed. Pp. 13–55. Chicago: University of Chicago Press.
Brader, Ted, Nicholas A. Valentino, and Elizabeth Suhay
2008   What Triggers Public Opposition to Immigration? Anxiety, Group Cues, and Immigration Threat. American Journal of Political Science 52(4):959–978.
Brimelow, Peter
1995   Alien Nation: Common Sense About America's Immigration Disaster. New York: Random House.
Buchanan, Patrick J.
2006   State of Emergency: The Third World Invasion and Conquest of America. New York: St. Martin's Press.
Camarota, Steven A.
2007   Immigrants in the United States, 2007: A Profile of America's Foreign-Born Population. Center for Immigration Studies, http://www.cis.org/articles/2007/back1007.pdf, accessed June 14, 2014.
Capps, Randolph, and Michael E. Fix
2005   Undocumented Immigrants: Myths and Reality. The Urban Institute, http://www.urban.org/publications/900898.html, accessed June 14, 2014.
Card, David
2005   Is the New Immigration Really So Bad? The Economic Journal 115(507):F300–F323.
Chavez, Leo R.
1997   Immigration Reform and Nativism: The Nationalist Response to the Transnationalist Challenge. In Immigrants Out! The New Nativism and the Anti-Immigrant Impulse in the United States. Juan F. Perea, ed. Pp. 61–77. New York: New York University Press.
2001   Covering Immigration: Popular Images and the Politics of the Nation. Berkeley: University of California Press.

2008   The Latino Threat: Constructing Immigrants, Citizens, and the Nation. Stanford, CA: Stanford University Press.

Cornelius, Wayne A.

2002   Ambivalent Reception: Mass Public Responses to the "New" Latino Immigration. *In* Latinos: Remaking America. Marcelo M. Suárez-Orozco and Mariela Páez, eds. Pp.165–189. Berkeley: University of California Press.

2005   Controlling 'Unwanted' Immigration: Lessons from the United States, 1993–2004. Journal of Ethnic and Migration Studies 31(4):775–794.

Cornelius, Wayne A. and Thomas J. Espenshade

2001   The International Migration of the Highly Skilled: 'High-Tech *Braceros*' in the Global Labor Market. *In* The International Migration of the Highly Skilled: Demand, Supply, and Development Consequences in Sending and Receiving Countries. Wayne A. Cornelius, Thomas J. Espenshade, and Idean Salehyan, eds. Pp. 3–19. La Jolla, CA: Center for Comparative Immigration Studies, University of California, San Diego.

Deaux, Kay

2006   To Be an Immigrant. New York: Russell Sage Foundation.

De Genova, Nicholas P.

2002   Migrant "Illegality" and Deportability in Everyday Life. Annual Review of Anthropology 31:419–447.

Department of Homeland Security, Office of the Inspector General

2005   Review of the Immigration and Customs Enforcement's Compliance Enforcement Unit. OIG-05-50. Washington, D.C.: Office of Inspections and Special Reviews. http://www.hsdl.org/?view&did=462216, accessed June 14, 2014.

Dinnerstein, Leonard, and David M. Reimers

2009   Ethnic Americans: A History of Immigration. New York: Columbia University Press.

Esbenshade, Jill, Benjamin Wright, Paul Cortopassi, Arthur Reed, and Jerry Flores

2010   The "Law and Order" Foundation of Local Ordinances: A Four-Locale Study. *In* Taking Local Control: Immigration Policy Activism in U.S. Cities and States. Monica W. Varsanyi, ed. Pp. 255–274. Stanford, CA: Stanford University Press.

Espenshade, Thomas J., and Charles A. Calhoun

1993   An Analysis of Public Opinion Toward Undocumented Immigration. Population Research and Policy Review 12(3):189–224.

Espenshade, Thomas J., and Katherine Hempstead

1996   Contemporary American Attitudes Toward U.S. Immigration. International Migration Review 30(2):535–570.

Fetzer, Joel S.

2000   Public Attitudes Toward Immigration in the United States, France, and Germany. Cambridge: Cambridge University Press.

Fix, Michael, and Jeffrey S. Passel

1994   Immigration and Immigrants: Setting the Record Straight. Washington, D.C.: The Urban Institute.

Geyer, Georgie Anne

1996   Americans No More. New York: Atlantic Monthly Press.

Gurcak, Jessica, Thomas Espenshade, Aaron Sparrow, and Martha Paskoff
2001   Immigration of Scientists and Engineers to the United States: Issues and Evidence. *In* The International Migration of the Highly Skilled: Demand, Supply, and Development Consequences in Sending and Receiving Countries. Wayne A. Cornelius, Thomas J. Espenshade, and Idean Salehyan, eds. Pp. 55–84. La Jolla, CA: Center for Comparative Immigration Studies, University of California, San Diego.

Hainmueller, Jens, and Michael J. Hiscox
2010   Attitudes Toward Highly Skilled and Low-Skilled Immigration: Evidence from a Survey Experiment. American Political Science Review 104(1):61–84.

He, Lilly
2002   Perceptions, Attitudes, and American Public Opinion Toward Skilled Asian Immigrants. Undergraduate Research Journal, The University of Texas at Austin 1:10–22.

Higham, John
1974   Strangers in the Land: Patterns of American Nativism, 1860–1925. New York: Atheneum.

Hjerm, Mikael
2009   Anti-Immigrant Attitudes and Cross-Municipal Variation in the Proportion of Immigrants. Acta Sociologica 52(1):47–62.

Hoefer, Michael, Nancy Rytina, and Bryan C. Baker
2010   Estimates of the Unauthorized Immigrant Population Residing in the United States: January 2009. Washington, D.C.: Department of Homeland Security, Office of Immigration Statistics, Policy Directorate. http://www.dhs.gov/xlibrary/assets/statistics/publications/ois_ill_pe_2009.pdf, accessed June 14, 2014.

Hood III, M. V., and Irwin L. Morris
1997   ¿Amigo o Enemigo?: Context, Attitudes, and Anglo Public Opinion Toward Immigration. Social Science Quarterly 78(2):309–323.

Huntington, Samuel P.
2004a   The Hispanic Challenge. Foreign Policy 141:30–45.
2004b   Who Are We? The Challenges to America's National Identity. New York: Simon and Schuster.

Jaeger, David
2006   Replacing the Undocumented Work Force. Washington, D.C.: Center for American Progress. http://www.djaeger.org/research/reports/replacing_undocumented.pdf, accessed June 14, 2014.

Johnson, Kevin
1997   The New Nativism: Something Old, Something New, Something Borrowed, Something Blue. *In* Immigrants Out! The New Nativism and the Anti-Immigrant Impulse in the United States. Juan F. Perea, ed. Pp.165–189. New York: New York University Press.

Joppke, Christian
2005   Selecting by Origin: Ethnic Migration in the Liberal State. Cambridge, MA: Harvard University Press.

Lapinski, John S., Pia Peltola, Greg Shaw, and Alan Yang
1997   The Polls—Trends: Immigrants and Immigration. Public Opinion Quarterly 61:356–383.

Lee, Ronald, and Timothy Miller
2000   Immigration, Social Security, and Broader Fiscal Impacts. The American Econom-
        ic Review 90(2):350–354.
Lowell, B. Lindsay
2001   The Foreign Temporary Workforce and Shortages in Information Technology. *In*
        The International Migration of the Highly Skilled: Demand, Supply, and Develop-
        ment Consequences in Sending and Receiving Countries. Wayne A. Cornelius,
        Thomas J. Espenshade, and Idean Salehyan, eds. Pp. 131–60. La Jolla, CA: Center
        for Comparative Immigration Studies, University of California, San Diego.
Muller, Thomas
1997   Nativism in the Mid-1990s: Why Now? *In* Immigrants Out! The New Nativism and
        the Anti-Immigrant Impulse in the United States. Juan F. Perea, ed. Pp. 105–118.
        New York: New York University Press.
Myers, Dowell, and John Pitkin
2010   Assimilation Today: New Evidence Shows the Latest Immigrants to America Are
        Following in Our History's Footsteps. Washington, D.C.: Center for American Prog-
        ress. http://cdn.americanprogress.org/wp-content/uploads/issues/2010/09/pdf/
        immigrant_assimilation.pdf, accessed June 14, 2014.
Nevins, Joseph
2002   Operation Gatekeeper: The Rise of the "Illegal Alien" and the Making of the U.S.-
        Mexico Boundary. New York: Routledge.
Office of Immigration Statistics
2004   Yearbook of Immigration Statistics. Washington, D.C.: Department of Homeland
        Security. http://www.dhs.gov/files/statistics/publications/yearbook.shtm, accessed
        June 14, 2014.
Ong, Aihwa
1996   Cultural Citizenship as Subject-Making: Immigrants Negotiate Racial and Cul-
        tural Boundaries in the United States. Current Anthropology 37(5):737–751.
Passel, Jeffrey S., and D'Vera Cohn
2011   Unauthorized Immigration Population: National and State Trends, 2010. Wash-
        ington, D.C.: Pew Hispanic Center. http://www.pewhispanic.org/2011/02/01/unau
        thorized-immigrant-population-brnational-and-state-trends-2010/, accessed June
        14, 2014.
Perea, Juan F., ed.
1997   *Immigrants Out!* The New Nativism and the Anti-Immigrant Impulse in the Unit-
        ed States. New York: New York University Press.
Sanchez, George J.
1997   Face the Nation: Race, Immigration, and the Rise of Nativism in Late Twentieth
        Century America. International Migration Review 31(4):1009–1030.
Saxenian, AnnaLee
2002   Brain Circulation: How High-Skill Immigration Makes Everyone Better Off. The
        Brookings Review 20(1):28–31.
Schneider, Silke L.
2008   Anti-Immigrant Attitudes in Europe: Outgroup Size and Perceived Ethnic Threat.
        European Sociological Review 24(1):53–67.

Smith, James P., and Barry Edmonston, eds.
1997   The New Americans: Economic, Demographic, and Fiscal Effects of Immigration. Washington, D.C.: National Academy Press.

Sniderman, Paul M., Louk Hagendoorn, and Markus Prior
2004   Predisposing Factors and Situational Triggers: Exclusionary Reactions to Immigrant Minorities. American Political Science Review 98(1):35–49.

Stephan, Walter G., Oscar Ybarra, and Guy Bachman
1999   Prejudice Toward Immigrants. Journal of Applied Social Psychology 29(11):2221–2237.

Tatalovich, Raymond
1997   Official English as Nativist Backlash. In Immigrants Out! The New Nativism and the Anti-Immigrant Impulse in the United States. Juan F. Perea, ed. Pp. 78–102. New York: New York University Press.

Telles, Edward E., and Vilma Ortiz
2008   Generations of Exclusion: Mexican Americans, Assimilation, and Race. New York: Russell Sage Foundation.

Tsuda, Takeyuki
2009   Diasporic Homecomings: Ethnic Return Migration in Comparative Perspective. Stanford, CA: Stanford University Press.

Usdansky, Margaret, and Thomas J. Espenshade
2001   The Evolution of U.S. Policy Toward Employment-Based Immigrants and Temporary Workers: The H-1B Debate in Historical Perspective. In The International Migration of the Highly Skilled: Demand, Supply, and Development Consequences in Sending and Receiving Countries. Wayne A. Cornelius, Thomas J. Espenshade, and Idean Salehyan, eds. Pp. 23–53. La Jolla, CA: Center for Comparative Immigration Studies, University of California, San Diego.

Varsanyi, Monica W., ed.
2010   Taking Local Control: Immigration Policy Activism in U.S. Cities and States. Stanford, CA: Stanford University Press.

Vigdor, Jacob L.
2008   Measuring Immigrant Assimilation in the United States. Civic Report, 53. New York: Center for Civic Innovation, Manhattan Institute. http://files.eric.ed.gov/fulltext/ED501689.pdf, accessed June 14, 2014.

Waslin, Michele
2010   Immigration Enforcement by State and Local Police: The Impact on the Enforcers and their Communities. In Taking Local Control: Immigration Policy Activism in U.S. Cities and States, Monica W. Varsanyi, ed. Pp. 97–114. Stanford, CA: Stanford University Press.

Wong-Rieger, Durhane, and Diana Quintana
1987   Comparative Acculturation of Southeast Asian and Hispanic Immigrants and Sojourners. Journal of Cross-Cultural Psychology 18(3):345–362.

12

Perceptions of Disruption

Media Representations and Medical Staffs' Perceptions of Undocumented Immigrants' Impact on Healthcare Services in Post–SB 1070 Arizona

JONATHAN MAUPIN

The implementation of Senate Bill (SB) 1070 in April 2010 firmly placed Arizona at the center of the national immigration debate. The proposal and subsequent adoption of the bill, which contained the strictest anti-immigrant policies of any state in the nation, prompted unprecedented response, as state, national, and international media focused on Arizona. While much of the debate about SB 1070 centered on states' rights versus federal jurisdiction and the legality of the statutes, the discussion also focused on the role of immigrants in the United States.

Central to this national and local debate is the extent to which immigrants are disruptive to U.S. society. As conceptualized in this volume, *disruptions* refer to interruptions of accustomed activities that significantly impact social structures on varying levels and scales. This definition highlights the fact that while the notion of disruption may be a generalized category, it emerges through concepts of multiple disruptions in several distinct, but interrelated, domains. And while notions of whether a group is disruptive may be driven by specific domains (such as the economy), it is also influenced by the cumulative impact across domains. The magnitude of disruption is not necessarily based on measureable impacts, however, but is strongly influenced by individual and group perceptions of disruption that emerge from diverse sources, including personal experience, second-hand accounts, generalized stereotypes, and media representations. These perceptions are important for considering individual or group action, particularly toward immigrants, as behaviors may be influenced more by our perceptions of the world (or groups of people) than measurable aspects.

Thus, perceptions of disruption may be more important to understand than documented impacts, which are themselves collected, measured, and presented in particular ways that both reflect and reinforce particular perceptions (see Maupin and Ross 2012).

Viewed in this way, "disruptions" strongly reflect the "integrated threat theory" (Stephan and Stephan 2000; Stephan et al. 2009). In this model, prejudice toward a group is influenced by the perceived threats they represent, which evoke fear and anxiety. According to Stephan et al. (2000), there are four types of threats: realistic threats that threaten the existence of the in-group, such as political and economic power, or the physical well-being of its members; symbolic threats referring to the in-group's morals, values, norms, customs, or traditions; intergroup anxiety, that is fears of embarrassment, rejection, or exploitation in interactions with out-group members; and negative stereotypes of the out-group, which also hinder intergroup interactions. These factors mediate more distal factors, including previous intergroup contact and conflict, status inequalities, knowledge of the out-group, and in-group identification in producing prejudice toward out-group members (Corenblum and Stephan 2001; Gonzalez et al. 2008). For example, Stephan et al. (2000) find that the quality and frequency of intergroup interactions influence individuals' perceptions of out-group members as threats, as increased and positive interactions reduce intergroup anxiety and negative attitudes toward out-group members.

Importantly, these are *perceived* threats and not necessarily measurable disruptions, raising the question of how perceptions of immigrants as disruptive threats emerge. Media may play a significant role in this process. While individuals may have strong opinions on sensitive topics, such as undocumented immigration, based on personal experience or as part of larger philosophical viewpoints (e.g., political or religious affiliation), there is significant potential for media to influence individuals' perceptions of immigrants. Media representations of immigrant populations, generally, are not unbiased or balanced. Rather, the ways in which media accounts frame issues or arguments influences the manner in which they are presented, and has been shown to influence both individuals' attitudes and their behavior (Comstock et al. 1978; McLeod and Detenber 1999; Sibley et al. 2006). These representations and framing devices draw on larger sentiments regarding undocumented immigrants and both reflect and reaffirm these perceptions. As such, media representations of immigration are an important source for examining the ways in which undocumented immigrants are perceived as disruptive in different domains.

For example, in a comparison of state and national media coverage of SB 1070, Fryberg et al. (2012) found that national media accounts supporting the bill frame undocumented immigrants as threats—threats to the public, economic threats, the need to protect welfare, and the need to protect jobs—more than state newspapers do. Conservative newspapers also presented arguments in terms of threats more than liberal newspapers, particularly in terms of public safety and the need to protect welfare. Luque et al. (2013) found similar patterns among Georgia newspaper coverage of House Bill 87, which is modeled after SB 1070. In this study, they found that metropolitan newspapers across the state had a higher proportion of arguments framing immigrants as disruptive compared to bilingual newspapers, particularly in terms of economic disruption. Importantly, however, Luque et al. (2013) found that economic arguments were the most common among those opposing the bill, which was not found in the analysis done by Fryberg et al. (2012). This difference may not be due to geographical variation but to shifting perceptions of disruption in the post–SB 1070 context.

In Arizona, the debate surrounding undocumented immigration remains central. In 2011, the Republican-led Senate proposed a set of five anti-immigrant bills aimed at extending the state's ability to enforce immigration policy and restricting the services available to undocumented immigrants. Included in this legislation, Senate Bill (SB) 1405 proposed requiring hospital staff to validate patients' documentation status either after treatment for emergency cases or prior to admission for non-emergency cases. While not generating the same level of media coverage as SB 1070, the introduction of the bills reaffirmed Arizona's position as the state driving the immigration debate. Yet the impact of SB 1070 changed the political and economic landscape in Arizona and influenced the types of arguments that proponents on both sides of the issues utilized in order to garner support. Although the arguments surrounding the senate bills have changed, public support or opposition to the bills is uncertain as both sides of the debate claim popular support for their actions.

In this chapter, media representations of the arguments surrounding SB 1405 are examined, with specific interest in the ways that the concept of "disruption" is utilized by both proponents and opponents of the bill. Health care is frequently cited as an example of the disruptive nature of undocumented immigration on federal, state, and local economies by driving uncompensated health care and thus negatively impacting the quality and cost of health care. Yet, while there is significant debate regarding undocumented immigrants' contribution to uncompensated healthcare costs, the extension of immigration policy into hospitals potentially presents new forms of disruption. To address this issue, I first examine estimates of undocumented immigrants' economic disruptions on healthcare systems. I then examine media representations of SB 1405. Finally, to determine how the arguments presented in the media reflect public opinion, I examine registered nurses' (RNs) responses to public opinion poll questions regarding health care and immigration reform. This discussion highlights the diverse ways in which the concept of "disruption" is utilized to frame the arguments both for and against Arizona's recent anti-immigrant bills, as well as how these notions of disruption reflect RNs' perceptions of undocumented immigrants' impact on health care.

Post–SB 1070 Anti-Immigrant Reform in Arizona

Following the momentum of SB 1070, the Arizona senate proposed a set of anti-immigrant bills in early 2011 that address a wide range of topics, including citizenship, as well as the rights and services available to undocumented immigrants:

SB 1611 is an omnibus bill focused on documentation verification and restricting rights for undocumented immigrants. The bill would require businesses to use E-verify; require individuals administering public benefits to verify individuals' documentation status; require legal proof to operate, purchase, or register a motor vehicle and to receive any type of license, including a marriage license. SB 1611 also directly addresses the use of federal and state services or subsidies, requiring proof of legal residence in order to enroll in K–12 schools, attend Arizona community colleges or universities, and receive federal public health benefits (including emergency medical services).

SB 1309 would define an Arizona citizen as someone who is born in this country with at least one parent who is a US citizen, national, or permanent resident. Related to this, SB 1308 would allow Arizona to create separate birth certificates for Arizona citizens (based on SB 1309 criteria) and to create compacts with other states to recognize these separate birth certificates.

SB 1407 would require school districts to collect data on students who cannot prove lawful residence in the U.S. The Department of Education would then compile a report for the governor that in-

274 · Jonathan Maupin

cludes research on the adverse impact of undocumented students'
enrollment in schools and an estimate of the total cost to taxpayers
for educating non-citizens, with a section on the cost of undocumented immigrants. Failure to comply would risk the loss of state
aid.

SB 1405 would require that hospital admissions officers confirm that
a person is a U.S. citizen or legal resident prior to admitting them
for non-emergency care. In the case of emergency care, hospital
admissions personnel must verify documentation status upon the
successful treatment of the patient, pursuant to the Emergency
Medical Treatment and Active Labor Act (EMTALA). In both
cases, hospital admissions must contact the local federal immigration office if the patient cannot demonstrate proof of U.S. citizenship or legal residence.

The senate bills received a large amount of local, state, and national attention. Significantly, the 2011 senate bill proposals generated reactions from
sectors of the Arizona community who were largely silent during the SB
1070 debates. In particular, representatives of the business community were
very vocal in their opposition to the bills, with dozens of CEOs from a wide
range of Arizona businesses opposing the measures. The Phoenix Chamber
of Commerce, along with several CEOs from Arizona businesses, sent a
letter to the state legislature stating their opposition to the bills and made
several public statements regarding their position. In terms of SB 1405, numerous CEOs of hospital systems in Arizona voiced their opposition, in
addition to the Arizona Hospital and Healthcare Association, the Physicians for Human Rights organization, the Arizona Nurses Association, and
the Mayo Clinic. Opposition to the bills thus included a larger, and more
influential, constituency than harnessed against SB 1070.

Even within the senate, support for the bills was not uniform. Despite a
Republican-led senate that supported the adoption of SB 1070 the previous
year, opposition threatened to prevent the bills from leaving their respective committees. Indeed, Senator Ron Gould, who proposed SB 1308 and
1309, pulled the two bills from the Senate Judiciary Committee, which he
led, due to lack of support. SB 1405 was pulled from the same committee
shortly after. In an attempt to move to the full senate, Senator Pearce reas-
signed them to the conservative Senate Appropriations Committee, which
also reviewed SB 1407 and 1611. On February 22, 2011, the committee passed
the set of five bills, although with some dissension among senators. SB 1611

was approved by a 7–6 vote, with one Republican voting against the bill, while SB 1308, 1309, 1405, and 1407 were approved by an 8–5 vote, with two Republicans voting against the bills.

The five bills went to the full senate for a vote on March 17, 2011. In a surprising outcome, all were voted down. Joining Democratic senators, several Republican senators voted against the bills. While proponents of the bills promised to revive them, only SB 1405 and 1407 were re-proposed in February 2012. However, the bills were assigned to two senate committees each and failed to move out of committee for a full senate vote.

While many of the bills extended the scope of reforms outlined in SB 1070, the inclusion of health care is a significant shift in immigration policy. The issue of undocumented immigrants' impact on uncompensated healthcare costs has been addressed at the federal level since the mid-1990s through 2000s. In 2003, the Local Emergency Health Services Reimbursement Act provided federal funds to compensate for the state and local costs for providing care to undocumented immigrants. The issue received national attention following Senator Joe Wilson's infamous "You lie!" outburst during the 2009 State of the Union address in which President Obama denied that the proposed healthcare reform would provide coverage to undocumented immigrants. Although debunked, the fear that undocumented immigrants would receive insurance under the health reform act sparked national debate concerning the cost of immigrants on health care. A central part of this debate focused on the role of citizenship verification for receiving federal coverage, although this discussion and proposals did not extend documentation verification into daily hospital operations. Arizona's expansion of immigration policy into hospitals and healthcare delivery thus pushes the limits of current immigration reform and concepts of immigrants as disruptive.

Estimating Immigrants' Disruption on Health Care

Undocumented immigrants' impact on the quality or cost of health care is difficult to estimate. In a 2004 report to Congress, the U.S. General Accounting Office (GAO; 2004:21) stated that the "lack of proven methods to estimate their numbers make it difficult to determine the extent to which hospitals treat undocumented aliens and the costs of their care. . . ." Part of this issue is the variation in the categorization of "undocumented." As the GAO report details, there are no standardized criteria among hospital systems for categorizing individuals as undocumented, but rather a range of idiosyncratic measures, including the lack of a social security card, being of Hispanic descent and lacking a social security card, or providing a foreign address. The lack of standardized criteria prevents us from adequately determining the economic disruption of undocumented immigrants on health care while also allowing for varying estimates based on different categorizations of undocumented immigrants.

For example, while the RAND corporation (Goldman et al. 2006) estimated that adult undocumented immigrants accounted for $1.1 billion of federal, state, and local funds in 2000, the Federation for American Immigration Reform (FAIR; Martin and Ruark 2011) states that if the U.S.-born children of undocumented immigrants are included, the true cost would be at least $3 billion in 2007. Indeed, the largest federal costs for undocumented immigrants in health care are Medicaid costs associated with the U.S.-born children of undocumented immigrants, including childbirth, Medicaid, and other insurance (Martin and Ruark 2011). In terms of adults, the FAIR estimates are based largely on assumptions of immigrants' treatment-seeking behavior. For instance, although Martin and Ruark (2011:15) note that "[o]nly anecdotal information is available about the amount of Medicaid usage by illegal aliens who use stolen identities of U.S. citizens or qualified 'green card holders,'" they estimate that it accounts for $2.47 billion a year in federal costs. Similarly, estimates of immigrants' role in uncompensated healthcare costs assume that undocumented immigrants without insurance "generally turn to emergency medical facilities for their treatment" (Martin and Ruark 2011:3), costing the federal government $250 million a year.

While there is a lack of verifiable data on undocumented immigrants' healthcare costs, data are available for native-born versus foreign-born populations, the latter including both authorized and unauthorized immigrants. Using these categories, several studies have documented that, though immigrants have a higher rate of uninsurance than native-born citizens, they account for a significantly smaller proportion of per capita healthcare costs than native-born persons (Gans 2006; Mohatny et al. 2005; Stimpson et al. 2010). Estimates also suggest that immigrants utilize healthcare services less than native-born individuals. Cunningham (2006) found that communities with low rates of immigrant populations, such as Cleveland, Ohio, have higher rates of emergency room (ER) visits than cities with large immigrant populations, including Miami-Dade, Florida, and Phoenix, Arizona. In general, uninsured individuals are no more likely to have ER visits than insured individuals and, in fact, Medicaid participants are more likely to have multiple ER visits in a one-year period (Garcia et al. 2010). While ER expenditures for immigrant children were three times higher than those of native-born children, immigrant children had 74 percent lower per capita healthcare expenditure than US-born children (Mohatny et al. 2005). Given the lower rates of healthcare utilization, these studies question the extent to which immigrants, much less undocumented immigrants, drive uncompensated healthcare costs.

Estimates of the impact of undocumented immigrants on uncompensated healthcare costs face similar limitations. In Arizona, the FAIR estimates that undocumented immigrants (and their U.S.-born children) account for $400 million per year. Gans (2008), however, estimates that the total uncompensated healthcare cost in the state was approximately $419.6 million in 2004, with foreign-born populations accounting for $149.3 million. Of this figure, non-citizens, including both authorized and unauthorized immigrants, accounted for $135.4 million. A similar disparity is found in the costs associated with the Arizona Health Care Cost Containment System (AHCCCS), Arizona's Medicaid agency, where the native-born population accounts for 84.9 percent of the approximately $4.3 billion in 2004. In comparison, foreign-born individuals accounted for $642 million, of which non-citizens contributed the most at $477.4 million. Thus, while immigrants do account for a portion of uncompensated healthcare and Medicaid costs, this portion is significantly smaller than that of the native-born population.

Yet these discrepancies between estimates of undocumented immigrants' disruption on healthcare costs may play a very small role in influencing popular perceptions of immigrants, as issues of methodology or analysis are rarely addressed. Rather, popular opinion may be influenced more by the ways in which these concepts are portrayed than the data on which they are based, thereby emphasizing the importance of examining media representation.

Media Representation of Senate Bill Proposals

Methods

To examine media representation of SB 1405, a review of newspaper articles published between January 1, 2011, and April 26, 2012, was conducted. Fourteen newspapers from around the state of Arizona were selected for analysis, although six of these newspapers had no searchable online database,

Table 12.1. Newspapers included in the sample

Newspaper	Number of Articles
Arizona Capital Times	8
Arizona Republic	6
Daily Courier	2
Daily Star	6
Daily Sun	4
Daily Sun News	3
La Voz	1
Yuma Sun	1
Total	31

did not contain any references to SB 1405, or did not specifically address the bill. The remaining eight newspapers provide a range of geographical coverage, as well as population demographics (see table 12.1). One of these newspapers, *La Voz*, is in Spanish and serves the Phoenix metro region.

Articles were selected from these eight newspapers through a systematic search through both LexisNexis and each newspaper's online archives, using the keywords "Senate Bill 1405," "SB 1405," "immigration hospital," "migrant hospital," "immigrant health care," and "migrant health care." There are significantly more articles that discuss the other senate bill proposals in detail; in fact, SB 1405 received the least amount of media exposure. In total, 79 articles that include SB 1405 were identified. However, only 31 of these articles discuss the bill specifically, whereas the other 48 only reference the bill in the context of the other senate bill proposals and were thus excluded from the analysis.

Not surprisingly, the three newspapers with the most extensive coverage of SB 1405 are the *Arizona Capital Times*, which focuses specifically on state politics and policy, the *Arizona Republic*, serving the greater Phoenix area, and the *Tucson Daily Star*. Newspapers serving smaller cities mention SB 1405 with much less frequency. Surprisingly, *La Voz*, the only Spanish-language newspaper included in this study, only had one article that specifically addresses the bill.

Procedure

Following the identification of articles, each was read to identify arguments in support of and against the proposal. A codebook for pro and con arguments was created, first identifying specific arguments and then aggregating these into larger thematic categories. Codes were dropped if they were

Table 12.2. Codes regarding SB 1405

	Description
ARGUMENTS IN SUPPORT OF SB 1405	
Economics	Undocumented immigrants are a significant cost to hospital systems and the state through uncompensated health care
Enforce Law	Bill would reinforce existing laws that prohibit aiding and abetting criminals, including undocumented immigrants
ARGUMENTS AGAINST SB 1405	
Turn into ICE	Verification requirements would effectively transform hospital staff into Immigration and Customs Enforcement officers
Economics	Verification requirements would cost hospital systems more money to implement and manage
Increase Hospital Workload	Verification requirements would increase hospital workload
Public Health	Deterring undocumented immigrants from health care would create a potential public health risk
Constitutionality/Civil Rights	Bill denies right to emergency care and threatens citizens or authorized immigrants' rights
Fed/State Relations	Immigration is a federal issue and action damages federal/state relations
Lower Quality of Care	Bill would lower the quality of care provided at hospitals

mentioned by less than five percent of the articles. In total, two arguments in support of the bill and seven arguments against it were identified (table 12.2).

Once the codebook was complete, each article was coded based on the presence of each argument ("1" if present and "0" if not present). As each article could, and most often did, have multiple arguments, more than one code could be applied to a single article. Articles were coded only for the presence or absence of each theme and not in terms of how many times the argument was made. The percentage of articles that contained the specific arguments for and against SB 1405 was then calculated.

Results

Table 12.3 shows the average percentage of articles that contain arguments in favor of and against SB 1405. In terms of support of the bill, there are only two primary arguments. Economics is the most common argument reported in support of the bill (35.5 percent). While supporters of the bill do not provide any estimates of the economic costs associated with undocumented immigrants, or uncompensated care in general, they draw on assumptions utilized by anti-immigrant organizations such as the FAIR that undocumented immigrants utilize emergency rooms as a primary source of care. As Senator Pearce describes (Girouard 2011): "But I get calls from doctors and nurses every day that work in the emergency room, talking about the abuse, the millions of dollars spent for folks who come in for pregnancy tests, sniffles . . . they use emergency room services as their primary care. When do we stand up for the taxpayers? . . . Quit inviting people over the border. We give them free stuff, free medical . . . enough is enough."

Tied to this issue is the argument that stricter verification processes will deter undocumented immigrants from seeking public services such as health care and education, thereby saving the hospital and state money. In reference to education and health care, Senator Steve Smith, who sponsored the bills in the 2012 session, stated, "Maybe we can deter the amount of money that is hemorrhaging out every year in free services for people that don't deserve it" (Howard Fischer Capitol Media Services, 2012).

The second argument made in support of SB 1405 is "enforce law" (9.7 percent). In reference to SB 1405 specifically, Senator Russell Pearce, the primary sponsor and supporter of the anti-immigrant legislation in Arizona, stated "It's the law. It's a felony to (aid and) abet. We're going to enforce the law without apology" (Associated Press, 2011).

The notion that hospital staff and/or employees may be held responsible for verifying documentation status is in fact the most common argument presented against SB 1405, as 42 percent of articles dealing specifically with the bill raise the concern of turning employees into Immigration and Customs Enforcement (ICE) agents. Not only are there questions regarding the legal responsibility, or penalty, of medical staff for verifying patients' documentation status, critics also suggest that the bill would violate the trust between physicians and patients and force them to "choose between the dignity of their profession and the indignity of violating the law" (Restrepo 2010:25).

Table 12.3. Frequency of themes regarding SB 1405 (n=31)

ARGUMENTS IN SUPPORT OF SB 1405	
Economics	35.5%
Enforce Law	9.7%
ARGUMENTS AGAINST SB 1405	
Turn into ICE	41.9%
Economics	32.3%
Increase Hospital Workload	32.3%
Public Health	22.6%
Constitutionality/Civil Rights	19.4%
Fed/State Relations	9.7%
Lower Quality of Care	6.5%

Critics of SB 1405 also raise the concern, linked to this argument, regarding the increased workload that this monitoring and verification of documentation status would require of hospital staff and/or hiring employees trained in immigration law, a topic included in 32.3 percent of articles about the bill. Additionally, while economics is the most common argument in support of SB 1405, it is also frequently used as an argument against the bill (32.3 percent). While not providing estimates of the costs of undocumented immigrants, critics argue that SB 1405 will neither reduce uncompensated healthcare costs for hospitals nor save the state money. Opponents of SB 1405 also cite the potential threat to public health (22.6 percent), as deterring undocumented immigrants from seeking health services may allow for infectious diseases to go unnoticed, potentially affecting the larger public, while the lack of preventative services such as prenatal care or vaccinations may result in future complications that require more intensive and costly services to remedy.

The fifth most common argument against SB 1405 is constitutionality/civil rights (19.4 percent), including the right to emergency care guaranteed under EMTALA. Critics also warn that, while the bill could deter undocumented immigrants from seeking health care, some also suggest that legal immigrants could be subject to discrimination and a denial of services, thereby impinging on the rights of legal residents.

Next, 9.7 percent of the articles addressing SB 1405 critiqued the bill for undermining federal authority in immigration enforcement and overextending the role of the state. Finally, only 6.5 percent of the arguments against SB 1405 stated that the bill would lower the quality of health care.

Discussion

The arguments for and against SB 1405 (and the set of 2011 senate immigration-related bills in general) represent a significant shift in media representation of the immigration debate from the portrayal of SB 1070. In Fryberg
et al.'s (2012) study regarding SB 1070, the most common argument in favor
of SB 1070 was federal in/action as well as threats to public safety (in terms
of crime, terrorism, or public health). Economic threats were mentioned
by a small percentage of articles, particularly in Arizona newspapers (only
8.5 percent). This pattern is inversed in the arguments regarding SB 1405, as
economic disruption is the primary argument in support of the bill (and is
the second most common argument supporting the set of bills as a whole).
Thus, while issues of public safety, federal in/action, states' rights, and constitutionality are still raised, the discourse around anti-immigration reform
has shifted to emphasizing the disruption of immigrants on the economy, a
pattern that reflects Luque et al.'s (2013) finding in Georgia.

Opponents of the bills also draw on the notion of disruption in their
arguments against the bills. However, rather than focusing on immigrants,
these arguments focus on the disruptive nature of the bills themselves. Following the negative economic impact generated by the implementation of
SB 1070, members of the business community strongly opposed the 2011
bills, arguing that they will further damage the tourism and business sectors while opening up the state to new lawsuits. In regard to SB 1405 specifically, arguments by hospital CEOs and associations largely focus on the
bill increasing hospital staffs' workloads and administrative overhead while
failing to reduce uncompensated healthcare costs and potentially creating
greater future costs by failing to provide curative and preventative care to
all individuals.

While arguments against the bills, and SB 1405 specifically, do address
civil liberties and constitutionality, these arguments are primarily framed
in terms of the rights of U.S. citizens, residents, or legal immigrants and
rarely address the issue of undocumented immigrants. Additionally, the
argument that the bills would transform teachers or hospital employees
into ICE agents is not framed necessarily in terms of negatively impacting
undocumented immigrants but on its impact to those employees' roles and
functions.

Surprisingly, the issue of discrimination, racism, or inequality is rarely
addressed in the critiques against the senate bill proposals. The issue of

discrimination was mentioned by only 3.2 percent of those articles addressing SB 1405 specifically (and only ten percent of the 79 articles discussing the bills in total). This low frequency is in stark contrast to Fryberg et al.'s (2012) finding that more than 50 percent of all articles contained arguments framing SB 1070. The decreased discussion of discrimination or racism as a critique of the senate bills signifies an important shift in opposition to immigration reform. Rather than critiquing the bills for being discriminatory or challenging the portrayal of immigrants as being disruptive in any sense, opponents of the bills focus almost exclusively on the disruption of the bills on the state economy, public and private services, and U.S. citizens, residents, and legal immigrants. Thus, undocumented immigrants themselves are largely ignored in arguments against the senate proposals, a neglect that potentially allows the perception of immigrants as a disruptive force to persist, as will be discussed.

Registered Nurses' Perceptions of Migrants as Disruptive

Analysis of media representation of the senate bill proposals highlights the ways in which media frame the arguments regarding the bills, as well as the themes that supporters and opponents draw upon to justify their positions. Though both supporters and opponents of the bills cite public support, they do not provide any data regarding public opinion regarding these issues. Even less understood are opinions of those individuals who would be greatly affected by the implementation of the bills. For example, while several hospital CEOs, healthcare associations, and individual providers publicly opposed SB 1405, it is not clear how medical staff working inside of hospitals consider the bill, or their perceptions of undocumented immigrants. Rather than media representation, medical staffs' perceptions of immigrants as disruptive to health care may derive from their clinical interactions with immigrants, their role within the hospital structure, and their perceptions of healthcare costs and structure. While Stephan et al. (2000) suggest that the quality and frequency of out-group interactions decreases negative perceptions, these interactions may also increase perceptions of disruption.

To address this issue, a second study of RNs' perceptions of undocumented immigrants as a disruptive force on health care, as well as their opinions regarding potential immigration reforms and hospital policy, was conducted.

Methods

A review of public opinion polls published by research organizations, such as Gallup and Rasmussen, regarding undocumented immigrants and health care, was performed on a sample of political, news, and immigration-related websites. From these sources, 15 public opinion poll questions were selected, three of which deal with perceptions of undocumented immigrants on the U.S. economy, three that address the impact of undocumented immigrants on healthcare quality and cost, two addressing the responsibility of the hospital to provide services to undocumented immigrants, six that deal with federal healthcare reform, and one addressing birthright citizenship. In order to ensure comparability, the exact wording from these published opinion poll questions was used. In addition, a question focusing on perceptions of which populations are responsible for the greatest majority of uncompensated healthcare costs was added.

Procedure

The questions were included in a larger survey administered online via SurveyMonkey. An electronic link to the survey was sent to RNs throughout the greater Phoenix, Arizona, area through an electronic listserv. The listserv includes a wide range of healthcare professionals working in different hospital systems throughout the valley. Participation in the survey was completely voluntary.

A total of 26 participants completed the questionnaire, although the completion rate for each individual poll question ranges between 17 and 19 individuals. All participants are registered nurses working primarily in hospitals, although there is a broad range of units represented, including women and infant's health (labor and delivery, postpartum, and NICU), pediatrics, oncology, and emergency room services. In terms of demographics, all participants self-identified as white non-Hispanic, and all but one is female. A total of eight individuals identified as bilingual, with four speaking German, four speaking Spanish, and one speaking French in addition to English. One person spoke both German and Spanish, which accounts for the discrepancy in numbers. On average, participants reported that 64.5 percent of their patients were from different ethnic/racial backgrounds than themselves, although these estimates range from 25 to 90 percent. Additionally, on average, participants reported that 37 percent of their patients speak a language other than English in clinical encounters, although there is an even greater variation in these estimates, ranging from five to 90 percent. However, these reports suggest that the RNs in our sample have a high degree of interaction with individuals from different ethnic and linguistic backgrounds, a factor that may influence their perceptions of undocumented immigrants on healthcare services compared to the public opinion polls conducted with a random sample of U.S. citizens.

Results

Figure 12.1 presents the results of the questions related to perceptions of undocumented immigrants' disruption on the economy for both the RNs and those of published public opinion polls. As is evident from the graph, a greater proportion of RNs than respondents in the public opinion poll view undocumented immigrants as a cost burden to the United States, as well as perceiving that undocumented immigrants do not pay their fair share of taxes (Gallup poll, 2010). Though a smaller percentage of RNs view undocumented immigrants as a significant strain on the U.S. budget than those in the public opinion poll (36.8 percent compared to 67 percent; Rasmussen poll, 2010a), nearly 95 percent of RNs view them as a moderate to significant strain on the budget.

In terms of their effects on health care (figure 12.2), the majority of RNs (73.7 percent, nearly the same rate found in a public opinion poll [Pulse Opinion Research poll, 2009a]) perceive that undocumented immigrants adversely impact the quality and cost of health care. However, RNs overwhelmingly think that providing care to undocumented immigrants increases healthcare costs (88.9 percent), a rate nearly double that found among liberals and progressives (48 percent; Pulse Opinion Research poll,

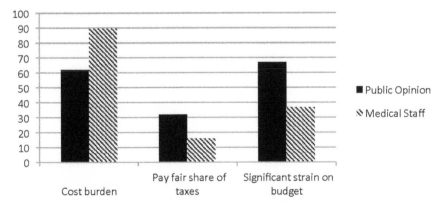

Figure 12.1. Perceptions of immigrants' disruption on the economy.

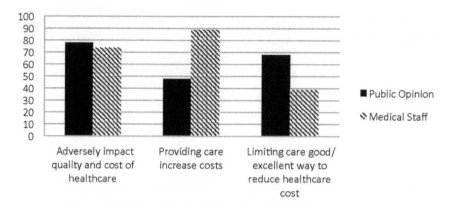

Figure 12.2. Perceptions of immigrants' disruption on healthcare costs.

2009b). Yet only 38.9 percent of RNs consider limiting care to undocumented immigrants a good or excellent way to reduce healthcare costs, a rate much lower than the 68 percent of respondents in the public opinion poll (Zogby poll, 2009).

While RNs perceive undocumented immigrants to be disruptive economically on health care, the public opinion poll questions do not address the relative impact of immigrants compared to other populations. To address this issue, one question asked participants to rate which population accounted for the largest proportion of uncompensated healthcare costs on a scale from 1–5 with 5 representing the greatest proportion. The groups included in this question are undocumented adults, undocumented children, authorized immigrant adults, authorized immigrant children, native-born adults, and native-born children. The results show that, on average, RNs rated U.S. native-born adults and children as accounting for the largest proportion of uncompensated healthcare costs (figure 12.3). Undocumented immigrant adults are rated third, above authorized adult and child immigrants, while undocumented children are rated the least responsible for uncompensated healthcare costs. Thus, even though RNs view undocumented immigrants as disruptive, they are not (on average) considered the most disruptive segment of the population in terms of uncompensated healthcare costs.

In terms of healthcare reform and coverage for undocumented immigrants (figure 12.4), the majority of RNs oppose extending coverage, and they express concern over the impact of Obamacare. Nearly 90 percent of RNs stated that individuals should prove that they are in the United States legally in order to receive government services or federal healthcare sub-

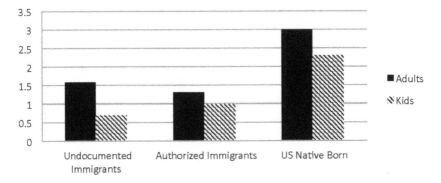

Figure 12.3. Perceptions of which population group accounts for the greatest proportion of uncompensated healthcare costs.

sidies, a rate similar to that reflected in public opinion polls (Rasmussen 2009a, Rasmussen 2009b). Additionally, 77.8 percent state that citizenship verification should be a part of federal health reform (Rasmussen 2009c). Interestingly, 76.5 percent responded that current healthcare reform proposals provide coverage to undocumented immigrants (Pulse Opinion Research 2009c), which 64.7 percent oppose (Rasmussen 2009d). Finally, 72.2 percent responded that providing insurance to undocumented immigrants would incentivize illegal immigrants (Pulse Opinion Research 2009d).

The concern over the economic disruption of undocumented immigrants on healthcare services also affects perceptions of the type of care that hospitals should provide to undocumented individuals, particularly

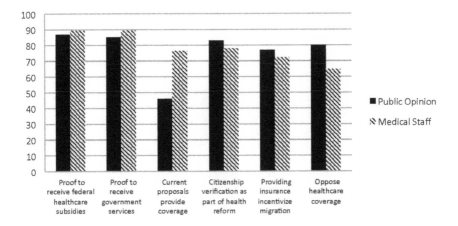

Figure 12.4. Perceptions of healthcare reform and access.

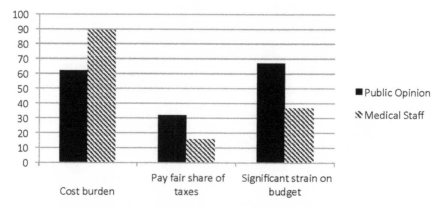

Figure 12.5. Perceptions of treatment and immigration actions for undocumented immigrants requiring long-term care.

for long-term conditions. A national poll conducted in 2009 found that nearly 50 percent of respondents believe that undocumented immigrants should be deported after receiving emergency care if it was determined that they required long-term care, while 38 percent stated that care should be provided under specific time and economic constraints, and a small proportion stated that long-term care should be provided (Pulse Opinion Research 2009e; figure 12.5). The majority of RNs in our sample (55.6 percent) stated that care should be provided with time and economic constraints, yet exactly one third stated that undocumented immigrants should be deported following the provision of emergency care, and only 11.1 percent stated that long-term care should be provided.

The final two questions directly concern the 2011 senate bill proposals. The first deals specifically with the content of SB 1405. In response to the

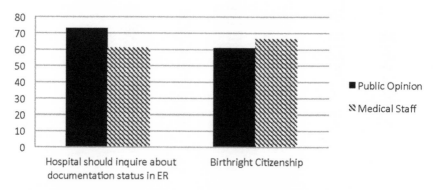

Figure 12.6. Perceptions of documentation status and healthcare operations.

question as to whether hospitals should inquire about and collect data on an individual's documentation status in the emergency room, without affecting the legal requirement that they provide emergency care, 61.1 percent of RNs responded affirmatively (figure 12.6). This figure is lower than that of a 2009 public opinion poll, in which 73 percent of respondents answered affirmatively (Pulse Opinion Research 2009f). When asked whether they believe that one or both parents of an infant born in the United States must be a U.S. citizens or resident in order for the infant to receive U.S. citizenship (the proposal in SB 1308/1309), two thirds of the RNs in our sample responded affirmatively, a figure closely reflecting the results of a public opinion poll (Rasmussen 2011).

Discussion

RNs' responses to the public opinion polls indicate a strong perception of undocumented immigrants as disruptive on the healthcare system, particularly in terms of economics. The fact that nearly nine out of ten RNs think that providing care to undocumented immigrants raises healthcare costs demonstrates the acute awareness of their disruption on the healthcare system in general, and for hospitals, providers, and medical staff in particular. While perceptions of the federal healthcare reforms may be influenced more by politics or public opinion than perceptions of undocumented immigrants themselves, the overwhelming support for documentation verification to receive federal and governmental services or subsidies, including health care, indicates a strong concern over healthcare access for undocumented immigrants, which the majority of RNs oppose. This concern is evidenced by RNs' belief that federal healthcare reform would provide coverage to undocumented immigrants.

Considering these responses, it is perhaps not surprising that RNs strongly support the content of SB 1405 and SB 1308/1309. Despite the opposition to the bills by healthcare CEOs and organizations, the majority of RNs support the proposal that hospitals inquire and collect data on the documentation status of ER patients, as well as the requirement that at least one parent be a U.S. citizen or resident in order for a newborn to receive citizenship.

Importantly, however, this concern over economic costs or citizenship/documentation verification does not necessarily imply that RNs oppose providing healthcare services to undocumented immigrants, as only 38.9 percent stated that limiting care was a good/excellent means of reducing healthcare costs, which is much lower than the results from the public opinion poll. Additionally, their responses to the question of whether un-documented immigrants with long-term-care issues should be deported, provided care under certain time and economic constraints, or provided long-term care suggest that there is concern over providing adequate health services within certain constraints.

These seeming disparities may be the result of two different factors. First, RNs' recognition that undocumented immigrants (both adults and children) account for a smaller proportion of uncompensated healthcare costs than U.S. citizens may foster the perception that limiting undocumented immigrants' access to health care would not significantly reduce healthcare costs in general. Second, the fact that RNs do not support limiting care to undocumented immigrants may reflect the concern that denying preventative services may result in more severe complications in the future. Additionally, denying curative care may create a public health threat, putting more individuals at risk for disease, and thereby increasing total healthcare costs, an argument used as a critique in the media representations of SB 1405.

Thus, while the RNs in our sample oppose extending healthcare coverage to undocumented immigrants and support reforms requiring citizenship verification for subsidies or services, they do not view limiting care as an effective way of reducing overall healthcare costs; this is a significant deviation from public opinion. Yet this recognition that limiting care will not reduce costs does not diminish the perception of undocumented immigrants as having a disruptive effect on health care and, in this sense, medical staff closely reflect public opinion regarding the negative impact of undocumented immigrants, as well as their support for reforms.

Conclusion

The extent to which immigrants are disruptive is difficult to measure. The concept of disruption is not necessarily an objectively definable measure, as the notion of what constitutes a disruption, how it is measured, and by whom influence estimates of the ways in which immigrants are portrayed as disruptive. The notion of disruption is also not uniform or consistent, as immigrants do not affect all sectors of society to the same extent, and the emphasis on disruptions in specific domains, or the framing of immigrants as disruptive, fluctuates depending on the context. This shift in the framing of undocumented immigrants as disruptive is evident in the media representation of SB 1405 and the larger set of 2011 senate bill proposals.

As Fryberg et al. (2012) detail, the primary argument in support of SB 1070 represented in national media, and to a large extent in Arizona, was undocumented immigrants' threat to public safety. Proponents of the bill thus drew on popular fears of immigrants' threatening the social fabric of American society to garner support for the bill. The impact of SB 1070, however, drastically changed the ways in which immigration reform, and immigrants themselves, are presented. As the analysis of SB 1405 demonstrates, the primary theme for arguments both supporting and opposing the bills is potential economic disruption. This notion of disruption is employed in very different ways. Whereas proponents of the bills framed undocumented immigrants as an economic threat, opponents focused on the negative economic impact the state has already experienced following the adoption of SB 1070, in addition to negatively impacting healthcare costs and operations. In response to the decreased tourism, boycotts, and negative publicity resulting from SB 1070, business leaders and healthcare associations throughout the state, which were quiet regarding SB 1070, actively opposed the bills, along with other sections of Arizona society. Luque et al. (2013) found a similar pattern in Georgia media representations of HB 87, in which the primary argument against the bill was its potential negative economic impact. Rather than focusing on the potential for racism and discrimination or the role of undocumented immigrants themselves, opponents of state immigration reform post–SB 1070 focus on the disruptive effects of the bills themselves to the state, businesses, social services, and citizens.

While the national economic recession and negative economic impact of SB 1070 undoubtedly played a large role in the failure of the bills, this shift in arguments against recent state immigration policies represents a significant change in the immigration debate. By focusing on the bills' potential disruption to Arizona businesses, healthcare systems, employees, and citizens, opponents of the bill fail to counter the arguments portraying undocumented immigrants as disruptive threats. Indeed, undocumented immigrants themselves rarely appear as a topic in arguments against the bills, and allegations of racism or discrimination are few. As such, these arguments still leave a space for the perception of undocumented immigrants as disruptive threats, though perhaps less threatening than the economic disruption of additional immigration legislation. However, as the economic recession declines and the impact of SB 1070 recedes, the persistence of these perceptions may support future reforms, particularly in domains such as health care.

While there are several signs that Arizona politics are moving to a less conservative position, including the 2012 recall of Senator Pearce, public opinion polls continue to reflect negative perceptions toward undocumented immigrants, as well as support for increased reform, including health care. Despite the strong opposition by hospital CEOs and provider associations against SB 1405, our sample of RNs indicates a predominant perception of undocumented immigrants as disruptive on healthcare costs and support for limiting care and requiring citizenship verification for receiving a wide range of healthcare services. More importantly, similar to public opinion polls, the majority of respondents support the content of SB 1405 and 1308/1309. Unfortunately, our sample size is too small to examine patterns of variation among RNs. However, it is important to note that 80.7 percent of our total sample of nurses (n=26) worked in labor and delivery, postpartum care, and NICU. All of these units are heavily influenced by the birthright citizenship issue, as they interact with individuals and families who may not have documentation. Contrary to Stephan et al.'s (2000) finding, it could be that greater intergroup interaction in this context may heighten perceptions of immigrants as disruptive threats and thus prejudice or negative attitudes.

One potential implication of this public support for reform and the opposition's neglecting to challenge the perception of undocumented immigrants as disruptive is that these reforms may re-emerge in different economic contexts. While expansive bills such as 1611 may not pass through the more conservative senate, health care is a domain where there is perhaps greater potential for reform. Though the impact of undocumented immigrants on healthcare costs is contested, the perception of immigrants as a disruption on healthcare quality and cost persists. If economic costs continue to comprise the central focus of the immigration debate, then the issue of immigrants' access to health care may slide even further into the margins.

References Cited

Associated Press
2011   Ariz. May Require Hospitals to Check Citizenship. Arizona Capitol Times, February 14. http://azcapitoltimes.com/news/2011/02/14/ariz-may-require-hospitals-to-check-citizenship/, accessed June 16, 2014.
Comstock, George A., Steven Chaffee, Natan Katzman, Maxwell McCombs, and Donald Roberts
1978   Television and Human Behavior. New York: Columbia University Press.

Corenblum, B., and Walter G. Stephan

2001   White Fears and Native Apprehensions: An Integrated Threat Theory Approach to Intergroup Attitudes. Canadian Journal of Behavioural Science/Revue anadienne des sciences du comportement 33(4):251–268.

Cunningham, Peter J.

2006   What Accounts for Differences in the Use of Hospital Emergency Departments Across US Communities? Health Affairs 25 (Supp. Web Exclusives): W324–W336.

Fryberg, Stephanie A., Nicole M. Stephens, Rebecca Covarrubias, Hazel Rose Markus, Erin D. Carter, Giselle A. Laiduc, and Ana J. Salido

2012   How the Media Frames the Immigration Debate: The Critical Role of Location and Politics. Analyses of Social Issues and Public Policy 12(1):96–112.

Gallup Poll, July 2010. http://www.gallup.com/poll/141113/Americans-Closely-Divided-Immigration-Reform-Priority.aspx, accessed November 30, 2014.

Gans, Judith

2006   Immigration and U.S. Health Care Costs. Udall Center Fact Sheet on Immigration Policy, 2. Tucson: Udall Center for Studies in Public Policy, University of Arizona. http://udallcenter.arizona.edu/immigration/publications/fact_sheet_no_2_health_care_costs.pdf, accessed June 16, 2014.

2008   Immigrants in Arizona: Fiscal and Economic Impacts. Tucson: Udall Center for Studies in Public Policy, University of Arizona. http://udallcenter.arizona.edu/immigration/publications/impactofimmigrants08.pdf, accessed June 16, 2014.

Garcia, Tamyra Carroll, Amy B. Bernstein, and Mary Ann Bush

2010   Emergency Department Visitors and Visits: Who Used the Emergency Room in 2007? NCHS Data Brief, 38. Hyattsville, MD: National Center for Health Statistics. http://www.cdc.gov/nchs/data/databriefs/db38.pdf, accessed June 16, 2014.

Girouard, April

2011   Arizona Immigration Debate Checks Into the Hospital. Foxnews.com, February 16. http://politics.blogs.foxnews.com/2011/02/16/arizona-immigration-debate-checks-hospital, accessed June 16, 2014.

Goldman, Dana P., James P. Smith, and Neeraj Sood

2006   Immigrants and the Cost of Medical Care. Health Affairs 25(6):1700–1711.

Howard Fischer Capitol Media Services

2012   Illegal Immigration Still a Legislative Cause. Arizona Daily Sun, January 8. http://azdailysun.com/news/local/state-and-regional/illegal-immigration-still-a-legislative-cause/article_a3354cd4-ea48-59d0-bf1e-7f36d0f00a74.html, accessed June 16, 2014.

Luque, John S., Angel Bowers, Ahmed Kabore, and Ric Stewart

2013   Who Will Pick Georgia's Vidalia Onions? A Text-Driven Content Analysis of Newspaper Coverage on Georgia's 2011 Immigration Law. Human Organization 72(1):31–43.

Martin, Jack, and Eric A. Ruark

2011 [2010]   The Fiscal Burden of Illegal Immigration on United States Taxpayers. http://www.fairus.org/publications/the-fiscal-burden-of-illegal-immigration-on-u-s-taxpayers, accessed June 16, 2014. Washington, D.C.: Federation for American Immigration Reform.

Maupin, Jonathan N., and Norbert Ross
2012   Expectations of Similarity and Cultural Difference in Conceptual Models of Ill-
        ness: A Comparison of Medical Staff and Mexican Migrants. Human Organization
        71(3):306–316.
McLeod, Douglas M., and Benjamin H. Detenber
1999   Framing Effects of Television News Coverage of Social Protest. Journal of Com-
        munication 49(3):3–23.
Mohatny, Sarita A., Steffie Woolhandler, David U. Himmelstein, Susmita Pati, Olveen Car-
        rasquillo, and David H. Bor
2005   Health Care Expenditures of Immigrants in the United States: A Nationally Rep-
        resentative Analysis. American Journal of Public Health 95(8):1431–1438.
Pulse Opinion Research Poll, August 2009a. http://www.fairus.org/facts/public-opinion,
        accessed November 30, 2014.
Pulse Opinion Research Poll, September 3, 2009b. http://www.progressivesforimmigra
        tionreform.org/healthcare-survey-of-600-progressives-and-liberals/, accessed
        November 30, 2014.
Pulse Opinion Research Poll, September 3, 2009c. http://www.progressivesforimmigra
        tionreform.org/healthcare-survey-of-600-progressives-and-liberals/, accessed
        November 30, 2014.
Pulse Opinion Research Poll, August 26, 2009d. http://www.fairus.org/facts/public-opin
        ion, accessed November 30, 2014.
Pulse Opinion Research Poll, August 26, 2009e. http://www.prnewswire.com/news-releases
        /national-poll-finds-most-americans-believe-immigration-adversely-affects-the-
        quality-and-cost-of-healthcare-62181357.html, accessed November 30, 2014.
Pulse Opinion Research Poll, August, 2009f. http://www.fairus.org/facts/public-opinion,
        accessed November 30, 2014.
Rasmussen Poll, November 2009a. http://www.fairus.org/facts/public-opinion, accessed
        November 30, 2014.
Rasmussen Poll, December 2009b. http://www.fairus.org/facts/public-opinion, accessed
        November 30, 2014.
Rasmussen Poll, September 2009c. http://www.fairus.org/facts/public-opinion, accessed
        November 30, 2014.
Rasmussen Poll, June 2009d. http://www.fairus.org/facts/public-opinion, accessed No-
        vember 30, 2014.
Rasmussen Poll, March 2010a. http://www.fairus.org/facts/public-opinion, accessed No-
        vember 30, 2014.
Rasmussen Poll, April, 19, 2011. http://www.fairus.org/facts/public-opinion, accessed No-
        vember 30, 2014.
Restrepo, Lucas
2010   Arizona Immigration Law and Medical Practice. New England Journal of Medi-
        cine 362(25):2432.
Sibley, Chris G., James H. Liu, and Steve Kirkwood
2006   Toward a Social Representations Theory of Attitude Change: The Effect of Message
        Framing on General and Specific Attitudes Toward Equality and Entitlement. New
        Zealand Journal of Psychology 35(1):3–13.

Stephan, Walter G., Rolando Diaz-Loving, and Anne Duran

2000   Integrated Threat Theory and Intercultural Attitudes: Mexico and the United States. Journal of Cross-Cultural Psychology 31(2):240–249.

Stephan, Walter G., and Cookie White Stephan

2000   An Integrated Threat Theory of Prejudice. *In* Reducing Prejudice and Discrimination. Claremont Symposium on Applied Social Psychology. Stuart Oskamp, ed. Pp. 23–46. Mahwah, NJ: Lawrence Erlbaum Associates.

Stephan, Walter G., Oscar Ybarra, and Kimberly Rios Morrison

2009   Intergroup Threat Theory. *In* Handbook of Prejudice, Stereotyping, and Discrimination. Pp. 43–59. Todd D. Nelson, ed. New York: Psychology Press.

Stimpson, Jim P., Fernando A. Wilson, and Karl Eschbach

2010   Trends in Health Care Spending for Immigrants in the United States. Health Affairs 29(3):544–550.

U.S. General Accounting Office (GAO)

2004   Undocumented Aliens: Questions that Persist about Their Impact on Hospitals' Uncompensated Care Costs. Report to Congressional Requesters. GAO-04-472. http://www.gao.gov/assets/250/242452.pdf, accessed June 16, 2014.

Velasco González, Karina, Maykel Verkuyten, Jeroen Weesie, and Edwin Poppe

2008   Prejudice towards Muslims in the Netherlands: Testing Integrated Threat Theory. British Journal of Social Psychology 47(4):667–685.

Zogby Poll, July 2009. http://www.fairus.org/facts/public-opinion, accessed November 30, 2014.

13

Conclusion

Migration and Disruptions from Prehistory to the Present

TAKEYUKI TSUDA AND BRENDA J. BAKER

The chapters in this book illustrate many of the similarities in migrations during the past and present. Using a set of unifying themes and a common analytical framework (Tsuda et al., chapter 1), contributors to this volume demonstrate the merits of interaction among scholars studying ancient and recent migrations in framing their investigations. In this conclusion, we wish to elaborate further on aspects of the common analytical framework developed in chapter 1, especially in the context of disruptions.

We reemphasize that a principal goal is gauging the *relative importance* of disruptions as a cause and consequence of human migration, and we do not assume that all migrations are related to disruptions. Whether disruptions in sending societies actually result in migration depends on the contextual vulnerability or resilience of local populations. In addition, not all consequences of migration in receiving societies are disruptive, and even those that initially are disruptive may eventually be reversed or lead to transformative changes.

Migrant-Sending Societies: The Relevance of Disruptions

A significant number of migratory flows in both the past and present can be attributed to the direct or indirect result of various types of environmental, political, and economic disruptions, including environmental degradation and natural disasters, regime instability or collapse, religious and ethnic conflict and persecution, warfare and invasions, and economic crises and decline. Such disruptions have produced three types of migrants: environmental migrants leaving habitats that can no longer sustain their livelihoods, political refugees fleeing ethnopolitical conflict or persecution, and commoner or labor migrants seeking better economic opportunities and livelihoods elsewhere.

According to the United Nations Department of Economic and Social Affairs (2012), the number of people living outside their country of birth increased 124 percent, from 95.5 million in 1970 to 214 million in 2010. Although this figure represents only three percent of the world's population of 6.8 billion, it is dwarfed by the total number of internal migrants who do not cross international borders.[1] What is not clear is how many of these international and internal migrants are responding to various types of disruptions. Therefore, even modern migration specialists must investigate the significance of disruptions as a factor stimulating migration.

While we recognize that the severity of a disruption depends on its size, scale, duration, and frequency, even serious social and environmental disruptions cannot always be assumed to produce migratory outflows. The chapters within this volume demonstrate that whether a disruption results in migration depends on a variety of other variables, including contextual social factors that contribute to the vulnerability or resilience of local populations. In addition, migration usually is not only the result of disruptive push factors since significant pull factors that attract migrants to receiving areas must also be involved. Finally, social barriers that inhibit migration must also be considered.

Migration as a Response to Environmental Disruptions

Among the various causes for ancient migrations identified by archaeologists and bioarchaeologists, environmental disruptions are cited frequently. Unstable or deteriorating environmental conditions such as climatic changes, droughts, floods, and overexploitation or resource depletion pushed people out of certain regional or local areas (e.g., Ahlstrom et al. 1995:126–127, 131–132; Anthony 1990:901, 906–907; Beekman, chapter 4; Beekman and Christensen 2003; Cabana et al. 2008:439–440; Cameron 1995:109; Clark 2001:2, 73–74; D'Andrea et al. 2011; Palkovich 1996:184–185; Storey et al. 2002:286–287). Entire settlements were sometimes abandoned, ranging from densely populated centers like the Mayan sites of Copán, Palenque, and Tikal by the end of the Classic period, ca. AD 1000 (Storey et al. 2002) to smaller towns or villages in sparsely populated regions such as the American Southwest, where a long-term pattern of settlement shifts, termed "serial migration" by Bernardini (2005:34, 2011:37), is evident among Puebloan peoples (see also Bernardini 1998; Cameron 1995; Clark

2001:90; Duff 1998:44; Fowles 2011:48–49; Palkovich 1996:184–186, 191–192). It is possible that ancient populations may have been more vulnerable to environmental disruptions because of their more limited technological means of mitigating them, although modern technology produces its own environmental impacts.

In the modern world, various types of environmental disruptions, including natural disasters, environmental degradation, technological disasters, and massive development projects that deprive local populations of their habitats are a significant factor in population displacement, especially among developing countries (e.g., the ongoing impact of dam construction on Nubian populations in the Nile Valley—see, for example, Dafalla 1975 and Hafsaas-Tsakos 2011). As construction of huge dams and irrigation projects alter ecosystems in once remote areas and natural disasters and coastal degradation related to global warming worsen in the future, more environmentally induced migrations will result (Black et. al. 2011:S7; Hugo 1996:113–117; Kolmannskog 2009:2; see also Loker 2003; Unruh et al. 2004). However, there are no reliable statistics on the number of environmental migrants, despite some exaggerated and alarmist estimates (see Myers 1997:167–168), largely because the extent to which environmental disruptions are a direct cause of out-migration is not always clear, except in cases of severe natural disasters (see Castles 2006:11–12). While some environmental catastrophes, such as massive floods, hurricanes, tsunamis, tornados, and nuclear disasters, are so sudden and severe that people have no choice but to flee en masse, such rapid-onset disasters tend to be relatively rare and usually result in short-term population displacements to nearby areas (Black et al. 2011:S7; Lonergan 1998:11). Therefore, the speed (or rate of change) of a disruption is a principal factor in determining its severity. When the same magnitude of disruption occurs suddenly over a shorter period, it will be more severe and will more likely result in out-migration than if it occurs over a long period (see also Renaud et al. 2011).

Environmental migration, therefore, cannot be understood through a "kinetic" model (Kunz 1973) in which external disruptive forces automatically produce migration through a simple cause and effect mechanism. Such oversimplified understandings have led some environmental migration scholars (called "maximalists") to envision progressively larger waves of refugees produced by the increasing severity of environmental disruptions (e.g., see Jacobson 1988; Myers 1997). Other scholars, however, question the extent to which environmental disruptions directly instigate out-migration because the decision to move is shaped by myriad demographic, socioeconomic, political, and institutional structures (e.g., Bardsley and Hugo 2010:246; Black et al. 2011:S4–S6; Hugo 1996:117; Kolmannskog 2009:3, Lonergan 1998:6, 11; Lubkemann 2008a:17–19; Morrissey, chapter 9). Migrants often respond to immediate economic hardships created by environmental disruptions (Afifi 2011). For example, migrants subjected to periodic flooding mostly cite economic and social reasons for moving instead of environmental factors (Dun 2011:e209–e212). Thus, the role of environmental disruptions in causing migration ranges from very important (especially in the case of rapid-onset, catastrophic disruptions) to being just one of many contributing factors (especially in the case of slow-onset disruptions; see Bardsley and Hugo 2010:241; Hugo 1996:109; Kolmannskog 2009:3).

Most environmental disruptions tend to be slow-onset, long-term changes, such as land degradation and coastal erosion, natural-resource depletion, climate change, drought, and desertification (see, for example, chapters in Unruh et al. 2004). Because affected populations have more time to respond and adapt in situ to such changes, the link between disruptions and out-migration is less direct. In fact, a prolonged period of drought initially may intensify a people's sociopolitical and cultural activities in an attempt to mitigate its effects, instead of triggering out-migration, as Beekman (chapter 4) demonstrates for northern Mesoamerica during the Epiclassic period. In the south-central Andes, however, Knudson and Torres-Rouff (chapter 6) show that gradual climate change and political disintegration actually resulted in decreased migration during the Late Intermediate Period as people became more insular with the disruption of social and economic ties.

Migration as a Response to Political Disruptions

Political disruptions are another commonly invoked reason for migrations in the distant past. External political conflicts with neighboring peoples (raids, wars, invasions, and other military threats) as well as internal conflicts, political disintegration, and persecution often forced threatened peoples to leave or flee their homes in the past (e.g., Bernardini 1998; Chapman and Hamerow 1997; Clark 2001:74; Cowgill, chapter 5; Fowler 2011; Hamerow 1997; Storey et al. 2002:286).

Political disruptions are an important cause of migration today, as in antiquity. Significant numbers of people are forced to flee persecution, political instability, wars, and other conflicts, although their numbers remain only a fraction of the world's migrants. For example, according to the United Nations High Commissioner for Refugees (2013), an estimated 16.3

million international refugees and asylum seekers, and a much larger number of internally displaced people (28.8 million), had fled some type of political disruption or persecution in 2012. The types of political disruptions that produce refugees include wars between states, but are more likely to be intrastate armed conflicts between ethnic, religious, or political groups, such as insurgencies or rebellions against states (Black et al. 2011:S6). Repressive regimes that persecute or commit genocide against specific groups have generated refugee flows, as have the collapse of governments, multiethnic nation-states, and empires. The creation of new nation-states in the recent past (including through decolonization) has also been politically disruptive and produced refugees, especially when it involved internal partitioning, wars for independence, conflicts over contested borders, and the repression or expulsion of unwanted ethnic minorities (see Schmeidl 2001; Weiner 1996; Zolberg et al. 1989:chapter 9). However, economic and sociocultural factors are also involved in shaping responses to war and violence (Lubkemann 2008a:introduction; Lucassen et al. 2010:9–10). For instance, political conflict and persecution often threaten the economic livelihoods of local peoples, making economic disruption the most proximate cause of refugee migration (e.g., see Ager 1999:3–4), again illustrating the complexity of intertwined factors that lead to migration.

Migration as a Response to Economic Disruptions

Although archaeologists and bioarchaeologists do not mention economic disruptions as a cause of prehistoric migrations very often, they may have played a greater role than generally known but may be harder to recognize using material cultural and skeletal remains. Environmental disruptions may also have led to various types of economic disruptions. Since much of contemporary migration is caused by economic pressures and opportunities elsewhere, this pattern must be extrapolated into the past to infer that similar economic forces influenced decisions to migrate among ancient households and social groups.

At present, most international migration is not a product of political or environmental disruptions, but a response to long-term structural economic and demographic inequalities between poorer, overpopulated developing countries and richer developed countries with declining populations and labor shortages (Castles and Miller 2003:22–26; Martin et al. 2006:3–13; Massey et al. 1993:432–444). Disparities between developed and developing countries and urban and rural areas within countries account for most economic labor migration today because population and labor market imbalances have created an oversupply of workers in economically under-developed sending areas and a strong demand for inexpensive unskilled migrant workers in developed receiving areas (Tsuda 2007:19). Therefore, the economic forces that drive contemporary labor migration are much more the product of the unequal distribution of capital and political power between developed and developing regions than temporary and cyclical economic disruptions in sending countries or communities (Castles and Miller 2003:25–26; Cornelius 1998; Massey 1988; Tsuda 1999b). A number of scholars have noted how the penetration of capital from rich developed countries into less developed countries (through direct foreign investment or free-trade zones) has disrupted less competitive rural economies, leading to mass migration to urban areas and international migration to developed countries (Hamilton and Chinchilla 1996; Massey et al. 1993:444–447; Sassen 1988). Thus, many internal population movements seem to consist of rural-to-urban economic migrants who cross a significant social boundary (Hugo 1996; International Organization for Migration 2008:173–183; Paul 2005:372–373). Rural-to-urban migration probably occurred commonly in the past, but it has not been a major focus of investigation. The extent to which unequal distribution of resources and power affected migration in antiquity would have varied considerably among different times and places, but they were undoubtedly factors drawing people from rural or marginal areas to centers of political, religious, and economic power (e.g., see Beekman, chapter 4).

Local Contexts of Vulnerability and Resilience

It is also important to remember that political or environmental disruptions cannot be viewed as automatic triggers of migration, because people's responses to a disruptive event vary and are influenced by numerous local contextual factors that determine a community's level of vulnerability or resilience. As a result, the same disruption can cause some people to abandon their homes, whereas others are able to absorb its effects without being forced to migrate (see also Black et al. 2011:S7; Lonergan 1998:11; Morrissey, chapter 9). Therefore, the threshold at which a disruption becomes significant enough to push people out of a sending area is not simply a mechanical reflection of its absolute severity.

Although a multitude of factors render certain populations more or less resilient to disruptions, perhaps the most important is access to resources such as wealth, income, land, and raw materials, as well as social networks, community/institutional support, political power, and government assistance (see also Castles 2002:4–5; Gilbert and McLeman 2010:13–16; Hewitt 1997:146–147, 153; Wisner et al. 2004:11–12). Such resources constitute "barrier effects" that James Morrissey discusses in chapter 9, which increase resilience and reduce vulnerability to environmental disruptions, lowering the possibility of out-migration. Access to resources is often influenced by variables such as class, gender, ethnicity, religious affiliation, health status, and age. Those with access to multiple resources generally are better able to weather environmental and political disruptions without resorting to migration (Gilbert and McLeman 2010:17; Julca 2011), whereas those who lack resources are more vulnerable and are more likely to be displaced (analogous to what Morrissey calls "additive" or "vulnerability effects" in chapter 9). Because people with the fewest socioeconomic resources are the most susceptible to disruptions and more likely to migrate (Gray and Mueller 2012; Hugo 1996:110; Lonergan 1998:10; Myers et al. 2008), most contemporary political and environmental refugee flows occur in poorer, developing countries (Hugo 1996:110, 113–115; Malkki 1995b:503; Suhrke 1994:473–474; Swain 1996:596).

The relative resilience of local populations is often more important than the absolute severity of disruptions in determining whether they migrate. As a result, different groups within the same society can have different thresholds at which they succumb to disruptive forces and are forced to migrate. Disruptions, therefore, cannot be given an artificial objectivity and physicality outside of the social and cultural relations through which they are constituted, since their impact is ultimately mediated by local contexts of resilience and vulnerability.[2] In addition, migration is not always an indication of a group's vulnerability or lack of resilience (cf. Adger 2000:357; Bardsley and Hugo 2010:243). Migration can be an adaptive strategy in the face of disruptions that, in turn, can enhance the resilience of local communities by providing them with economic and social resources, as well as new opportunities (Adger 2000:355; Julca 2011; Locke et al. 2000; Lubkemann 2008a:introduction). This strategy is especially true for sending communities where migration has become so pervasive and entrenched that a "culture of migration" has developed in which a high regard for the benefits of out-migration creates an enduring cultural propensity to relocate elsewhere as a life-course strategy (Cornelius 1992; Kandel and Massey 2002; Tsuda 1999a). Such a "migration mentality" was evident among historic Pueblo peoples, whose continual mobility was reinforced by rituals of movement in anticipation of (and to practice) future migrations (Fowles 2011). As a result, the population movements caused by disruptions often follow prior and preexisting migratory pathways (Bardsley and Hugo 2010:243–244; Beekman, chapter 4; Lubkemann 2008b:458–461).

Because of the inherently complex and varied nature of local responses to disruptive events, it is problematic to refer to politically or environmentally induced migrations simply as "forced" or "involuntary" refugee flows (Black et al. 2011:S4; Morrissey, chapter 9; Zolberg et al. 1989:30; see also Lucassen et al. 2010:8–9). Except in the most severe cases, local peoples threatened by disruptions have a choice to leave or stay and are not necessarily expelled by force or by threat of death (see also Schaeffer 2010). In most cases, their migration is an active decision shaped by local social contexts. Some decide they must move when faced with disruptions, whereas others choose to remain and cope with the environmental risks or political violence. Clearly, the degree of coercion is a continuum that ranges from migrants who have little control to those who have considerable control over their relocation (Bates 2002:467–468; Hugo 1996; Renaud et al. 2011). Therefore, to refer to such peoples as simply forced or involuntary refugees is to overemphasize the determinative impact of disruptions on migration and to ultimately portray them as mere victims without agency (Lubkemann 2008a:5–6).

Migration Pull Factors and Barriers

When assessing the relative importance of disruptions in instigating population flows, pull forces that draw migrants to receiving societies as well as barriers that make it difficult for some people to relocate must also be considered. Migration usually is not initiated without significant pull factors that attract people to receiving areas, such as better economic or educational opportunities, environmental conditions, or political stability (what Morrissey calls mobility "enabling effects" in chapter 9). If pull factors are strong enough, people may migrate even if the disruptive push factors are moderate.

Even in the distant past, archaeologists have noted that migrants used kin and other social networks, as well as trade routes, seasonal movements, and religious pilgrimages to obtain necessary information about destination areas (Anthony 1990:896, 903–904; Beekman and Christensen 2003:147; Cameron 1995:109; Clark 2001:74; Duff 1998:32–33) and were pulled to regions that had better environmental conditions and subsistence opportunities (e.g., Ahlstrom et al. 1995:126–127, 131–132; Anthony 1990:901, 906–907; Beekman and Christensen 2003; Cabana et al. 2008:439–440; Cameron 1995:109; Clark 2001:2, 73–74; Cowgill, chapter 5). In chapter 4,

Christopher Beekman even surmises that some polities in Mesoamerica attempted to attract migrants from surrounding areas, constituting an early immigration policy. Invaders and conquerors were also "pulled" to other regions in order to exploit human and environmental resources and better habitats (e.g., European colonization of the New World and Africa and ancient Egyptian incursions into Nubia). Likewise, the political disintegration of states and civilizations not only caused out-migration, but instigated the in-migration of populations intending to take advantage of the political collapse and the resulting power vacuum (e.g., Beekman and Christensen 2003:149; Cowgill, chapter 5). In such cases, a political disruption in another region becomes a migratory pull factor. Despite their importance, however, pull factors alone usually do not instigate population movements unless significant push factors are also present in the sending area. Ultimately, migration results from a combination of push and pull factors and is more likely to occur if both are present (see Morrisey, chapter 9; Tsuda 1999a).

Finally, even if compelling disruptive push factors are simultaneously coupled with pull factors, their impact can be limited if there are factors that deter or prevent people from migrating (see Morrisey's "barrier effects" in chapter 9). These factors can include age (the very old can find it difficult to relocate), strong attachments to one's native territory, or lack of opportunities elsewhere. People can also lack the economic resources and social network connections necessary to migrate. Disruptions of established economic and social networks that enabled migration can impede mobility, as suggested by Knudson and Torres-Rouff (chapter 6). In the case of contemporary international migration, the world's poorest, who have few economic and social network resources, do not migrate (Castles and Miller 2003:23), except in response to extreme disruptions that literally force them to move. Repressive nation-states have sometimes prevented their citizens from emigrating as well.

Migrant-Receiving Societies: Disruptions and Resilience

Not only can various types of disruptions contribute to the displacement of peoples, migratory inflows may have disruptive consequences for the host societies that receive them. Some migrant groups are absorbed easily by the receiving population, whereas others have been known to disrupt economic, environmental, ethnic, and political systems and even cause social disorder and state collapse. Whether migratory inflows lead to disruption depends on both the characteristics of the migrants and the resilience of the host society. In addition, the short-term impact of migration and its long-term consequences must be distinguished since initial impacts eventually may be reversed or transformative in the long run depending on the resilience of the receiving society and its environment.

Most research on past migrations has been devoted to identifying newcomers to an area, but more recent work has begun deciphering the impact of migrants on receiving societies. Many examples in the archaeological record have suggested that in-migration often contributed to the collapse of local communities, polities, and even empires. In many world regions, different nonlocal people are apparent at particular times and places, as at Mesoamerican centers (e.g., Beekman, chapter 4; Cowgill, chapter 5; Beekman and Christensen 2003:152; Storey 1992), within and outside of Andean polities (e.g., Buzon et al. 2012; Knudson 2008; Knudson and Torres-Rouff, chapter 6); throughout Europe during the first millenium AD (e.g., Burmeister 2000:548–552; Heather 2010; Hills, chapter 2; Zakrzewski 2011, chapter 3), and between Egypt and Nubia (e.g., Buzon 2006; Buzon et al. 2007; Buzon and Bowen 2010; Buzon and Simonetti 2013; Morkot 2000; Smith 2003). Military invasion by conquering peoples was a prevalent form of migration (e.g., see Chapman and Hamerow 1997). Conquests typically result in subsequent colonization with severe disruptive consequences for the receiving population, which have been a focus of many scholars interested in past migrations. For example, the impact of European intrusion on New World populations has garnered considerable attention among anthropologists, demographers, and historians (e.g., Baker and Kealhofer 1996; Crosby 1972; Denevan 1992; Dobyns 1983; Fitzhugh 1985; Hassig 1994; Hutchinson 2007; Jennings 1975; Larsen and Milner 1994; Ramenofsky 1987; Reff 1991; Rouse 1992; Spicer 1962; Stannard 1992; Stearn and Stearn 1945; Steele 1994; Stojanowski 2010; Thomas 1989, 1990, 1991; Thornton 1987; Trigger 1985; Verano and Ubelaker 1992).

Although migration in the distant past may indeed have been very disruptive, this perception may partly reflect the inherent limitations of archaeological methods. Archaeologists traditionally have traced in-migrations mainly by identifying sudden shifts in local material culture, settlement patterns, and funerary practices (see Adams et al. 1978; Anthony 1990; Burmeister 2000; Cabana 2011). Changes in material culture in the archaeological record, however, do not necessarily mean that the local population was replaced or re-peopled by a large wave of newcomers. Migratory groups cannot always be identified by a specific material style or a distinctive set of artifacts (Beekman and Christensen 2003:135; Buzon 2006:683–684; Burmeister 2000:540; Cabana 2011; Cowgill, chapter 5; Zakrzewski, chapter 3). Others may simply choose not to emphasize their ethnic identity through material culture and may not leave a material trace of their presence (Beekman, chapter 4; Beekman and Christensen 2003:135).

Alternatively, even if immigrants were a minority in the new region, they may have attained political or ethnic/cultural dominance over the indigenous populace, disproportionately influencing local material culture, settlement patterns, and mortuary practices (e.g., Cowgill, chapter 5; Smith 2003). Elucidating such possibilities in the past is aided by multifaceted investigations that combine cultural and biological data (e.g., Hills, chapter 2; Knudson and Torres-Rouff, chapter 6; Zakrzewski, chapter 3). The careful contextualization of biological data within its cultural setting—the bioarchaeological approach—has improved our detection of migrants and our understanding of these processes. For example, Buzon (2006) investigated ancient Nubian mortuary remains from Tombos, an Egyptian colonial town during the New Kingdom (a component dating ca. 1400–1050 BC) Although burial styles and grave goods suggest a predominance of Egyptian settlers at Tombos, analysis of cranial morphology shows biological affinities with both Egyptians and Nubians, indicating coresidence of these groups. Thus, most of the indigenous Nubians adopted Egyptian styles in death. Subsequent stable isotope analyses confirm the presence of some first-generation Egyptian settlers at Tombos, although the majority of those interred in Egyptian style have local isotope signatures (Buzon and Bowen 2010; Buzon and Simonetti 2013; Buzon et al. 2007).

The effects of modern migration are rarely as disruptive as they often are portrayed in the distant past. Today, cases of migrations that lead to the collapse of entire societies or nation-states or the wholesale displacement of local populaces are rare (Tsuda 2011:325). Nonetheless, there remain serious concerns about the potentially disruptive consequences of migration on receiving societies. Immigrants can be economically disruptive for labor markets by reducing employment opportunities and wages for native workers while burdening public services and social welfare systems (e.g., see Maupin, chapter 12; Tsuda, chapter 11). Expanding immigrant populations can also contribute to degradation and depletion of limited environmental resources, which is a concern in developing countries (Curran and Agardy 2004; Eder, chapter 10; Pradhan 2004). Since migrants often consist of biologically and culturally different peoples, they are often seen as a threat to the national identity and unity of host countries. Migration has been politically disruptive to various receiving societies as well. The rising volume of international illegal immigration has seriously challenged the sovereignty of nation-states and their ability to control territorial borders (Cornelius and Tsuda 2004) and has led to significant political backlashes and anti-immigrant movements at both the national and local levels (Chavez 2008; Maupin, chapter 12; Tsuda, chapter 11; Varsanyi 2010).

Disruptions and the Characteristics of Migration Flows

Certain attributes of migrants can make them more disruptive to host societies. The factors we have considered in this book are the size, duration, and frequency of the migration flow and the type of migrant involved. Size is the most apparent variable, since larger migrant groups tend to place a greater strain on limited resources and are less likely to be integrated smoothly into the host populace. Social disruption theory from rural boomtown studies claims that rapid population growth caused by in-migration leads to a period of crisis that disrupts social ties and community cohesion, cultural worldviews, collective identities, and even individual mental health (England and Albrecht 1984; Park and Stokowski 2009).

Size, of course, must be viewed in relation to the size of the host population, since the same number of immigrants may have a greater disruptive impact on smaller host societies than larger ones. Therefore, even a small immigrant group can have significantly disruptive consequences in sparsely populated areas, as seems to have been the case in the ancient American Southwest, where local populations were occasionally displaced by migrants, although they more frequently coresided with newcomers (e.g., see Clark 2011). Even in modern societies, small indigenous groups can be overwhelmed by in-migrating populations, causing the reverse assimilation of the host population to the migrants, instead of the other way around (e.g., see Eder, chapter 10).

The size of the migrant group relative to the host society, however, may not always correlate with its disruptive magnitude. Certain types of migrants generally are more disruptive than others, even if their numbers are limited. Invaders and conquerors are much more disruptive than labor migrants, for instance, since they plan to seize political power through violence and warfare and impose their sociocultural system on the native populace. Despite prevalent images of hordes of invaders overrunning local populations, "invasions" can consist of relatively small numbers of migrants who are able to have a disproportionate impact because of their military and political power, as shown by Catherine Hills in chapter 2, and by the Egyptianized Nubians previously described (Buzon 2006; Smith 2003).

Duration and frequency, however, must be considered along with the size of the influx to gauge its disruptive impact. Although a sudden, one-time arrival of a large number of immigrants is short on duration and low on frequency, it is usually much more disruptive than frequent but small influxes of migrants over extended periods of time. Sustained migration of larger numbers of people, however, will be more likely to overwhelm the receiving society, as demonstrated by European colonization of the Americas.

Several contributors to this volume also considered the extent of difference between immigrants and the host populace as an important factor that determines potential disruption to the receiving society. In general, immigrants who differ more, both biologically and culturally, from the majority host population have greater disruptive consequences since they are more likely to disturb the dominant status quo by introducing new technologies, subsistence and settlement patterns, ethnic groups, and ideology. Such groups also have a greater tendency to cause tensions and conflict with members of the receiving population. In contrast, those who are similar to the receiving society are more likely to be incorporated smoothly and assimilated into the local society with significantly less disruption. Consequently, modern nation-states have had ethnic-preference policies that prioritize immigrants who are ethnically related to the host population, usually drawing from the country's pool of diasporic descendants born abroad (Joppke 2005; Tsuda 2009).

In antiquity, migrants who had significantly different material cultures, settlement patterns, and biological characteristics are most likely to have left a mark on the material and skeletal record. Although cultural differences of migrants sometimes are hard to detect through material remains because, as previously noted, newcomers may not always correspond with a bounded assemblage of artifacts, their biological differences can be identified through skeletal morphology (see Frankenberg and Konigsberg 2011; Konigsberg 2006; Stojanowski and Schillaci 2006), genetic makeup (see Bolnick 2011; Stone 2008), and biogeochemical analyses that identify first-generation immigrants based on their bone and tooth composition (see Knudson 2011). Certain repetitive activities can leave indicators on skeletons that help distinguish groups of people, such as the religious practices discussed by Sonia Zakrzewski in chapter 3. In contrast, migrants who biologically or socially resembled host populations are less traceable. In the contemporary world, migrants who are ethnically and linguistically different from the host populace (e.g., Mexican immigrants in the United States) cause considerable disruption and controversy, whereas those who are ethnically and linguistically similar easily blend in with the dominant majority and are hardly noticed (e.g., Canadian immigrants in the United States).

Migrants who cross major boundaries are more likely to differ from host populaces and be more disruptive than people who move within the same ecological, economic, sociocultural, or political region. Most modern migrants (including internal migrants) are boundary crossers, and migrants in the past often seem to have covered considerable distances over geographical, political, or ethnolinguistic boundaries as well. Of course, ancient migrations were likely to have been much shorter distance on average than today, since modern transportation has greatly increased the speed and ease of international travel to distant regions. Nonetheless, migration in the past was often the cumulative result of many shorter-distance migrations that took place over decades or longer (the "wave of advance" and "village drift" theories; see Anthony 1990:901–902; Darling 2011) that eventually became long-distance movements across significant boundaries. In addition, there were plenty of short-distance migrations over significant boundaries and borders. Even boundaries that were traversed readily in the past persisted through time as markers of spatial zones of difference (see Anthony 2010; Smith 2003) and continue to do so today despite increased migration of peoples across them in an era of globalization.

Migratory movements across certain boundaries of difference, however, are more likely to be disruptive than others. The contemporary migration of predominantly poor peoples from developing countries to developed countries (across a significant economic boundary) is often seen as quite disruptive if migrants are perceived as an economic burden on host societies. Population movements that occur over significant cultural and linguistic (or ethnic) boundaries are also likely to be more disruptive because they often threaten a country's ethnonational unity. Although ancient migrants who traversed environmental/ecological boundaries sometimes brought different technologies and subsistence or settlement patterns, modern migrants who cross such boundaries today are less likely to be disruptive. Current international migration across political borders is not necessarily disruptive when they do not correspond with boundaries of significant economic or cultural/ethnic/linguistic difference (again, Canadian immigration to the United States). In contrast, Mexican immigrants in the United

States have crossed a political border that overlaps with major economic, linguistic, cultural, and ethnic boundaries, making them more different and disruptive.

Even when migrants cross boundaries and differ from local populaces, their eventual impact ultimately depends on their rate of cultural and social assimilation and incorporation into the receiving society. Immigrants who are unwilling or unable to assimilate and therefore maintain their cultural and socioeconomic differences tend to be more disruptive than those who assimilate. They can be considered a threat to the ethnic cohesion and identity of the host society and provoke hostility and discrimination from the majority populace (see Maupin, chapter 12; Tsuda, chapter 11).

Among the numerous factors that influence the rate of assimilation of an immigrant group to the host society, its size and cohesion, identity, and amount of discrimination it experiences are the most important. In general, larger and more internally cohesive immigrant groups tend to assimilate slower to the host society than those that are smaller. Immigrants who are residentially segregated or confined to specific low-status occupations or castes have limited interaction with the majority population, making it difficult for them to adopt majority cultural norms or become socioeconomically incorporated into mainstream society. There are many contemporary examples of large unskilled immigrant minority groups living in self-contained ethnic and economic enclaves where they can conduct their daily lives among family and compatriots in culturally familiar settings without much contact with mainstream society (e.g., Smith 2006; Tsuda 2003). Ethnic neighborhoods also appear to have separated immigrants from the host populace in many ancient cities (e.g., at Teotihuacan—see Cowgill, chapter 5; Storey 1992).

Migrants may also maintain particularly strong minority identities (especially if their racial and ethnic differences are significant), often causing them to continue to emphasize their differences from mainstream society instead of assimilating. Even if such migrant groups are willing to assimilate, they may experience strong ethnic discrimination from the host populace, making it difficult for them to acculturate, achieve social mobility, and become integrated into mainstream society. Such marginalization and alienation among migrants may cause them to develop a "reactive ethnicity" against mainstream society (Portes 1999:465–466; Portes et al. 1999:228; see also Tsuda 2003:chapter 3), eventually leading to downward segmented assimilation to the permanent underclass (see Portes and Zhou 1993). In general, immigrant assimilation is quicker and smoother in multiethnic societies than mono-ethnic ones. In the former types of societies, immigrants generally experience more tolerance and less discrimination so it is easier for them to become socially accepted and mobile even if they retain some cultural differences.

In modern, developed countries, many first-generation immigrants do not fully assimilate. However, most of their second-generation descendants eventually become culturally assimilated, although their socioeconomic integration sometimes takes longer and some have joined the permanent underclass (Alba and Nee 1997; Waters and Jiménez 2005). In general, elite, high-skilled, and professional immigrants tend to assimilate faster than unskilled commoner immigrants because they are better educated, tend to live in mainstream suburban neighborhoods, and their occupations make them more socially mobile (e.g., Tsuda, chapter 11). Refugees have greater difficulties because they often have less social and economic capital and poorer mental and physical health, especially if they have been through traumatic experiences (e.g., Ager 1999; Connor 2010; Potocky-Tripodi 2003).[3]

Archaeological evidence of ethnically different migrants coexisting, intermingling, and assimilating to local societies is increasing, especially in cases where small groups migrated over extended periods of time (Cordell 1995:205; Stone 2003:50–54, 59, 61) or lived in more highly populated locales and multiethnic states (e.g., Adams et al. 1978:489–496, Beekman and Christensen 2003; Buzon 2006; Buzon et al. 2007; Buzon and Simonetti 2013; Cowgill, chapter 5; Smith 2003; Zakrzewski, chapter 3). Migration currently is viewed more often as a "social mixer" than a cultural replacer compared with earlier archaeological interpretations (Clark 2011:85–86). Homogeneity in material culture and settlement patterns in migrant-receiving societies can exemplify how ethnic differences between migrants and hosts were de-emphasized (Beekman, chapter 4; Stone 2003:47–50). Even invaders can be assimilated and incorporated into the host society over an extended period of time, especially if they were smaller in number (e.g., Zakrzewski, chapter 3). In contrast, large and sudden intrusions of migrants can lead to residential segregation, the persistence of differences in material culture and identity, and hostility with the host populace (e.g., Stone 2003:54–59, 61–62).

The Socially Relative Nature of Migrant Disruptions

Although there are general reasons why certain immigrant groups are more disruptive than others, the disruptive effects of any migratory inflow are socially relative. Therefore, an immigrant group may be more disruptive for certain segments of the receiving society than others. For instance, in modern host societies, native workers often find immigrants who compete for the same jobs as disruptive, but employers benefit from and depend on the lower cost of immigrant labor to stay in business. The cultural differences of immigrants may be disruptive to conservative elements of the receiving society who wish to maintain their ethnic homogeneity, but not disruptive to liberal groups or ethnic minorities that espouse multicultural diversity. Likewise, migrations in the distant past sometimes had a disproportionate impact on certain segments of the host populace, whereas others were less affected.

In addition, there is often a disconnect between the host society's perceptions of immigrant disruptions and their actual disruptive impact, as measured by objective, empirical indices. For example, unskilled Mexican immigrants are often seen as a threat to native workers and an economic burden by the public, even if there is little empirical evidence of their negative impact, as shown by Takeyuki Tsuda in chapter 11. According to James Eder (chapter 10), although agricultural migrant settlers have been more environmentally, demographically, and culturally disruptive than Muslim migrants in Palawan (Philippines), the latter are seen as more controversial among the Philippine public. Lisa Meierotto (chapter 8) discusses public perceptions about the negative environmental impact of Mexican migrants crossing a wildlife refuge on the U.S.-Mexican border, despite evidence that the U.S. Border Patrol is causing more damage. Likewise, Jonathan Maupin (chapter 12) notes that, although the uncompensated healthcare costs of undocumented immigrants is very small compared to native-born Americans, such data have little impact on the public. In all of these cases, the mass media (and other widely read publications) often shape public attitudes about immigrant disruptions.

The perceptions that host societies have about immigrants can actually influence the amount of disruption that they cause. Even if an immigrant group is not that disruptive, negative public perceptions can exacerbate its disruptive impact by leading to increased political controversy, ethnic tension, and anti-immigrant backlashes. Contemporary illegal immigrants have become a source of disruptive public wrath in many countries, since they are usually seen in an exaggerated manner as a threat to national sovereignty and public safety as well as a serious economic burden. Large numbers of refugees, especially from poor, war-torn countries, are also often seen negatively as a public burden, although a number of them do assimilate and become socially successful. Much of the disruptive anti-immigrant backlash in Western European countries is against so-called bogus asylum seekers, whom the public suspects are not actual refugees but illegal economic migrants who take advantage of generous asylum policies and feed off social welfare systems. Often, immigrants are used as a scapegoat and unfairly blamed for many of society's ills, which can become quite disruptive for the immigrants themselves, who must endure discrimination, hostility, and anti-immigrant legislation, as shown by a number of the chapters in part III of this volume.

On the other hand, even if immigration *is* actually disruptive, its negative effects may be mitigated if the host populace does not perceive it as disruptive. For instance, although a significant number of Asian immigrants in the United States are unauthorized and those who are highly skilled may have adverse effects on the employment of native IT workers, the American public generally sees them as model minorities who contribute important skills to the economy. As a result, there is very little anti-immigrant backlash against Asians (Tsuda, chapter 11).

The perceptions that ancient host populations had of migratory inflows are much harder to study using fragmentary material remains from the distant past, particularly in preliterate societies. Where documentary/historical records can be consulted, however, such perceptions may be accessible. For example, ancient Egyptians clearly portrayed foreigners of differing ethnicities, often cast as enemies on which pharaohs trod, as captives, or as tribute bearers. Such documentation, however, was typically produced by and for literate elites or by members of the dominant culture, making it more challenging to discover the attitudes of commoners toward a group of in-migrants. For example, historical documentation concerning indigenous people's reaction to and perceptions of European invaders, colonists, and settlers exists, but it is almost always written by a male European.

Host Society Resilience and Transformations

Whether migration results in social and environmental disruptions is not determined simply by the characteristics of the migrant themselves but also by the nature of the host societies that receive them. The most important factor in this respect is the resilience of receiving societies to withstand migratory disruptions. Resilience is a concept used most often in the complex adaptive socioecological systems literature, pertaining to the interaction between people and their ecological environments. Although it is employed to a much more limited extent in the urban planning literature (e.g.,

Gotham and Campenella 2010; Prosperi and Morgado 2011), the concept has not been used to analyze migration. The complex-systems literature usually defines resilience as the ability of a society to withstand disruptions without fundamental structural change (Carpenter et al. 2001:765; Gunderson et al. 2006; Holling 1973:17; Walker et al. 2004). If a social or ecological system is not resilient, disruptions can cause them to eventually weaken and decline, and even disintegrate and collapse.

Undoubtedly, there are many factors that determine a society's resilience to migratory disruptions. Receiving societies that have more economic and environmental resources to share with new migratory groups may be able to avoid social disruption (ethnic competition and conflict over scarce resources) and environmental disruption (depletion and degradation of natural resources and habitats due to expanding populations). In the contemporary world, therefore, developing countries with fewer resources have experienced more environmental disruption from immigration to both urban and rural areas (Curran and Agardy 2004; Pradhan 2004; see also Eder, chapter 10).

We also emphasize ethnic and social diversity as a key variable for resilience. A number of researchers studying socioecological systems have noted that the diversity of biological and environmental systems enhances their adaptive capacity and resilience (Carpenter et al. 2001:778; England and Albrecht 1984:233; Folke 2006:257–258; Holling 1973:18–19; Walker et al. 2004). Diversity seems to produce complex, heterogeneous systems of interdependent units with built-in functional redundancy so that deterioration of one component because of disruptions can be compensated for by others (Gotham and Campenella 2010:10, 13).[4]

As noted earlier, diverse, multiethnic societies may be able to incorporate and assimilate ethnically different immigrants into the national fabric without major disruption better than more mono-cultural and ethnically homogenous societies. Not only do they tend to have a more ethnically tolerant, multicultural ideology, culturally different immigrants are more likely to find ethnic niches and communities in which they can develop a sense of belonging and that can assist in their social integration even if they face discriminatory marginalization by the majority society. Diversity may also apply to economic and environmental resilience. A diversified economy that has many industries may weather a shock to one economic sector caused by an influx of immigrants while insulating native workers employed in other sectors (or allowing them to move to other industries).

A society with more diverse environments may be better able to withstand the deterioration of certain habitats caused by population growth without endangering others.

By definition, a truly resilient society will be able to reduce and eventually reverse the effects of a disruption without undergoing fundamental change. This standard conceptualization of resilience, however, is restrictive and seems to imply a simple binary outcome for the consequences of disruptions—either the society is able to negate the effects of the disruptive change and maintain the status quo or it is threatened with social deterioration and disintegration. As discussed in chapter 1, resilience is not simply resistance to change (Folke 2006:259) but the ability to withstand disruption by eventually returning to a state of equilibrium. In fact, one of the keys to resilience may be the ability of societies to change in sustainable ways in response to disruptions without falling into a state of disorder. Indeed, a number of complex-systems scholars have noted that the flexibility within a system to learn, innovate, and transform is an important aspect of resilience (Carpenter et al. 2001; Folke 2006:253; Gotham and Campenella 2010:9, 12; Gunderson et al. 2006). An inflexible system that cannot be changed when affected by disruptions may actually be more subject to disintegration and collapse and, thus, lacks resilience (see also Christensen 1997; Janssen et al. 2003:723).

As outlined in chapter 1, migration may initially disrupt the equilibrium of the host society. If the society is resilient, however, migration may not end up being disruptive in the long term, since the host society may eventually return to the original status quo/equilibrium or a new, transformative status quo may be established over time (a "new normal," according to Eder, chapter 10). Migrants have often introduced new ethnic groups, cultures, technologies, or subsistence systems that challenge the receiving society's status quo and may initially appear disruptive, but eventually may transform the host society by producing greater ethnic diversity, new belief systems, and new lifestyles. For example, Sonia Zakrzewski (chapter 3) shows how the Arab and Berber invaders of Spain were initially disruptive because of their ethnic differences and Islamic religion, but eventually coexisted with the local populace and were religiously and demographically incorporated into a transformed Spanish culture and populace. Likewise, James Eder (chapter 10) discusses how the initially disruptive Islamic influence of Muslim immigrants in Palawan has produced a transformation as it has become incorporated into the island's already diverse religious landscape. Takeyuki Tsuda (chapter 11) also speculates that the currently disruptive sociocultural and racial differences of Mexican immigrants eventually may transform American race relations and social class structure.

In this sense, migrants who cross more significant boundaries of environmental, cultural, and social difference may be more disruptive but are also more likely to transform host societies over the long run because they bring new and different social and cultural forms to local areas. According to Patrick Manning (2012), such cross-community migration has been a primary way in which innovations and changes have been spread throughout human history. An ancient example from Egypt is the influx of the Hyksos people from Syro-Palestine, which began during the Middle Kingdom but led to their control of the Nile delta (Lower Egypt) during the Second Intermediate Period (ca. 1674–1567 BC) and a period of warfare with competing rulers to the south. The domesticated plant and animal species and technological innovations introduced by the Hyksos, however, were rapidly adopted and adapted by indigenous Egyptians, transforming their society by the advent of the New Kingdom. In contrast, local population movements of similar peoples within the same area are less disruptive, but they are less likely to lead to transformations and may simply reinforce the existing status quo.

Thus, a certain amount of initial disruptive change caused by migrant differences may be a prerequisite to eventual transformation. Sometimes people do not acknowledge or remember the extent to which their current societies are a product of previous waves of (initially disruptive) immigrants, whose transformative contributions have been incorporated into the status quo. Such historical amnesia is more likely to occur if the migrations were in the distant past (e.g., Zakrzewski, chapter 3). Although we do not make the normative assumption that migrant transformations are always positive and desirable or an advancement over the previous status quo (cf. Folke 2006:260; Gotham and Campenella 2010:9–10), it is certainly possible that they have made an important contribution to social change.

Nonetheless, we must also be careful not to equate all the transformative changes in human history to migration since they may have spread through simple borrowing and dissemination of technologies and knowledge across societies and were not always the product of massive waves of migrants (see O'Connor 1995). Because archaeologists usually cannot observe actual population movements in the material record but can only infer them from impacts in sending and receiving areas, migration frequently has been invoked to explain transformative changes in local material artifacts, subsistence systems, and settlement patterns (Bolnick 2011:263; Cabana 2011; Rouse 1986:9). Whether such transformations were a product of a new population migrating into the area with a different material culture, the diffusion of new artifacts and lifestyles into the region (through trade, borrowing, and acculturation from neighboring peoples), or in situ development often is difficult to determine. As Cowgill (chapter 5) notes, however, local changes in decorative styles of artifacts suggest emulation of foreign styles (without migration), whereas changes in technology or manufacture suggest that migration was involved.

Future Research Directions

Despite some obvious differences between migrations in the contemporary world and those in the past, this book has shown that there are also significant continuities and common patterns. As a result, scholars investigating migrations in the present and in the distant past can certainly benefit from greater dialogue and collaboration to develop unifying concepts and common frameworks for analysis of population movements over time.

As is always the case with such broad conceptual frameworks, there are some significant shortcomings to our analysis that can be addressed in future research and collaborations. A number of scholars may take issue with our use of disruptions as the central, unifying concept for studying migration through time, although we have repeatedly emphasized that disruptions should not be considered an automatic trigger for out-migration and that contextual factors in receiving societies influence the extent to which in-migrations are disruptive. Nonetheless, since our project focused on assessing the relative importance of disruptions to human migration (see Baker and Tsuda, introduction; Tsuda et al., chapter 1), we have not emphasized the nondisruptive causes of migration or population inflows that are not associated with disruptions. Some scholars, therefore, may find that other unifying concepts are more relevant for analyzing various aspects of migration in human history.

Our conceptual framework is also based on some artificial dichotomies. The first is the present and the past. Our case studies are either from the contemporary world or the distant past, and we have no studies from the more recent past (i.e., between the fifteenth and twentieth centuries). We attempted to recruit several historians, but they were unavailable or unable to contribute. Although we have refrained from making vast generalizations that compare the present to the distant past, the binary persists and we do not account for the temporal gap between these two time periods. Nonetheless, we have attempted in this chapter to provide a number of examples that span this temporal gap. In so doing, the continuity of common features of migrations and disruptive consequences through time is demonstrated.

The other dichotomy is sending versus receiving societies. With the exception of Beekman's chapter, our contributors have tended to examine migration and disruptions separately in these two social contexts. More research directed toward specific migration flows in both sending and receiving societies and the social connections that develop across boundaries between immigrants and those left behind in sending areas is needed. For instance, it is difficult simply to examine the impact of immigrants in destination areas without an understanding of what caused them to migrate into that area in the first place. Although contemporary migration studies have focused mainly on immigrants in the host society (and sometimes in sending communities), researchers are increasingly interested in the transnational connections and relationships immigrants maintain with their home countries across territorial borders and how they simultaneously impact both sending and receiving countries (see Basch et al. 1994; Levitt and Jaworsky 2007; Portes et al. 1999; Tsuda 2012). Studying such dynamic interconnections across geographical or sociopolitical boundaries in the past is more challenging, but it has been accomplished successfully (e.g., Goldstein 2005; Ross 2013). Increased attention to this aspect of migration is needed.

Research on the actual *process* of migratory movement between various locales also is scarce. In chapter 7, Jason De León et al. examine migrants during their movement across the Mexico-U.S. border. This chapter demonstrates the information that may be gleaned directly about the process of migration from the material traces that migrants leave behind as they move. Significantly, they show how it is possible to study such migratory actions in the past using archaeological methods.

Despite (or because of) the shortcomings evident in this book, we hope that it will inspire other anthropologists to collaborate across subdisciplinary and disciplinary boundaries to provide a more comprehensive understanding of population movements throughout human history. In turn, anthropological perspectives are very useful for other disciplines studying human migration, especially history (Lucassen et al. 2010:19–20) and international relations. The ultimate goal is to reach an interdisciplinary understanding of population movements from prehistory to the present.

Notes

1. For instance, the total volume of internal migration in China and India alone is double the total number of international migrants (King et al. 2008:3). There seem to be no reliable estimates for the total number of internal migrants in the world.

2. Even the literature on disasters acknowledges that they are not just a natural phenomenon, per se, because their impact is a very social process (Bolin 1998; Kreps 1984; Myers et al. 2008:272; Oliver-Smith 1996; Wisner et al. 2004:4–5, 10–11).

3. Refugees who live in camps tend to assimilate more slowly than those who settle in towns and cities, since they are segregated and often maintain a temporary exile mentality. In contrast, the latter intend to have long-term or permanent stays and interact more with local populations (see, e.g., Ager 1999:9; Malkki 1995a; Westin 1999:28–29).

4. Other studies, however, claim that diverse social and ecological systems are not always high in resilience (Adger 2000; see also Gotham and Campenella 2010:14).

References Cited

Adams, William Y., Dennis P. Van Gerven, and Richard S. Levy
1978   The Retreat from Migrationism. Annual Review of Anthropology 7:483–532.
Adger, W. Neil
2000   Social and Ecological Resilience: Are They Related? Progress in Human Geography 24(3):347–364.
Afifi, Tamer
2011   Economic or Environmental Migration? The Push Factors in Niger. International Migration 49(S1):e95–e124.
Ager, Alastair
1999   Perspectives on the Refugee Experience. *In* Refugees: Perspectives on the Experience of Forced Migration. Alastair Ager, ed. Pp. 1–23. London: Pinter.
Ahlstrom, Richard V. N., Carla R. Van West, and Jeffrey S. Dean
1995   Environmental and Chronological Factors in the Mesa Verde–Northern Rio Grande Migration. Journal of Anthropological Archaeology 14(2):125–142.
Alba, Richard, and Victor Nee
1997   Rethinking Assimilation Theory for a New Era of Immigration. International Migration Review 31(4):826–874.
Anthony, David W.
1990   Migration in Archeology: The Baby and the Bathwater. American Anthropologist 92(4):895–914.
2010   The Horse, the Wheel, and Language: How Bronze-Age Riders from the Eurasian Steppes Shaped the Modern World. Princeton: Princeton University Press.
Baker, Brenda J., and Lisa Kealhofer, eds.
1996   Bioarchaeology of Native American Adaptation in the Spanish Borderlands. The Ripley P. Bullen Series. Gainesville: University Press of Florida.
Bardsley, Douglas K., and Graeme J. Hugo
2010   Migration and Climate Change: Examining Thresholds of Change to Guide Effective Adaptation Decision-Making. Population and Environment 32(2/3):238–262.

Basch, Linda G., Nina Glick Schiller, and Cristina Szanton Blanc
1994   Nations Unbound: Transnational Projects, Postcolonial Predicaments, and Deterritorialized Nation-States. Amsterdam: Gordon and Breach Publishers.
Bates, Diane C.
2002   Environmental Refugees? Classifying Human Migrations Caused by Environmental Change. Population and Environment 23(5):465–477.
Beekman, Christopher S., and Alexander F. Christensen
2003   Controlling for Doubt and Uncertainty Through Multiple Lines of Evidence: A New Look at the Mesoamerican Nahua Migrations. Journal of Archaeological Method and Theory 10(2):111–164.
Bernardini, Wesley R.
1998   Conflict, Migration, and the Social Environment: Interpreting Architectural Change in Early and Late Pueblo IV Aggregations. In Migration and Reorganization: The Pueblo IV Period in the American Southwest. Katherine A. Spielmann, ed. Pp. 91–114. Arizona State University Anthropological Research Papers No. 5. Tempe: Department of Anthropology, Arizona State University.
2005   Reconsidering Spatial and Temporal Aspects of Prehistoric Cultural Identity: A Case Study from the American Southwest. American Antiquity 70(1):31–54.
2011   Migration in Fluid Social Landscapes. In Rethinking Anthropological Perspectives on Migration. Graciela S. Cabana and Jeffery J. Clark, eds. Pp. 31–44. Gainesville: University Press of Florida.
Black, Richard, W. Neil Adger, Nigel W. Arnell, Stefan Dercon, Andrew Geddes, and David S. G. Thomas
2011   The Effect of Environmental Change on Human Migration. Global Environmental Change 21(Suppl. 1):S3–S11.
Bolin, Robert C., with Lois Stanford
1998   The Northridge Earthquake: Vulnerability and Disaster. London: Routledge.
Bolnick, Deborah A.
2011   Continuity and Change in Anthropological Perspectives on Migration: Insights from Molecular Anthropology. In Rethinking Anthropological Perspectives on Migration. Graciela S. Cabana and Jeffery J. Clark, eds. Pp. 263–277. Gainesville: University Press of Florida.
Burmeister, Stefan
2000   Archaeology and Migration: Approaches to an Archaeological Proof of Migration. Current Anthropology 41(4):539–567.
Buzon, Michele R.
2006   Biological and Ethnic Identity in New Kingdom Nubia: A Case Study from Tombos. Current Anthropology 47(4):683–695.
Buzon, Michele R., and G. J. Bowen
2010   Oxygen and Carbon Isotope Analysis of Human Tooth Enamel from the New Kingdom Site of Tombos in Nubia. Archaeometry 52(5):855–868.
Buzon, Michele R., Christina A. Conlee, Antonio Simonetti, and Gabriel J. Bowen
2012   The Consequences of Wari Contact in the Nasca Region During the Middle Horizon: Archaeological, Skeletal, and Isotopic Evidence. Journal of Archaeological Science 39(8):2627–2636.

Buzon, Michele R., and Antonio Simonetti

2013   Strontium Isotope (^{87}Sr/^{86}Sr) Variability in the Nile Valley: Identifying Residential Mobility During Ancient Egyptian and Nubian Sociopolitical Changes in the New Kingdom and Napatan Periods. American Journal of Physical Anthropology 151(1):1–9.

Buzon, Michele R., Antonio Simonetti, and Robert A. Creaser

2007   Migration in the Nile Valley during the New Kingdom Period: A Preliminary Strontium Isotope Study. Journal of Archaeological Science 34(9):1391–1401.

Cabana, Graciela S.

2011   The Problematic Relationship between Migration and Culture Change. In Rethinking Anthropological Perspectives on Migration, Graciela S. Cabana and Jeffery J. Clark, eds. Pp. 16–28. Gainesville: University Press of Florida.

Cabana, Graciela S., Keith Hunley, and Frederika A. Kaestle

2008   Population Continuity or Replacement? A Novel Computer Simulation Approach and Its Application to the Numic Expansion (Western Great Basin, USA). American Journal of Physical Anthropology 135(4):438–447.

Cameron, Catherine M.

1995   Migration and the Movement of Southwestern Peoples. Journal of Anthropological Archaeology 14(2):104–124.

Carpenter, Steve, Brian Walker, J. Marty Anderies, and Nick Abel

2001   From Metaphor to Measurement: Resilience of What to What? Ecosystems 4(8):765–781.

Castles, Stephen

2002   Environmental Change and Forced Migration: Making Sense of the Debate. New Issues in Refugee Research, Working Paper, 70. Geneva: Evaluation and Policy Analysis Unit, United Nations High Commissioner for Refugees. http://www.unhcr.org/3de344fd9.html, accessed June 17, 2014.

2006   Global Perspectives on Forced Migration. Asian and Pacific Migration Journal 15(1):7–28.

Castles, Stephen, and Mark Miller

2003   The Age of Migration: International Population Movements in the Modern World. 3rd edition. New York: Guilford Press.

Chapman, John, and Helena Hamerow, eds.

1997   Migrations and Invasions in Archaeological Explanation. British Archaeological Reports International Series, 664. Oxford: Archaeopress.

Chavez, Leo R.

2008   The Latino Threat: Constructing Immigrants, Citizens, and the Nation. Stanford: Stanford University Press.

Christensen, Clayton M.

1997   The Innovator's Dilemma: When New Technologies Cause Great Firms to Fail. Boston: Harvard Business School Press.

Clark, Jeffery J.

2001   Tracking Prehistoric Migrations: Pueblo Settlers Among the Tonto Basin Hohokam. Anthropological Papers of the University of Arizona, 65. Tucson: University of Arizona Press.

2011   Disappearance and Diaspora: Contrasting Two Migrations in the Southern U.S. Southwest. *In* Rethinking Anthropological Perspectives on Migration. Graciela S. Cabana and Jeffery J. Clark, eds. Pp. 84–107. Gainesville: University Press of Florida.

Connor, Phillip
2010   Explaining the Refugee Gap: Economic Outcomes of Refugees Versus Other Immigrants. Journal of Refugee Studies 23(3):377–397.

Cordell, Linda S.
1995   Tracing Migration Pathways from the Receiving End. Journal of Anthropological Archaeology 14(2):203–211.

Cornelius, Wayne A.
1992   From Sojourners to Settlers: The Changing Profile of Mexican Immigration to the United States. *In* U.S.-Mexico Relations: Labor Market Interdependence. Jorge A. Bustamante, Clark W. Reynolds, and Raúl A. Hinojosa Ojeda, eds. Pp. 155–95. Stanford: Stanford University Press.
1998   The Structural Embeddedness of Demand for Mexican Immigrant Labor: New Evidence from California. *In* Crossings: Mexican Immigration in Interdisciplinary Perspective. Marcelo Suárez-Orozco, ed. Pp. 114–144. Cambridge: Harvard University Press.

Cornelius, Wayne A., and Takeyuki Tsuda
2004   Controlling Immigration: The Limits of Government Intervention. *In* Controlling Immigration: A Global Perspective. 2nd edition. Wayne A. Cornelius, Takeyuki Tsuda, Philip L. Martin, and James F. Hollifield, eds. Pp. 3–48. Stanford: Stanford University Press.

Crosby Jr., Alfred W.
1972   The Columbian Exchange: Biological and Cultural Consequences of 1492. Westport, CT: Greenwood.

Curran, Sara, and Tundi Agardy
2004   Considering Migration and Its Effects on Coastal Ecosystems. *In* Environmental Change and Its Implications for Population Migration. Advances in Global Change Research, vol. 20. Jon D. Unruh, Maarten S. Krol, and Nurit Kliot, eds. Pp. 201–229. Boston: Kluwer Academic Publishers.

Dafalla, Hassan
1975   The Nubian Exodus. London: C. Hurst in association with the Scandinavian Institute of African Studies, Uppsala.

D'Andrea, William J., Yongsong Huang, Sherilyn C. Fritz, and N. John Anderson
2011   Abrupt Holocene Climate Change As an Important Factor for Human Migration in West Greenland. Proceedings of the National Academy of Sciences of the United States of America 108(24):9765–9769.

Darling, J. Andrew
2011   S-cuk Kavick: Thoughts on Migratory Process and the Archaeology of O'odham Migration. *In* Rethinking Anthropological Perspectives on Migration. Graciela S. Cabana and Jeffery J. Clark, eds. Pp. 68–83. Gainesville: University Press of Florida.

Denevan, William, ed.

1992   The Native Population of the Americas in 1492. 2nd edition. Madison: University of Wisconsin Press.

Dobyns, Henry F.

1983   Their Number Become Thinned: Native American Population Dynamics in Eastern North America. Knoxville: University of Tennessee Press.

Duff, Andrew

1998   The Process of Migration in the Late Prehistoric Southwest. *In* Migration and Reorganization: The Pueblo IV Period in the American Southwest. Katherine A. Spielmann, ed. Pp. 31–52. Arizona State University Anthropological Research Papers No. 51. Tempe: Department of Anthropology, Arizona State University.

Dun, Olivia

2011   Migration and Displacement Triggered by Floods in the Mekong Delta. International Migration 49(S1):e200–e223.

England, J. Lynn, and Stan L. Albrecht

1984   Boomtowns and Social Disruption. Rural Sociology 49(2):230–246.

Fitzhugh, William W., ed.

1985   Cultures in Contact: The European Impact on Native Cultural Institutions in Eastern North America, AD 1000–1800. Washington, D.C.: Smithsonian Institution Press.

Folke, Carl

2006   Resilience: The Emergence of a Perspective for Social-Ecological Systems Analyses. Global Environmental Change 16(3):253–267.

Fowles, Severin M.

2011   Movement and the Unsettling of the Pueblos. *In* Rethinking Anthropological Perspectives on Migration. Graciela S. Cabana and Jeffery J. Clark, eds. Pp. 45–67. Gainesville: University Press of Florida.

Fowler, Catherine S.

2011   A Numic Migration? Ethnographic Evidence Revisited. *In* Rethinking Anthropological Perspectives on Migration. Pp. 191–206. Graciela S. Cabana and Jeffery J. Clark, eds. Gainesville: University Press of Florida.

Frankenberg, Susan R., and Lyle W. Konigsberg

2011   Migration Muddles in Prehistory: The Distinction Between Model-Bound and Model-Free Methods. *In* Rethinking Anthropological Perspectives on Migration. Pp. 278–292. Graciela S. Cabana and Jeffery J. Clark, eds. Gainesville: University Press of Florida.

Gilbert, Genevieve, and Robert McLeman

2010   Household Access to Capital and Its Effects on Drought Adaptation and Migration: A Case Study of Rural Alberta in the 1930s. Population and Environment 32(1):3–26.

Goldstein, Paul S.

2005   Andean Diaspora: The Tiwanaku Colonies and the Origins of South American Empire. Gainesville: University Press of Florida.

Gotham, Kevin Fox, and Richard Campenella
2010 Towards a Research Agenda on Transformative Resilience: Challenges and Opportunities for Post-Trauma Urban Ecosystems. Critical Planning 17:9–23.

Gray, Clark, and Valerie Mueller
2012 Drought and Population Mobility in Rural Ethiopia. World Development 40(1):134–145.

Gunderson, Lance H., Steve R. Carpenter, Carl Folke, Per Olsson, and Garry Peterson
2006 Water RATs (Resilience, Adaptability, and Transformability) in Lake and Wetland Social-Ecological Systems. Ecology and Society 11(1):Art. 16.

Hafsaas-Tsakos, Henriette
2011 Ethical Implications of Salvage Archaeology and Dam Building: The Clash Between Archaeologists and Local People in Dar al-Manasir, Sudan. Journal of Social Archaeology 11(1):49–76.

Hamerow, Helena
1997 Migration Theory and the Anglo-Saxon 'Identity Crisis.' In Migrations and Invasions in Archaeological Explanation. Pp. 33–44. John Chapman and Helena Hamerow, eds. British Archaeological Reports International Series, 664. Oxford: Archaeopress.

Hamilton, Nora, and Norma Stoltz Chinchilla
1996 Global Economic Restructuring and International Migration: Some Observations Based on the Mexican and Central American Experience. International Migration 34(2):195–228.

Hassig, Ross
1994 Mexico and the Spanish Conquest. London: Longman.

Heather, Peter
2010 Empires and Barbarians: The Fall of Rome and the Birth of Europe. New York: Oxford University Press.

Hewitt, Kenneth
1997 Regions at Risk: A Geographical Introduction to Disaster. London: Longman.

Holling, C. S.
1973 Resilience and Stability of Ecological Systems. Annual Review of Ecology and Systematics 4:1–23.

Hugo, Graeme
1996 Environmental Concerns and International Migration. International Migration Review 30(1):105–131.

Hutchinson, Dale L.
2007 Tatham Mound and the Bioarchaeology of European Contact: Disease and Depopulation in Central Gulf Coast Florida. Gainesville: University Press of Florida.

International Organization for Migration
2008 World Migration Report 2008: Managing Labour Mobility in the Evolving Global Economy. IOM World Migration Report Series, vol. 4. Geneva: International Organization for Migration.

Jacobson, Jodi L.
1988 Environmental Refugees: A Yardstick of Habitability. Worldwatch Paper, 86. Washington, D.C.: Worldwatch Institute.

Janssen, Marco A., Timothy A. Kohler, and Marten Scheffer
2003   Sunk-Cost Effects and Vulnerability to Collapse in Ancient Societies. Current An-
        thropology 44(5):722–728.
Jennings, Francis
1975   The Invasion of America: Indians, Colonialism, and the Cant of Conquest. Chapel
        Hill: University of North Carolina Press.
Joppke, Christian
2005   Selecting by Origin: Ethnic Migration in the Liberal State. Cambridge: Harvard
        University Press.
Julca, Alex
2011   Multidimensional Re-creation of Vulnerabilities and Potential for Resilience in
        International Migration. International Migration 49(S1):e30–e49.
Kandel, William, and Douglas S. Massey
2002   The Culture of Mexican Migration: A Theoretical and Empirical Analysis. Social
        Forces 80(3):981–1004.
King, Russell, Ronald Skeldon, and Julie Vullnetari
2008   Internal and International Migration: Bridging the Theoretical Divide. Paper pre-
        sented at the International Migration Institute "Theories of Migration and Social
        Change Conference," St. Anne's College, Oxford, July 1–3. http://www.imi.ox.ac.
        uk/pdfs/russell-king-ron-skeldon-and-julie-vullnetari-internal-and-international
        -migration-bridging-the-theoretical-divide/view, accessed June 17, 2014.
Knudson, Kelly J.
2008   Tiwanaku Influence in the South Central Andes: Strontium Isotope Analysis and
        Middle Horizon Migration. Latin American Antiquity 19(1):3–23.
2011   Identifying Archaeological Human Migration Using Biogeochemistry: Case Stud-
        ies from the South-Central Andes. In Rethinking Anthropological Perspectives on
        Migration. Graciela S. Cabana and Jeffery J. Clark, eds. Pp. 231–247. Gainesville:
        University Press of Florida.
Kolmannskog, Vikram
2009   Climate Change, Disaster, Displacement and Migration: Initial Evidence from Af-
        rica. New Issues in Refugee Research, Research Paper 180. Geneva: Policy Devel-
        opment and Evaluation Service, United Nations High Commissioner for Refugees
        (UNHCR). http://www.unhcr.org/4b18e3599.pdf, accessed June 16, 2014.
Konigsberg, Lyle W.
2006   A Post-Neumann History of Biological and Genetic Distance Studies in Bioar-
        chaeology. In Bioarchaeology: The Contextual Analysis of Human Remains. Jane
        E. Buikstra and Lane A. Beck, eds. Pp. 263–279. Burlington, MA: Academic Press.
Kreps, G. A.
1984   Sociological Inquiry and Disaster Research. Annual Review of Sociology 10:309–
        330.
Kunz, E. F.
1973   Refugee in Flight: Kinetic Models and Forms of Displacement. International Mi-
        gration Review 7(2):125–146.
Larsen, Clark S., and George R. Milner, eds.
1994   In the Wake of Contact: Biological Responses to Conquest. New York: Wiley-Liss.

Levitt, Peggy, and B. Nadya Jaworsky

2007   Transnational Migration Studies: Past Developments and Future Trends. Annual Review of Sociology 33:129–156.

Locke, Catherine, W. Neil Adger, and P. Mick Kelly

2000   Changing Places: Migration's Social and Environmental Consequences. Environment 42(7):24–35.

Loker, William M.

2003   Dam Impacts in a Time of Globalization: Using Multiple Methods to Document Social and Environmental Change in Rural Honduras. Current Anthropology 44(S5):S112–S121.

Lonergan, Steve

1998   The Role of Environmental Degradation in Population Displacement. In Environmental Change and Security Project Report 4. Geoffrey D. Dabelko, ed. Pp. 5–15. Washington, D.C.: The Woodrow Wilson International Center for Scholars. http://www.wilsoncenter.org/sites/default/files/ACF1493.pdf, accessed June 17, 2014.

Lubkemann, Stephen C.

2008a   Culture in Chaos: An Anthropology of the Social Condition in War. Chicago: University of Chicago Press.

2008b   Involuntary Immobility: On a Theoretical Invisibility in Forced Migration Studies. Journal of Refugee Studies 21(4):454–475.

Lucassen, Jan, Leo Lucassen, and Patrick Manning

2010   Migration History: Multidisciplinary Approaches. In Migration History in World History: Multidisciplinary Approaches. Jan Lucassen, Leo Lucassen, and Patrick Manning, eds. Pp. 3–35. Boston: Brill.

Malkki, Liisa H.

1995a   Purity and Exile: Violence, Memory, and National Cosmology Among Hutu Refugees in Tanzania. Chicago: University of Chicago Press.

1995b   Refugees and Exile: From "Refugee Studies" to the National Order of Things. Annual Review of Anthropology 24:495–523.

Manning, Patrick

2012   Migration in World History. 2nd edition. London: Routledge.

Martin, Philip, Manolo Abella, and Christiane Kuptsch

2006   Managing Labor Migration in the Twenty-first Century. New Haven: Yale University Press.

Massey, Douglas S.

1988   Economic Development and International Migration in Comparative Perspective. Population and Development Review 14(3):383–413.

Massey, Douglas S., Joaquín Arango, Graeme Hugo, Ali Kouaouci, Adela Pellegrino, and J. Edward Taylor

1993   Theories of International Migration: A Review and Appraisal. Population and Development Review 19(3):431–466.

Morkot, Robert G.

2000   The Black Pharaohs: Egypt's Nubian Rulers. London: Rubicon Press.

Myers, Candice A., Tim Slack, and Joachim Singelmann
2008   Social Vulnerability and Migration in the Wake of Disaster: The Case of Hurricanes Katrina and Rita. Population and Environment 29(6):271–291.

Myers, Norman
1997   Environmental Refugees. Population and Environment 19(2):167–182.

O'Connor, Richard A.
1995   Agricultural Change and Ethnic Succession in Southeast Asian States: A Case for Regional Anthropology. Journal of Asian Studies 54(4):968–996.

Oliver-Smith, Anthony
1996   Anthropological Research on Hazards and Disasters. Annual Review of Anthropology 25:303–328.

Palkovich, Ann M.
1996   Historic Depopulation in the American Southwest: Issues of Interpretation and Context-Embedded Analyses. In Bioarchaeology of Native American Adaptation in the Spanish Borderlands. Brenda J. Baker and Lisa Kealhofer, eds. Pp. 179–197. Gainesville: University Press of Florida.

Park, Minkyung, and Patricia A. Stokowski
2009   Social Disruption Theory and Crime in Rural Communities: Comparisons Across Three Levels of Tourism Growth. Tourism Management 30(6):905–915.

Paul, Bimal Kanti
2005   Evidence Against Disaster-Induced Migration: The 2004 Tornado in North-Central Bangladesh. Disasters 29(4):370–385.

Portes, Alejandro
1999   The Origins and Effects of Transnational Activities. Ethnic and Racial Studies 22(2):463–475.

Portes, Alejandro, Luis E. Guarnizo, and Patricia Landolt
1999   The Study of Transnationalism: Pitfalls and Promise of an Emergent Research Field. Ethnic and Racial Studies 22(2):217–237.

Portes, Alejandro, and Min Zhou
1993   The New Second Generation: Segmented Assimilation and Its Variants. Annals of the American Academy of Political and Social Science 530(1):74–96.

Potocky-Tripodi, Miriam
2003   Refugee Economic Adaptation: Theory, Evidence and Implications for Policy and Practice. Journal of Social Service Research 30(1):63–91.

Pradhan, Pushkar K.
2004   Population Growth, Migration, and Urbanisation. Environmental Consequences in Kathmandu Valley, Nepal. In Environmental Change and Its Implications for Population Migration. Advances in Global Change Research, vol. 20. Jon D. Unruh, Maarten S. Krol, and Nurit Kliot, eds. Pp. 177–199. Boston: Kluwer Academic Publishers.

Prosperi, David C., and Sofia Morgado
2011   Resilience and Transformation: Can We Have Both? In Change for Stability: Lifecycles of Cities and Regions. Manfred Schrenk, Vasily V. Popovich, and Peter Zeile, eds. Pp. 819–829. Proceedings, 16th International Conference on Urban Planning,

Regional Development and Information Society, Real Corp 2011. http://programm. corp.at/cdrom2011/papers2011/CORP2011_92.pdf, accessed June 17, 2014.

Ramenofsky, Ann F.
1987   Vectors of Death: The Archaeology of European Contact. Albuquerque: University of New Mexico Press.

Reff, Daniel T.
1991   Disease, Depopulation, and Culture Change in Northwestern New Spain, 1518–1764. Salt Lake City: University of Utah Press.

Renaud, Fabrice G., Olivia Dun, Koko Warner, and Janos Bogardi
2011   A Decision Framework for Environmentally Induced Migration. International Migration 49(S1):e5–e29.

Ross, Douglas E.
2013   An Archaeology of Asian Transnationalism. Gainesville: University Press of Florida and The Society for Historical Archaeology.

Rouse, Irving
1986   Migrations in Prehistory: Inferring Population Movement from Cultural Remains. New Haven: Yale University Press.
1992   The Tainos: Rise and Decline of the People Who Greeted Columbus. New Haven: Yale University Press.

Sassen, Saskia
1988   The Mobility of Labor and Capital: A Study in International Investment and Labor Flow. Cambridge: Cambridge University Press.

Schaeffer, Peter
2010   Refugees: On the Economics of Political Migration. International Migration 48(1):1–22.

Schmeidl, Susanne
2001   Conflict and Forced Migration: A Quantitative Review, 1964–1995. In Global Migrants, Global Refugees: Problems and Solutions. Aristide R. Zolberg and Peter M. Benda, eds. Pp. 62–94. New York: Berghahn Books.

Smith, Robert Courtney
2006   Mexican New York: Transnational Lives of New Immigrants. Berkeley: University of California Press.

Smith, Stuart Tyson
2003   Wretched Kush: Ethnic Identities and Boundaries in Egypt's Nubian Empire. London and New York: Routledge.

Spicer, Edward S.
1962   Cycles of Conquest: The Impact of Spain, Mexico, and the United States on the Indians of the Southwest, 1533–1960. Tucson: University of Arizona Press.

Stannard, David E.
1992   American Holocaust: Columbus and the Conquest of the New World. New York: Oxford University Press.

Stearn, E. Wagner, and Allen E. Stearn
1945   The Effects of Smallpox on the Destiny of the Amerindian. Boston: Bruce Humpries.

Steele, Ian K.

1994   Warpaths: Invasions of North America. New York: Oxford University Press.

Stojanowski, Christopher M.

2010   Bioarchaeology of Ethnogenesis in the Colonial Southeast. Gainseville: University Press of Florida.

Stojanowski, Christopher M., and Michael A. Schillaci

2006   Phenotypic Approaches for Understanding Patterns of Intracemetery Biological Variation. Yearbook of Physical Anthropology 131(S43):49–88.

Stone, Anne C.

2008   DNA Analysis of Archaeological Remains. In Biological Anthropology of the Human Skeleton. 2nd edition. M. Anne Katzenberg and Shelley R. Saunders, eds. Pp. 461–83. Hoboken, NJ: John Wiley & Sons.

Stone, Tammy

2003   Social Identity and Ethnic Interaction in the Western Pueblos of the American Southwest. Journal of Archaeological Method and Theory 10(1):31–67.

Storey, Rebecca

1992   Life & Death in the Ancient City of Teotíhuacan: A Modern Paleodemographic Synthesis. Tuscaloosa: University of Alabama Press.

Storey, Rebecca, Lourdes Marquez Morfin, and Vernon Smith

2002   Social Disruption and the Maya Civilization of Mesoamerica. In The Backbone of History: Health and Nutrition in the Western Hemisphere. Richard Steckel and Jerome Rose, eds. Pp. 283–306. Cambridge: Cambridge University Press.

Suhrke, Astri

1994   Environmental Degradation and Population Flows. Journal of International Affairs 47(2):473–496.

Swain, Ashok

1996   Environmental Migration and Conflict Dynamics: Focus on Developing Regions. Third World Quarterly 17(5):959–973.

Thomas, David Hurst, ed.

1989   Columbian Consequences, vol. 1: Archaeological and Historical Perspectives on the Spanish Borderlands West. Washington, D.C.: Smithsonian Institution.

1990   Columbian Consequences, vol. 2: Archaeological and Historical Perspectives on the Spanish Borderlands East. Washington, D.C.: Smithsonian Institution.

1991   Columbian Consequences, vol. 3: The Spanish Borderlands in Pan-American Perspective. Washington, D.C.: Smithsonian Institution.

Thornton, Russell

1987   American Indian Holocaust and Survival: A Population History since 1492. Norman: University of Oklahoma Press.

Trigger, Bruce G.

1985   Natives and Newcomers: Canada's "Heroic Age." Montreal: McGill-Queens University Press.

Tsuda, Takeyuki

1999a   The Motivation to Migrate: The Ethnic and Sociocultural Constitution of the Japanese-Brazilian Return Migration System. Economic Development and Cultural Change 48(1):1–31.

1999b The Permanence of "Temporary" Migration: The "Structural Embeddedness" of Japanese-Brazilian Immigrant Workers in Japan. Journal of Asian Studies 58(3):687–722.

2003 Strangers in the Ethnic Homeland: Japanese Brazilian Return Migration in Transnational Perspective. New York: Columbia University Press.

2007 Bringing Humanity Back into International Migration: Anthropological Contributions. City and Society 19(1):19–35.

2009 Diasporic Homecomings: Ethnic Return Migration in Comparative Perspective. Stanford: Stanford University Press.

2011 Modern Perspectives on Ancient Migrations. In Rethinking Anthropological Perspectives on Migration. Graciela S. Cabana and Jeffery J. Clark, eds. Pp. 313–38. Gainesville: University Press of Florida.

2012 Whatever Happened to Simultaneity? Transnational Migration Theory and Dual Engagement in Sending and Receiving Countries. Journal of Ethnic and Migration Studies 38(4):631–649.

United Nations Department of Economic and Social Affairs
2012 Migrants by Origin and Destination: The Role of South–South Migration. Population Facts, 2012/3. New York: United Nations Department of Economic and Social Affairs, Population Division. http://www.un.org/en/development/desa/population/publications/pdf/popfacts/popfacts_2012-3_South-South_migration.pdf, accessed June 17, 2014.

United Nations High Commissioner for Refugees
2013 New UNHCR Report Says Global Forced Displacement at 18-Year High. June 19. http://www.unhcr.org/51c071816.html, accessed June 16, 2014.

Unruh, Jon D., Maarten S. Krol, and Nurit Kliot, eds.
2004 Environmental Change and Its Implications for Population Migration. Advances in Global Change Research, vol. 20. Boston: Kluwer Academic Publishers.

Varsanyi, Monica W., ed.
2010 Taking Local Control: Immigration Policy Activism in US Cities and States. Stanford: Stanford University Press.

Verano, John W., and Douglas H. Ubelaker, eds.
1992 Disease and Demography in the Americas. Washington, D.C.: Smithsonian Institution.

Walker, Brian, C. S. Holling, Stephen R. Carpenter, and Ann Kinzig
2004 Resilience, Adaptability and Transformability in Social-Ecological Systems. Ecology and Society 9(2):Art. 5.

Waters, Mary C., and Tomás R. Jiménez
2005 Assessing Immigrant Assimilation: New Empirical and Theoretical Challenges. Annual Review of Sociology 31:105–125.

Weiner, Myron
1996 Bad Neighbors, Bad Neighborhoods: An Inquiry into the Causes of Refugee Flows. International Security 21(1):5–42.

Westin, Charles
1999 Regional Analysis of Refugee Movements. In Refugees: Perspectives on the Experience of Forced Migration. Alastair Ager, ed. Pp. 24–45. London: Pinter.

Wisner, Ben, Piers Blaikie, Terry Cannon, and Ian Davis
2004 At Risk: Natural Hazards, People's Vulnerability and Disasters. 2nd edition. London: Routledge.
Zakrzewski, Sonia
2011 Population Migration, Variation, and Identity: An Islamic Population in Iberia. *In* Social Bioarchaeology. Sabrina C. Agarwal and Bonnie A. Glencross, eds. Pp. 183–211. Malden, MA: Wiley-Blackwell.
Zolberg, Aristide R., Astri Suhrke, and Sergio Aguayo
1989 Escape from Violence: Conflict and the Refugee Crisis in the Developing World. New York: Oxford University Press.

Contributors

Brenda J. Baker is associate professor of anthropology at Arizona State University and coeditor-in-chief of *Bioarchaeology International.*

Christopher S. Beekman is associate professor of anthropology at the University of Colorado at Denver. He is an archaeologist who uses multiple lines of evidence (archaeological, biological, linguistic, and ethnohistoric) to study migrations in Mesoamerica during and after the decline and fall of the Teotihuacan state, circa AD 500–1000.

George L. Cowgill is professor emeritus in the School of Human Evolution and Social Change at Arizona State University. He is an anthropological archaeologist focusing on ancient states and cities: their rise, functioning, and fall. He has worked especially at Teotihuacan, an immense prehistoric city in central Mexico. His interests include large-scale migration and its consequences.

Jason De León is assistant professor of anthropology at the University of Michigan and director of the Undocumented Migration Project (www.undocumentedmigrationproject.com). He uses ethnography, archaeology, and forensic science to study the causes and social dynamics of undocumented Latin American migration into the United States.

James F. Eder is professor of anthropology in the School of Human Evolution and Social Change at Arizona State University. His research interests concern the indigenous and migrant-origin inhabitants of Palawan Island, the Philippines, and include the foraging economy of forest dwellers, occupational diversification in upland farming communities, livelihood and resource management in the coastal zone, and ethnic identity and religious expression among the island's Muslim peoples.

Anna Forringer-Beal is an undergraduate studying anthropology and Spanish at the University of Michigan–Ann Arbor. Her work focuses on the experiences of undocumented female migrants crossing the Mexico–Arizona border and the archaeological footprint this population leaves behind.

Cameron Gokee is research assistant professor of anthropology at Appalachian State University. His research focuses on the archaeology of village communities in West Africa and of undocumented migration in southern Arizona, where he collaborates with the Undocumented Migration Project.

Catherine Hills is a senior fellow of the McDonald Institute for Archaeological Research at the University of Cambridge. She is an archaeologist who studies early Anglo-Saxon migration and material evidence during the fifth through seventh centuries AD in Britain and the North Sea region.

Kelly J. Knudson is associate professor of anthropology in the School of Human Evolution and Social Change at Arizona State University. She is a bioarchaeologist specializing in archaeological bone chemistry, particularly social identities, paleomobility, and paleodiet in the ancient Andes.

Patrick Manning is professor of world history at the University of Pittsburgh. He is well known for his work on migration in world history, with an emphasis on Africa and the African diaspora. He will serve as president of the American Historical Association in 2016.

Jonathan Maupin is assistant professor in the School of Human Evolution and Social Change at Arizona State University. He is a sociocultural anthropologist specializing in medical anthropology. He examines how conceptual models of illness among Mexican immigrants in Nashville, Tennessee, change as they access biomedical services. He is specifically interested in the perceived disruptive impact of undocumented immigrants on the U.S. healthcare system and also conducts fieldwork among the Maya in Guatemala.

Lisa Meierotto is a lecturer in Foundational Studies at Boise State University. She is a sociocultural and environmental anthropologist who examines the actual and perceived environmental disruptions caused by unauthorized immigration across protected nature preserves on the U.S.-Mexican border.

James Morrissey is an international development scholar at the University of Oxford who examines migration caused by environmental stress in Africa and the effects of environmental change on rural-urban migration in northern Ethiopia. He fuses political ecology and migration theory to understand "environmental refugees."

Rachel E. Scott is assistant professor of anthropology at DePaul University in Chicago. She is a bioarchaeologist who specializes in medieval Ireland. Her research integrates human skeletal, archaeological, and historical data in order to examine the processes of identity formation and the social construction of disease.

Christina Torres-Rouff is associate professor of anthropology at the University of California at Merced and a bioarchaeologist focusing on health and identity in the ancient Andes.

Takeyuki Tsuda is professor of anthropology at Arizona State University.

Sonia Zakrzewski is a senior lecturer in the department of archaeology at the University of Southampton in the United Kingdom. She is a bioarchaeologist who has studied population affinities and morphological change in ancient Egyptian populations and, more recently, mobility and movement in Islamic Andalucía, Spain, and the impact of religion and population groups on biological and social identities.

Index

Lightning Source UK Ltd.
Milton Keynes UK
UKHW040612251019

352274UK00003B/123/P